LONDON LORE

Steve Roud recently retired from his position as Local Studies Librarian for the London Borough of Croydon and has served as Honorary Librarian of the Folklore Society for over fifteen years. He has been researching British folklore for over thirty years and is the joint author of the *Oxford Dictionary of English Folklore*. His other books include the *Penguin Guide to the Superstitions of Britain and Ireland*, which won the Katherine Briggs Folklore Award in 2004, *Monday's Child is Fair of Face ... and other traditional beliefs about babies and motherhood* and *The English Year*, a month-by-month guide to festivals. He also compiles the Folk Song Index and the Broadside Index, two internationally acclaimed computer databases of traditional folk and popular song.

Praise for *London Lore*

'A wonderful collection of stories and legends, to be recommended to anyone who is at least half in love with the dark side of London's past.'
Peter Ackroyd, *The Times*

'I've been enthralled . . . The book's real strength lies [in] its exposure of deeper levels of custom, tradition and magical thinking that lie beneath the smooth Tarmac of contemporary realism.'
Will Self, *Evening Standard*

'A spellbinding study of our city's folklore . . . digs through layers of hearsay and speculation to investigate how and why the stories and traditions arose in the first place.'
Newham Recorder

'[An] absorbing compendium by folklore expert Steve Roud. He excavates the history of the capital, from obscure suburban streets to famous sites like the Tower of London.'
The London Paper

'A fascinating new book of London tales of lore and legend . . . admirably put together'
Camden New Journal

'Brings to life the surprising, sometimes gruesome, history of the city.'
Croydon Advertiser

'An absorbing and fascinatingly thorough book'
Harrow Observer

London Lore

*The legends and traditions of
the world's most vibrant city*

STEVE ROUD

arrow books

Published by Arrow Books 2010

14

Copyright © Steve Roud 2008

Steve Roud has asserted his right under the Copyright, Designs
and Patents Act, 1988, to be identified as the author of this work

First published in Great Britain in 2008 by
Random House Books
Random House, 20 Vauxhall Bridge Road,
London SW1V 2SA

www.randomhouse.co.uk

Addresses for companies within The Random House Group Limited can be found at:
www.randomhouse.co.uk/offices.htm

The Random House Group Limited Reg. No. 954009

A CIP catalogue record for this book
is available from the British Library

ISBN 9780099519867

Typeset in Fournier MT by SX Composing DTP, Rayleigh

Penguin Random House is committed to a sustainable future for
our business, our readers and our planet. This book is made from
Forest Stewardship Council® certified paper.

Printed and bound in Great Britain by Clays Ltd, Elcograf S.p.A.

For Jacky and Jack, Geoff and Ann, Peter and Diana,
and Hazel and Malcolm – Londoners all

ACKNOWLEDGEMENTS

Many thanks, as always, to my ex-colleagues at Croydon Local Studies Library: Chris Corner, Lizzie Mould, Francesca Debenham, Gillian Butler, and Chris Bennett; also the staff at all the local studies libraries around London and the staff of the London Library, without whom the book would have been impossible; and the many folklore friends who have helped with information, support and advice over the years, in particular Jacqueline Simpson, Caroline Oates, Roy Vickery, Roy Palmer, Gillian Bennett, Marion Bowman, Malcolm Taylor, John Clark, and the late Jennifer Chandler (Westwood); and my editors Sophie and Emily at Random House for knocking the book into shape.

The author is grateful for the quotations from John Emslie by kind permission of the Folklore Society.

Every effort has been made to contact all copyright holders. If notified, the publisher will be pleased to rectify any errors or omissions at the earliest opportunity.

ILLUSTRATIONS
All black and white illustrations are from the author's private collection, except for the following:
p. 78 Bible and Key Scene from *The Mayor of Casterbridge* © Dorset County Library; p. 127 The Confession of Richard Brandon © Ann Ronan/Heritage-Images/Imagestate; p. 155 Holland House © Royal Borough of Kensington & Chelsea Libraries; p. 171 Chelsea Pensioners in the Retiring Room © Royal Borough of Kensington & Chelsea Libraries; p. 180 Boudicca © National Portrait Gallery, London; p. 198 Mother Damnable © Wellcome Library, London; p. 208 Pearly King © The Print Collector/Heritage-Images/Imagestate; p. 238 Witch Bottle © Norfolk Museums & Archaeology Service; p. 355 Dan Leno © Getty Images.

CONTENTS

INTRODUCTION

'There's a lot of history around in London,' a taxi-driver told me the other day, and he was right. Interestingly, though, most of what he then went on to talk about was not verifiable historical fact at all, but was instead a series of seemingly authentic stories about buildings, streets and people which were either unprovable or untrue. They were not history, but legends: part of the realm of folklore, which can be defined as the unofficial culture of the people, passed on informally from person to person in the home, the workplace, the pub, the school, or, indeed, the taxicab.

There is certainly a lot of folklore around, and *London Lore* brings together a representative sample from past and present, and from every corner of the capital. Legends are covered extensively, but many other customs and traditions are also included – children carrying garlands around the streets on May Day, for example, or building grottoes in August; men selling their wives in the local market; Pearly Kings and Queens talking in rhyming slang; people telling fortunes, going to fairs, carrying mascots, prophesying doom, writing eccentric wills, and worrying about death omens. As a result, you will find a whole cast of characters here: kings and queens, lords and ladies, clergymen, chimney sweeps, milkmaids, innkeepers, highwaymen, rough musickers, murderers, vampire-hunters, cuckolds, Jacks-in-the-Green, rioters, bonfire boys, quacks, charlatans, witches, cunning women, astrologers, and quite a few ordinary Londoners too. Royal and civic pageantry, however, are largely omitted from the book, partly because the subject is so well-covered in tourist books and guides, but also because they are 'official' and have not been subject to the 'Chinese whispers' effect that underlies real folklore.

Even so, a single book can only hope to include a selected sample of the mass of lore which exists, covering only the smallest tip of the largest iceberg. Although we do not normally realise it, folklore is all around us, and everybody knows some. Every London schoolchild, for example, has a head full of rhymes, jokes, games, stories, superstitions, and beliefs learned from their family and playmates. And every London adult, however sophisticated they think they are, will also have a repertoire of traditional bits and pieces picked up from here and there.

FACT OR FICTION?

While people tend to accept traditions and customs for what they are – or were – when it comes to legends, the natural tendency seems to be to believe what we are told, or at least to give the story some qualified credence. This is a small example of the astonishing power of *narrative* in our everyday lives. Not only do we devour novels and read our children bedtime stories, but we avidly follow the continuing television sagas of soap operas, crime or costume dramas, and even the makers of documentaries strive to give their subjects a coherent storyline. On the personal level, we follow the same instincts whenever we relate something which has happened to us or someone we know. We recast the 'facts' into story form, arranging them into narrative order, placing the emphasis for the best effect, exaggerating or underplaying, giving comic or dramatic asides, adding a punchline or a moral as a coda.

It is important to be clear how the term *legend* is used in this book, as its basic meaning is changing rapidly in everyday use. For our present purposes, a somewhat simplistic definition is the following: *a legend is a story which is told as being true, but is not*, and much of my discussion and analysis revolves around questions of belief, truth and evidence. As regards the legend itself, it is *belief* which matters most, or at least *believability*, and another defining characteristic of a legend is that it includes elements which support and legitimise its message. In each re-telling, little details are added or changed – recognisable names and places, a real-sounding chronology, spurious but credible historical 'facts', and so on. My premise is therefore that it is not just what the stories say which is important but also how and why they say it; how they have developed, why they are believed, and whether they have any historical truth in them. It seems that the biggest deception of all is the general notion that all legends must have a grain of truth in them. In fact, they rarely do, and are often completely invented like any other story. If there is a grain of anything in their origin, it is *untruth*, because they are based on a misunderstanding, false reasoning, or prejudice and this is where the darker side of folklore comes in. There is no social prejudice or area of concern, including especially racism and anti-Semitism, which is not sustained and legitimised by traditional stories, jokes and assumptions about the victim group. Similarly, witch-hunts and vigilante actions are usually sparked and fed by rumour and legend.

But most legends are not sinister, and it is fascinating to study them in their natural habitat. One good example occurred a few years ago, when a college near Croydon Library (where I worked for many years as Local Studies Librarian), was demolished and a routine archaeological investigation of the site organised. Two trenches were dug at right angles to each other, and nothing was found, but within days the rumour was circulating that the archaeologists had discovered a Roman villa whose foundations you could plainly see. Similarly, at Pollards Hill, in Norbury, there is a somewhat strangely shaped housing estate. It was laid out in the mid nineteenth century, but only built up in the 1920s, and it has roads that run in circles. Not far away from the estate, horse races were held in the fields for a short time in the mid nineteenth century. A local teacher saw 'entrance to race course' in an old directory, and immediately told her class that the reason why the Pollards Hill estate is such a strange shape is that it was previously a race course. One of the parents then claimed to have paced out one of the roads and discovered it was the 'exact number of furlongs of a flat race'; another stated that the reason why the local railway station had ramps down to the platforms instead of steps was because they brought the horses down by train; in Croydon Library we subsequently received a succession of visitors trying to work out where the grandstand would have been.

Incidentally, Pollards Hill itself is a bit of an anomaly, as it is a prominent isolated hill in an otherwise flat area. For at least twenty years the story has been told that it is a man-made structure, consisting solely of the earth and rock they dug out when constructing the London Underground (a story told of many other places).

The ways such narratives accumulate is nicely shown in the following letter, published in the *Daily Mirror* on 24 November 1975:

> I wonder if you could give me any information on the house at number
> 37 Stepney Green, London E1. My mother was once caretaker there. We
> were told it was built by a sea captain about four hundred years ago and that

a lot of ship's timbers were used to build it. Also, the greens outside are the burial place of plague victims. The only information I could find in our local library was that it was once owned by a Lady Mico, who had the Almshouse built alongside in 1699. There is supposed to be a ghost – a little old lady who walks through one of the rooms, but I can assure you we never hung around long enough to find out. Not after dark anyway.

From a folklorist's point of view, what is interesting about the three distinct stories that have grown up about this particular house is that none of them is unique; they are all tales that have a general currency and are widely told about other buildings and at other times. The plague pit idea, for example, is particularly common among legend-makers (see p. 120). It is of course true that in areas of central London where the plague was rife, the churchyards became too full and ad hoc burial grounds were used, but the historical record shows that these were few, and they have been pretty well documented. Yet for many years any unused piece of land seems to have attracted the story to explain its condition, and in the last fifteen years or so, there has been a veritable explosion of these stories. Every supposed ghost or uncanny feeling is put down to the building being on the site of a pit, and this is as true for outer London boroughs, which were hardly affected by the pestilence, as for the central areas.

Apart from the plague, there are several motifs which are so widespread that they do not figure largely in this book. They would take up all the available space by themselves, and there is often little more to say than to report yet another version of a common story. These ubiquitous tales include the following:

Tunnels

Any old building, and many that are quite recent, is likely to have a 'secret tunnel', often reportedly running to another named building. Occasionally, cellars, bricked-up vaults, or even sewers have been seen, but in most cases the legend has not even needed this stimulus, and seems to have been made up completely out of the blue. These tunnels are often said to have been used by monks, nuns, smugglers, Roman Catholic priests, highwaymen, or assorted kings and queens, with motives criminal, religious, amorous, or, if possible, all three. Sometimes tunnels do exist, of course, but prosaic functionality is not sufficient and it is actually the frisson of the word *secret* that really attracts people. In Croydon, for example, the late Victorian Town Hall and the two 1970s council office buildings face each other across two roads. They are very sensibly joined, at second-floor level, by a covered walkway, and, under the roads, by a service tunnel. I have many times been told, in hushed tones, that there is a *secret* tunnel joining these buildings, but nobody thinks the second-floor walkway, which is in plain sight, at all interesting.

Land given to the people

Whenever any piece of land, especially if previously an allotment or open ground, or a building which was previously a school or hospital, is to be sold for development, the rumour is circulated that the land was 'given to the people' and can 'never be built on or sold off'. It is astonishing how firmly convinced people are of this fact, even though they have probably only recently been told it. In extreme cases, they take a failure to find any corroboration as proof of a conspiracy by the Council to keep the truth hidden.

Buildings built wrong

A particular building (especially one of striking or ugly appearance) was built that way by mistake. The architect had the plans upside down, or they were printed out back to front, and by the time they realised their mistake it was too late to rectify it. In some versions, the architect was so mortified that he committed suicide.

Ghosts

Probably the most common folkloric genre in current circulation at local level is the ghost story, and a plethora of booklets, ghost walks and local newspaper features confirm their continued popularity. There have been a number of good social histories of ghost beliefs, and a fascinating story they tell. But one thing that is clear is that ghosts have changed dramatically over the years, in their physical appearance, their reasons for staying around, their behaviour, and how the living can interact with them. The fact that these attributes have all altered with the times is one of the most telling reasons to be sceptical as to whether ghosts really exist.

As already indicated, one of the occupational hazards of being a folklorist is that we cannot leave anything alone. Faced with a story, we can never say simply 'That's a good story', but we have to pick at it, deconstruct it, analyse why it is a good story, isolate the motifs and compare them with other stories, investigate why it is believed or how it has survived, find its roots and examine its forbears. We find this approach fascinating; others find it extremely irritating. However, if you are the kind of person who likes to probe rather than simply accept, the following pointers may help you when you next want to weigh the likelihood of a story you have been told:

(1) Always try reversing the story. The *story* is that the house is empty because it is haunted; the *fact* is that it is believed to be haunted because it is empty. The patch of land is not unused because it is a plague pit; it is believed to be a plague pit because it has been left unused.

(2) Recognise recurrent motifs. If the same story is told about three buildings, it is unlikely to be true of any of them. If it is told of six buildings, it is even less likely to be true.

(3) Identify the assumptions. Current assumptions include the notion that all items of folklore are ancient and probably pagan, but there is never any evidence to support the idea. 'Touch wood' does not go back to prehistoric times when we believed in tree spirits (which we probably did not), but stems from an early nineteenth century children's game. Mistletoe was not banned from churches because the Druids regarded it as sacred, and so on.

(4) Recognise the formulae. Folklore thrives on formulae which pop up regularly: 'Did you hear what happened to my wife's cousin . . . ?' warns that a contemporary legend is about to be told, in the same way as the phrases 'Once upon a time' or 'Knock knock' herald fairy tales or jokes.

(5) Investigate the chronology. Did 'Ring a Roses' exist during or just after the plague? (No, its first recorded existence is in the 1880s.) When did people start saying the rhyme is about the plague? (About the 1950s.)

(6) Recognise spurious legitimating details. ' "Ring a Roses" is about the plague because sneezing was the first symptom of the disease' (no, it was not), and 'the sores were big red circles' (no, they were not).

(7) Beware of tour guides. They *may* know a lot about their particular subject or building, but they are under immense pressure to make their talks fun and interesting, and they are not always overly concerned with the niceties of historical accuracy. Whenever a guide says 'That's why we say . . .' take what follows with a pinch of salt.

(8) The more closely an explanation matches the modern facts, the more likely it is to be spurious, because one of the basic rules of folklore is that

items change and develop over time. An old 'custom' will probably have changed dramatically over the years, so if the legend which explains it covers all the current details, it is bound to be itself quite modern. The principle is even more obvious with place-name 'meanings'.

(9) But, most importantly of all, ask yourself: 'Is the story at all likely?'

FOLKLORE AND SOCIAL HISTORY

It may be felt that an openly sceptical approach to legends and stories destroys one of life's pleasures, but it is quite possible to enjoy a story without actually believing it. We do it all the time with fiction and television drama, and the tooth-fairy and Father Christmas have their uses without adults having to believe in them. And a story is often made more interesting when its development is revealed. To give one example, detailed in Westwood and Simpson's excellent *Lore of the Land* (2005): we know that Margaret Pole, Countess of Salisbury, was executed at the Tower of London in 1541 on the orders of Henry VIII. A hundred years later, a story was circulating that she initially refused to submit to the executioner's axe. By Victorian times she was said to have attempted to flee from her executioner, who proceeded to chase after her with his axe and hew her to the ground, and it is this gruesome scene, which never happened, that her ghost reputedly re-enacts on each anniversary of her death. Each retelling added a detail to the original account, adding a fresh twist to capture the imagination of each new generation.

The question of belief is not only crucial to an understanding of narratives, but is also central to other folklore genres, superstition in particular. A rule-of-thumb definition would be that a superstition is *an irrational belief in luck, omens, spells and supernatural powers*. It is astonishing how many superstitions existed in the past, but have largely been forgotten. Anything to do with health, childbirth and good fortune was cause for endless speculation and worry during periods of history when life could be very precarious, hence, for example, the widely held belief that the wearing of a necklace of blue beads kept bronchitis at bay. Although we like to pretend we are still superstitious, as a society we are infinitely more rational than we were only a century ago.

Another common genre of folklore is what were once called 'vulgar errors', which were often false scientific or legal misconceptions. It really was believed by probably the majority of the population in the mid nineteenth century, for example, that a horsehair thrown into a rainwater-butt would grow into an eel. It was also genuinely believed that pregnant women could not take a valid oath, and that what someone saw 'through glass' could not be admissible as evidence in court. We have our own 'vulgar errors' nowadays, of course. It is still sometimes said that putting a stamp upside down on an envelope is illegal – it being disrespectful to the Queen, and therefore treason – or that if you put a human tooth overnight in a glass of Coke it will have completely dissolved by morning.

The bulk of modern folklore is therefore a complex web of legends, rumours, superstitions, and vulgar errors. A few selections from the *Talking Folklore* online discussion list in 2008 gives a good flavour of this range: the height of Nelson's Column is carefully designed so that Nelson can see the sea from up there; the pyramid top of the Canary Wharf tower is a Masonic design, deliberately designed as an anti-Christian symbol; the arrow of Eros in Piccadilly Circus is pointing at something significant (but the contributor had forgotten what); the three-legged water tower on Addington Hills was the inspiration for H. G. Wells' *War of the Worlds*; everyone knows that Henry VIII 'exploded' in his coffin outside the London Apprentice pub in Isleworth when being transported down the Thames; the lions at the north entrance of the British Museum stand up and stretch when they hear the clock strike midnight; the lions in Trafalgar Square face outwards, to guard Nelson, but the sphinxes around Cleopatra's Needle face inwards, to protect London from its occult power; the reason why there is a kink in the Piccadilly line as it passes under Brompton Oratory is that it is swerving to avoid a plague pit; a black statue of Horus hawk in the Egyptian collection at the British Museum used to stand by a much-used corridor and its beak was splendidly polished by passers-by touching it; the foot of the statue of St Peter in Westminster Cathedral is well polished by the kisses of the Roman Catholic faithful; a public fire burned continuously in Spitalfields from 1682 to the 1980s as part of the market's charter to always provide a fire for the homeless; there is no number 13 in Fleet St, Park Lane, Oxford Street, Praed Street, St James's Street, Haymarket, and Grosvenor Street, and so on.

THE RANGE OF THIS BOOK

Geographically speaking, the idea of London is not simple, and has meant different things to different people at different times. In some cases the name signifies just the square mile of the City of London, but at other times it encompasses the central districts such as the City and Westminster, and bits of the borough of Camden, which reaches as far south as Holborn. But then there is the old London County Council area (1888–1965), which included all the present inner London boroughs, and later the Greater London Council (1965–86), which created the London Borough system, abolished Middlesex as an administrative unit, and took in huge chunks of Kent, Surrey, Hertfordshire, and Essex.

But the whole thing is complicated by the Post Office, which went its own sweet way in labelling areas to suit its own purposes. Back in the nineteenth century, it gave London postal district numbers to many parts of the outer area, which were still administratively in other counties. People could therefore live in, say, Surrey, but have an SW or SE London postal address. Even further confusion has resulted since 1965, and many people who now live in outer London still have Essex or Kent postal addresses, even though their houses have technically been in London for over forty years. More recently, businesses have started referring to the M25 area as if it were synonymous with Greater London.

For the purposes of this book, London comprises the London boroughs, as defined in 1965, although I occasionally cheat a little and include some areas which extend beyond the boundary, such as Epping Forest. Boroughs are grouped together into areas, such as West, North, East, and so on, which works reasonably well, but throws up a few anomalies where the areas overlap. Please use the index and the maps if you feel you are getting lost.

It is only remains to say that if you find this book and its lore interesting and would like to contribute any material for a future edition or second volume, I would be pleased to hear from you; either c/o the publishers or at sroud@btinternet.com.

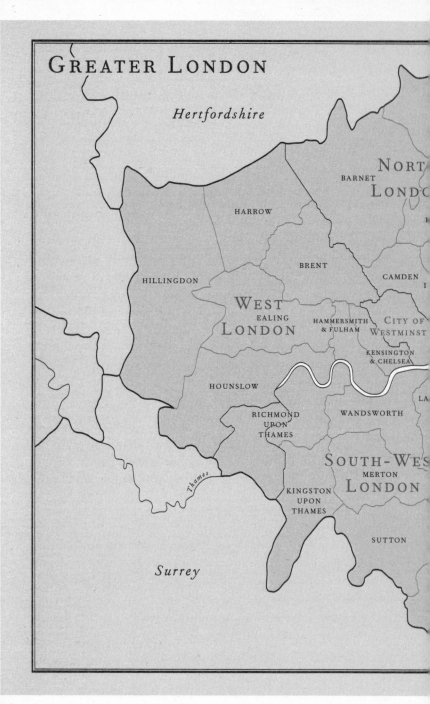

GREATER LONDON

Hertfordshire

NORT
LONDO

BARNET

HARROW

BRENT

CAMDEN

HILLINGDON

WEST
EALING
LONDON

HAMMERSMITH
& FULHAM

CITY OF
WESTMINST

KENSINGTON
& CHELSEA

HOUNSLOW

RICHMOND
UPON
THAMES

WANDSWORTH

LA

Thames

SOUTH-WES
MERTON
LONDON

KINGSTON
UPON
THAMES

SUTTON

Surrey

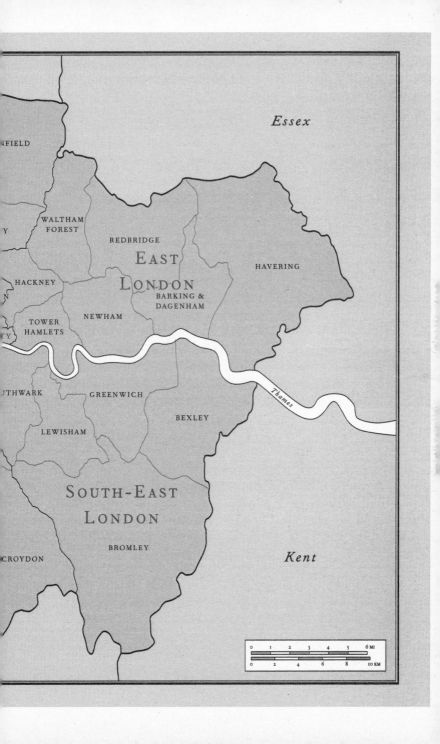

CITY OF LONDON

Aldgate High Street: St Botolph's church

At St Botolph's church, Aldgate High Street, in late February or early March, a commemorative service is held in honour of Sir John Cass (1660?–1718). Sir John was a wealthy member of the City's commercial elite and served as Alderman, Sheriff, and Member of Parliament, making enough money to contribute significantly to education in his community. The service is therefore attended by the staff and pupils of Sir John Cass Foundation Primary School, the only primary school in the City but one of three educational institutions to bear Cass's name.

All the congregation carry or wear red feathers in his honour, as this has become his identifying symbol. The story is told that he suffered a major haemorrhage while writing his will, and that the quill pen in his hand was dyed red as a result. It is more likely that the red feathers are a reference to one on his coat of arms. Sir John was actually buried at St Mary's, Whitechapel, but was baptised at St Botolph's, which is why they claim him as their own.

Modern legends are quite fond of body parts turning up in odd places, and according to one rather bizarre notion, St Botolph's has a severed head on show in a glass case. Hapless Henry Grey, Duke of Suffolk (1517–54), was executed at the Tower of London for his part in the conspiracy to prevent Queen Mary's marriage to Philip of Spain. According to a letter in the *Essex Countryside* (1959/60):

> By some strange chance, Henry Grey's head rolled away into some loose shavings, where it lay for many years. The shavings acted as a preservative and when the head was eventually discovered it was found to be in a remarkable state of preservation. Even today this head is unusually intact

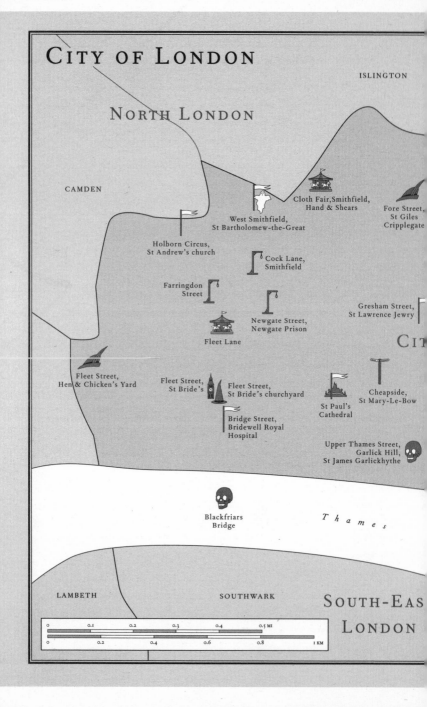

CITY OF LONDON

ISLINGTON

NORTH LONDON

CAMDEN

Cloth Fair, Smithfield,
Hand & Shears

Fore Street,
St Giles
Cripplegate

West Smithfield,
St Bartholomew-the-Great

Holborn Circus,
St Andrew's church

Cock Lane,
Smithfield

Farringdon
Street

Gresham Street,
St Lawrence Jewry

Newgate Street,
Newgate Prison

CIT

Fleet Lane

Fleet Street,
Hen & Chicken's Yard

Fleet Street,
St Bride's

Fleet Street,
St Bride's churchyard

Cheapside,
St Mary-Le-Bow

St Paul's
Cathedral

Bridge Street,
Bridewell Royal
Hospital

Upper Thames Street,
Garlick Hill,
St James Garlickhythe

Blackfriars
Bridge

T h a m e s

LAMBETH

SOUTHWARK

SOUTH-EAS
LONDON

| 0 | 0.1 | 0.2 | 0.3 | 0.4 | 0.5 MI |
| 0 | 0.2 | 0.4 | 0.6 | 0.8 | 1 KM |

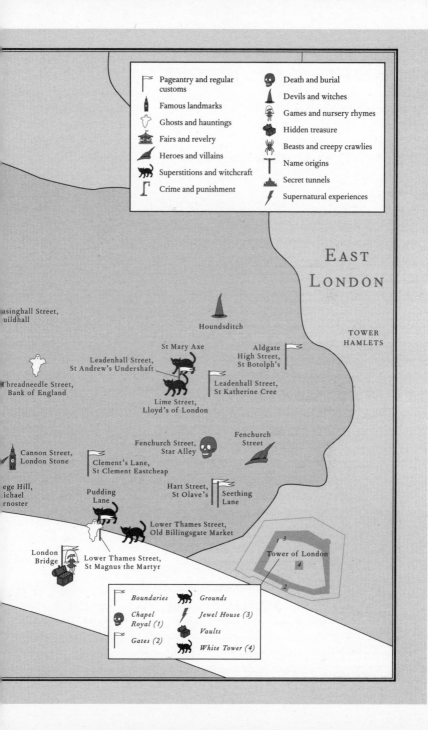

	Pageantry and regular customs		Death and burial
	Famous landmarks		Devils and witches
	Ghosts and hauntings		Games and nursery rhymes
	Fairs and revelry		Hidden treasure
	Heroes and villains		Beasts and creepy crawlies
	Superstitions and witchcraft		Name origins
	Crime and punishment		Secret tunnels
			Supernatural experiences

EAST
LONDON

TOWER
HAMLETS

Basinghall Street,
Guildhall

Houndsditch

St Mary Axe

Aldgate
High Street,
St Botolph's

Leadenhall Street,
St Andrew's Undershaft

Threadneedle Street,
Bank of England

Leadenhall Street,
St Katherine Cree

Lime Street,
Lloyd's of London

Cannon Street,
London Stone

Fenchurch Street,
Star Alley

Fenchurch
Street

Clement's Lane,
St Clement Eastcheap

College Hill,
Michael
Paternoster

Pudding
Lane

Hart Street,
St Olave's

Seething
Lane

Lower Thames Street,
Old Billingsgate Market

London
Bridge

Lower Thames Street,
St Magnus the Martyr

Tower of London

	Boundaries		Grounds
	Chapel Royal (1)		Jewel House (3)
	Gates (2)		Vaults
			White Tower (4)

considering its age, the sword-cuts at the base of the skull being clearly visible. I would urge your less squeamish readers to view this unique phenomenon. It is kept at the church, and may be seen on application.

Leaving aside the highly dubious notion that wood shavings are such an effective preservative, the story presumes that there were no rats or other creatures around to bother the head while it was quietly mummifying itself. Nevertheless, it is true that the church had a mummified head on show in the past, although the identity of the owner was not known. It has now been buried.

BASINGHALL STREET: GUILDHALL

For most Londoners before the Second World War, Gog and Magog were the names of the two wooden giants, fourteen feet tall, who guarded the entrance to the Guildhall, although learned people maintained that one was named Gogmagog and the other Corineus. These figures had been carved by Captain Richard Saunders in 1708, and would be there still if they had not been destroyed in an air raid in 1940. Two statues were commissioned to replace them, but they now stand inside the Guildhall building – presumably for their own protection.

Gog and Magog have had a long association with London, even if their names and early history are complex. The words appear in the Bible (Ezekiel 38–9 and Revelation 20), but not in any context which connects them with giants, and it was in medieval times that this link is first made clear, in the *History of the Kings of Britain*, the mythical history of Britain compiled by Geoffrey of Monmouth in around 1136 – although it is not apparent how much of the story was invented by him and how much was based on existing traditions.

According to Geoffrey, Brutus of Troy arrived in Britain and found it peopled with giants which he and his followers set about destroying. While in Cornwall the Trojans killed all of the giants except one, Goemagot, who was set to wrestle in single combat with their champion Corineus. The latter won the fight by throwing his opponent off the cliffs on to the rocks below. In a later edition of the story, however, Gog and Magog have become two giants who Brutus captures and chains to the doors of his palace in London

According to legend, Gog and Magog were two giants captured
by Brutus, the Trojan prince who was popularly believed to have
founded the kingdom of Britain. Their statues, shown here in a
rather crude nineteenth-century engraving, guarded the entrance
to the Guildhall until they were destroyed by an air raid in 1940.
They have since been replaced.

to act as porters, and this is the root of their connection with the Guildhall
and their association with the centre of the City's government.

Giants were also popular figures, in Britain as elsewhere in Europe, in
processions and pageants from at least the Middle Ages to the seventeenth century. For this purpose, they were made of wickerwork and cloth,
and were light enough for someone to stand inside and carry along.
Processional figures such as these needed frequent repair and replace-
ment, but when not in use they were put on display at the Guildhall, so
that people grew accustomed to their presence. When the building was
rebuilt after the Great Fire, Saunders' wooden statues replaced the old
portable ones.

There are indications that Gog and Magog were used by parents as
'frightening figures' to keep their children in line, and the following long-
running story was reported by London writer Walter Bell in his *More About
Unknown London* (1921):

Every day, I learnt [when about six years old], when the giants hear the
clock strike twelve they come down to dinner. How anxious I was to be in
Guildhall at that hour of noon, to see them clamber off their pedestals and

stalk hungry away. In what gigantic cooking-pot was that gargantuan meal prepared? Where was it served?

BLACKFRIARS BRIDGE

The bridges over the Thames all have reputations for being magnets for those wishing to commit suicide, and this forms the background for one of Elliott O'Donnell's ghost stories in his *Ghosts of London* (1932). As a postman was walking across Blackfriars Bridge early one autumn morning, a tall woman in black and a policeman were the only people in sight:

> Suddenly the woman commenced climbing on to the wall of the bridge. Feeling sure she was about to commit suicide, the postman ran towards her, to try to prevent her, but was too late, for she had disappeared. However, off came his coat, and he was about to jump into the river, to try to save her, when the policeman, who, as he must have seen what had just taken place, appeared to be somewhat callous, stopped him. 'Put on your coat again,' he said, catching him by the arm. 'It is of no use jumping in. What you saw was no living person, it was a ghost.'

He claimed to have seen exactly the same thing before, and suggested that if the postman did not believe him he should come back at the same time the next day.

> The same hour the following morning, found him again on the bridge, and the very same thing occurred . . . 'Well,' the same policeman who was standing by, observed, 'didn't I tell you so? I've seen her do the same thing, at the same hour, for seven consecutive mornings. I'm told it won't happen again (it's what they call periodical haunting) for a good many years, and I'm thankful for that, as it's a bit trying on one's nerves.'

See also KINGSWAY, p. 235.

BRIDGE STREET: BRIDEWELL ROYAL HOSPITAL

Bridewell Royal Hospital was founded in 1553, in the old royal palace of Bridewell, situated between Fleet Street and Blackfriars. The palace had been built by Henry VIII thirty years previously, but was lying empty when Nicholas Ridley, Bishop of London, suggested to Edward VI that it be used as a new institution for the poor and unemployed. The hospital became a combination of workshop, school, and workhouse, and other similar institutions also became known as *Bridewells*, but they gained an unpleasant reputation for harsh treatment, and were also used as prisons. By the mid nineteenth century, however, the various aspects of the institutions were separated, and the school began to build the solid reputation for education for which it is still known today. When the school moved to Witley, Surrey, in 1867, its name was changed to King Edward's School, but the staff and students remember their City origins when they attend a founder's day service at St Bride's church in Fleet Street each year on the second Tuesday in March. The service is often attended by the Lord Mayor.

CANNON STREET: LONDON STONE

Set into the wall of an empty building in Cannon Street, behind a fancy iron grille, and totally ignored by the office workers rushing past, is a stone that some people believe is the most important piece of masonry in the city, and is almost certainly one of the oldest above ground. It is called the London Stone. The metal plaque on the site records:

> This is a fragment of the original piece of limestone once securely fixed in the ground now fronting Cannon Street Station. Removed in 1742 to the north side of the street, in 1798 it was built into the south wall of the church of St Swithun London Stone which stood here until demolished in 1962. Its origin and purpose are unknown, but in 1188 there was a reference to Henry, son of Elwyn de Londenstane, subsequently Lord Mayor of London.

Even earlier references exist. The London chronicler John Stow, for example, claimed in 1598 that he had found a reference to the stone in a book dating from the reign of the Saxon king Ethelstane (925–40), although it is

Roman milestone or part of the first Lord Mayor's house? The original purpose of the London Stone has been the cause of ceaseless speculation for centuries. This engraving shows the stone as it appeared when it was built into the south wall of the church of St Swithun. When the church was demolished in 1962, the London Stone was reset into the wall of a now empty building in Cannon Street.

now suggested that the document to which he referred actually dates from between 1098 and 1108. From that time onwards, the stone is mentioned in passing in a variety of documents, and by numerous chroniclers, poets, playwrights, and others.

As the plaque states, the origin of the stone is not known, but it has long had the unfortunate capacity to attract theories about origin and purpose that are at best conjectural and often completely fanciful. The more down-to-earth ideas can be summarised as follows: it was the central Roman milestone, from which all distances in England were measured; it marked the boundary of the Roman city; it marked the exact centre of the medieval city; it was where people met their creditors to pay their debts; it was a place where people pinned up important notices; or it is the last remaining part of the first Lord Mayor's house, which was special at the time because it was the only one made of stone.

But present-day theorists are more concerned with the stone's symbolic meaning rather than its practical use, and it has been widely argued that the stone has previously been imbued with religious, civic or patriotic meaning and power. The wilder end of these claims includes the idea that it was brought by Brutus when he founded the city; that it is the last remaining evidence of a series of sacred monoliths (like a version of Stonehenge), used by Druids in their worship; or even that it is an integral part of the ley-line system which underlies the secret psychogeography of London. But the most pervasive of all, because in one sense or other it nourishes all the 'symbolic' theories, is the idea that the stone embodies the soul of the city, and it is therefore intimately concerned with the capital's welfare; if it falls or is destroyed, then London will fall.

Another persistent thread in the mythical history built around the stone stems from the scene in Shakespeare's *Henry VI, Part 2*, first performed about 1591. Jack Cade, the leader of the Kentish Rebellion, strikes the stone with his sword (although in some editions it is his staff) and declares, of himself, 'Now is Mortimer lord of this city.' It is not clear whether or not this was a real historical incident. Shakespeare based this scene on one or more of the historical chronicles that were available in his time, only some of which include this incident, and their accuracy is not guaranteed. But even if Cade did this, there is no indication from any other source that this was any more than a dramatic impromptu action. Yet later writers have taken this scene as firm evidence of an ancient belief that striking the stone in such a way was the key part of a ritual which legitimated any leader's claim to authority, in particular that no Lord Mayor could take office until he had struck the stone with his sword.

All these invented traditions and spurious histories are fully examined, and found wanting, in a so-far unpublished paper, 'London Stone: The Stone of Brutus?' by John Clark of the Museum of London. Clark demonstrates that a survey of writings on the London Stone is an object lesson in how legend is a poor basis on which to build a history. He examines the work of writers who have either simply invented a history to suit their own purposes, or who have taken an isolated incident, real or imagined, assumed it to be indicative of a long-standing tradition, and have then extrapolated to build a history with no foundation. Later writers accept these suggestions and build further, but it is a game of smoke and mirrors.

The truth is extremely prosaic. All that can be said safely is that the London Stone has been a landmark since at least the eleventh century, sufficiently well known to give its name to the surrounding area, but there is no evidence that it was imbued with any symbolic or ritual power or meaning.

CHEAPSIDE: ST MARY-LE-BOW CHURCH

The earliest known written reference to the word *cockney* appeared in 1521, and in all the early sources the word is used in derision, to denote a stupid or even effete Londoner, ignorant of country ways and of the real world. John Minsheu's *Ductor in Linguas* (1617), as quoted in the *OED*, provides an origin-story:

The Lord Mayor's Show

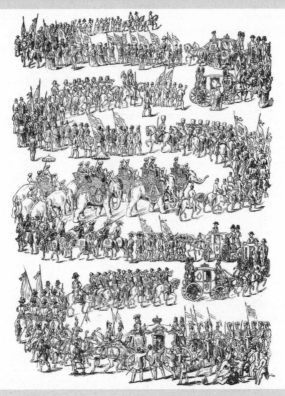

A depiction of the Lord Mayor's Show taken from the 1877 edition of *St Nicholas Magazine for Boys and Girls*.

The Lord Mayor's Show is one of the major high points of London pageantry. Popular with visitors and locals alike, it attracts over half a million spectators in person and many more who tune in to watch it on the television. It previously took place on 9 November, but in deference to the tourist trade, and to avoid gumming up the City streets on a weekday, it is now held on the second Saturday in November. The event is organised by a pageantmaster, and the procession takes a circular route from the Guildhall, covering 1.7 miles and taking at least an hour to pass one spot. The 2007 event included over 6,000 people in 250 vehicles and 70 floats.

Technically speaking, of course, it is not the thousands of people in the procession who are important, but the one person in the ceremonial gilded horse-drawn coach, which dates from 1757. The new Lord Mayor is elected by the members of the Court of Aldermen on or around 29 September (Michaelmas Day), and his or her first official act is to visit the Royal Courts of Justice in order to swear the oath of allegiance to the Crown. This tradition dates from 1215, about twenty-five years after the Mayoralty was established, when a charter of King John stipulated that an oath of allegiance must be taken. In the earliest times, the new Mayor simply rode over to the Courts from his residence, or went by barge, with a few attendants, but this journey gradually grew in pomp and circumstance as the office grew in importance.

The Show has had its ups and downs, and its content has reflected the political and economic preoccupations of the time. Before the Reformation it was primarily a religious event, but later on patriotic and military themes were drawn into the celebrations, and during the time of the Commonwealth it fell into abeyance. The middle of the nineteenth century was a particularly low point, when, according to Robert Chambers' *Book of Days* (1864), many people deemed it 'simply ludicrous'. Twenty years later, however, things had improved and the focus had become a typically late Victorian combination of education, technological advances, and the celebration of Britain's imperial might, as can be seen in this extract from the *Illustrated London News* of 17 November 1883:

> The procession contained no men in armour, or meaningless family costumes, but it included Grace Darling's boat, a life-boat with its crew, and a rocket apparatus, for saving lives from shipwreck; a trophy of the Fisheries, composed of nets, spars and oars, ropes, buoys, baskets, and other fishing-gear, from the late Exhibition; and several trophies of India and the Colonies, which were original, if not quite appropriate in design. That of India consisted of natives standing among palm-trees, with a stuffed tiger above, followed by two elephants; that of Canada, a backwoodsman, amidst pine-logs and piles of corn-sacks with beavers and bears.

A Cockney or Cockny, applied only to one born within the sound of Bow-bell, that is within the City of London, which term came first out of this tale: That a citizen's son riding with his father . . . into the country . . . asked, when he heard a horse neigh, what the horse did, his father answered the horse doth neigh; riding farther he heard a cock crow, and said doth the cock neigh too? and therefore Cockney or Cocknie, by inversion . . . raw or ripe in country-men's affairs.

The real origin of the word is obscure, and it has therefore attracted a number of theories and guesses. Minsheu's story implies that the word was originally pronounced *cock-nay*, and this agrees with the best suggestion, given in the *OED*, that it derives from *cocken*, meaning 'cock's', and *ay*, an early pronunciation of 'egg'. Certainly, in many country districts, any small, malformed or useless egg has long been called a *cock's egg* and is said to have been laid by the cockerel.

CLEMENT'S LANE: ST CLEMENT EASTCHEAP CHURCH

There was a strong and popular tradition in local parishes for Easter to be seen as a time for good neighbourhood and brotherly love, which often resulted in customary meals or the sharing of bread or cakes in the church. A bequest in the will of Robert Halliday, dated 6 May 1491, gave five shillings to the churchwardens of St Clement, Eastcheap, each year, to entertain local people who were 'at variance with each other', to induce them to 'better neighbourhood, and to beget brotherly love amongst them'. If there happened to be nobody in such a condition, the money was to be spent on the parishioners at the local tavern, on Shere Tuesday (the Tuesday before Good Friday).

See also CHURCH ROAD, TWICKENHAM: ST MARY THE VIRGIN CHURCH, p. 369.

CLOTH FAIR, SMITHFIELD: HAND AND SHEARS PUB

For 722 years, a regular highlight of the Londoner's summer entertainment was a trip to Bartholomew Fair at Smithfield. Of all the fairs in reach of London – Barnet, Southwark, Greenwich, Fairlop – St Bartholomew's was the oldest, the greatest and the one that Londoners claimed as their own local fair. It was founded by a charter of Henry I, granted to the Prior of St Bartholomew's church and priory, Smithfield, in 1133. At the dissolution of the monasteries in 1539, it was taken over by the City of London, and from then on was officially proclaimed each year by the Lord Mayor himself. The fair started, appropriately, on St Bartholomew's Day (24 August) but its duration varied over the years, from three days to three weeks.

Once the formalities of opening were over, the Mayor and Alderman went for a ceremonial dinner, and the fun of the fair could commence. A German traveller called Keutzner noted in 1598 that:

> A parcel of live rabbits are turned loose among the crowd, which are pursued by a number of boys, who endeavour to catch them with all the noise they can make.

Bartholomew was originally designed as a trade fair, and for many years it was the most important event in the year for the cloth industry. Chambers' *Book of Days* (1864) noted that the clothworkers had previously had their own customs at the fair, including a burlesque proclamation the evening before by a company of drapers and tailors. They met at the Hand and Shears, their local pub, in a lane called Cloth-Fair, running parallel to Bartholomew Close,

For over 700 years – until 1855 – Bartholomew Fair was one of the highlights of London life, its theatrical booths proving particularly popular. This nineteenth-century engraving shows a troupe of actors playing out the biblical story of the beautiful Hebrew widow Judith, who beheaded the Assyrian general Holofernes.

from whence they marched, shears in hand, to the same place that the Lord Mayor would stand for the real opening. A road called Cloth Fair survives in Smithfield, and there is still a Hand & Shears pub.

In its heyday, Bartholomew Fair was particularly known for its large theatrical booths, presenting everything from Shakespeare to the latest comedies and farces; in addition there were puppet shows, dancing booths, menageries, wild-beast shows, tightrope walkers, freak shows, gingerbread stalls, and of course every kind of food and drink imaginable, but particularly roast pork. It is difficult in these days of ready money, and the abundance of shops and places of entertainment, to understand how important were the few days of fun and freedom that events like these provided for the working-class Londoner of the past. James Grant's *Sketches in London* (1840) gives an indication in just one small area:

> In the sweetmeat and toy department of the Fair, the variety and abundance are so great that you are quite confounded with the scene. I have heard a young man ask his sweetheart what she would like, pointing to a stall on which were displayed, in rich abundance and most tempting condition, sweetmeats innumerable: and I have seen her so completely at a loss to make up her mind as to which she would prefer, that the fable of the ass perishing of hunger between two bundles of hay, has come across my mind . . . In fact it is no uncommon thing, in such circumstances, for the lover to be obliged to decide, as well as to pay, for the object of his affections.

By the turn of the nineteenth century, many of the country's older fairs were under pressure because they had outgrown their original purpose and had become notorious for rowdy behaviour. The inner-city fairs like Bartholomew had also outgrown their physical bounds, as building developments grew up around them, and the new local residents began to complain. The opposition to Bartholomew Fair came from many quarters: religious people deplored the moral depravity of the proceedings; magistrates condemned the crime the fair engendered; and local people hated the noise, the mess and the crowds. As early as 1786 *The Times* was complaining:

> Much has been said relative to the return of Bartholomew Fair and of the great nuisance it is to the neighbouring inhabitants, whilst it continues. That it collects together a numerous tribe of thieves and pickpockets we readily admit, and, without question, a total suppression of it is devoutly to be wished.

But the opposition took a long time to suppress the fair and it lingered on for many years, finally going out with a whimper rather than a bang. Because the fair belonged to the Corporation of London rather than a private individual or other institution, the authorities decided to use various powers to remove its 'abuses' piecemeal, instead of tackling it head-on. The rent that the showmen had to pay was sharply increased, the length of the fair was strictly confined to three days, regulations about the restriction of pavements were tightened, and so on. Perhaps the real deathblow was the Act for Regulating Theatres (1843), which gave the Corporation the power to ban all theatrical performances at the fair. As this included every 'tragedy, comedy, farce, opera, barletta, interlude, melodrama, pantomime, or other entertainment of the stage, or any part thereof', many of the shows for which the fair was famous were removed at a stroke. By 1850, hardly any stallholders were bothering to turn up, and the great Bartholomew was proclaimed for the last time in 1855.

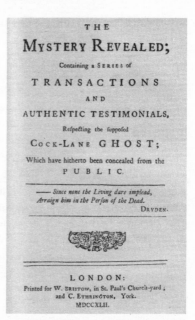

THE

MYSTERY REVEALED;

Containing a SERIES of

TRANSACTIONS

AND

AUTHENTIC TESTIMONIALS,

Respecting the suppofed

COCK-LANE GHOST;

Which have hitherto been concealed from the
PUBLIC.

—— Since none the Living dare implead,
Arraign him in the Perfon of the Dead.
DRYDEN.

LONDON:
Printed for W. BRISTOW, in St. Paul's Church-yard;
and C. ETHRINGTON, York.
MDCCXLII.

The title-page of an eighteenth-century pamphlet written by Oliver Goldsmith claiming to tell the truth about the Cock Lane ghost. Note the mistake made with the printing date: 1742 predates the alleged ghostly events by seven years.

See also ST MARGARET'S HILL, SOUTHWARK, p. 343.

COCK LANE, SMITHFIELD

Cock Lane is an inconspicuous, narrow thoroughfare, off Giltspur Street, Smithfield, which suddenly acquired international fame in 1762 when a house in the road became the scene of one of the best-known hauntings in London's history. The proceedings were heavily reported in many of the newspapers and pamphlets of the time, and were briefly the talk of the town, but it is unlikely that such an obscure and ultimately unconvincing ghost story would have had such a lasting impact if the ghost had not accused somebody of its murder. It is because of this fame that we know so much more about this incident than many other scares which were, in comparison, mere nine-day wonders.

In 1749, William Kent, recently arrived from Norfolk, was living with his late wife's sister Fanny. They were posing as man and wife, and lodging at the home of Richard Parsons and his family, in Cock Lane. Parsons owed money to Kent, and relations between them were becoming strained. While Kent was away, Fanny shared a room with Parsons' twelve-year-old daughter Elizabeth and became aware of odd scratching noises in her room. On William's return, the Kents changed their lodgings, but sadly Fanny died of smallpox a short time later. Back at Cock Lane, it was suggested that it was the ghost of Kent's first wife who was causing the scratching noise, but all went quiet until two years later when the noises returned with new vigour. It was now claimed that the renewed rappings were in fact Fanny's ghost, which could not rest because Kent had, it claimed, poisoned her with arsenic in her drink. The house already had something of a local reputation for being haunted, but rumours of this new development spread like wildfire across London, and crowds began flocking to hear the noises, which would sometimes answer individual questions (once for yes, twice for no). Parsons charged an admittance fee, and local pubs did a roaring trade; the events were avidly reported in the papers, and songs and plays on the subject rapidly followed.

By all accounts the crowds that gathered were drawn from every class, and ranged from awestruck believers to those out for a laugh, but the Parsons family had many respectable supporters, in particular the Revd John Moore, a young clergyman of Methodist leanings, who avidly believed in the ghost. Nevertheless, another group of gentleman, including Dr Johnson and others with connections to Kent, decided to investigate, and arranged to visit and stay in the house. Particular attention focused on young Elizabeth Parsons, who claimed to be the only one who could see the spirit, which only seemed to be active when she was around.

The tide of educated public opinion turned when the ghost rashly promised that on a certain day she would rap on Fanny's coffin in the crypt at St John's, Clerkenwell, but although the investigating committee gathered at the appointed time, nothing happened. With the approval of the Lord Mayor, Elizabeth was taken to another house and closely interrogated and secretly watched, and she was seen to hide a piece of wood in her nightclothes. It became clear that the whole thing had been a fraud from start to finish, with Elizabeth, and probably both parents, as the perpetrators.

William Kent was understandably highly vexed by the whole affair, which he claimed had ruined his business and his life, and he was adamant that the imposture should be publicly exposed so that he could clear his name. He ensured that the principals involved, including Parsons and his wife, Moore, and some of those involved in publishing the accusations against him, were arrested and charged 'for conspiracy to take away the life of William Kent by charging him with the murder of Frances Lynes by giving her poison whereof she died'. They were all found guilty, and Parsons was placed in the pillory three times, and then served two years in jail. But the feelings of the local populace were made plain when instead of throwing stones and rotten vegetables at him, they took up a collection to help ease his time in prison.

Supporters and detractors continued to carry out a war of words in the newspapers, but the sceptics had gained the upper hand, and there followed a torrent of mockery against those who had believed in the ghost. The affair was given extra edge by being caught up in one of the major religious controversies of the day, caused by the rise of John Wesley's Methodists. These individuals were already under fire for their gullibility over things supernatural and their penchant for whipping up their congregations into a frenzy, and Revd Moore's role in giving the Parsons family's story widespread credibility was particularly open to criticism. Within months of the affair, Hogarth had published his savagely satirical print *Credulity, Superstition and Fanaticism: A Medley*, which portrayed a Methodist meeting and included references to a number of exposed supernatural frauds, including the Cock Lane ghost.

But there are always those who regard any exposure as a conspiracy, or as rigged in favour of the establishment, and whose belief is actually strengthened by a little opposition. Thus it was claimed at the time that Elizabeth had been forced to cheat by the aggressive treatment of her interrogators, and also that the reason why the ghost could not appear in the crypt was that Kent had secretly moved Fanny's coffin to another place. In response, a group of worthies accompanied Kent into the crypt to prove that Fanny's body was where it should be, and they found it to be in an advanced state of decay. Similarly, other traditions lingered on, or were created. Charles Mackay's *Extraordinary Popular Delusions* (1841), for example, includes a footnote which claims that about seven years previously, one J. W. Archer was sketching in the crypt of St John's, Clerkenwell, when a coffin was pointed out to him as that of 'Scratching Fanny'. The body inside was of a young woman, extremely well preserved, but bearing no marks of smallpox, and the state of the body was claimed to be consistent with arsenic poisoning.

Despite countless articles and at least three books on the subject, some modern writers still claim that the Cock Lane haunting has 'never been explained'.

COLLEGE HILL: ST MICHAEL PATERNOSTER CHURCH

Lord Mayor Richard Whittington (*see* DICK WHITTINGTON, p. 228) made many benefactions in his will, and one of these was for the rebuilding of St Michael Paternoster church, in College Hill, where he and his wife were buried in an ornate and costly tomb. The almsmen of another of his charitable creations, the Whittington Hospital, were instructed to gather round his tomb after divine service to pray for his and his wife's souls, but poor Richard was not to rest easy for long. According to John Stow's *Survey of London* (1598):

> This Richard Whittington was in this church three times buried: first by his executors under a fair monument; then in the reign of Edward VI, the parson of that church, thinking some great riches, as he said, to be buried with him, caused his monument to be broken, his body to be spoiled in his leaden sheet, and again the second time to be buried; and in the reign of Queen Mary the parishioners were forced to take him up, to lap him in lead as afore, to bury him the third time, and to place his monument, or the like, over him again, which remaineth, and so he resteth.

St Michael Paternoster was rebuilt by Wren between 1686 and 1694, a steeple was added in 1713, but it was also damaged in the Second World War. The church is now the chapel and headquarters of the Missions to Seafarers, and features a modern Whittington window, by John Hayward, and a memorial tablet detailing the position of his original tomb.

When the Second World War bomb damage to the church was being repaired, the builders discovered a mummified cat, which immediately started the notion that Whittington's cat must have been buried with him. Oddly enough, however, mummified cats are not particularly rare in old buildings. They have been reported in various parts of the country, hidden in walls and attics, and mostly in domestic settings. There seems to be no documentary evidence as to why they were placed there, but the known examples strongly suggest a symbolic or even magical purpose. By far the most likely explanation is that they were believed to keep rats and mice away from the building.

FARRINGDON STREET

If you walk up Farringdon Street from Fleet Street, you are following the line of the Fleet Ditch, or River, which is now underground, having been incorporated into the sewer system in the 1860s. The Fleet was previously one of the most important watercourses that ran into the Thames; rising at Hampstead, and flowing through what is now Camden Town, King's Cross, Farringdon and reaching the Thames near Blackfriars Bridge. Until the sixteenth century it was used for river transport, and its banks were lined with mills, wharves and factories. But it was also the main sewer for the surrounding area and became a major health hazard. Only those who could afford nothing better would choose to frequent its banks, and this is the setting for the following account in Elliott O'Donnell's *Haunted Waters* (1957):

> Numbers 2 and 3 West Street, demolished in the 1860s, close to the Fleet River . . . Built by an affluent Gipsy, they served conjointly the purpose of a tavern and an inn, which became the resort of fences, robbers, and every kind of criminal. There were sliding panels, secret staircases, cupboards for storing stolen goods, and trapdoors, which afforded a means of escape and of dropping bodies of victims into the Fleet, to be borne speedily by the current into the Thames. Many cruel, dark deeds were perpetuated in the inn. Strangers in London were decoyed by attractive women, confederates of the robbers, to the inn, where they were robbed and murdered. Once within the walls of the inn there was no hope of escape and no mercy. It

was small wonder that stories of ghostly happenings in the inn and in the Fleet were constantly circulated.

The motif of the murderous inn-keeper is widespread throughout the country, and towns from Colnbrook in Buckinghamshire to Shepton Mallet in Somerset have local versions of this story.

FENCHURCH STREET

In 1707, the mysterious 'E.B.' of Ludgate printed a chapbook entitled *The Constant, but Unhappy Lovers*, a story set in Fenchurch Street. As is common with this type of publication, the title-page provides an excellent synopsis:

> Being a full and true relation of one Madam Butler, a young gentlewoman, and a great heiress at Hackney boarding-school, who being by her father forced to marry Mr Harvey a rich merchant's son near Fanchurch [*sic*] Street, against her will; one Mr Perpoint, a young gentleman of considerable estate, who had courted her above two years, grew so discontented that he went a volunteer to the wars in Spain, where being mortally wounded at the late Battle of Almanza, he writ a letter with his own blood, therein putting a bracelet of Madam Butler's hair, and then ordering his servant to bake his heart to a powder after his death, he charg'd him to deliver them in a box to the abovesaid gentlewoman. His man came to England, and went on the 6th of June to deliver the present to Madam Butler, but it was took away by her husband, who gave her the powder in a dish of tea, which when she knew what she had drank, and saw the bloody letter and bracelet, she said it was the last she would ever eat and drink and accordingly going to bed, she was found dead in the morning, with a copy of verses lying by her on a table, written in her own blood.

As David Blamires pointed out in an article in *Folklore* (1993), this is a version of an old and widespread tale, called by folklorists 'The Eaten Heart', which has been recorded from oral traditions in India and North America as well as across Europe. But the key point about E.B.'s *The Constant, but Unhappy Lovers* is the skilful way in which the writer has updated the story (drinking tea, fighting in Spain) and localised it

(Hackney, Fenchurch Street), so that the reader of the day would certainly have related to its content, and would have been much more likely to regard it as a true story.

FENCHURCH STREET: STAR ALLEY

Until the Burial of Suicides Act of 1823, the bodies of suicides were deliberately treated badly, and friends of the deceased often tried to circumvent official procedures by carrying out a quiet burial of their own. Sometimes the authorities turned a blind eye, but usually they did not, as revealed in this brief reference from the *Gentleman's Magazine* of August 1755:

> One Barlow a bookseller in Star Alley, Fenchurch Street, shot his child of two years old which died instantly, and then himself in at the mouth . . . After a few days he died of the wound, and the jury upon the inquest found him guilty of felo de se. His friends took away the body and buried it; of which the Lord Mayor being informed, ordered it to be dug up, and put in a hole made for that purpose in the cross roads at the upper end of Moorfields, and a stake drove through the body.

See also SUICIDE BURIALS, p. 260.

FLEET LANE

This brief mention of the surprisingly widespread custom of 'selling a wife' appeared in the *Country Journal* on 6 September 1729:

> Last Wednesday one Everet, of Fleet Lane, sold his wife to one Griffin of Long Lane for a 3s bowl of punch; who, we hear, hath since complained of having a bad bargain

See also WIFE-SELLING, p. 102.

Wife-selling, particularly at local markets, was formerly widespread, one instance being recorded at Fleet Lane in 1729. It was commonly believed that such transactions were a legal form of divorce.

FLEET STREET: HEN AND CHICKEN'S YARD

The tale of Sweeney Todd, the demon barber of Fleet Street, is one of those remarkably tenacious stories which is re-launched for every generation with a new adaptation, stage play, or film, and which, despite its origins as an archetypal 'penny dreadful', continues to capture the public imagination as a true story. The story, which is either horrific or ludicrous, depending on whether you find Gothic novels gripping or ineffably silly, clearly strikes a chord with many people, and was a major influence on many other hits of the genre, such as *Dracula* and *Dr Jekyll and Mr Hyde*.

The core of the story is that a barber, Sweeney Todd, has a special chair that precipitates selected customers into the basement, where their throats are cut and their valuables and clothes stolen. As if this were not sufficiently horrible, Todd has an arrangement with Mrs Lovett, a nearby pastry cook, to dispose of the bodies in her famous pies.

The true beginnings of the Sweeney Todd story as we know it are suitably murky, and despite a great deal of scholarly attention being devoted to the question in recent years, we still do not know for sure who wrote it. It is likely that the author was one of the anonymous hacks who made their living writing for the publisher Edward Lloyd. He specialised in pirated editions, plagiarised versions of popular authors such as Dickens and Ainsworth, sensational horror stories and what came to be known as penny dreadfuls. The two leading contenders are Lloyd's best-known hacks, Thomas Prest and James Rymer, but we will probably never know for sure which one.

What is known is that the story first appeared in print as *The String of Pearls: A Romance*, which was serialised in Lloyd's short-lived periodical *People's Periodical and Family Library*, from November 1846 to March 1847. It was popular enough to be adapted for the stage before the last part was even published, and Lloyd published a much-expanded version of the story as *The String of Pearls or A Sailor's Gift* in 1850. From then on, there were countless reprints, adaptations, stage versions and even pantomimes, as the story entered the general consciousness of popular culture, and the name of the main character became adopted as the title of the piece.

It is also clear that Lloyd's staff-writer did not invent the story from scratch, but was recycling existing elements, and the core motif was already in the air some years before the public birth of the story. Charles Dickens, for example, had obviously heard of people being made into pies in London at least two years earlier. In *Martin Chuzzlewit* (1844), at the end of Chapter 36 and beginning of Chapter 37, Tom Pinch gets lost in the big city:

> 'I don't know what John will think of me. He'll begin to be afraid I have strayed into one of those streets where the countrymen are murdered; and that I have been made meat-pies of, or some such horrible thing.' Tom's evil genius did not lead him into the dens of any of those preparers of cannibalistic pastry, who are represented in many standard country legends as doing a lively retail business in the Metropolis.

In the next few sentences Dickens briefly mentions other stories of what happens to country bumpkins in the evil city. The theme of the demon barber and meat pies was certainly not new at the time, and had several other published antecedents, for example the short story in the periodical *Tell-Tale* of about 1824, set in Paris; a report in the *London Chronicle* from 2 December 1784; and stories in France set in the time of the French Revolution, and others in Venice. In addition to the literary investigations into the story and its antecedents, there has been a sub-stratum of those who argue, not particularly convincingly, that Todd was a real person, but there is no evidence to support such wishful thinking.

The Great Plague

Daniel Defoe, whose *Journal of the Plague Year* provides a fascinating insight into the beliefs and superstitions that were in circulation around the time of the Great Plague.

It is a truism of folklore research that the incidence of superstition in society rises sharply in times of uncertainty and danger, so it is no surprise that an outbreak of disease on the scale of the 1665 plague, whose cause and treatment were unknown at the time, engendered countless examples of rumours, panics and legends that circulated widely and rapidly among a bewildered and frightened population.

A superb source of information is Daniel Defoe's *A Journal of the Plague Year*, first published in 1722, although the book's historical accuracy should not be taken for granted. Despite being written convincingly in the first person, it is not the eyewitness diary it purports to be, as Defoe himself was born in 1660, and was only five when the outbreak occurred. His claim that the journal was compiled by one 'H.F.', a saddler from Whitechapel, is also unsubstantiated, but it has been shown that he used many genuine contemporary sources, and the book is best viewed as a particularly accurate form of historical fiction. Many of his descriptions are corroborated by other writers of the time, in particular diarists such as Samuel Pepys.

Defoe's account teems with prophecies, rumours, stories, superstitions, and methods of prevention and cure, but he retains a healthy degree of scepticism, and is acutely aware that hearsay is often unreliable. He is one of the earliest writers to recognise the type of story which we would now call 'contemporary legend', and he even suggests characteristics by which they can be identified:

> But these stories had two marks of suspicion that always attended them, which caused me always to slight them, and to look on them as mere stories that people continually frighted each other with. That wherever it was that we heard it, they always placed the scene at the farther end of town ... In the next place, of what part soever you heard the story, the particulars were always the same ... so that it was apparent, at least to my judgement, that there was more of Tale than Truth in those things.

Many of the stories that circulated were about whether or not this great catastrophe could have been predicted. Both Pepys and Defoe mention the comets that appeared in December 1664 and April 1665, as well as the almost universal idea that these were a sign from God of major disasters to come. In the early days of the plague, the city fairly swarmed with fortune-tellers, cunning men, and mountebanks, who Defoe regarded as parasites on society, and he comments, with some satisfaction, that none of those fortune-tellers who perished had been able to predict their own fate.

The items sold by these charlatans to protect against infection included a wide range of herbal remedies and a number of magically protective amulets. One such charm described by Defoe was the word *abracadabra* written out six times, one under the other, with letters missed out at each end, to make an inverted triangle. Written in this way and worn or carried about the person, it was said to protect the bearer from evil influences as well as disease, and was widely popular in seventeenth-century England. The earliest known version is in a Latin document from the second century AD, and it most probably entered British tradition in translation in the sixteenth century.

Of the common substances believed to keep the infection at bay, vinegar, garlic, and tobacco were three of the most popular. In any transaction in which money had to change hands, the coins were placed in bowls of vinegar, and a sexton who carried dead bodies to his cart described holding garlic and rue in his mouth and smoking tobacco. His wife, who acted as nurse to infected people, swore by washing her head and sprinkling her head-cloths with vinegar.

Stories at the time included rumours that people were going round deliberately infecting others with the disease. These are echoed in modern legend cycles such as 'Typhoid Mary' and 'Welcome to the World of Aids', which rely on the same idea. A more upbeat story given by Defoe tells of a piper who was lying in the street in a drunken stupor one night when he was taken up by the dead-cart by mistake. Waking up just as the cart reached the pit, he called out, 'Where am I?' When told he was in the cart, he exclaimed, 'But I ain't dead yet, am I?' Defoe commented that he had heard other versions in which the piper woke up and started to tune up his pipes, which frightened the cart attendants out of their wits, thinking the Devil was in the cart. The story of the drunken piper was not new, and had been around at least since the turn of the seventeenth century, but in true folklore form was given a new lease of life in this way.

See also PLAGUE PITS, p. 120.

FLEET STREET: ST BRIDE'S CHURCH

The impressive spire of St Bride's was built in 1703, and includes four octagonal tiers of diminishing size. One of the countless mini-legends about London landmarks relates that the modern tiered wedding cake was invented by William Rich, a pastry cook, who was directly inspired by the view of the church from his shop window.

FLEET STREET: ST BRIDE'S CHURCHYARD

Man's Amazement is the title of a broadside ballad, dating from about the 1650s, which tells the story of a meeting between Tom Cox, a poor coachman, and the Devil. It is printed in black-letter, the old-fashioned Gothic script that was common for this type of publication at the time, and is typical of the tales of amazing wonders that were then very popular. Only one copy seems to have survived, and that is in the collection made by Samuel Pepys, housed at Magdalene College, Cambridge.

The ballad begins with Tom Cox setting down his fare in Water Lane, then driving to the end of the road to turn round. A figure appeared who he thought was another customer, so he stopped, got down and opened the door. The man asked to be taken to 'Brides Low churchyard'. Tom climbed up to start, but:

> The horses possest with a habit of fear
> They snorted and started as it did appear
> The coachman his hat it fell off to the ground
> The night being dark it could not be found
> This gentleman told him though he did not see it
> His hat it lay under his horse's fore-feet
> There finding his hat and the words to be true
> He then was amazed to think how he knew.

They reached St Bride's churchyard with great difficulty, as the horses continued to play up. The man held out his hand:

Built in 1703, the impressive spire of St Bride's is said to have inspired a local pastry cook, William Rich, to have devised the modern tiered wedding cake.

> Here's money enough I will bountiful pay
> Then as he did proffer to feel for his hand
> Yet there was no substance he could understand
> Nor there was no money the coach-man could see.

As the passenger got down from the coach he suddenly appeared in the form of a bear, which stared upon him with 'great flaming eyes'. The coachman lashed at it with his whip, and it seemed to pull back and then vanish 'in great flashes of fire'. Tom turned his horses homeward but only just managed to get there:

> The coach-man was speechless like one almost dead
> But they took him down and convey'd him to bed
> Where five or six days he did speechless remain
> But then at length it returned again.

He was eventually able to say what had happened to him, but had 'lost the sense and the use of his limbs' and lived on in a languishing state. He could no longer follow his calling.

What the seventeenth-century audience for ballads made of this story is unrecorded, but in the early nineteenth century a parody version called *The Devil and the Hackney Coachman* was widely known.

FORE STREET: ST GILES CRIPPLEGATE CHURCH

On the north wall of St Giles's church is a memorial to Sir William Staines, an Uxbridge man who had a touch of the Dick Whittingtons about him. He used to tell the story of how he had started work as a bricklayer's labourer and was working on repairs to a parsonage when the vicar's wife, to his great surprise, told him that she had twice dreamed that he would be Lord Mayor of London. He did indeed prosper as a mason and builder and, after moving to London, he served as Alderman for Cripplegate ward from 1793 to 1807, and Lord Mayor from 1800 to 1801. Staines pioneered a number of philanthropic schemes, including the erection of almshouses. Nevertheless, he was illiterate, and it appears in some accounts that his contemporaries did not forget his humble origins but made jokes about his putting butter on his meal 'with a trowel', and the terse comment in the *City Biography* (1800) that he had 'married his cook-maid'.

GRESHAM STREET: ST LAWRENCE JEWRY CHURCH

A colourful piece of London pageantry takes place each year when the Lord Mayor, Court of Common Council, Court of Aldermen, and other City dignitaries, all walk in procession to St Lawrence Jewry church in Gresham Street to hear the annual 'spital sermon'. The usual date is the second Wednesday after Easter, but this varies a little, to accommodate the Lord Mayor's busy schedule.

The term *spital* comes from the same root as *hospital*, and similarly denoted a place where the needy and sick were cared for, but spitals became closely associated with the care of the destitute, beggars and people suffering from 'foul' diseases. These charities were often supported by endowed sermons, and, because of the nature of the institution and its inmates, the annual sermons were delivered outdoors.

The spital sermons that now take place at St Lawrence's pre-date the Reformation, and were originally given each year at the priory church of St Mary Spital. They have had many different homes since, including St Paul's Cross, and Christ Church, Newgate Street, and have been at their present home since the Second World War. Until the end of the nineteenth century there were two sermons – on Monday and Tuesday in Easter week.

Christ's Hospital (often called the Bluecoat School, after its distinctive uniform) was founded in Newgate in 1552, and for centuries the boys of the school always attended the spital sermons en masse. Samuel Pepys recorded a visit:

2 Apr 1662
Mr Moore came to me and he and I walked to the Spittle, an hour or two before my Lord Mayor and the Blewe coate boys came, which at last they did, and a fine sight of charity it is indeed. We got places and stayed to hear a sermon; but it being a presbyterian one, it was so long, that after above an hour of it we went away.

Indeed, the event was so closely associated with Christ's Hospital that when that institution moved to Horsham, West Sussex, in 1902, it was seriously thought that the sermons would cease. But they did not, and the schoolchildren still attend each year.

Another outdoor spital sermon takes place at Magdelen College, Oxford, in June.

HART STREET: ST OLAVE'S CHURCH

St Olave's church, Hart Street, is one of the smallest of the City churches, dating from the fifteenth century. It survived the Great Fire, but was quite badly damaged in the Blitz. This was Samuel Pepys's parish church and is where his wife Elizabeth was buried in 1669, and he too, after his death on 26 May 1703. There is an original monument to Elizabeth, erected by Samuel, but the one to him is late Victorian (1883). Every year, on or near the date of his death, there is a well-attended commemoration service, organised by the Pepys Club, which was founded in 1903. The Lord Mayor often attends and lays a wreath in front of Samuel's memorial. There is much seventeenth-century music, to reflect the keen interest Pepys took in that sphere, and an address by an eminent scholar.

Pepys was a regular, but not always enthusiastic, churchgoer, often going twice on a Sunday, and as a member of the Navy Office, he sat in the gallery (now removed). He quite often recorded his views on the sermon here and at other churches he visited, but he regularly slept through the whole thing, and on many occasions his mind was on other matters entirely: at Greenwich church on 13 January 1661 he wrote of 'a good sermon, a fine church, and a great company of handsome women'; and at St Margaret's, Westminster, where he had gone to meet Mrs Martin:

26 May 1667
. . . there much against my will, stayed out the whole church . . . but I did entertain myself with my perspective glass up and down the church, by which I had the great pleasure of seeing and gazing a great many very fine women; and what with that and sleeping, I passed away the time till sermon was done.

HOLBORN CIRCUS: ST ANDREW'S CHURCH

St Andrew's church in Holborn was only just saved from THE GREAT FIRE OF LONDON (p. 48) by a change of wind, but as it was already in a state of disrepair it was decided to rebuild it and Christopher Wren took on the task. According to the Charity Commissioners' Report for the parish:

> Mr Thomas Tuck, who died in the year 1670, gave by will 40s per annum, for ever, to this parish; viz 20s for a sermon on the 4th day of September in every year, to deplore the calamity of the dreadful fire in London in 1666, and 20s to be distributed in bread among the poor of the same parish. But it is not known that this gift was ever paid.

See also LOWER THAMES STREET: ST MAGNUS THE MARTYR CHURCH, p. 40.

HOUNDSDITCH

Satan was very real to the people of seventeenth-century England. There were many tales in which he walked the earth, in various guises, going about his daily business of opposing God and everything He stands for. In addition to causing major mayhem with plagues and earthquakes, the Devil also had the personal touch, and there were many stories in which he appeared to individuals or small groups, to carry them off to Hell, to bargain for their souls or simply to tempt them into sin and wickedness.

In the latter category is the story of poor George Gibbs, who lived with his wife at Houndsditch, and who was persuaded to commit suicide. It appears as a ballad on a black-letter broadside, written by C.H. (Charles Hammond), probably in 1663. As is often the case with ballads of this time, the extended title tells most of the story:

> *The Divils Cruelty to Mankind being a true relation of the life and death of George Gibbs, a sawyer by his trade, who being many times tempted by the Divil to destroy himselfe, did on Fryday being the 7th of March 1663, most cruelly ripp up his own belly and pull'd out his bowells and guts and cut them in pieces; to the amazement of all the beholders, the sorrow of his friends, and the great grief*

of his wife, being not long married, and both young people. To the tune of the Two Children in the Wood.

And the first verse sets the moral tone:

> Good Christian people lend an ear
> To this my doleful song
> A sadder tale you nere did heare
> Exprest by any tongue
> The Divil hath very busie been
> Now in these latter dayes
> For to entrap, and to draw in
> Poor souls by severall wayes.

The description of George tearing out his own innards is presumably designed to be horrific, but to modern sensibilities is faintly comic, and one wonders if that is the way many people would have taken the story even in the 1660s.

LEADENHALL STREET: ST ANDREW'S UNDERSHAFT CHURCH

On or near the date of 5 April each year, a simple ceremony takes place in the church of St Andrew Undershaft, Leadenhall Street, to commemorate the life and work of John Stow (1525–1605). Stow was the son of a tailor, and apprenticed to that trade, but later gave it all up to follow his passion for books. His first book, *A Summarie of Englysh Chronicles*, was published in 1561 and went through eleven editions in his lifetime, but it is his *Survey of London* of 1598, revised in 1603, that puts him at the forefront of London historians, and gives him a permanent place in the chronicles of the city.

Stow was buried at St Andrew's, and his wife paid for a terracotta monument in his memory, but this was replaced in 1905 by a life-size marble effigy, which shows him sitting at his desk, writing. The Lord Mayor, or an alderman representing the Lord Mayor, attends the church on the day, and as part of the commemoration places a quill pen in Stow's hand, which stays there until the following year.

AUT SCRIBENDA AGERE AUT LEGENDA SCRIBERE

Every year, the Lord Mayor, or an Alderman representing him, visits the church of St Andrew Undershaft in Leadenhall Street to celebrate the life of the first great historian of London, John Stow, and to replace the quill pen in his hand. This engraving shows the original funerary monument that was replaced in 1905.

John Stow's *Survey of London* is immensely readable, and is not only the first real history of the city, by one of the best scholars of the day, but also a wonderful source of information about the daily lives of Elizabethan Londoners. It is no exaggeration to say that it ranks alongside Samuel Pepys's *Diary* as one of the most important historical accounts of life in London, and it is no surprise that it is still in print 400 years after being written.

For the folklorist the book is a real treasure: Stow describes midsummer pageants with giants and morris dancers; rough-music punishments (*see* ALBERT ROAD: ADDISCOMBE, p. 358 for a description of these); bear-baiting and cock-fighting; fairs; summer bonfires; Christmas lords of misrule; and many more customs and festivals. He is particularly useful on May Day practices, and he also supplies the reason why St Andrew's has such a strange name:

> At the north-west corner of this ward, in the said high street, standeth the fair and beautiful parish church of St Andrew the Apostle; with an addition, to be known from other churches of that name, of the knape or undershaft; and so called St Andrew Undershaft because that of old time every year on May-day in the morning, it was used, that an high or long shaft, or May-pole, was set up there, in the midst of the street, before the south side of the said church; which shaft, when it was set on end and fixed in the ground, was higher than the church steeple.

A *knape*, in this case, was the bunch of flowers set at the top of the maypole. Stow also tells us of the sad end of this maypole. In 1517, during their May

Day celebrations, the London apprentices staged a major riot, turned on foreigners living in the city and ransacked their houses. The day was referred to as Evil May Day, and apprentices' celebrations were banned for a while. The St Andrew's maypole was not erected from then on, but was stored on hooks 'along over the doors' of a row of houses in Shaft Alley. In 1549, a local curate had the maypole sawn into pieces in an excess of Puritan zeal, but he did not succeed in changing the name of the church, and 'Undershaft' it remained.

LEADENHALL STREET: ST KATHERINE CREE CHURCH

At St Katherine Cree on Leadenhall Street, an endowed sermon called the Lion Sermon, has been delivered every year on or near 16 October for over 350 years. Sir John Gayer (1584?–1649) was a successful London merchant who was involved in the Levant and East India Companies, and active in City politics, as Alderman, Sheriff, and, finally, Lord Mayor from September 1646. When he died, in addition to bequests to the poor in London, Surrey, Coventry, and Plymouth, he bequeathed £200 to endow an annual sermon to be preached 'in memory of his deliverance from the paws of a lion in Arabia'. The straightforward story of this deliverance is that on one of his trading expeditions he became separated from his companions and was suddenly confronted by lions. Remembering the story of Daniel, he prayed fervently for deliverance, and the lions turned aside and left him alone. But the more romantic version is that after uttering the prayer he fell asleep, and when he woke in the morning there were lions' paw prints all around him, while he had been left unharmed.

Incidentally, the 'Cree' in the name of the church is probably a contraction of 'Christ Church', the parish in which the church was built. John Gayer also donated the font, which can still be seen in the church.

Another regular event was the flower sermon, a form in vogue in the later nineteenth and early twentieth centuries. The first of these was probably held at St James's church, Mitre Court, and was reported in *The Times* on 21 May 1902:

The first flower sermon was provided in 1853 by the Rev Dr Whittemore to please some young friends who desired an annual service. He resolved that the sermon would always be on a floral subject, thinking it would afford a good opportunity of leading his youthful hearers to a closer contemplation of God's wisdom and love as manifested by the beautiful flowers which He has scattered in such profusion.

The church was always decorated with flowers for the occasion, and the congregation also brought bunches of flowers with them. St James's church was demolished in 1874, and its congregation merged with St Katharine Cree church, Leadenhall Street. The sermons were still being preached each year in the 1950s, but it is not known how long it survived after that date.

See also HIGH ROAD, SHOREDITCH: ST LEONARD'S CHURCH, p. 275.

LIME STREET: LLOYD'S OF LONDON

The Lutine Bell hangs in the headquarters of Lloyd's of London, probably the most famous insurance market in the world. *La Lutine* (the Sprite) was a French ship that was captured by the British at Toulon in 1793. She joined the British fleet, but in October 1799 she was wrecked off the coast of Holland. The ship's bell, which measures eighteen inches in diameter, was salvaged in 1859 and placed in the Lloyd's underwriting room. The bell was rung when some maritime announcement was made – normally, one stroke for bad news, such as a ship that was overdue at its destination, and two for good, when the ship arrived safely. Either way, the sound of the bell always brought instant silence across the underwriting room, as everyone present anxiously awaited the announcement. Nowadays the bell is only rung on special occasions, to honour important visitors or to announce the beginning and end of a commemorative period of silence.

The Lutine Bell is often cited as the basis of the fairly widespread twentieth-century superstition that when a drinking glass 'rings' after being accidentally struck, the sound must be stopped immediately, 'to save a sailor from drowning'. But there is no evidence that there is any connection between the bell and this superstition.

The old London Bridge – inspiration for a nursery rhyme and the popular legend of the Swaffham pedlar. Note the heads of criminals displayed on spikes at the entrance to the bridge.

LONDON BRIDGE

The first London Bridge was built in Roman times, and there were probably several successors which were burnt or swept away in Anglo-Saxon times. The first stone bridge was started in 1136, and soon afterwards it was recorded that houses were being built on the bridge. These were a major feature until the mid-eighteenth century. Until the erection of Putney Bridge in 1727 and Westminster Bridge in 1738, London Bridge was the only way to cross the river apart from getting a ferry, and its strategic value was recognised by the drawbridge at the Southwark end to prevent possible incursions. It was naturally the site of numerous ceremonial entries to London by various royals and other dignitaries, and until the 1660s it was the place where the severed heads of traitors and other enemies could be displayed.

Thanks to the nursery rhyme 'London Bridge is Falling Down', it is probably the most famous bridge in the English-speaking world. The rhyme's mysterious words have attracted numerous theories of the bridge's ancient origins and even of human sacrifice having taken place there, but as is usual in these cases, the earliest known version of the words dates only from *Tommy Thumb's Pretty Song Book*, published about 1744, so the ritual origin is based on speculation.

The bridge has also attracted its own lore, as for example this piece recorded by Chris Roberts in his *Cross River Traffic* (2005):

> Braving the turbulent waters beneath Old London Bridge was known as 'shooting the bridge' because of the speeds with which boats were hurled through by pressure of the river and the drop of up to two metres either side. It was a dangerous and fatal activity with thousands of people dying over the centuries, including in 1290 a shipload of Jews who were being expelled from England by Edward I. It is alleged that their cries can still be heard on quiet nights from the embankment near Customs House.

Another belief was noted by John Emslie in *London Studies* (1974):

> On account of the very rapid current through the narrow arches of London Bridge, it was a somewhat dangerous and very delicate matter to make the boats pass safely through them. North-west country bargemen, when approaching it, would say: 'Gord bless Lon'on Bridge; Lon'on Bridge never did I any harm', repeating this until they had passed safely to the other side, when they would turn round and exclaim: 'Damn an' blast thee Lon'on Bridge!'

There is also a popular legend that tells the story of the Swaffham Pedlar, who came all the way to London Bridge because a dream told him that he would meet someone who would tell him some joyful news there. So he went, and stood there for two or three days, but heard nothing. Finally, a shopkeeper, who had noticed him standing idly all day, came over and asked what he was doing. The pedlar told him, but the shopkeeper laughed and called him a fool for taking such a long journey on a silly errand. 'I myself have had a dream that if I went to an orchard in Swaffham and dug under a particular oak tree, I would find a great treasure, but I am not such a fool as to follow dreams.' The pedlar went home, dug under the tree, and found a pot holding great treasure. Some versions add the following coda: after a time, someone visiting the pedlar's house discovered that the pot bore a Latin inscription, which was translated as 'Under me doth lie/Another much richer than I', and they then found even more treasure under the same tree.

This is, in fact, an internationally known folktale, found in *The Arabian Nights* and other collections and given the standard title of 'The Treasure at Home'. It has probably been localised to Swaffham because the church there has medieval carved figures of a man with a pack on his back and a dog at his heels, along with a woman looking over a shop door, and these form a rebus, or visual pun, on the name Chapman, which is an old name for a pedlar. The first known mention of the Swaffham story is in a letter written by Sir William Dugdale in 1652–3, and it was very popular in chapbooks in the eighteenth and nineteenth centuries.

London Bridge also has an important role to play in Doggett's boat race, which takes place on the Thames every year as near as possible to 1 August, and starts from the bridge. It is named after its founder, Thomas Doggett (c.1670–1721), who was born in Dublin, but was a major figure in English drama from about 1691 until his death. He was a popular actor, particularly well known for his comic parts, but also wrote plays and was involved in theatre management. Doggett was an enthusiastic supporter of the new Hanoverian dynasty, represented by the accession of George I in 1714. The following year he inaugurated the race in George's honour, and left money in his will to support its continuance, charging the Fishmongers' Company to organise it in perpetuity. It has been run every year since, except during the Second World War.

The original race involved young boatmen racing their ordinary passenger wherries four and a half miles against the tide, from London Bridge to Chelsea, which could take a gruelling five hours, but nowadays the boats are much lighter, and the race goes with the tide and takes less than half an hour. The course still runs from London Bridge to Chelsea. The winner gets a bright red coat (originally orange, the symbolic colour of the Hanoverians) and a large fancy silver badge to wear on his left arm. Previous winners are expected to assist at official Company functions and other formal Thames events, such as the payment of the Knollys Rose to the Lord Mayor every 24 June (see SEETHING LANE, p. 52).

It is not clear why Doggett chose this particular way of announcing his political allegiance, and so the field has been left open to legend. One explanation, reported in the *Guardian* on 19 July 1974, is that one stormy night he was late for the theatre, but was stranded on the wrong side of the river. The ferry would not take him, but a young lighterman came to his rescue and rowed him across.

See also LAMBETH PLACE ROAD, LAMBETH: ST MARY'S CHURCH, p. 396; MONTAGUE CLOSE: SOUTHWARK CATHEDRAL, p. 340.

Billingsgate Market as it was in 1820. A local superstition held that fishermen had to throw a penny into the sea 'to buy wind'.

LOWER THAMES STREET: OLD BILLINGSGATE MARKET

Before moving to the Isle of Dogs in 1982, Billingsgate Market was the main wholesale fish market in the capital, and the nearby wharf was where the catches were landed. In one of his many ramblings around the out-of-the-way parts of London, Edward Lovett came across a fishermen's superstition, which he included in his *Magic in Modern London* (1925):

> One day I was somewhere near Billingsgate, it was about the year 1912, and whilst chatting with some of the men I noticed a penny nailed to the mast of a small boat. As I looked at it and wondered what it meant, one of the men said: 'I bet you don't know what that means.' I admitted that I did not. So he said, 'Well, we found that in a cod's stomach.' That sounded so like a 'yarn' that I naturally said: 'But how on earth did it get there?' And then he told me how, when sailing boats are becalmed, one of the crew will climb the mast and throw a penny into the sea, 'to buy wind'. Then, he added: 'Them pennies never reach the bottom; as they sink they wobble about, and some fish – usually a cod – sees 'em and goes for 'em.'

LOWER THAMES STREET: ST MAGNUS
THE MARTYR CHURCH

The parish church of St Magnus the Martyr, near London Bridge, has been bothered by fire several times in its long history. It was destroyed in THE GREAT FIRE OF LONDON (p. 48) in 1666 and rebuilt by Wren, but was then severely damaged by fire again in 1760 when the bridge was being rebuilt to remove the buildings that lined its sides. It had also clearly had a close shave in a previous conflagration. Susanna Chambers, by a will dated 28 December 1640, gave money to the poor, and the sum of twenty shillings a year to the parson of the parish church of St Magnus to preach a sermon on each 12 February, 'in commemoration of God's merciful preservation of the said church of St Magnus from ruin in that late and terrible fire on London Bridge.' The Fire Sermons had disappeared by the turn of the nineteenth century, but have since been restarted and can be heard at the church every February.

According to the indefatigable ghost-writer Jack Hallam, the apparition of a 'short black-haired priest wearing a cassock' has been seen by church staff. There is a marked tendency for ghosts to be identified with the most famous person associated with the particular building, so it is no surprise that this one is thought to be Miles Coverdale (1487–1569), who oversaw the first complete translation of the Bible into English, even though his remains were moved here only in 1840.

The expensive clock that projects from the tower was the gift, in 1709, of Sir Charles Duncombe (c.1648–1711), wealthy financier and one-time Lord Mayor of London. The legend is that it was erected in memory of the occasion, during his apprenticeship, that he missed an important appointment for want of a reliable public clock, a story that is told of other clocks around the country. The clock was originally adorned with gilt figures of St Magnus, St Margaret, Atlas, Hercules and two cupids.

See also HOLBORN CIRCUS: ST ANDREW'S CHURCH, p. 31.

Newgate Street: Newgate Prison

Newgate Prison was situated where the Central Criminal Court now stands. There had been a prison on the site since at least the twelfth century, but it was rebuilt many times, including after the Great Fire, and again when wrecked in the Gordon Riots in 1780. In 1783, public hangings ceased at Tyburn and from then on took place in the open space in front of Newgate. This meant that much of the theatre of the Tyburn hangings was dispensed with, in particular the trip in the cart, but many thousands of spectators still turned up every time an execution was scheduled. Public hanging was abolished in 1868, as reported in *The Times* on 27 May:

> London yesterday witnessed the last of those hideous spectacles familiar enough to the hard eyes of our predecessors, but more and more repulsive to the taste of these days.

However, executions at Newgate were simply moved indoors and continued until the prison was finally demolished in 1902. Throughout most of its miserable existence, Newgate was infamous for its squalor, disease, brutality, and degradation, which hardly needs repeating here, but it was a fertile breeding ground for gruesome legends and rumours.

Some interesting information about the latter days of Newgate comes from the writings of R. Thurston Hopkins (1884–1958). A number of his relatives, including his father, worked in the prison service, and he was familiar with the workings of Newgate and other penal institutions. He wrote about them in his books *Life and Death at the Old Bailey* (1935) and *Ghosts over England* (1953) but, as he says, things were not what they used to be:

> The Old Bailey should, by all the canons of the spirit world, be crowded with ghosts. If, as it is commonly supposed, the spirits of those who have suffered a violent or untimely death wander about their former surroundings, it should not be more than an everyday occurrence to meet a ghost in the court rooms. But the ghost who returns to haunt the Old Bailey will receive a cruel shock, for the old cells, gallows, and oozy exercise yards have vanished and over the site stands the new Central Criminal Court. In place of Newgate Prison, with its interminable dusky corridors and galleries, and

41

Public hangings at Newgate took place until 1868. Not suprisingly, various sightings of ghosts have been recorded over the years, one of which is reported to have had a tell-tell mottled mark around its throat. The prison was demolished in 1902, and the Central Criminal Court was built in its place.

the Old Sessions House, stands a spacious pile with hardly a darksome corner in the whole building.

Hopkins wrote about Dead Man's Walk, a narrow passage through which prisoners passed to and from their court appearances, and under whose flagstones executed criminals were buried. The alternative nickname 'Bird Cage Walk' was given to it because although it was open to the air, it was covered with a strong wrought-iron grille. One of old warders told Hopkins what he had experienced there in December 1891. He was working late, when he heard footsteps approaching. The footsteps were stealthy, and seemed to drag like the shuffle of a limping man:

I got up and walked to the great doors which led out to Dead Man's Walk. This door, a ponderous piece of work with enormous bolts and locks, was fitted with a sliding grille. I did not feel inclined to unlock it at that moment, and I pulled back the shutter. I was horrified to see a man's face pressed close to the grille, and it was a great deal whiter than it should have been. The face only remained a few seconds, but long enough for me to see that the skin around the throat was bruised and had turned a mottled green colour. Instantly I thought of the mark left by the hangman's rope. I mustered up sufficient courage to open the door and walk along the passage, but the phantom did not display any other physical manifestations that night.

He heard the steps on other nights, and learned from older staff that the haunting was quite well known. One even said, 'It's a strange thing that several of the Old Bailey housekeepers have refused to stay on at their jobs, and, as you know, two of them had the horrors so badly that they committed suicide.' He also learned that the last man buried in the Walk had walked with a limp.

One of the most notorious of Newgate's residents was Jack Sheppard (1702–24), who was famous for his daring escapes from various prisons. In 1948, according to Hopkins, a clergyman who had rooms in Amen Corner, opposite the old prison wall, reported seeing Sheppard up to his old tricks. The clergyman was at work by his window one evening, and suddenly saw a man creeping along the top of the old prison wall. The figure was dressed in eighteenth-century costume:

> His hair was long and tangled, and he had chains on his legs; his appearance was sufficiently unusual to impress the witness deeply. He seemed to hear the noise made by the window being opened for he remained still and fixed the clergyman with a long and hostile stare. They remained thus looking at each other for about a minute; then the figure floated down from the wall, feet first, and made for the ancient gateway, which leads from Amen Court down to the Old Bailey.

Another notorious inmate was Mrs Amelia Dyer, the famous Reading 'baby farmer', who murdered babies placed in her care. Hopkins's informant, Chief Warder Scott, admitted to being unnerved by her presence in the jail, and after she was executed in 1896, her memory still gave him the creeps. Sure enough, the night before Newgate was closed for good:

Suddenly Scott felt aware that someone's eyes were fixed on him, and he heard a voice ringing in his head: 'Meet you again . . . Meet you again some day, sir.' It struck him that he had heard that voice before, but how long ago and where he could not at once determine. Then, he looked towards the door and Mrs Dyer's face was framed in the grille. There was no mistaking her oily benevolent smile, the little dark, snake-like eyes and the thin lips trying to look kind and harmless. She gave Scott one sad enigmatical look and passed on. Scott jumped up and opened the door and saw nothing except a woman's handkerchief which fluttered at his feet on the wet flagstones.

When a photo of the warders was taken later that day, it showed something over Scott's shoulder, which might have been a woman's face.

According to many reports, burglars and thieves were, perhaps still are, particularly superstitious. Scott gives an almost touchingly pathetic example when he describes seeing two or three suspicious-looking men rubbing their shoulders against the ironwork of the old prison gate. When he asked them what they were up to, they replied, 'Lor', governor, don't you know that if you don't come up and rub yourself against the old Newgate once a year, you'll spend half your life in quod and die a fool?'

Superstitions are not confined to the criminal class, of course. Hopkins also tells of a High Court judge, Sir William Horne (1774–1860), who apparently believed that if he was called upon to administer the death penalty he would himself soon die. He resigned his post rather than run the risk. The *Oxford Dictionary of National Biography* confirms that Horne was against the death penalty, but says nothing about why.

A different aspect of superstition is inextricably linked to Newgate, Tyburn, and other places of execution, and concerns the 'dead man's hand' cure for illnesses such as tumours and goitres. One of the bizarre underlying principles of many superstitions is that the really bad can be really good, and worse is better. Many cures, for example, have involved moss from skulls, earth from graves, and so on, but the most prevalent belief in this sphere was that certain ailments could be cured by the touch of a 'dead hand'. However strange it may seem to modern eyes, this attempted cure was widely practised in Britain from at least the 1590s until the late nineteenth century. In most cases it was only the hand of an executed criminal or a suicide that was believed to be effective, and the

The notorious Jack Sheppard (1702–24) makes good his escape over the roof of Newgate's prison.

abolition of public hanging in 1868 made it much more difficult for ordinary people to get access to the right kind of dead body.

The thinking behind the procedure has never been satisfactorily explained, but it is possible that the principle involved is the very common one of *transference*. The idea here is that the affliction is transferred to the dead body, and will diminish as the corpse rots in the grave. Similar principles underlie the cures for other conditions, from warts to whooping cough, but this does not explain why an executed criminal or suicide was singled out in this context. The same belief was found in classical times, and mentioned in Pliny's *Natural History* (AD 77), so perhaps it entered British tradition when antiquarians started translating classical sources and making them more widely available.

Naturally enough, the hangman expected to be paid for allowing people to touch the corpse, and another of the perks of the public hangman's job was to claim the clothes of the criminals, which he could sell. A third valuable asset was the rope that had been used, and pieces of this were sold by the inch, traditionally in the Green Dragon in Fleet Street. Many of those who bought pieces of rope were probably simply after souvenirs, but at least some were bought because they were thought to have intrinsic properties. Foremost of these were curative powers. The following cure for a headache, for example, was published in Reginald Scot's *Discoverie of Witchcraft* (1584): 'Tie a halter about your head, wherewith one hath been hanged'; and over 330 years later a Lincolnshire folklorist collected the advice: 'Fits can be cured by procuring a strand from a rope with which a man has hung himself, and wearing it always round the neck.'

But later evidence, from *Notes and Queries* in 1868, points to another useful property:

> It is held by certain gamesters that a bit of a hangman's rope is a charm for success at cards. It costs eight pounds – they're very difficult to get now.

See also EDGWARE ROAD, TYBURN, p. 80.

PUDDING LANE

See THE GREAT FIRE OF LONDON, p. 48.

ST MARY AXE

St Mary Axe, on which the ultra-modern Gherkin building now stands at No. 30, was the location of one of the many cases of theft by FORTUNE-TELLING (p. 78) recorded in the records of the Old Bailey. In this once-popular trick, the victim is told that he or she will find some hidden money if he or she supplies some money and personal items to complete the spell.

22 February 1758: Mary Beaumont

In October last I lived at Mr Alveringo's, in St Mary Axe. On the 24th of that month the prisoner came and knock'd at the door, which I went and open'd. She asked me if I had any china to mend. I said no. Then she said it was a blessed moment, the first time I ever saw you, will you have your fortune told? I did not want to have it told. She said she could tell me of things that would do me a great deal of good, and also to a person that had been dead a long time, to give that soul rest, and went on with a good deal of this discourse. I said I did not believe what she talk'd of. She said, it is as true as God is in heaven, telling me of a pot, in which was £200 hid by that deceased person. She told me I must go down into the cellar, fetch up a bit of earth, and put it in a handkerchief, which I did. When I came up again she asked me if I had any silver in my pocket. I said I had. She bid me pull it out, and hold it in my hand with the blessing of God. She said she did not desire a farthing. I pull'd out a crown piece, and six shillings in silver. She said I must put it into these things, then pull'd out a bit of earth and some black dust, put it into the handkerchief and, as I thought, put it into my bosom; but I found afterwards when I went to look, it was only some halfpence, and a medal piece . . . She said also that she must have some of my clothes, or else she could not recover the things, nor give the spirit rest; so I gave her a white apron, a silk handkerchief, a linen one, a cotton one, a colour'd apron and a cap. She said she would come again with them again in the evening. I never saw her afterwards.

See also BERKELEY SQUARE, p. 67; FRYING PAN ALLEY, TOWER HAMLETS, p. 274.

The Great Fire of London

A nineteenth-century engraving of London aflame. Eye-witness accounts of the disaster show that some people just stood back and watched the city burn, believing that the fire fulfilled one of Mother Shipton's prophecies.

The Great Fire of London started with a small house-fire at Farriner's bakery, in Pudding Lane, early on 2 September 1666. Remarkably few lives were lost, but well over 13,000 buildings were destroyed. Part of the blame for the damage and its aftermath can be laid at the door of superstition and legend. Just as a belief in witches can break out into terrifying witch-hunts, so belief in 'prophecies' can lead people to stand back and watch as a catastrophe unfolds instead of acting to prevent it. Not only that, but wild rumour can also lead to the victimisation of particular groups who hearsay has declared to be guilty.

In his seminal collection *Extraordinary Popular Delusions* (1841), Charles Mackay quotes an eyewitness account published in the transactions of the Royal Society of Antiquaries on the credulity of Londoners at the time:

> The writer, who accompanied the Duke of York day by day through the district included between Fleet-bridge and the Thames, states that, in their efforts to check the progress of the flames, they were much impeded by the superstition of the people. Mother Shipton, in one of her prophecies, had said that London would be reduced to ashes, and they refused to make any efforts to prevent it. A son of the noted Sir Kenelm Digby, who was also a pretender to the gifts of prophecy, persuaded them that no power on earth could prevent the fulfilment of the prediction; for it was written in the great book of fate that London was to be destroyed.

He comments on the effect this had on the ground:

> Hundreds of persons, who might have rendered valuable assistance, and saved whole parishes from devastation, folded their arms and looked on. As many more gave themselves up, with less compunction, to plunder a city they could not save.

It was widely believed that 'Mother Shipton' had prophesied that 'London in sixty-six shall be burnt to ashes', but she had not, of course. She was a purely fictional character, invented sometime around 1640, and her so-called prophecies do not predict the Great Fire, except in the vaguest terms, which, as with all prophecies, can be interpreted in any number of ways. Samuel Pepys recorded a mention of Mother Shipton's prophecy on 20 October 1666, but four months later the talk was of another prophet:

3 Feb 1667

. . . among other discourse, we talked much of Nostradamus, his prophecy of these times and the burning of the City of London, some of whose verses are put into Booker's Almanac this year.

In Century II, para 51 of Nostradamus's prophecies, apparently written in the 1550s, he wrote of London's being struck like lightning, and *vingt trois les six*, or 'twenty three the sixes', which is usually glossed as sixty-six. If Nostradamus had written (in French, of course), 'London will burn down in 1666', we would be more impressed with his foresight, but instead we are left to ask what is the point of a prophecy that can only be understood after the event it was meant to foretell.

The question of who was to blame for the fire was quick to take a very nasty turn. In the autobiography of William Taswell (1651–82), published in the *Camden Miscellany* 2 (1853):

The ignorant and deluded mob, who upon the occasion were hurried away with a kind of phrenzy, vented forth their rage against the Roman Catholics and Frenchmen; imagining these incendiaries (as they thought) had thrown red-hot balls into the houses. A blacksmith, in my presence, meeting an innocent Frenchman walking along the street, felled him instantly to the ground with an iron bar. I could not help seeing the innocent blood of this exotic flowing in a plentiful stream, down to his ankles. In another place I saw the incensed populace divesting a French painter of all the goods he had in his shop; and, after having helped him off with many other things, levelling his house to the ground under this pretence, namely, that they thought himself was desirous of setting his own house on fire, that the conflagration might become more general. My brother told me he saw a Frenchman almost dismembered in Moorfields, because he carried balls of fire in a chest with him, when in truth they were only tennis balls.

See also HOLBORN CIRCUS: ST ANDREW'S CHURCH, p. 31; LOWER THAMES STREET: ST MAGNUS THE MARTYR CHURCH, p. 40.

Designed by Christopher Wren after the Great Fire of 1666, the
current St Paul's Cathedral is reputed to be honeycombed with
secret passages and stairs. Its medieval predecessor witnessed the
annual custom of electing a Boy Bishop.

ST PAUL'S CATHEDRAL

Like many lesser buildings, St Paul's has its share of ghost stories and
secret-tunnel legends, and these sit alongside its secular and religious
customs. R. Thurston Hopkins supplies plenty of secret passages in his
Ghosts over England (1953):

> Few people are aware that St Paul's Cathedral is simply honeycombed with
> secret passages and stairs and many of them may yet remain undiscovered.
> A secret passage runs round the inner cupola of the Dome, and two
> corkscrew staircases are contained in the thickness of the walls of the main
> entrance facing Ludgate Hill. More secret passages run inside the walls of
> the North and South transepts – I happen to know this is true because I
> spent a morning exploring these passages with Charles G. Harper, the topo-
> graphical writer, some forty years ago.

Unfortunately, the cathedral is not quite so rich in ghosts. In standard
works of London ghost-lore, writers describe an elderly clergyman who
haunts All Souls' Chapel at the west end of the cathedral, just by the

visitors' entrance. When this chapel was redesigned after the First World War, a secret stairway was revealed at the exact spot where the ghost was always said to appear. It is sometimes suggested that this stair leads directly to the dome, but J. A. Brooks, the best of the writers on London ghosts, comments: 'this is clearly ridiculous since the length of the nave separates the chapel from the crossing.' This ghost has one strange characteristic: he is reputedly accompanied by (or emits) a high-pitched tuneless whistle.

Jack Hallam's *Ghosts of London* (1975) records that St Paul's Deanery, just across the road from the cathedral, is haunted, although nothing specific is known. He comments:

> But what about those secret passages and stairways which are thought to honeycomb the Cathedral? Is it not possible that a yet-to-be discovered passage connects the Deanery and the Cathedral deep beneath the road and that the ghost which haunts All Souls' Chapel could also haunt the Dean's house?

In such a way are legends made.

Old St Paul's, the building that was destroyed in the Great Fire, was the location of the annual custom of electing a Boy Bishop. This procedure seems distinctly odd to modern sensibilities, but for centuries it was an integral part of the church year, and took place in some form or other at most of the cathedrals in England, including St Paul's, and across the Continent. It had been introduced to Britain, probably from Germany, by the twelfth century, and was a popular institution with congregations, although the authorities sometimes found it difficult to control. Originally part of the main church festival that concerned children, Holy Innocents' Day (28 December), the focus later moved to St Nicholas's Day (6 December) as that saint grew in popularity. By starting on the 6th and ending on the 28th, the custom became firmly associated with Christmas in the popular mind.

A choirboy was elected, sometimes by his peers, sometimes by the adult clergy, to take the place of the bishop for a short time. He was dressed in a bishop's clothes and, supported by his fellow choirboys, fulfilled many of the usual ceremonial functions, although he was not allowed to take Mass. Two popular set pieces of the custom were his delivery of a sermon (written by the regular clergy), and the carol-singing that he and his colleagues would perform later as they went around the neighbourhood.

Much is now made by modern writers of the role-reversal aspect of the custom, and the idea that this period of misrule acted as a psychological safety valve, but in fact the boys' behaviour was severely circumscribed and monitored, and although some high spirits were tolerated, they were certainly not allowed to parody or poke fun at the Church, its personnel, or its teachings. The Boy Bishop custom was abolished by Henry VIII, briefly revived by Mary and abolished again by Elizabeth I.

SEETHING LANE

Every year, on the feast of St John the Baptist (24 June), a single red rose is presented to the Lord Mayor at the Mansion House. This presentation is a revival of a ceremony that started in the fourteenth century, in which Sir Robert Knollys (d. 1407) paid a similar tribute each year to the City. Knollys was a professional soldier who was involved in numerous conflicts on the Continent, in the King's service, and he took a leading role in the suppression of the Peasants' Revolt of 1381.

There are several versions of the story of the rose. In earlier accounts, Knollys was said to have paid the rose for permission to build a balcony overlooking Seething Lane. In a more colourful account, he owned two properties on either side of Seething Lane, and in 1381, while he was away fighting, his wife built a footbridge to join the two properties, without asking permission of the City authorities. Given his importance in London affairs, Knollys was only fined one red rose every year. The payment lapsed a long time ago, but the idea was revived by the Revd Philip Thomas Byard ('Tubby') Clayton (1885–1972). Revd Clayton was a tireless worker in a number of religious fields, including service in both world wars, and was a well-known and flamboyant figure in his day. From 1923 he was the vicar of All Hallows-by-the-Tower church, Byward Street, which is very close to Seething Lane, and, learning of the old payment, he decided to revive it. It is not clear exactly when the new custom was first carried out, but an article in *The Times* on 24 June 1936 described it as having taken place the previous day, in terms that suggest it was not yet a regular occurrence.

To ensure its continuation, the Company of Watermen and Lightermen of the River Thames, which also has strong links with All Hallows, was charged with carrying out the ceremony every year. The Master of the Company now cuts a rose in Seething Lane Gardens and proceeds to the Mansion House, with, as guard of honour, the Doggett Badge winners (*see* LONDON BRIDGE, p. 36).

THREADNEEDLE STREET: BANK OF ENGLAND

R. Thurston Hopkins, who worked in the banking industry as well as writing about the supernatural, tells the story of the Black or Bank Nun ghost who haunts the Bank of England in his *Ghosts over England* (1953). According to Hopkins, this sad tale started with a young clerk named Philip Whitehead, who worked at the Bank in the early nineteenth century. Whitehead got into bad company, lost his job, began forging cheques, was caught and was finally condemned to death in November 1811. He had a devoted younger sister, who unfortunately lost her reason after his execution and started turning up at the Bank every day asking for him. This she did for the rest of her life, and was apparently pitied, and quietly supported, by the Bank's staff, although she became quite abusive and began accusing major figures of cheating her out of her fortune. After her death, her ghost was often seen about the Bank, and in its garden, still searching for her brother, and she was called the Black or Bank Nun because of her nun-like head-dress. Hopkins stated that all the clerks at the Bank were familiar with the story in his time, and he even claimed to have seen the ghost himself.

Hopkins' account has an unusual amount of detail for a ghost story, which enables us to look into it more thoroughly than usual. The records of the Old Bailey reveal that there was indeed an ex-bank clerk, *Paul* Whitehead, condemned to death for forgery on 30 October 1811. Furthermore, *The Times* of 22 February 1828 reported that a Sarah Whitehead had appeared before the magistrates at Union Hall, asking

Sarah Whitehead, also known as 'the Black Nun' or 'Bank Nun', was the younger sister of a former clerk at the Bank. He was sentenced to death for forging cheques and, after his execution, she used to come looking for him at the Bank, a habit which apparently continued even after her death.

for help in preventing a conspiracy against her to defraud her of her money, and poison her into the bargain. A person present in the court explained that Sarah's brother had worked at the Bank, and so on.

So the bones of the story are correct, and the ghost believer would be satisfied that this proves the story – and the spirit – to be true. But there are coincidences of wording in the official reports and in Hopkins' story that are suspicious – in particular those concerned with Sarah's habitual appearance: in black, with a heavily rouged face. It is possible that Hopkins was quoting an earlier source, but on present evidence it seems clear that he had access to these records, or similar newspaper reports, which he used to give an interesting back-story to a ghost. Whether or not he actually saw the ghost, or if it existed before his time, is another matter.

TOWER OF LONDON: BOUNDARIES

In former times, the custom of BEATING THE BOUNDS (p. 370) was carried out regularly in every parish in the country. Before the Reformation the custom had strong religious overtones of 'blessing the fields', but from the mid sixteenth century the main focus was on the need for the secular local authority to ensure that the boundaries of their jurisdiction were known and respected. The procession around the whole boundary, by local officials, clergy, and local inhabitants, thus served the dual purpose of inspecting the boundary and fixing it into the memories of the young who might in future be called upon to testify.

The production of detailed maps and other forms of reliable records made the old beatings obsolete, and the custom gradually died out during the nineteenth century, but the Tower is one of the few places that continue to do it on a regular basis. Every three years, on Ascension Day, a group assembles to carry out the custom. The day starts with a short service in St Peter ad Vincula, then the Chief Yeoman Warder, in full dress and carrying his mace, leads a procession that includes the Resident Governor and other officials, and a group of children dressed in white surplices, carrying willow wands. The procession perambulates the boundaries of the Tower Liberty, guided by the thirty-one markers bearing the unromantic symbol *WD* (War Department). At each marker, the Chief calls out, 'Cursed be he who removeth his neighbour's landmark – Whack

Few places in London are home to more traditions, superstitions and ghost stories than the Tower of London. This fanciful Victorian engraving seeks to depict the Tower as it would have appeared four hundred years earlier.

it, boys, whack it!', and they beat it with their wands. In places where the markers are not safely accessible, he shouts, 'Mark it well', and they all reply, 'Marked!' Back in the Tower, they sing the National Anthem and then have refreshments.

TOWER OF LONDON: CHAPEL ROYAL

It is a ghost writer's cliché that if ghosts are created in places where torture, violence and death take place, the Tower of London must be full of them, and headless ghosts should be prominent in their number. Most of the writers on English ghosts include examples from the Tower, but G. Abbott's *Ghosts of the Tower of London* (1980) contains the most, and there is also a good summary of them in J. A. Brooks's *Ghosts of London* (1991). Abbott was a yeoman warder, so he must have known the Tower well.

To represent the many hundreds of famous people executed in the Tower over the centuries, many of whom have been seen haunting the place in recent years, we must choose Anne Boleyn, whose fame seems to grow with the years rather than diminish. J. A. Brooks writes:

> Her ghost has frequently been seen on the Green and, more spectacularly, in the Chapel Royal situated in the White Tower. Here a captain of the Guard saw a light burning in the locked chapel late at night. Finding a ladder, he was able to look down on to the strange scene being enacted within. A nineteenth-century account described it thus: Slowly down the aisle moved a stately procession of knights and ladies, attired in ancient costumes, and in front walked an elegant female whose face was averted from him, but whose figure resembled the one he had seen in reputed portraits of Anne Boleyn. After having repeatedly paced the chapel, the entire procession, together with the light, disappeared.

Tower of London: Gates

A unique piece of pageantry takes place every evening at seven minutes to ten. The Chief Yeoman Warder, accompanied by the Watchman, a lantern carrier and an armed escort led by a sergeant, visits each of the Tower's gates to lock them for the night, with the ceremonial keys. Each sentry they pass salutes the Queen's keys, and at the Wakefield Tower the ritual challenge takes place:

SENTRY: Halt!
SERGEANT: Escort to the keys, Halt!
SENTRY: Who comes there?
CHIEF YEOMAN WARDER: The keys.
SENTRY: Whose keys?
CHIEF YEOMAN WARDER: Queen Elizabeth's keys.
SENTRY: Pass, Queen Elizabeth's keys, all's well.

The Chief Yeoman Warder passes along to meet the Main Guard, who present arms, and the Chief shouts, 'God preserve Queen Elizabeth!', to which the Guard replies, 'Amen', and the 'Last Post' is played on the bugle. The whole affair takes only ten minutes or so, and is open to the public, by ticket only.

TOWER OF LONDON: GROUNDS

The best-known Tower superstition in the present day, lovingly related by tour guides and guidebooks, is the idea that if the resident ravens ever leave the Tower then something desperately bad will happen to Britain. The birds are therefore protected and fed by a yeoman raven master, and are an important feature of the Tower experience. It is generally assumed that they have been there for many centuries, and indeed some pieces of official tourist literature confidently state that the ravens have been in residence for 900 years. Another, less ambitious tradition claims that it was Charles II who donated the first pair, while others say that Charles was simply the first to officially decree their protection, and did so because he was aware of the already existing tradition.

There was an understandable flurry of anguished articles in the daily press in 2004 when Dr Geoff Parnell, 'official Tower of London historian', announced that he could find no reference to ravens in Tower records before 1895, and a subsequent piece by Boria Sax in *History Today* in January 2005 confirmed that no record of them could be found before the mid nineteenth century. Indeed, the earliest reference he could find to the legend that Britain will fall if the ravens leave the Tower is as late as 1955. This being so, the legend is probably an example of tourist-lore – items made up by tour guides to spice up their guided walks.

It is interesting to note that the adoption of the raven as a protective symbol runs directly counter to their usual reputation in British tradition as bad omens. The appearance or raucous cry of a raven as an omen of death or disaster appears so often in tradition and literature that it could be called a cliché, and yet it was genuinely believed, as the Revd Francis Kilvert recorded in his diary:

26 May 1873

John Vincent said that a man was sick at Derry Hill. Two ravens flew over the house [crying:] 'corpse, corpse.' The man died the next day.

The few scattered references to ravens being protected from harm, for fear of bad luck, are most likely an extension of their malevolent reputation.

A whole corpus of beliefs has now accumulated around the Tower ravens, which will not disappear simply because historians and folklorists have identified the original superstition as a recent invention, and these beliefs will no doubt increase as the years go by. In *London's Secret History* (1983) Peter Bushell writes:

It is widely believed that certain misfortune awaits anyone who kills a raven; and they are said to possess the power to revenge themselves on those who harm them. Between the wars a guardsman stationed here kicked one of them. He later walked in his sleep and fell into the moat, breaking both legs. During the same period a visiting Nazi officer was being shown round the Tower by the Constable when they encountered one of the ravens on Tower Green. The German remarked on its disreputable appearance and apparent ill-temper, adding, 'For our own emblem, we Nazis prefer the eagle.' The raven waddled over and promptly bit him on the ankle.

Even though the need to protect the ravens at the Tower has been shown to be a recent invention, it is most likely to be a simple extension of a much older idea. Long before the arrival of the ravens, the Tower was the site of the Royal Menagerie, housing exotic beasts for about 600 years. There had been the odd unusual animal at royal residences before, but the real beginning of the Tower menagerie is usually thought to be the gift to Henry III in 1235 of three 'leopards' (probably lions) from Frederick II, Holy Roman Emperor, on his marriage to Henry's sister Isabella. Not long after, in 1252, the King of Norway gave Henry a 'pale' bear (possibly a polar bear), which could regularly be seen sitting on the banks of the Thames catching its own dinner. They were joined by an elephant in 1255, and many other animals followed over the years, until the Tower menagerie became a well-known feature of London life. The lions, in particular, were immensely popular, and it was said that anyone prepared to feed their unwanted pets to the lions was admitted to the menagerie free of charge. John Ashton gives a flavour of eighteenth-century attitudes to the lions in his *Social Life in the Reign of Queen Anne* (1882):

> 'I took three lads, who are under my guardianship, a-rambling, in a hackney coach, to shew them the town; as the lions, the tombs, Bedlam' (*The Tatler*, 1709). These were the three great sights of London: the lions at the Tower, the tombs in Westminster Abbey, and the poor mad folk in Bedlam. 'To see the lions' is proverbial, and these had to be visited by everyone new to the city. In 1703 there were four – two lions and two lionesses, one with a cub. In this reign three of the lions died almost at the same time, and it was looked upon as an event of dire portent.

In fact, it is from around this time that we have the first documentary evidence of the tradition that if the lions of the Tower die then the sovereign of the day would also die. Several superstitions focused on lions in general British tradition, and they were often, for some unknown reason, linked to human fertility. But the idea of a direct link between the 'king of the beasts' and the reigning monarch was specific to the Tower lions. The animals were moved to the Zoological Gardens in 1835, which perhaps accounts for the dying out of the tradition.

The lions feature in another piece of amusing lore, as recorded in Chambers' *Book of Days* (1864):

> In March 1860, a vast multitude of people received through the post a card having the following inscription, with a seal marked by an inverted sixpence at one of the angles, thus having to superficial observation an official appearance: 'Tower of London – Admit the Bearer and Friend to view the Annual Ceremony of Washing the White Lions, on Sunday April 1st 1860. Admitted only at the White Gate. It is particularly requested that no gratuities be given to the Wardens or their Assistants.' The trick is said to have been highly successful. Cabs were rattling about Tower Hill all that Sunday morning, vainly endeavouring to discover the White Gate.

This was certainly not the first time this hoax had been perpetrated, and 'washing lions in the Tower' became a catchphrase for a trick or wild goose chase.

TOWER OF LONDON: JEWEL HOUSE

One famous unexplained 'supernatural' occurrence was related by Edmund Lenthal Swifte, then eighty-three, in *Notes and Queries* (1860–61). In October 1817, when Swifte was serving as Keeper of the Crown Jewels in the Tower, he was sitting at dinner one night in the sitting room of the Jewel House with his wife, son and sister-in-law:

> I looked up and saw a cylindrical figure, like a glass tube, seemingly about the thickness of my arm, and hovering between the ceiling and the table: its contents appeared to be a dense fluid, white and pale azure, like to the gathering of a summer cloud, and incessantly rolling and mingling within the cylinder. This lasted about two minutes, when it began slowly to move before my sister-in-law; then, following the oblong shape of the table, before my son and myself; passing behind my wife, it paused for a moment over her right shoulder . . . Instantly she crouched down, and with both hands covering her shoulder, she shrieked out, 'Oh, Christ! it has seized me!' Even now, while writing, I feel the fresh horror of that moment. I caught up my chair, struck at the wainscot behind her . . . Neither my sister-in-law nor my son beheld this 'appearance'.

No appreciable after-effects manifested themselves, and indeed the account rings all the more true because there is no climax, punchline or narrative closure. In the same correspondence, Mr Swifte also mentioned another incident that took place soon after his family's unnerving experience:

> . . . a night-sentry was alarmed by a figure like a huge bear issuing from underneath the door. He thrust at it with his bayonet, which stuck in the door, even as my chair dinted the wainscot; he dropped in a fit, and was carried senseless to the guard-room.

Two or three days later he was dead.

It is interesting to compare these spectacular occurrences with the incidents recorded in Roy Baker (ed.)'s *Strange Stories from the Tower of London* (1983), which were based on testimony from existing security staff who patrolled the building at night, in particular Mr 'Taff' Cullen, Custody Guard. These men do not talk of headless ghosts in period costume, but of far more subtle, and in a way more frightening, sensations as they passed through the empty rooms – sudden sounds, smells, chills, a touch on the shoulder, and so on:

> Immediately he stepped into the room he was gripped by a feeling of crushing pressure, which he described as like wearing a heavily weighted deep-sea diving suit. At first he thought he was having a heart attack, but, realising that the pressure was not increasing, he shuffled towards the Chapel of St John. As he did so the pressure lifted as suddenly as it had come.

TOWER OF LONDON: VAULTS

Last but not least in the traditional lore of the Tower is the story of John Barkstead's treasure. Barkstead, at one time a goldsmith in the Strand, held various positions in the Puritan army and administration, and was Lieutenant in the Tower from 1652 to 1659. At the Restoration he escaped to Germany, but was later apprehended in Holland, brought back to England, and executed as a regicide in April 1662. A rumour was soon abroad that he had hidden a large sum of money before fleeing the country, which he had not had time to recover.

Only six months after Barkstead's death, Samuel Pepys was invited to join a small group who had definite knowledge to offer, which was apparently based on information from a woman who claimed to be Barkstead's 'friend':

> *30 October 1662*
> £7000 hid in the Tower, of which he was to have two for discovery, my Lord himself 2, and the King the other 3 when it was found . . . We went into several cellars and then went out-a-doors to view, and then the coleharbour; but none did answer so well to the marks which was given him to find it by as one arched vault. Where after a great deal of counsel whether to set upon it now or delay for better and more full advice, we set to it; and to digging we went till almost 8 o'clock at night – but could find nothing. But however, our guides did not at all seem discouraged; for that they being confident that the money is there they look for, but having never been in the cellars, they could not be positive to the place and therefore will inform themselves more fully.

They tried again on 1 and 7 November, and for the last time on 19 December, and Pepys then falls silent on the subject. This is, in fact, a classic story of treasure-seeking, with all the usual elements: the information on which the treasure-seekers act turns out to be much more vague than it had originally seemed, and shifts around somewhat; the mood of certainty and excitement keeps the seekers going for a while, until disillusion begins to set in; and above all, there is a need for secrecy, in case someone else gets there first.

There is a fascinating echo of Pepys's involvement in this quest for buried treasure some five years later. In June 1667, with London in the grip of a panic occasioned by the Dutch fleet sailing up the Thames as far as Chatham, Pepys decided to evacuate his wife and father to the family home in Brampton, Huntingdonshire. He sent with them all his worldly store – about £1,300 in gold, which they duly buried, for safe keeping. Unfortunately, when Pepys came in October to retrieve it, they were somewhat imprecise about its exact location, and it took some effort, under the cover of darkness, to find it. Getting the gold back home was also fraught with worry, and Pepys's final comment on the affair was that it was 'some kind of content to remember how painful it is sometimes to keep money as well as to get it' (11 October 1667).

Several attempts have been made since Pepys's time to find Barkstead's treasure, including one official archaeological investigation from May to October 1957, which was reported in *The Times*, but all to no avail.

The Tower of London proves to be disappointingly short of secret tunnels. A surprisingly sensible work on the subject is Granville Squiers's *Secret Hiding-Places* (1933), which has this to say:

> The Tower of London is popularly supposed to be riddled with secret passages, thanks to the traditions launched by Harrison Ainsworth and nurtured by some of the guides that conduct parties there. Unfortunately the best authorities that one can consult on the subject of the Tower have found nothing that can properly be called secret . . . There are traditions of a secret way under the moat which emerged somewhere on Tower Hill. There is no official confirmation of this, unless one cares to accept the word of a Tower warder in that sense. Such a one informed me that the passage went to a nunnery, though he didn't say how he knew . . . Those who refuse to relinquish the secret passage story can always console themselves with the idea that if their favourite tunnel is not mentioned, then it must be more mysterious than ever.

Harrison Ainsworth was an extremely popular writer of historical fiction, and his *Tower of London* was a best-seller in 1840.

TOWER OF LONDON: WHITE TOWER

Two beliefs mentioned in passing in Peter Bushell's *London's Secret History* (1983) are that women would stick pins in Henry VIII's codpiece, on show in the White Tower, in order to enhance their own chances of getting pregnant, and that so much royal and noble blood has been spilt in the Outer Ward that grass refuses to grow there. The same writer also relates a more developed story:

> [One] of the Jacobites incarcerated within the Tower after the rebellion of 1715 was Sir William Wyndham, an exceptionally superstitious man. Having twice been warned by soothsayers to beware 'of a white horse', he took great care to see that he never mounted such an animal. But on being carried into the Tower he happened to glance up at the Hanoverian coat-of-arms above the gate. At its centre was a white horse. On his release, thinking the prophecy 'spent', Sir William bought himself a magnificent white charger. It promptly threw him and kicked him in the head.

UPPER THAMES STREET, GARLICK HILL: ST JAMES GARLICKHYTHE CHURCH

Until recently, visitors to the church of St James Garlickhythe, in Upper Thames Street, could view a mummified body, nicknamed Jimmy Garlic, which was kept in a cupboard at the back of the church. In a private communication (2008), the verger, Ellis Pike, explained what is known of him:

> A great deal of misinformation has circulated regarding 'Jimmy' since he was first discovered either during repairs to the church in 1837 or in the 1850s, when the vaults were cleared. Most commentators have described him as a young man, which is incorrect.

I was able to have some tests done on the body a couple of years ago, which have shown that he was undoubtedly an older man, probably of very high standing, possibly a wealthy merchant. Carbon testing was inconclusive but it showed that the most likely time of death was around the time of the Great Fire of London, and the building of the new church. He had been temporarily embalmed (possibly while the church was being built), during which time he became completely desiccated, which accounts for his current remarkable state of preservation.

Church authorities have decided that it is inappropriate to treat such bodies as curios, so Jimmy is no longer on show and now resides in a purpose-built elm casket below the tower. It is planned that he will be buried in the relatively near future. Jimmy narrowly missed destruction by a bomb in the Second World War, which crashed through the roof but failed to explode, and inevitably there are stories of his ghost being seen about the church.

West Smithfield:
St Bartholomew-the-Great church

Every Good Friday, the ceremony of the Butterworth Dole takes place at St Bartholomew's. The traditional form was described by Christina Hole in her *English Custom and Usage* (1944):

> At the church of St. Bartholomew-the-Great in Smithfield, twenty-one sixpences are given to as many poor widows every Good Friday. The coins are placed on a tombstone in the churchyard, and each widow kneels by the stone to pick up her sixpence. She then walks over the stone and is given a hot cross bun and half a crown. No one knows who gave the money for this charity, for all the papers concerning it perished with the other parish records in the Great Fire of London.

From the 1970s, no poor widows have presented themselves, so the buns are nowadays given to children. The lack of founding documents has led to some exaggerated claims about how old the custom is, with 500 years and more often being quoted. As it was made clear in a letter to *The Times* on 21 April 1919, there is no mention of the dole in church records in 1662, but the next surviving volume, of 1686, records 'paid Mr Burgess for his sermon and the poor widows £1'. It is a safe bet that the dole was founded between these two dates. By 1888, like many other charities, the dole had fallen into disuse and was revived by an endowment by G. W. Butterworth, and it now bears his name.

The traditional place for executions in London, before the famous Tyburn took over the honour, was at The Elms, Smithfield. Presumably, as the sixteenth-century chronicler John Stow commented, the area had originally been famous for its real elm trees, but these had all gone by the early fifteenth century, and by then the name 'The

Two very different aspects of London life could once be witnessed at the church of St Bartholomew-the-Great: public executions and the granting of an annual dole to poor widows.

Elms' had become synonymous with 'place of execution'. Tradition states that these executions were carried out almost on the doorstep of St Bartholomew's church, and in addition to innumerable nameless criminals and martyrs a number of high-profile figures were despatched here, including the Scottish patriot William Wallace, who was executed, appropriately enough, on St Bartholomew's Eve in 1305. Particularly barbaric methods were used on the site, including burning and drawing and quartering, and according to Walter Thornbury's *Old and New London* (Vol. 2, 1872):

> In March 1849, during excavations necessary for a new sewer, and at a depth of three feet below the surface, immediately opposite the entrance to the church . . . the workmen laid open a mass of unhewn stones, blackened as if by fire, and covered with ashes and human bones, charred and partially consumed. This was believed to have been the spot generally used for the Smithfield burnings.

So much blood and pain can hardly go unremembered in the spirit world. As J. A. Brooks in his *Ghosts of London* (1991) comments:

. . . small wonder that their ghostly cries still echo through the ether, and these, with the sound of crackling faggots, have been heard by people passing by here alone, on dark nights. Some people have even spoken of also smelling the hideous stench of charred flesh.

This is disappointingly vague, but the ghosts within the church are far more specific.

The Revd Sandwith, rector of the church, told Mrs Stirling, for her book *Ghosts Vivisected* (1957):

I was taking two ladies round the church, and quite suddenly, looking at the pulpit, I saw in it a man in the black gown of Geneva, evidently a Divine of the Reformation period, preaching away most earnestly to an invisible congregation. No sound was to be heard, but he appeared to be exhorting the unseen audience with the greatest fervour, gesticulating vehemently . . . for fully a quarter of an hour I remained in the church seeing that man as clearly as I see you beside me.

The ladies with him saw nothing. The Reverend's wife, however, had previously seen the figure of a monk, whose cowl hid his face, gliding through the church into the vestry, and the following day the rector himself saw a cowled face looking at him while he was conducting the service. Unlike those who have felt ghostly activity at the execution site, people who have seen or felt these ghosts have reported a feeling of comfort and benevolence. The apparitions are usually explained as sightings of Rahere, who founded his priory of St Augustine on the site in 1123. He was a courtier who underwent a religious conversion on a trip to Rome, decided to found a hospital, and was told by St Bartholomew, in a vision, to found a church as well. Even today, entering the church is like stepping back 800 years.

See also EDGWARE ROAD: TYBURN, p. 80.

CITY OF WESTMINSTER

BERKELEY SQUARE

A small window on the world of Londoners in the 1820s is provided by a piece that appeared in *The Times* on 29 March 1825. It concerns a lost £10 note, and is a good example of how much faith people put in the power of fortune-tellers, and also highlights the fact that some residents, such as Gypsies, could trade on their 'otherness' to claim occult powers. The Bible and key (*see* FORTUNE-TELLING, p. 78) procedure mentioned here was a widespread method of detecting thieves:

> Marlborough Street: A few days ago, a woman of colour, named Elizabeth Dodd, was brought to this office upon a charge of fortune-telling. It appeared that a woman named Mary Edmonds, living as cook in the family of Mr Prendergast, MP, in Berkeley Square, had a sum of money given to her by Mrs Prendergast, to pay the butcher,

THE
GIPSY
FORTUNE
TELLER

CONTAINING

JUDGMENT FOR THE 29 DAYS OF THE MOON, THE SIGNIFICATION OF MOLES, AND THE ART OF TELLING FORTUNES BY DICE, DOMINOES, &c., &c.

LONDON:
PUBLISHED BY T. GOODE. "LION" PRINTING WORKS. CLERKENWELL GREEN.

Gypsy fortune-tellers once enjoyed considerable popularity – and notoriety – as an early nineteenth-century court case, arising from recent events in Berkeley Square, attests. This popular pamphlet sets out some of the procedures that fortune-tellers used.

CITY OF WESTMINSTER

Maida
Vale

St John's
Wood

CITY OF

WESTMINSTER

Portman

Portman Square,
Montagu House

Sussex Gardens,
St James

Edgware Road
Tyburn

Hyde Park

	Pageantry and regular customs
	Famous landmarks
	Ghosts and hauntings
	Fairs and revelry
	Heroes and villains
	Superstitions and witchcraft
	Crime and punishment
	Death and burial
	Devils and witches
	Games and nursery rhymes
	Hidden treasure
	Beasts and creepy crawlies
	Name origins
	Secret tunnels
	Supernatural experiences

KENSINGTON
& CHELSEA

WEST

LONDON

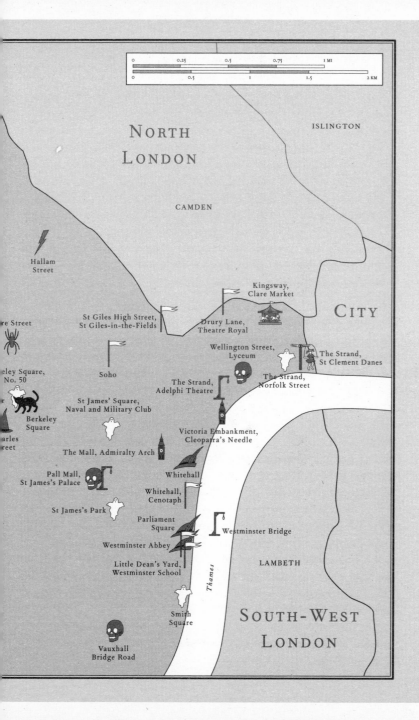

baker, &c.; this sum consisted of five £10 notes, which Mr Prendergast had received from Child's bank, as part payment of a check drawn in his favour by Mr Fleeming, MP, of Gloucester Place, for £130. The cook, in the course of her disbursements, by some accident or other lost one of these £10 notes; and having heard of a very high character of the dark-coloured prophetess, and much of her repute and success in recovering lost property, she invited her to Mr Prendergast's house, for the purpose of at once fixing on the thief. The prophetess having gone through the usual ceremony practised in her profession, with a Bible and key, pointed out a young girl, a nursery-maid in the family, named Susan Watkins, as the depredator. But Susan Watkins, having a little more common sense than usually falls to the lot of servant maids on such subjects, instead of being alarmed at the dread power of the 'witching woman', sent for a constable, and had her brought to the office to answer, upon some rational or human grounds, why it was she fixed upon the poor nursery-maid as the thief.

The magistrate gave the fortune-teller two months in a House of Correction, but the article goes on to state that the cook was still convinced that her prophecy was correct, and Susan Watkins was discharged from her situation.

BERKELEY SQUARE: NO. 50

No. 50 Berkeley Square is possibly the most famous haunted house in London, and during the mid Victorian period it was discussed in drawing rooms and at dining tables all over the capital. Indeed, even modern ghost-writers hold it up as an example of a well-attested truly haunted house. Over the years, many competing stories have attached to this seeming hotbed of supernatural activity, so it is extremely interesting to follow the thread of the reports published about the house. Fortunately for us, it has not been only the popular press who have picked up on the tale, but also the contributors to *Notes and Queries* who, in the main, were less likely to succumb to the temptations of sensationalism.

The first public attention to the story came with a question about the property in *Notes and Queries* in November 1872, which was answered by Lord Lyttelton:

> Haunted Houses: Can your readers inform me of any houses now *closed*, as being haunted? Is there a house in Berkeley Square (London), with this repute, as I have been informed? H.A.B.

> It is quite true that there is a house in Berkeley Square (No. 50) said to be haunted, and long unoccupied on that account. There are strange stories about it, into which this deponent cannot enter. LYTTELTON

In January 1873, a further correspondent (E.M.P.) wrote to say that he had been to the house, which was *not* unoccupied, and to ask Lyttelton if he had 'any further reason for supposing the house to be haunted'. Lord Lyttelton did not reply, and he died, by his own hand, in 1876, before the next flurry of interest in the topic. However, although 'the mystery of Berkeley Square' seemed to go quiet in the public journals for a few years, things were far from quiet on the ground.

It all burst forth again in 1879, and it is clear that by this time the haunted house in Berkeley Square had been the talk of the town for some time, and was extremely widely known. As one off-hand comment in the 25 December 1880 edition of *Notes and Queries* reveals, this was not a case of peasants sitting round the fireplace telling tales, which is what folklore is often thought to be, but of the chit-chat of a middle-class dinner party: 'For many years the lady one took down to dinner was sure to tell you of the strange horrors connected with No. 50 Berkeley Square.'

Between August 1879 and February 1881, the *Notes and Queries* fraternity carried out a leisurely conversation on the topic, in which hearsay and fact were aired, challenged, and chewed over. They printed one particularly important piece of evidence in December 1880: a letter, addressed to the late Bishop Thirlwall, dated 22 January 1871, which gives us a rare opportunity to find out what was really being said in the wider community, unfiltered by journalists or other writers.

> Ghosts remind me that I never told you a story Mrs — related to us when she was here last, about the haunted house in Berkeley Square; S— pointed it out to me last spring . . .The dilapidated, forsaken, dusty look of the house quite suits a reputation for ghosts . . .

> Miss H— (who repeated the tale to Mrs P—) was told by some R.C. friends of hers that a family they knew hired the haunted house – wherever it was – in Berkeley Square for a London season, as there were daughters to be brought out, one of whom was already engaged. They spent a short time

in the house without finding anything amiss; then they invited the young lady's lover to join them, and the next bedroom, which they had not occupied, was made ready for him, and the housemaid was either sleeping there, or else still busy with her preparations at twelve o'clock the night before his arrival. The hour had no sooner struck than piercing shrieks were heard, loud enough to rouse the whole household. They rushed upstairs, flung open the door of the haunted room, and found the unfortunate housemaid lying at the foot of the bed in strong convulsions. Her eyes were fixed, with a stare of expressive horror, upon a remote corner of the chamber, and an agony of fear seemed to possess her, yet the bystanders saw nothing. They took her to St George's Hospital, where she died in the morning, refusing to the last to give any account of what she had seen; she could not speak of it, she said it was far too horrible. The expected guest arrived that day. He was told the story, and that it was arranged that he should not occupy the haunted room. He voted it all nonsense, and insisted upon sleeping there. He, however, agreed to sit up until past twelve, and to ring if anything unusual occurred. 'But,' he added, 'on no account come to me when I ring first; because I may be unnecessarily alarmed and seize the bell on the impulse of the moment. Wait until you hear a second ring. 'His betrothed expostulated in vain. He did not believe in apparitions, and he would solve the mystery. She listened, in a misery of suspense, when the time of trial drew near. At last the bell rang once, but faintly. Then there was an interval of a few dreadful minutes, and a tremendous peal sounded through the house. Everyone hurried breathless to the haunted room. They found the guest exactly in the same place where the dead housemaid had lain, convulsed as she was, his eyes fixed in horror upon the same spot where hers had been fixed the night before, and, like her, he never revealed his experiences. They were too awful, he said, ever to mention. The family left the house at once.

Following the printing of this letter, there was a flurry of communication from people who claimed to have lived in the house in the 1850s and 1860s, during which time there was no talk of it being haunted. There was also a letter in January 1881 from a doctor at St George's hospital, in response to the element in the story that describes the servant girl being taken there, stating that no such case had been admitted in over twenty years. An attempt to get the writers of the letter to Bishop Thirlwall to back up their story met with evasion and refusal, a situation very familiar to anyone who has tried to trace the transmission of any 'true' contemporary legend.

On top of this, several of the *Notes and Queries* writers were aware of the similarity with a published ghost story, and this was soon identified as 'The Truth, the Whole Truth, and Nothing but the Truth', by Rhoda Broughton, first published in *Temple Bar* in February 1868, and then in book form as *Tales for Christmas Eve* (1872), renamed as *Twilight Stories* (1879). On being asked about it, Ms Broughton stated quite categorically in the February 1881 edition of *Notes and Queries* that the tale had nothing to do with Berkeley Square and admitted that it was a country story:

> . . . and I clothed it in fictitious characters and transposed it to London, which I have since regretted, as so many people have thence assumed that it must refer to the house in Berkeley Square.

In trying to make sense of what happened, chronology is everything. The earliest indication of any story attached to the house is the Thirlwall letter, written in January 1871 but referring to the previous spring – i.e. about March 1870. We have some evidence, from people who lived in the house, that the stories were not in circulation in 1859, and Rhoda Broughton's story was published in February 1868.

The most likely explanation is simple and prosaic: an apparently empty and neglected house in an otherwise respectable neighbourhood began to attract speculation, and a recently published article was immediately drafted in to explain it, and became more and more indelibly connected to the house with each retelling. This scenario fits perfectly with how folklore works, although it will disappoint those who prefer to believe that there are real supernatural occurrences at the root of all ghost stories.

But there is more to be said about Berkeley Square. Other stories were told, either at the time or since, and while some can be seen to be derived from the Broughton story, others seem to have arisen completely independently. Indeed, the writer of the Thirlwall letter also gave a completely different story, before talking of ghosts:

> This house, she says, is watched strictly by the police. None of its inhabitants ever cross its doorstep, and false coining is supposed to be carried on there, but has never been detected.

Another recurrent theme in the tales is that the house had been prepared for a new bride, but that she had ditched her fiancé at the altar, sending him mad. Naturally, he wandered the empty house at all hours of day and night, and the only visitor allowed to visit was his sister. Another story, which, like the Broughton story, is focused on a particular room, tells of how the house was occupied only by an old couple as caretakers. One room in the house was always locked and only the owner had the key. He would occasionally visit the house, lock the couple in the basement and then spend some time in the locked room, doing who knows what.

Yet another story, along fairly standard 'madman in the attic' lines, is noted in Augustus Hare's journal. He quotes Mrs Stuart Wortley, who had come to luncheon:

27 December 1872

She told us that the secret of 'the haunted house in Berkeley Square' is that it belonged to a Mr Du Pré of Wilton Park. He shut up his lunatic brother there in a cage in one of the attics, and the poor captive was so violent that he could only be fed through a hole. His groans and cries could be distinctly heard in the neighbouring houses. The house is now to be let for £100 the first year, £200 the second, £300 the third, but if any tenant leaves within that time, he is to forfeit £1000. The house will be furnished in any style or taste the tenant chooses.

Not to be left out, the prolific ghost writer Elliott O'Donnell published a completely different story in his *Ghosts of London* (1932), repeated in *Phantoms of the Night* (1956), which again focuses on the evil-room motif. Sometime in the 1870s two penniless sailors came across the empty house one winter's night, and went inside to spend the night. They made a fire in one of the upstairs rooms and eventually fell asleep. They were awakened by sounds in the house, and footsteps on the stairs – not ordinary ones, but 'soft, stealthy steps, more like some great animal than of a human being'. The door opened slowly and some horrible shape entered the room. One sailor managed to dodge past and flee down the stairs, as he heard his companion scream. On reaching the street he collapsed in fright, but his fellow sailor was later found dead in the back yard, where he had jumped or fallen from the upstairs window.

Later writers have cheerfully incorporated this into the corpus of Berkeley Square stories, but there is no evidence that O'Donnell did not simply make it up, and no coroner's report or newspaper report has been found to confirm any part of the story. However, one thing that O'Donnell says about the aftermath of the house's reputation is of interest:

When I first visited London in the early nineties I soon found my way to Berkeley Square, and although No. — was no longer a topic of conversation, having lost its ghostly notoriety, I was nevertheless thrilled when I saw it . . . Then few people questioned the truth of its once having been really haunted, the stories told about it were generally accepted as facts.

One key aspect of the Berkeley Square saga that no writer seems to have commented on is the recurrent motif of the *empty house*, and its central importance in all the stories and explanations. This may seem like an insignificant detail, but it is crucial to any understanding of this particular outbreak of ghost-lore, and many others. Indeed, it occurs so frequently in ghost stories that it could be termed the Empty House Syndrome (EHS), as in *these strange things happened in the house, and now it can't be let, and stands empty . . .*, or *some people rented an empty house, at an unusually low rent, and they could not understand why it was empty . . .* In most cases it is used as a small but important legitimating element in the story; however, it can take on much more narrative weight.

Empty or dilapidated houses often seem to attract ghost stories, and EHS is found throughout the ghost-lore literature; indeed, it is difficult to find a book of ghost stories that does not include at least one example. In the Berkeley Square *Notes and Queries* correspondence, the first two letters, quoted above, focus on the notion of a house standing empty because it is haunted, and the main thrust of much of the following correspondence was concerned with the questions 'Is the house empty?' and 'Why is the house empty?'

In folklore terms, what is happening here is a clear example of another common principle, which could be termed the *reversal of causation*. So, for example, it is often believed that legends attached to traditional customs satisfactorily explain those customs because the details of the legend match those of the custom. But it is actually the case that the legend was invented *after* the custom existed, and tailored to fit. In the ghost story, the confirmatory detail – *the house is empty because it is haunted* – should always be understood as *the house is believed to be haunted because it is empty*.

A last word on Berkeley Square: A. W. M. Stirling ends a chapter on mysterious happenings in *The Merry Wives of Battersea* (1956) with a short piece about Berkeley Square told to her by 'the late Lady C.'. Unfortunately, she does not say which house, but it would be a fitting end to the stories of poor old No. 50.

A house in Berkeley Square was alleged to be badly haunted, so a priest was called in to exorcize the ghosts or poltergeists who were infesting it. Apparently they were extremely up-to-date spooks for, after the priest had departed, it was found that a typewriter had been moved from a writing-table in a distant corner of the drawing-room and placed conspicuously on a table in the centre of the room, while in it was left a badly typed script which bore the message: 'Most uncomfortable. Have gone, never to return.'

CHARLES STREET, WESTMINSTER

There were several ways of dealing with malevolent witchcraft of the day-to-day kind, and one of the commonest methods was to draw blood from the person who had cast the spell, 'above the breath', i.e. on the face or head. There are numerous records of innocent people, usually old women who fitted the local stereotype of the witch figure, being attacked for this reason, as in the following court case heard at Bow Street court and reported in *The Times* on 2 June 1862. Charles Tilbrook, aged twenty-seven, recently discharged from the army, was accused of attempting to murder his grandmother, 75-year-old Mary King, in Charles Street, Westminster. Mrs King stated:

> On Sunday, April 13, about dinner time, I was putting on my cap, having just finished dressing, in the presence of my husband and grandson (the prisoner), when, without a word being spoken, the latter rushed upon me and gave me two cuts with something which he held in his hand. He cut my face and the top of my head, and then took up a wooden copper-stick and attacked me with it until my poor head was beaten in . . . I had not had any words with my grandson, but about a week ago I remember saying to him, 'May-Day will be a gay one this year', to which he replied, 'You will never live to see it.'

When Tilbrook was arrested, he declared: 'Serve her right. She ought to have been dead long ago. I did not care to kill her. I wanted to shed her blood, and I have done it', and later, in court, he announced: 'I wish it to be known that she is a very bad character, and not fit to live at all. She is a witch, in daily intercourse with the devil.'

See also WITCH BOTTLES, p. 238.

DRURY LANE: THEATRE ROYAL

Every Twelfth Night, the cast of the current production at the Theatre Royal, Drury Lane, gather in the green room, still in costume after their performance, to eat a slice of cake and toast the memory of one of their predecessors, Robert Baddeley (1733–94). Baddeley was a popular English actor who had been a cook and a valet before joining the stage in 1760. In private he led an unconventional life, eloping with Sophia Snow, another player of the time, with whom he had a stormy marriage until they separated and both lived with other partners. He fought at least two duels, but remained popular with the theatre-going public, and was active in setting up charities for actors and their families. Baddeley died in November 1794, while dressing for the part of Moses in Sheridan's *School for Scandal*, a role for which he was particularly well known, and he left money in his will to help theatrical folk who had fallen on hard times, plus a small annual sum to supply the slice of cake and glass of punch or wine to the cast. It was no accident that he chose Twelfth Night for his annual celebration, as there was a very long tradition of special cakes on that day, until the Victorian remodelling of the season pulled the custom towards Christmas Day. Nevertheless, it was reported in *Notes and Queries* in 1916 that Baddeley happened into the green room one day and:

> . . . noticed all the company were dull and moping round the fire; so he immediately sent out for cake and punch, and said, as long as he could prevent it such a thing should never occur again, meaning, of course, the depression of his brother and sister artists.

The money from Baddeley's bequest ran out long ago, but the theatre management still honours his wishes every year, although a correspondent in *Notes and Queries* (1940) revealed that the cake had not been made in the last years of the First World War, because of a sugar shortage, and that there had been no company, and therefore no cake, when the theatres were closed in 1940.

Fortune-Telling

A nineteenth-century engraving taken from the original serialisation in *Cornhill Magazine* of Thomas Hardy's *Far from the Madding Crowd*. Bathsheba Everdene and her maid have decided to try the 'Bible and key' method to discover who she might marry.

The eighteenth century saw the educated classes gradually turning away from superstition, but most folk still believed implicitly in witchcraft and fortune-telling. Evidence of these occult beliefs is not always easy to find, but a trawl through the archives of the Old Bailey from 1729 to 1834 brings up a number of cases of fortune-tellers being charged with theft or deception, and they provide a valuable insight into this aspect of daily life and belief in the city. It is interesting to note that in each of these cases the fortune-tellers acted in almost exactly the same way as confidence tricksters today, with a combination of fast talking, wheedling, bullying and sleight of hand designed to prey on the victim's gullibility and greed. Apart from the straightforward telling of a fortune for a set fee, a common trick was to get the victim to provide money, valuables or saleable clothing. The fortune-teller would then take these items away, saying that they needed to be hidden in order to locate some buried treasure, or be used in some occult astrological rite to obtain more money or divine the future. The fortune-teller promised to return these valuables in a few days, but of course they were never seen again.

Another recurrent feature was recourse to the 'Bible and key', an extremely widespread procedure designed to tell the future, or to resolve some difficult decision or question. It could be used for any type of fortune-telling because it was meant to provide a response to questions posed to it, but the two areas most often put to this test were love divination and the location of lost or stolen property. The basic method was simple, but it varied somewhat in practice. A large key, sometimes specifically the main house key, was placed in a Bible at a particular passage. The Bible was then tied tightly and held lightly between two people, usually by each holding an end of the key, or the Bible, on their fingertips. Some kind of formula was spoken to set the scene, usually based on the chosen Bible passage, and then questions asked, such as 'Who stole my brooch? Was it A—, or D—, or L—,' and so on. At the mention of the guilty name, the Bible would twist or move in the people's hands.

As with most folk-based uses of the Bible, the real meaning of the chosen passage does not seem to have been important, as long as the words approximated to the setting. The passages could be from any part of the Bible, but for retrieving stolen goods, the most often reported were Ruth 4:4, which contains the words, 'If thou wilt redeem it, redeem it', and Psalm 50: 18, which includes, 'When thou sawest a thief'. For love divination, the two most common verses were the Song of Solomon 8: 6–7, which contains the words, 'Set me as a seal upon thine heart', or Ruth 1:16, 'whither thou goest, I will go'.

The first known reference to the procedure is in 1303, and the early versions are all concerned with unmasking thieves, but by Victorian times it had also developed into a party game for love divination. Nevertheless, its serious use lasted well into the twentieth century, and it is astonishing how much blind faith people put into these fortune-telling procedures, especially when it came to stolen property.

See BERKELEY SQUARE, p. 67; FRYING PAN ALLEY, TOWER HAMLETS, p. 274; ST MARY AXE, p. 47.

EDGWARE ROAD: TYBURN

CLOWN: What is he that builds stronger than either the mason, the
shipwright, or the carpenter?
OTHER: The gallows-maker; for that frame outlives a thousand tenants.
(*Hamlet*, v:1)

Tyburn was the main place of public execution in London from at least
1388 until 1783, when it was replaced by Newgate. It takes its name from
the Tyburn stream, which ran from Hampstead to the Thames near
Vauxhall Bridge, and was so well known that the word became, for a time,
synonymous with *gallows*. Tyburn gallows stood close to where Marble
Arch is now, and the approximate site is marked by a stone in the traffic
island at the junction of Edgware Road and Bayswater Road. An iron
plaque is located about fifty yards west of Marble Arch.

The first permanent gallows, in the triangular shape so characteristic of
the site, called the Triple Tree, was erected in 1571 and stood until 1759,
when the New Drop was installed. The timber from the old bloodstained
triple tree was reputedly sold to a carpenter who turned it into beer-butt
stands for the cellar of the Carpenters' Arms public house close by.

Until the New Drop was introduced, the condemned simply stood in
the cart in which they had been brought, drawn up under the gallows. The
noose was placed around their neck, and the horse then made to move on,
and they were left suspended. A broken neck was the best they could hope
for, but slow strangulation was most likely. At smaller gallows, the
condemned were simply forced to climb a ladder and were then pushed off
into eternity.

The details of executions make gruesome reading. They were often badly
bungled, and chaos ensued. Friends and relatives tried to cut criminals down
quickly in order to revive them or keep them from the hands of the
anatomists, and methods were so haphazard that the occasional unfortunate
criminal survived and woke up on the dissection table, or in their coffin.
On other occasions, friends would pull on the feet of the hanged person to
hasten their death. There was little crowd control, and things could turn
nasty if the crowd felt it had been cheated of its entertainment.

Silas Told (1711–78), who came under the influence of John Wesley,
began visiting condemned prisoners at Newgate in order to minister to

their spiritual needs, and he even accompanied many of them in the cart that took them to the gallows. In his memoirs, published in 1786, Told describes an incident which he attributed to God moving in mysterious ways, but which to modern eyes looks like a rumour or legend. Told was ministering to a prisoner, who was on his way to the gallows:

> John Lancaster had no friend who could procure for his body a proper interment; so that, when they had hung the usual space of time, and were cut down, the surgeon's mob secured the body of Lancaster, and carried it over to Paddington.

As usual, there was a vast concourse of people for the hanging, but the crowd had mostly dissipated when:

> A company of eight sailors, with truncheons in their hands, having come to see the execution, looked up to the gallows with an angry countenance, the bodies having been cut down some minutes previous to their arrival. The old woman . . . who sold gin, observing these tars to grow violent, by reason of their disappointment, mildly accosted them and said, 'Gentlemen, I suppose you want the man that the surgeons have got?' 'Aye', replied the sailors, 'where is he?' The poor affrighted woman gave them to understand that the surgeons' crew had carried him over to Paddington, and she pointed out to them the direct road thereto.

The sailors hastened off to Paddington, and with the threat of violence demanded Lancaster's body.

> Two of them cast it on their shoulders, and carried him round by Islington. They being tired out with its pressure, two others laid themselves under the weight of the body, and carried it from thence to Shoreditch. Then two more carried it from Shoreditch to Coverley's Fields.

Eventually tiring of their burden, and their game, they decided to leave the body on the next doorstep they came to, which they promptly did, and marched off. Hearing a noise at her door, the old woman of the house came out to investigate.

> When she saw the corpse lie at the step of the door, she proclaimed, with an agitated spirit, 'Lord, here is my son, John Lancaster!' This being spread abroad, came to the knowledge of the Methodists, who made a collection, and got him a shroud and a good strong coffin.

Public hanging was, of course, deliberately horrible, as it was designed to deter criminals, but there is little evidence that it succeeded at all in this respect. Indeed, the people subverted the proceedings by making an execution into some kind of vast street theatre, and many of the condemned played up to their role of temporary star performer, dressing flamboyantly, throwing oranges or flowers to the crowds, making speeches and cracking jokes. Some, on the other hand, were meek and mild, and many were catatonic with fear. The route from Newgate to Tyburn was lined with sightseers, and whole families turned up, treating the occasion as a carnival day. Side-shows, food and drink stalls, ballad singers selling the 'Last Dying Speeches' of the condemned, prostitutes, pickpockets and all London humanity gathered for what was known colloquially as Tyburn Fair.

But there was a worse horror than a hanging – burning alive, the required punishment for women convicted of treason, murdering their husbands (as this was counted as treason), and coining (making counterfeit money). Contrary to popular notions, witches were not burnt at the stake in England, they were hanged. Daniel Lysons, in his *Environs of London: Middlesex* III (1795), described just one of many burnings:

> The public place of execution for criminals convicted in the county of Middlesex was formerly in the parish of Marybone, at the end of Park-lane, not far from Tybourn-turnpike. There suffered the infamous Catherine Hayes, for the murder of her husband (in this parish), which was attended with circumstances of uncommon atrocity. It is recorded in a well-known ballad, beginning, 'In Tybourn-road there liv'd a man'. Catherine Hayes suffered the utmost severity of her sentence, being literally burnt alive, in consequence (as it was said) of the indignation of the populace, who would not suffer the executioner to strangle her (as is usual) before the fire was kindled.

As indicated here, the usual 'humane' way of executing women in this way was to strangle them first, and then burn them.

The last woman to be executed by burning was Christian Murphy, who was killed on 18 March 1789 having been convicted, with her husband, of coining offences. Oddly enough, burning was seen by many as a more humane method of execution for certain offences: whereas men were stripped naked, castrated, drawn, quartered, and so on, women were simply burnt alive.

Every year, on the first Sunday in May, Tyburn is again visited by a crowd, but there are no gin sellers or ballad singers in evidence. This is the annual Tyburn Walk, a pilgrimage to commemorate all the Catholics who were martyred for their faith at Tyburn over the centuries. Modern traffic makes it difficult, but the walk tries to follow the route taken from Newgate in the Strand to Marble Arch, and it has taken place every year since 1910.

See also NEWGATE STREET: NEWGATE PRISON, p. 41; WEST SMITHFIELD: ST BARTHOLOMEW-THE-GREAT CHURCH, p. 64.

HALLAM STREET

A well-known incident in the annals of ghost-lore rests on the testimony of the biographer and historian A. W. M. Stirling, in her *The Merry Wives of Battersea* (1956). It concerns a friend of hers, Mr Sherard Cowper Coles (1866–1936), metallurgist and inventor, who had invited her to his flat in Hallam Street.

The reason for Coles's invitation was to show Mrs Stirling an album of photographs taken in the flat, which clearly showed figures in a variety of period dress, despite the fact that the room was known to be completely unoccupied when the photos were taken. He had discovered the first figure quite by accident, when he took a photograph of his sitting room to send to his wife, and discovered the image of a man sitting in an armchair by the window. He started taking regular photographs in the same room, and gathered quite a heterogeneous collection, including a warrior in ancient armour with a winged helmet, and a man in a military coat of the period of Wellington. They appeared to be photographs of living people, not those of unsubstantial wraiths. Only one of the people seemed to have any connection with Coles himself. His older brother recognised the family's old nurse among them. When Mrs Stirling asked, 'Did you ever get repulsive or evil things?', he replied, 'Sometimes, but I destroy these.'

From the brief description given, it seemed that the phantoms used Mr Coles's furniture rather than bringing their own. Mrs Stirling clearly believed Mr Coles's assertion that the photos were genuine, but there is no reason for us to be so credulous. Coles was known to be interested in psychic matters, as well as being an experimental photographer, which is a potent combination. There is also an uncertainty about the timing of events in Stirling's account, which is characteristic of her vague style of writing. She specifically states that she was invited to visit Coles in 1934, but also writes that he had the Hallam Street flat during and after the First World War. The events described may therefore have taken place anything up to twenty years before her involvement. The photographs are most likely to be as real as the famous ones of the Cottingley Fairies.

HYDE PARK

Hyde Park is the largest of the London ROYAL PARKS (p. 90), and was opened to the public in the early seventeenth century. It has proved popular for a wide variety of purposes ever since. During the day and summer evenings, Hyde Park is a charming slice of rural tranquillity in the middle of London, but at night it can be spookier than any country spot. It is no surprise to learn that there are many stories of unnerving occurrences. To begin, let us consider a ghost story given in Jacob Larwood's *Story of the London Parks* (c.1881):

> Owing to the number of violent deaths which happened in the Park by means of duels, murders, suicides, and Tyburn closely adjoining, it is no wonder that weak-minded people could be made to believe that awful and supernatural events were witnessed there in the dead hour of night. This was the case in 1798, when two soldiers belonging to the 1st Regiment of Footguards for some time greatly imposed upon the credulity of their comrades and acquaintances in the following manner. One of them, who had long pretended to be inspired with an 'inward spirit', used to declare that he had frequently seen and conversed with the spirit of the Lord, and if any of his comrades would accompany him any night to Hyde Park, he would convince them of the truth of what he asserted.

Two acquaintances therefore accompanied him to a certain tree, where he proceeded to draw a magic circle and muttered incantations, and a white spirit duly appeared. His companions took fright and ran off. The reputation of the wizard was thereby enhanced, and he agreed to another demonstration with others in attendance. Again the spirit was conjured, but a corporal in their midst, instead of running away, advanced towards the spirit, and it was the latter who tried to beat a hasty retreat. It turned out to be another soldier of the same regiment dressed up.

A popular recreational spot for centuries, Hyde Park is also home to numerous ghost stories – in part, possibly, because the Serpentine was associated with suicide.

Of all the modern writers on the ghosts and strange phenomena of London parks, Elliott O'Donnell is the only one who claims to have done original research, by talking to local people such as 'down-and-outs' who slept there, regular users, and park-keepers, and his books seem to be the source of many of the stories that subsequent writers have reprinted, often without acknowledgement. O'Donnell had well-developed ideas about the reason why parks attract strange occurrences, which he explained in his *Ghosts of London* (1932):

> That certain localities tempt people to commit homicidal acts is never more proven than in the case of Hyde Park and St James's Park. If the deeds were confined to the immediate vicinity of the water in these parks, one might think it was the fascination still water has for people of certain temperaments, but homicidal deeds have been very common in parts of the Park where there is no water. I am of the opinion that the key to the mystery lies in the combination of the Unknown, in superphysical forces that are attracted by still water and by certain trees, and which, in their turn, attract

and influence people of certain temperaments. It is not merely the appearance of the still water glimmering in the golden sunshine or cold moonbeams that inspires a person with a sudden impulse to drown themselves or someone else, it is a power, a force lurking near the water that, magnet-like, attracts some people to its shore and there fills them with homicidal thoughts. The same applies to trees.

O'Donnell drew parallels with 'other countries' which had beliefs in spirits inhabiting trees, rocks, and other physical locations, and he cited what in Greece are called *stichios*, or spirits for which certain trees have a peculiar fascination. He therefore coined the word *stichmonious* to describe the phenomenon, which he used extensively in his books, although it has not yet made it into the *OED*.

His hypothesis is extremely useful, as it is so infinitely adaptable that it can be used to explain any number of strange phenomena. In the same book, for example, he tells the story of 'All Button Mary', so called because she had so many buttons on her jacket, who slept under a particular elm tree and in the morning declared that a voice had kept whispering to her all night. The voice had insisted that the next world was a wonderful place and she should kill herself to get there sooner. She was found dead in the Serpentine later that day. O'Donnell gives the following comment:

> The elm, when stichmonious, would usually seem to be haunted by a grotesque type of spirit that affects people of certain temperaments in a very unpleasant way. If it does not tempt them to suicide or murder, it generates in them vicious desires and strange manias. Women appear to come under its influence more than men.

And in another tree-based Hyde Park story, from the same writer:

> I was strolling across the grass, close to here, one night . . . when I suddenly became conscious of someone in front of me, and upon raising my head – I had been walking with head bent in deep thought – I saw a woman a few yards ahead of me. She was going along in the same direction as I was, and the moonlight was so strong on her that I could see every item of her dress. It was a shabby turnout, a grey woosted shawl, a rusty black skirt, very bedraggled and frayed, an old battered bonnet, and a pair of boots, with splits in the back of them, through which I could see her bare skin. She looked so poor and solitary that a wave of pity went through me, and I hastened my steps to give her the wherewithal for a night's lodging. Fast as

I walked, however, the distance between us invariably remained the same, although she never seemed to make any alteration in her pace.

The pair continued in this fashion across the park:

I then perceived, some little distance off, to my right, a huge, solitary tree with very curiously-shaped branches, one of which, in particular, riveted my attention. It stretched out from the trunk, at a height of six or seven feet from the ground, like a great arm, and it terminated in what looked exactly like fingers, long bony fingers, slightly curved, as if to clutch hold of one. The woman ahead of me now turned sharply and made straight towards it. She was entirely in the open, the ground on either side of her being quite bare, and, as I gazed, I perceived a certain indistinctness, a something shadowy about her that I had not noticed before . . . The moment she came under the shadow of the tree she turned round. As she did so, one soft brilliant ray of light fell on her face, and made every feature in it stand out with frightful clearness. I say frightful clearness, because the thing that looked at me was not living, it was dead – long, long dead.

He then 'got the wind up' and ran out of the park into the Bayswater Road, but he returned the following day and despite a thorough search could not find the tree, or anything like it. Finally, he asked a very old man:

He took me to a broad open space, which I seemed to recognize, and pointing to a certain spot, said, 'That's where the tree you are looking for stood, about twenty years ago. I remember it very well. It had a branch exactly like a human arm and hand, and it fascinated people, fascinated them so much that they used to like to sleep under it, and quite a number who tried to do so were found dead in the morning. One or two, I believe, hanged themselves on its branches. It was cut down eventually, partly, I understood, because of these suicides, and partly because it was said that queer things had been seen and heard in its vicinity at night.

Nevertheless, trees are not the only scary things in the vicinity:

With regard to suicides in the Park, however, I think the spot most favoured by them is the Serpentine. Among those who drowned themselves there in the past was Harriet Westbrook Shelley, the unhappy wife of the poet Shelley . . . in 1816, and rumour has it that her ghost, as well as numerous other ghosts, haunts the Serpentine at night.

O'Donnell also tells the story of two women who were walking by the Serpentine one fine autumn afternoon, when they remarked on some unexplained ripples on the water's surface. As they spoke, a white, slim woman's hand appeared, fingers clutching at the air convulsively, like those of someone drowning. On the middle finger of the hand was a plain gold ring that flashed and sparkled in the daylight. After about a minute, the hand slowly sank out of sight, and the horrified women ran out of the park as fast as they could.

See also EPPING FOREST: SUICIDE POOL, p. 269.

KINGSWAY: CLARE MARKET

Clare Market, situated between Lincoln's Inn Fields and the Strand, was a purpose-built market created by the Earl of Clare in the mid seventeenth century. It housed various greengrocers, fishmongers, and other provision merchants, but was particularly famous for its butchers and the animals they slaughtered there. By the nineteenth century it had become a crowded, dirty and unsavoury place, and it was mostly swept away when Kingsway and Aldwych were redeveloped in 1900.

One of the regular sights in the streets of eighteenth- and early nineteenth-century London was a group of butchers' apprentices and assistants serenading a newly married couple with marrowbones and cleavers. Hogarth's print *The Industrious 'Prentice out of his Time and Married to his Master's Daughter* (1747), for example, shows two men so armed elbowing away a 'proper' musician to get to the newlyweds' door. The meat cleavers were beaten with the bones, and although this would appear to be akin to the cacophonous sounds made by bands of 'rough music' (*see* ALBERT ROAD, ADDISCOMBE, p. 358), it seems, in fact, that the butchers tried to make real music, of a sort, as Chambers' *Book of Days* (1864) explains:

> Sometimes, the group would consist of four, the cleaver of each ground to the production of a certain note; but a full band – one entitled to the highest grade of reward – would be not less than eight, producing a complete octave – and where there was a fair skill, this series of notes would have all the fine effect of a peal of bells . . . It was wonderful with what quickness and certainty, under the enticing presentiment of beer, the serenaders got wind

Butchers' apprentices and assistants serenading a newly married couple with marrowbones and cleavers, one of the regular sights in Clare Market in the eighteenth and early nineteenth centuries.

of a coming marriage, and with what tenacity of purpose they would go on with their performance until the expected crown or half-crown was forthcoming. The men of Clare Market were reputed to be the best performers, and their guerdon was always on the highest scale accordingly. A merry rough affair it was; troublesome somewhat to the police, and not always relished by the party for whose honour it was designed . . . yet the marrowbone-and-cleaver epithalamium seldom failed to diffuse a good humour throughout the neighbourhood, and one cannot but regret that it is rapidly passing among the things that were.

LITTLE DEAN'S YARD: WESTMINSTER SCHOOL

On Shrove Tuesday each year, the boys of Westminster School celebrate their pancake game, called The Greaze, which apparently mans a 'scrum' or 'crowd'. The school cook prepares a large pancake, stiffened with horsehair, and then tosses it over a metal bar that runs across the room high above the boys' heads. As the pancake lands, each boy strives to obtain a piece. Until the 1880s the whole upper school would take part, but now it is restricted to elected boys from each form, and many of them wear fancy dress.

After a minute, a whistle is blown and the boy who holds the largest piece (as determined by a pair of antique scales kept for the purpose) is presented with a gold guinea by the Dean of Westminster, who is also ex officio chairman of the school governors.

The tradition of eating pancakes on Shrove Tuesday goes back to medieval times, as this was the last day before the beginning of Lent, and

Royal Parks

A nineteenth-century engraving of fashionable Londoners parading in Hyde Park during the 'season'.

The royal parks – BATTERSEA PARK (p. 363), Brompton Cemetery, Bushy Park, HYDE PARK (p. 84), Green Park, Greenwich Park, Kensington Gardens, Regent's Park, Richmond Park, and ST JAMES'S PARK (p. 105) – are often called the 'lungs of London', but their website just as appositely calls them 'London's personal space'. Their long and varied histories are peppered with examples of their use not just as public arenas but also as places for private rendezvous. One of their prime purposes over the centuries has been for military reviews, manoeuvres, processions and parades, and they are still the locale for all kinds of ceremonial occasions, including the famous gun salutes. These salutes are fired in Hyde Park and at the Tower of London, although for state visits, the Opening of Parliament and the Queen's Birthday Parade, Green Park is used instead. Salutes are fired by the King's Troop Royal Horse Artillery, and the number of rounds fired depends on the place and occasion. The basic salute is twenty-one rounds, but in Hyde Park and Green Park an extra twenty rounds are fired because they are royal parks.

The parks have also long functioned as playgrounds for Londoners, rich and poor. Blood sports such as hare-coursing, and deer-, otter- and duck-hunting, were regular occurrences in the days when the parks were in a wilder state, and innumerable boxing matches, impromptu fairs, open-air concerts, and every other kind of entertainment have taken place there. They were also known during the Regency period as the primary locale for the weekly parading and socialising of the fashionable rich during the London 'season'. These social occasions were regulated by a complex set of rules which only the elite knew and understood, but there was clearly something about the 'open air' which encouraged the relaxation of normal social conventions, and what was permitted in the park did not always meet with approval in some quarters.

A play called *St James's Park: A Comedy*, for example, written in 1733, protested against the moral laxity of the times:

> One of the customs most shocking, according to our notions, still continued – viz, that the ladies allowed any well-dressed man to talk to them without the previous formality of introduction. These hours of park-walking are times of perfect carnival to the women. She that would not admit the visits of a man without his being introduced by some relation or intimate friend, makes no scruple here to commence acquaintance at first sight; readily answers to any question shall be asked of her, values herself on being brisk at repartee; and to have *put him to it* (as they call it), leaves a pleasure on her face for a whole day. In short, no freedoms that can be taken here are reckoned indecent, all passes for raillery and harmless gallantry.

All kinds of events now take place in the parks, including some less well-known annual customs. Since 1968, for example, horse-riders of all kinds have gathered at noon on a Sunday in September for their annual Horseman's Sunday service and parade, to celebrate and encourage horse-riding in central London. The vicar of St John and St Michael's, Hyde Park Crescent, arrives on horseback and leads his congregation back to the church for the service; each horse is given a commemorative rosette and they then hold a parade across the park. Another annual equestrian event, the Easter Monday Harness Horse Parade, which was formerly held in Hyde Park, now takes place in Battersea Park.

But for earlier generations the parks were dangerous places, with highwaymen, robbers, and murderers of all sorts lurking to attack the unwary traveller, and they were also a handy meeting place for those who wished to fight a duel. London's parks have therefore generated a wealth of legends of their own, including stories of mystery and murder and a host of ghost stories, but also many little traditions, such as the idea that no flowers will grow in Green Park because it was previously the burial ground for St James's leper hospital, and that Rotten Row in Hyde Park is a corruption of *Route du roi* (King's Road).

A Victorian depiction of 'The Greaze', a traditional Shrove Tuesday game that still takes place every year at Westminster School.

therefore the final chance to eat well for forty days. According to the school's website, the earliest known reference to the pancake custom dates from 1753, nearly 200 years before the modern pancake-race tradition, which was invented in 1948.

MAIDA VALE

In *Haunted Highways and Byways* (1914), Elliott O'Donnell tells the tale of one dark night in March 1912, when, armed only with an electric torch, he set out to investigate rumours of a pig-faced lady who haunted a garden in Maida Vale. This character does not sound very alarming on paper, but our intrepid ghost-hunter found it decidedly upsetting:

It was the most sublimely horrible thing I ever saw. It was human and yet not human; the top part of the head covered with a tangled mass of long hair was that of a woman; the lower, with two obliquely set eyes and a thin, leering mouth, was that of a pig. Apart from the hair, which was of a very vivid yellow and the eyes, which were of a very steely blue, there was a total absence of colour, the whole face was of a gleaming, leaden white. The expression was hellish. I could conceive nothing more diabolical.

A fortnight later, O'Donnell returned to the garden with a friend, and again saw the dreadful sight. Presumably, the nightly hauntings continue to this day; if he had only given the actual location of the house, we would be able to find out.

THE MALL: ADMIRALTY ARCH

According to an article in *The Lady* on 11 July 1986, Admiralty Arch has often been criticised for its vulgarity, and an interesting story explains why. It claims that Queen Victoria was so well known for her bad taste in artistic and architectural matters that when a competition was launched to design the building, everyone shuddered when she announced that she would be the judge. The committee gathering the designs quietly decided to submit only two for her perusal, the very best and the very worst, in the hope that she would see the difference. Needless to say, she chose the worst one. The fact is, however, that the Arch was designed by Sir Aston Webb and built in 1910, as part of the Queen Victoria Memorial scheme. Apparently poor Queen Victoria's taste was so bad it lasted nine years after her death.

One feature of the Arch is a small protuberance on the inside of the north arch which is, more or less, in the shape of a human nose. It is said by some to be Napoleon's nose, and also that one should rub it as one passes through – but you have to be on horseback to reach it.

MAYFAIR

It is one of London's little ironies that one of the capital's most select and expensive districts is named after something as disreputable as the May Fair. This fair was held on the east side of Hyde Park from 1 May, and lasted for about sixteen days each year. It was not an ancient fair, but granted by James II in 1689 for 'the buying and selling of all manner of goods and merchandises'. Notwithstanding this laudable attempt to foster local trade, the fair rapidly became known as a pleasure fair, pure and simple, and almost immediately came under fire for encouraging bad behaviour and crime.

The fair was apparently quite fashionable for a short time, as a piece from 1701 quoted in John Timbs's *Walks and Talks About London* (1865) indicates:

> I wish you had been at May Fair, where the rope-dancing would have recompensed your labour. All the nobility in town were there, and I am sure even you, at your years, must have had your youthful wishes to have beheld the beauty, shape, and activity of Lady Mary when she danced . . . There was the city of Amsterdam . . . every street, every individual house was carved in wood.

But Ned Ward, whose satirical view of life in the city, *The London Spy* (1703), is justly famous, was not impressed:

> Where the harsh sound of untunable trumpets, the catterwauling scrapes of thrashing fiddlers, the grumbling of beaten calves-skin, and the discordant notes of broken organs, set my teeth on edge, like the filing of a hand-saw, and made my hair stand as bold upright as the quills of an angry porcupine . . . [We] could not, amongst many thousands, find one man that appeared above the degree of a gentleman's valet. In all the multitudes that ever I beheld, I never in my life saw such a number of lazy rascals, and so hateful a throng of beggarly, sluttish strumpets, who were a scandal to the Creation, mere antidotes against lechery, and enemies to cleanliness.

In 1702, the constables of St Martin's attempted to close the fair, in line with the recently published document *Her Majesty's Proclamation for the Encouragement of Piety and Virtue, and for the Preventing and Punishing of Vice, Prophaneness, and Immorality*, but they were so vigorously opposed that one of their number was killed. The fair was closed down in 1708, but was revived a short time later, and lasted until 1764 at the insistence of local residents and developers.

As well as a raucous May Fair, the area was also famous for duck-hunting, as recorded by George Daniel in *Merrie England in the Olden Time* (1842):

25 June 1748

At May Fair ducking pond, on Monday next, the 27th inst., Mr Hooton's dog Nero (ten years old, with hardly a tooth in his head to hold a duck, but well known for his goodness to all that have seen him hunt) hunts six dogs for a guinea against the bitch called the Flying Spaniel, from the Ducking Pond on the other side of the water, who has beat all she has hunted against excepting Mr Hooton's Good-Blood. To begin at two o'clock. Mr Hooton begs his customers won't take it amiss to pay twopence admittance at the gate.

See also ISLINGTON, p. 232.

PALL MALL: ST JAMES'S PALACE

In his *Accredited Ghost Stories* of 1823, T. M. Jarvis recounts a tale concerning the Duchess of Mazarine, the former mistress of Charles II. She had an apartment in St James's Palace, as did one Madame de Beauclair. There was much discussion at the time about the truth, or otherwise, of the afterlife, and these two friends agreed that whoever died first would appear to the other, if at all possible. The Duchess died first, and when her apparition failed to keep the agreed appointment, Madame de Beauclair became inclined to doubt that anything survived after death. Some years later, however, another friend received an urgent message to come and see Madame de Beauclair, who agitatedly explained to her:

I have seen my dear Duchess of Mazarine. I perceived not how she entered; but turning my eyes to yonder corner of the room, I saw her stand in the same form and habit she was accustomed to appear in when living: fain would I have spoke, but had not the power of utterance: she took a little circuit round the chamber, seeming rather to swim than walk; then stopped by the side of that Indian chest, and looking on me with her usual sweetness, 'Beauclair,' said she, 'between the hours of twelve and one this night you will be with me.' The surprise I was in at first being a little abated, I began to ask some questions concerning that future world I was so soon to visit; but, on the opening of my lips for that purpose, she vanished from my sight, I know not how.

When Madame de Beauclair finished her story, it was just before midnight, and she seemed not in the least bit ill. Then suddenly she cried out, 'O! I am sick at heart!' and she died about half an hour later – at exactly the time the apparition had foretold.

The Duchess of Mazarine, born Hortense Mancini (1646–99) was an extremely well-known beauty of her day, immensely rich and involved in numerous scandals and adventures, including being an acknowledged mistress of Charles II. In modern times she would be constantly in the tabloids and certain glossy magazines. Even strait-laced John Evelyn mentions her in his diary, a year after she came to England:

6 Sep 1676
Supped at the Lord Chamberlain's, where also supped the famous beauty and errant lady, the Duchess Mazarin (all the world knows her story).

He also recorded her death on 11 June 1699. The Duchess is just the sort of celebrity to be adopted for a legend such as this, but the sparse details given in the story do not ring true. She did not retire gracefully, but continued her extravagant lifestyle to the end, and died in Chelsea in poverty, of drink (or some say by suicide).

Madame de Beauclair, however, has eluded any attempts to identify her as a real person, and may well be fictional.

St James's Palace was also the scene of more sinister courtly intrigue. Ernest Augustus, Duke of Cumberland (1771–1851), was George III's fifth son, and, in the general opinion of the day, a thoroughly bad lot. An outspoken high Tory, anti-Catholic and anti-radical, Cumberland made enemies very easily. Although his bad behaviour resulted mostly in rumours rather than in concrete scandals, he was a major embarrassment to his family. The low point in his reputation came in May 1810, when his valet, Joseph Sellis, was found with his throat cut. Cumberland insisted that Sellis had attacked him, then fled to his own room and committed suicide. While the inquest jury accepted this explanation, very many people in the country did not, and there were persistent rumours that Sellis knew too many of Cumberland's dark secrets, and had been silenced, or that the Duke had seduced his daughter. Cumberland was booed and pelted in the street. Nevertheless, he became King of Hanover in June 1837, and was surprisingly popular in the role. Joseph Sellis, on the other hand, lingered on as a ghost in the palace, and was reportedly seen sitting up in a blood-soaked bed with his throat cut from ear to ear. It is not clear, however, who has actually seen this terrifying spectre.

PARLIAMENT SQUARE

Oliver Cromwell (1599–1658) is considered by some to be perhaps the greatest Englishmen who ever lived, and by others to be the Devil incarnate. Every year, on the day of his death, 3 September, the Cromwell Association celebrates his life with a service in front of his statue outside the Houses of Parliament, and they lay a wreath at its foot. The Association was founded in 1935 and exists to commemorate Cromwell and to stimulate interest in his life and times, and it holds other events throughout the year. Members of the Society of King Charles the Martyr do not attend.

When it comes to historical characters, English folklore has a definite A-list of celebrities who pop up in various situations: in local legends; as ghosts; as quasi-historical explanations for things, and so on. Nell Gwynne, Dick Turpin, and Oliver Cromwell are the top three in this list, although Elizabeth I, Henry VIII, and Boudicca come close behind.

Even in his own day, there were numerous beliefs and legends about Cromwell, but those were unbelievably credulous times, when all sides believed implicitly in omens, portents, signs, apparitions, prophecies, and predictions, and always sought to use them as proof that their own side was favoured by God, and by fortune. As Christina Hole comments in her *English Folk-Heroes* (1946):

> Oliver Cromwell was supposed by Royalists to have made a compact with the Devil for a term of years and to have been carried away by the fiend on the night of his death, 3 September 1658. The fierce storm which then raged was believed to be of the Devil's raising. The Roundheads, for their part, whilst attributing their leader's success to God's will and his own merits,

asserted that Prince Rupert's great military skill was due to witchcraft. It was generally believed by those on the Puritan side that his favourite dog, Boy, who went everywhere with him and was killed at Marston Moor, was his familiar spirit and spied for him upon the opposing armies . . .

The idea that storms accompanied the deaths of great figures was particularly widespread in the seventeenth century. Samuel Pepys, for example, noting some overnight damage on 18 February 1662, comments:

> In the streets, which were everywhere full of brick bats and tiles flung down by the extraordinary wind the last night (such as hath not been in memory before, unless at the death of the late Protector) . . .

And on 19 October 1663:

> Waked with a very high wind, and said to my wife, 'I pray God I hear not of the death of any great person, this wind is so high', fearing that the Queen might be dead.

There was also a storm on the day that Cromwell's body was exhumed.

In a different vein, John Aubrey, in his *Miscellanies* (1696), used Cromwell's life as evidence of lucky and unlucky days:

> 3 September was as remarkable day to the English Attila, Oliver. In 1650 he obtained a memorable victory at Dunbar, another at Worcester 1651. And that day he died, 1658.

And elsewhere in the same book:

> A little before the death of Oliver a whale came into the River Thames and was taken at Greenwich – foot long. 'Tis said Oliver was troubled at it.

Then there is the long-running debate about what happened to his body, and his head, after the Restoration. The official version is that he was buried in Westminster Abbey, in Henry VII's Chapel, after lying in state and receiving a full state funeral. But in 1661 Charles II ordered his body, along with those of the other regicides Ireton and Bradshaw, to be exhumed. They were hung at Tyburn, decapitated, and their bodies thrown unceremoniously into a deep pit at the foot of the gallows, while their heads were displayed on stakes at Westminster, until they rotted away and fell off.

As with all such legends, individual notions feed off and build on each other, and, as will be seen, most of them rest on the uncertain premise that

Cromwell himself, or his colleagues, knew that their bodies would not be safe from Royalist wrath in later years, and so took certain precautions.

There is one germ of fact on which some theories have been based. It is fairly well documented that the embalming procedure necessary for a body to be exhibited as it lay in state went badly wrong in Cromwell's case, and the real body was therefore buried quickly, in private. An effigy was put on show and given the state burial sometime later. This was apparently not uncommon in the period.

But it has given rise to rumours that the 'secret' burial was designed to disguise the location of his grave, which was therefore not in Westminster Abbey, but somewhere else. The battlefield of Naseby, scene of one of Cromwell's most important victories, is a favourite candidate, but some hold that his body was placed in a lead coffin and sunk in the deepest part of the Thames. Proponents of these particular ideas often maintain that Cromwell himself dictated the subterfuge before he died. Other suggested locations are on his estate in Huntingdonshire, in St Nicholas's church in Chiswick, St Andrew's church in Northborough, Newburgh Priory, and RED LION SQUARE, HIGH HOLBORN (p. 241).

The next link in this chain of legend came with the exhumation. Some say that his tomb was found to be empty (because he had been buried elsewhere), and the people charged with finding him simply supplied another body to cover their failure. But perhaps the most delicious theory of all is that Cromwell had contrived to have Charles I's body placed in his tomb, and that when the public hangman came to string up 'Cromwell', he found that the corpse's head had been sewn back on. Needless to say, some think that when Cromwell's body was cut down it was spirited away by a secret Roundhead society and buried with honour in a secret location.

When Cromwell's head came down from its ignominious perch, either in a storm or by design, it started a journey of its own. Different dates are given for this occurrence, ranging between 1672 and 1703, but it is generally accepted that it passed into private hands as a curio, and was owned, and often exhibited, by various people over the next 250 years or so. A number of skulls have been claimed as his, but the main contender for the title of 'true Cromwell' is the one called the 'Wilkinson' head, after the owner who acquired it in 1815. This one is fairly well documented, and was finally immured in the chapel of Sidney Sussex, Cambridge, Cromwell's old university, in 1960, where it remains, although its exact location is kept secret.

Several of the Cromwell legends still refuse to lie down, and as they rely heavily on the notion of a conspiracy (on one side or the other), every attempt to scotch them becomes part of the story.

PORTMAN MARKET

Sale of a Wife: On Tuesday afternoon at 2 o'clock, a number of persons assembled in the neighbourhood of Portman Market to witness an exhibition of the above description. At the appointed time the husband, accompanied by his wife, entered the crowded arena, the latter having been led to the spot in the usual manner, with a halter round her neck. The business then commenced amid the hissings and booings of the populace, who showered stones and other missiles on the parties. The first bidding was a 4s, and the next 4s 6d, after which an interval elapsed, amidst the call of 'Going, going' from the auctioneer. At last a dustman stepped forward, and exclaimed, 'I wool give five bob' (5s). The woman was 'knocked down' for the sum, and the dustman carried her off, nothing loth, amidst the hisses of the crowd.

This incident, reported in *The Times* on 4 July 1833, is an example of a surprisingly widely held belief that a man could legally end a marriage by selling his wife to another.

See also WIFE-SELLING, p. 102.

PORTMAN SQUARE: MONTAGU HOUSE

In local folklore, there is a strong connection between traditional customs that take place each year, and the legends that grow up to explain their origin and purpose. In the eighteenth and nineteenth centuries, the sight of chimney sweeps dancing in the streets on May Day was very common, and the stories that were told of sweeps duly incorporated both this custom and fashionable romantic and philanthropic concerns about the use of 'climbing boys' (and girls) in the sweeps' daily work, into one complex of traditions.

The core of the most common legend told to explain the chimney sweeps' May Day exuberance was that once upon a time a noblewoman lost a child, who years later was found to be working as a climbing boy, and she decreed the celebrations to commemorate his safe return. As indicated elsewhere, a legend often works best when it becomes attached to a named 'celebrity', and in this case it was it was Mrs Elizabeth Montagu (1720–1800), author and society leader, who from 1781 lived in the very grand Montagu House built on the corner of Portman Square.

Mrs Montagu was involved in many philanthropic causes, but one of the most famous, because the most piquant, was her decision to entertain all the sweeps of London who cared to turn up at her house on May Day to al fresco entertainment and a meal, which always consisted of the archetypal English dinner of roast beef and plum pudding. Elizabeth was not alone in her concern for the welfare of sweeps, as the plight of 'climbing boys' had

Chimney sweeps celebrating May Day with a traditional garland. The story goes that their celebrations commemorated the time when one of their number was found to be a nobleman who had been stolen at birth – possibly from a house in Portman Square.

been in the air since social reformer James Hanway (1712–86) raised the subject in the early 1770s, although the practice of using children to clean chimneys was not finally abolished by Act of Parliament until 1875.

It is not known exactly when the Montagu gatherings first started, but they were certainly in place by 1793, as Hannah More wrote to her sister in that year: 'I have been invited to dine at Portman Square with the chimney-sweepers on May-day, a feast I should have liked much had I been well enough.'

Mrs Montagu's partiality for sweeps was therefore well known, and is the reason why an existing legend of the time became associated with her name. Even *The Times* was taken in and mentioned the story in 1799, prompting Mrs Montagu to write and categorically deny it. But you cannot keep a good

Wife-Selling

A woodcut of the sale of a wife, taken from a nineteenth-century broadside.

At an early hour a young couple came into the market. The lady was dressed neat and clean, and so attractive were her rosy cheeks and sparkling eyes, that all the folks in the market soon collected about her (she being to be sold). Well, good folks, says the lady's spouse, here's a rare bargain to dispose off! Here's my pretty sweet wife, who will try all she can, to please any man, who's willing to take her for life.

So begins the text of a broadside entitled *Particular and Merry Account of a Most Entertaining and Curious SALE OF A WIFE*, printed by James Catnach in London, about 1830. In lively prose, typical of the broadside press, the piece details the enthusiastic bidding from, among others, the butcher, the cobbler, the miller, and the tallow-chandler, until:

> A gallant publican, hearing the fun, bounced forward with such haste that he upset the barber and tailor in the mud, and almost trod the fiddler's toes off. He instantly paid down fifteen pounds, and took them all to an inn, where they had a capital dinner, and after emptying a dozen of wine, the happy couple mounted a gig, and set off in full glee.

This incident is fiction, of course, as is the famous scene in Thomas Hardy's *Mayor of Casterbridge* (1886), when Michael Henchard sells his wife in a drunken fit at the fair. Nevertheless, up and down the country, since at least the mid sixteenth century, hundreds of real wife-sales have been reported, and there must have been many hundreds more which went unrecorded. Not every sale realised fifteen pounds, however, as can be seen in this article that appeared in the *Hereford Journal* on 17 March 1894:

SELLING A WIFE FOR FOURPENCE

One of the few remaining common lodging-houses in Middle-Row, Croydon was on Sunday night the scene of a curious transaction, a labouring-man selling his wife for a pot of fourpenny-ale. The purchaser adopted the precaution of taking a receipt for his money, and when the newly-mated couple adjourned to a neighbouring public house, the document was the object of much curiosity. It is said the husband and wife parted on very friendly terms.

From the extensive number of cases, it is clear that many of those involved genuinely believed that such transactions were a legal form of divorce, as long as certain rules were adhered to. The local market was the commonest place for the auction, and in some cases the wife was led in wearing a halter to emphasise the connection with a livestock sale. The husband would be careful to pay the toll he would normally pay for selling an animal, and be equally careful to get a receipt. The wife might be dressed only in her shift, which symbolised the fact that the purchaser took her as she stood, and could make no further claim on the husband. If all this sounds dreadful in our post-feminist age, it must be noted that in at least some of the cases we know that the wife had agreed to the proceedings and had, in fact, already arranged who was going to bid for her.

See FLEET LANE, p. 21; PORTMAN MARKET, p. 100.

story down, and it continued to appear, with variations, throughout the nineteenth century, in publications as well as the oral tradition. It was still being told well into the twentieth century:

> About the middle of the eighteenth century, a little boy between three and four years of age was lost in London (he was of noble birth) by his nurse. It was supposed he was kidnapped for his fine clothes. Search was made, but no tidings could be obtained of his whereabouts. Some years afterwards a little boy of between eight and nine years of age was put to sweep a chimney upon the first of May at a gentleman's house in London. After he came down the chimney he saw a picture of his mother hanging in the room against the wall. The people of the house came in and found him crying. He told them it was the picture of his mother whom he had lost. They at once recognised that he was their lost child. That is why the sweeps used formerly in most towns of England to make a holiday on the first of May, dressing up in coloured paper and linen, and with dancing and gala processions through the streets.

This was how it appeared in the *Evesham Notes and Queries* volume for 1911, but there were many other versions. According to Charles Dickens's *Sketches by Boz* (1836), the scene was slightly different:

> Being hot and tired when he came out of the chimney, he got into the bed he had so often slept in as an infant, and was discovered and recognised therein by his mother, who, once every year of life, thereafter, requested the pleasure of the company of every London sweep, at half past one o'clock, to roast beef, plum pudding, porter, and sixpence.

The famous social investigator and campaigner Henry Mayhew gave more than one version of the lost-boy story in his *London Labour and the London Poor* (1861), and he also quoted evidence given to the Parliamentary Committee that showed it was taken as established fact that children were kidnapped and sold to sweeps, or that poor parents sold them to become climbing boys. It is difficult to be sure how prevalent this practice really was, but the descriptions themselves have all the hallmarks of legends. Mayhew also recorded yet another tradition that is clearly related to this nexus of belief and tale:

> I am told that a considerable sum of money was left for the purpose of supplying every climbing-boy who called on the first of May at a certain place, a shilling and some refreshment, but I have not been able to ascertain

by whom it was left, or where it was distributed; none of the sweepers with whom I conversed knew anything about it. I also heard, that since the passing of the Act, the money has been invested in some securities or other, and is not accumulating, but to what purpose it is intended to be applied I have no means of learning.

See also MAY DAY IN LONDON, p. 318.

ST GILES HIGH STREET: ST GILES-IN-THE-FIELDS CHURCH

One of the men who helped Charles II escape after his army was routed at Worcester in 1651 was Richard Penderel, a yeoman farmer. He took charge of the hapless monarch, cut his hair with a pair of shears, gave him some of his own clothes to wear, and hid him in a local wood. Over the next days he accompanied Charles until his final escape, and was rewarded handsomely at the Restoration. He died in London on 8 February 1671, and was buried at St Giles-in-the-Fields, and it was previously the custom for local people to decorate his tomb with oak branches, Charles II's particular symbol, every year on 29 May.

ST JAMES'S PARK

Hard on the heels of the Hammersmith Ghost (p. 145), in January 1804, *The Times* ran a report that a headless ghost had been seen by members of the Coldstream Guards on duty in St James's Park, and that two soldiers were already gravely ill in hospital after the fright of seeing the dreadful sight. Another reported that someone, or some thing, had been busy in an uninhabited house close by, opening and shutting windows, and repeatedly calling out for a light.

It seems that the paper was challenged to back up its story, because three days later a second report appeared, which included further details along with the signed statements of George Jones and Richard Donkin. The former stated:

St James's Park, the setting for one ghost story that turned out to have a natural explanation, and one that did not.

I do solemnly declare, that, whilst on guard at the Recruit House, on or about the 3rd instant, about half past one o'clock in the morning, I perceived the figure of a woman, without a head, rise from the earth, at the distance of about three feet before me . . . I distinctly observed that the figure was dressed in a red striped gown with red spots between each stripe, and that part of the dress and figure appeared to me to be enveloped in a cloud.

The article also supplied a reason for the spectre's strange condition:

It was not until the other day, that the old women about the Park were able to account for the ghost's appearance, and they now recollect, that, about sixteen years ago a serjeant murdered his wife in the Park, by cutting off her head and they therefore attributed the phantom's appearance to that circumstance.

Nevertheless, six days later a small piece appeared offering a more prosaic explanation:

The ghost in St James's Park, we understand, originated in an application of the Phantasmagoria, by two unlucky Westminster scholars, who having got possession of an empty house on the side of Bird-Cage Walk, were enabled to produce the appearance which so greatly alarmed the sentinels on duty in the immediate vicinity of the spot.

The Phantasmagoria was a startling new apparatus, exhibited in London by Mr Philipstal in 1802, that projected images by way of a magic lantern to produce 'spectres, skeletons, and terrific figures . . . [which] suddenly advanced upon the spectators, becoming larger as the approached them, and finally vanished by appearing to sink into the ground' (*OED*).

But not all the ghosts in the neighbourhood are explained away so easily. A classic haunted-house story appears in John Ingram's *Haunted Homes and Family Traditions of Great Britain* (1912):

> It is not many years since a house in St James Street, the number of which it is as well to omit, acquired considerable notoriety on account of the unpleasant noises which took place in it. It had stood empty for a long time, in consequence of the annoyances to which various tenants who had tried it had been subjected. There was one apartment in particular which nobody was able to occupy without being disturbed.

A young man who had been abroad and therefore knew nothing of the house's reputation was given the room:

> . . . in the morning, however, he complained sadly of the terrible time he had had in the night, with people looking in at him between the curtains of his bed and he avowed his determination to terminate his visit at once, as he could not possibly sleep there any more.

Even more mysterious, when the building was being renovated, the master builder was alone in the house when he repeatedly heard footsteps behind him as he moved about. Entering the drawing room:

> . . . he took hold of a chair, and drawing it resolutely along the floor, he slammed it down upon the hearth with some force, and seated himself in it; when, to his amazement, the action, in all its particulars of sound, was immediately repeated by his unseen companion, who seemed to seat himself beside him on a chair as invisible as himself. Horror-stricken, the worthy builder started up and rushed off out the house.

See also ROYAL PARKS, p. 90.

St James's Square: Naval and Military Club

In March 1994, the press reported a ghost that had been sighted in one of the rooms of the Naval and Military Club in Piccadilly. A porter saw the apparition early one morning, and described his appearance, which included the detail that he wore a full-length trench coat. From this description, the ghost was identified as Major Braddell, a member of the club, who had miraculously survived an air raid on the building in 1941, but was killed a week later in another raid. Relatively sensible accounts of the manifestation appeared in *The Times* on 15 and 19 March and the *Evening Standard* on 11 March 1994, but on 16 March the *Sun* could not resist adding a characteristic little detail: 'Officials at a posh club say a ghost there will not be exorcised – because he is still a member.'

St John's Wood

The sight of a Jack-in-the-Green and his attendants dancing in the streets of London on May Day was a regular occurrence in the late eighteenth and nineteenth centuries. Many adults enjoyed the spectacle, but several descriptions by people remembering their childhood experiences record how frightening this greenery-clad giant could be to young people. A particularly evocative account is given in the first part of E. H. Shepard's delightful autobiography, *Drawn from Memory* (1957). Shepard was born in 1879 in St John's Wood, and is best known for his definitive Winnie the Pooh illustrations.

> It was on the first of May that I had one of the frights of my life. I was playing alone in the Terrace garden when I heard the jingling of bells and went to the end of the garden to investigate. A motley group of men rigged up for 'Jack-in-the-Green' was turning into the Terrace. One fellow completely covered with greenery, so that only his legs were showing, was jogging up and down. Another had his face smeared with paint to represent a clown, and a third, in striped cloth coat and trousers, with a huge collar and a blackened face, was beating a tambourine. But the one that really frightened me was a man got up as a woman, in a coloured, ill-fitting dress, a wig made of tow, and showing brawny arms above dirty white gloves. Brandishing a tattered

parasol, he, or she, held out to catch coins thrown by passers-by or from the houses. Fascinated, I watched their progress from behind the bushes. Then I made a bolt for home. But I had left it too late. As I emerged from the gate the man-woman spotted me and came prancing up, calling out, 'What have you got for Jack-in-th'-Green, little gentleman?' Petrified with fear, I ran back into the garden, and made for the sloping tree we always climbed. I was up it in a jiffy, but the dreadful creature, grinning like a satyr, followed me into the garden and started to dance around while the others clattered and banged and shouted encouragement from the gateway. I was fast losing my reason when a welcome face appeared at the area steps – it was Lizzie. She took in the situation at a glance and up she came. Her indignation was more for the state of my clothes than anything else, but the enemy gave way before her and, blowing kisses and still dancing, the troupe passed on. I must have been almost hysterical when I was taken in and washed, and I never could bear the sight of a man dressed as a woman after that.

See also HIGH STREET, LEWISHAM, p. 334.

SMITH SQUARE

A long ghost story set in Smith Square, Westminster, can be found in Townshend and Ffoulkes's *True Ghost Stories* (1936). It is from the pen of Miss Estelle Stead, daughter of W. T. Stead, famous journalist and magazine proprietor, who perished on the *Titanic*. It started when Estelle was allotted an attic room in her parents' house in Smith Square. One night:

I was awakened, after about a couple of hours' sleep, by the sound of footsteps coming quickly upstairs and along the passage leading to my room. The door was thrown wide open, and a little man wearing a long black cloak and a large black hat walked in! As he entered, the character of the whole room changed, much in the way that a scene changes in a theatre. My bedroom was no longer the comfortable modern dedication to sleep . . . Except for two wooden chairs and a large table littered with papers, it was now entirely destitute of furniture and furnishings. The little man flung his hat on the table, and seating himself on one of the chairs he began to write, ignoring me completely. I sat up in bed, entirely fearless, wondering what on earth would happen next . . .

But then she fell asleep, and in the morning the only thing to show for her night vision was that the door was open. Nevertheless, a few nights later it all happened again, and she decided to consult her father. He suggested they try to contact the spirit with a Spirit Indicator, a device popular at the time, and they quickly discovered that the man was Gordon Knight, an extremely minor poet who specialised in 'rollicking songs of the sea'. Gordon and Miss Stead happily shared the room from then on, and he even started opening the door quietly rather than crashing it open, so as not to disturb her, and taught her father how to keep in contact with Estelle after his death.

SOHO

London's Chinatown, around Leicester Square, is a surprisingly recent addition to the city, having only developed in the area in the late 1960s. The first Chinatowns in Britain were close to major ports such as East London and Liverpool, where Chinese nationals employed on merchant ships started to set up homes, and as settled communities formed, people found work, particularly in the laundry trade and food provision. More families arrived after the Second World War, and Chinese people started to diversify their business interests into other areas. At the 2001 census there were nearly a quarter of a million Chinese-born residents in the country.

The now-famous Chinese New Year celebrations started in 1973, and were a deliberate move to establish the community's presence in the eyes of the wider community. As reported in the *Daily Telegraph* on 5 February 1973:

LION TRIES MAGIC ON PLANNERS

A processional lion pranced through the streets of Soho, London, yesterday, as part of the Chinese New Year celebrations. Mr Kuk Sang, manager of a Lisle Street restaurant, and one of the organisers, said this was the first New Year lion-dance in the streets of the area. He explained, 'We decided to do it this year because there are now a lot of Chinese people in this country. We want to show people that there is now a China Town here. We have heard that Westminster council mean to pull down Gerrard Street to rebuild. Gerrard Street is the main China Town street. We are having a lion-dance to ward off the bad luck.'

Whether or not the lion's magic works on town planners, it certainly does on tourists, and the celebrations rapidly have become an integral part of London's festive calendar. Since 1978, the event has been organised by the London Chinatown Chinese Association, and in recent years the Greater London Authority has taken an active interest and supported its growth and rapid development. Chinese New Year has spilled out of Chinatown into neighbouring areas and become more spectacular. Some people fear that these developments threaten the intimate connection between the community and the celebrations, but the audience grows each year.

The Chinese year is primarily lunar and does not synchronise well with the solar calendar of the West, and so their New Year usually falls some time between 21 January and 21 February.

THE STRAND: ADELPHI THEATRE

One of the best-known theatre ghost stories is that of the actor William Terriss (real name William Charles James Lewin, 1847–97), who has the distinction of haunting two places – the Adelphi Theatre, in the Strand, and Covent Garden Underground Station. At the height of his career Terriss was a popular actor, particularly well known for his performances in nautical melodramas. On the night of 16 December 1897, when he was starring in William Gillette's play *Secret Service*, he arrived at the stage door in Maiden Lane and was stabbed to death by unemployed actor Richard Archer Prince (a man known to Adelphi staff as 'Mad Archer'), apparently in a fit of jealousy.

Terriss died in the arms of his leading lady (and mistress) Jessie Millward, and according to some ghost books, his last words were 'I will be back', but more reliable sources say that he cried, 'Sis! Sis!', his nickname for Jessie. This in itself was remarkable, because for some time Jessie had been having a recurrent dream in which William was trapped in a locked room crying for help with those very words. But there is more. According to a report in *The Times* on 17 December, Terriss's understudy, Frederick Lane, also had warning of the crime:

> I dreamt about this very thing last night, and when I came to the theatre
> this morning for the rehearsal I told all the 'boys' about it. I dreamt I saw

Mr Terriss lying in the landing, surrounded by a crowd, and that he was raving. I seemed to see it all, and then it all seemed to fade away. It was a horrible dream, and I could not tell what it meant. I tried to forget it during the day, but tonight again, when I came to the theatre, I was going down Bedford Street when something seemed to say, 'Do not go there.'

And there is still more. When Jessie Millward's autobiography, *Myself and Others*, was published in 1923, she revealed that Terriss had been warned that his life would be short by a palmist just before his murder. Apparently, the editor of the *Era*, the trade magazine for the acting profession, asked various stars to have their palms read. Jessie had hers done, and tried to persuade Terriss to do the same:

When I broached the subject he roared with laughter, and flatly refused to waste his time. But I had promised to do my best, and at last he grudgingly consented and paid his visit. On his return he was as sceptical as ever as to the value of palmistry. 'I've got quite a nice character, Jessie,' he laughed; 'so nice, in fact, that it seems a pity that I'm booked for a sudden death. I'm very clever, I've got a kind heart, and I'm coming to a violent end. Pleasant, cheery person, your palmist!'

After all this, it is not surprising that Terriss refuses to rest in peace. He seems to have been quiet until about 1928, when a stranger walking in Maiden Lane encountered a figure, dressed in a grey turn-of-the-century suit, who disappeared before his eyes. He later recognised the ghost when shown a photograph of Terriss. In the same year, an actress reported that the chaise longue on which she was resting in her dressing room began to lurch and shake, and she felt blows and a tight grip on her arms. A greenish light appeared above her dressing-table mirror, and two sharp taps sounded, from the same direction. She found out later that the dressing room had been the favourite of Jessie Millward, and that Terriss was in the habit of giving her door two sharp raps with his cane as he passed by. Other workers have since reported encounters with Terriss around the theatre, despite the fact that the current building only dates from 1930.

Jack Hallam's *Ghosts of London* (1975) also details several sightings of a ghostly man in grey by the staff at Covent Garden Underground Station in the mid 1950s and 1960s, but there was nothing to connect the spirit with Terriss until a spiritualist medium identified it as him.

The Strand: Norfolk Street
(between Surrey Street and Arundel Street)

The novelist Winifred Graham recorded her personal experiences of ghosts in Townshend and Ffoulkes's *True Ghost Stories* (1936). One supernatural event was witnessed by Winifred and her mother in Norfolk Street:

> [We] had asked the hall porter to whistle for a four-wheeler. It was before taxis were to be seen regularly in the streets, and we stood in the porch of the building until the cab came up. Then I noticed the dark figure of a man, apparently wearing a loose black cape, who was leaning out of the window of the four-wheeler, gesticulating violently. I was certainly impressed by the strange blackness of his clothing, and it crossed my mind that he was either making signs to the driver to stop, or else wishing to indicate that he was going in the wrong direction – nothing uncanny entered my mind. Then, to my amazement, the cab drew up *empty*, and as the porter advanced to open the door, I said quickly to my mother: 'I saw the figure of a man in the cab, waving his arms. He must have been signalling to us not to get in, I'm sure if we do so, we shall probably be killed.'
>
> Again, I had a surprise. My mother, who believes in ghosts, and is psychic, being the seventh child of a seventh child, entirely discarded my warning ... I had no choice but to follow, and we had not been two seconds in that four-wheeler before the horse bolted, swerved violently across the road, and came to a standstill on the pavement, landing the cab against the railings of the opposite building. Naturally we got out as quickly as possible, and I can only surmise that the man in the black cape deliberately frightened the horse and made it shy in order to clear us out. I cannot help believing if we had remained in the cab something very terrible would have happened ...

See also HAMPTON COURT ROAD: ST ALBANS, p. 389.

The Strand: St Clement Danes church

Stuck in the middle of the present-day Strand, with traffic flowing on both sides, is St Clement Danes parish church. There has been a church on the site since the tenth century, but it has been rebuilt several times over the years; most notably by Wren in 1682, and again after severe damage by enemy action in 1941. St Clement's is the centre of a number of separate threads of tradition, which often get tangled, but the three specific questions that are often asked of the church are: why is it called St Clement *Danes*, what is the connection with oranges and lemons, and what is the original meaning of the rhyme of that name?

On the question of Danes, there is no simple answer. The London historian John Stow stated in 1598 that it was:

> ... because Harold, a Danish King and other Danes were buried there. This Harold, whom King Canutus had by a concubine, reigned three years and was buried at Westminster; but afterwards Hardicanutus, the lawful son of Canutus, in revenge of a displeasure done to his mother, by expelling her out of the realm, and the murder of his brother Alured, commanded the body of Harold to be digged out of the earth, and to be thrown into the Thames, where it was by a fisherman taken up and buried in this churchyard.

King Harold I (nicknamed 'Harold Harefoot') died in 1040. The story of the desecration of his body has all the hallmarks of a legend, and is only given in one historical source, Florence of Worcester's *Chronicon ex Chronicis*. But as Florence died in 1118, his account was written not long after the events described, and his chronicle is usually trusted by historians.

Stow then gives another suggestion, quoting William of Malmesbury; that in the reign of King Ethelred, a party of Danes who had destroyed Chertsey Abbey were later 'by the just judgment of God all slain at London in a place which is called the church of the Danes'.

Either of these explanations could be taken to imply that the area was already called 'Dane' and so are not necessarily useful in pinning down the origin. Yet another explanation, also made in the sixteenth century, was that when King Alfred expelled the Danes from the City of London, he permitted those with English wives to settle just outside the City walls, and they founded a Danish community on that spot. As Alfred took London from the Danes in 886, this, if true, would long pre-date the other suggestions. So the real problem is that it is not clear when the parish first became known as St Clement Dane, and until we know that, all is speculation.

Turning to the rhyme 'Oranges and Lemons', we are in similarly murky waters, with not even the equivalent of a medieval chronicler to guide us. What is known is that 'Oranges and Lemons' was the name of a dance tune in the 1660s, but the earliest version of the words that has so far come to light is to be found in *Tom Thumb's Pretty Song Book* of about 1744. These early words are quite different from the standardised version most people sing nowadays:

> Two sticks and an apple, Ring ye bells at Whitechapel,
> Old father bald pate, Ring ye bells Aldgate,
> Maids in white aprons, Ring ye bells at St Catherines,
> Oranges and lemons, Ring ye bells at St Clemens,
> When will ye pay me, Ring ye bells at ye Old Bailey,
> When I am rich, Ring ye bells at Fleetditch,
> When will that be, Ring ye bells at Stepney,
> When I am old, Ring ye bells at Pauls.

It was not at all unusual for people to make up rhymes that incorporated local churches and their bells, and similar rhymes have been reported from other towns; nor is there the slightest evidence that this is any more than a children's rhyme made up for fun and entertainment. But for some time there has been a widespread notion that all nursery rhymes have a hidden secret history, and a vigorous cottage industry is devoted to revealing their true meaning, whether they have one or not. The usual method here is simply to extrapolate from words in the rhyme.

The first assumption is therefore that the coupling of the bells with the words that precede them has some intrinsic meaning. But the most likely explanation is simply the need to make things rhyme – what else can you rhyme with 'Clements'? Of all the suggested meanings, the one seeming to lead the pack nowadays is that the rhyme details the churches which a condemned criminal had to pass on his or her way to the gallows. There is no clue to this in the rhyme itself, but it is suggested by the fact that some versions of the children's game that use the rhyme end with the children filing through an arch to the words: 'Here comes a candle to light you to bed/Here comes a chopper to chop off your head/Chop, chop, chop.' But as these words do not appear in the earlier versions of the rhyme, this theory has no basis. In the measured words of Iona and Peter Opie in their 1985 book *The Singing Game*:

> Since the bells of St Clements, and the oranges and lemons, feature in only two of the four known texts of the 18th century, and then not prominently, and since the head-chopping figures not at all, stories about the ancient significance of the game have a counterfeit look to them.

Other explanations include the idea that the rhyme is a commentary on the fate of the wives of Henry VIII, although it is not clear how, and the silliest of all, that it is all concerned with sex, and describes a wedding night. Then there are more prosaic suggestions, which seek a historical link between the church and fruit, such as the 'fact' that the porters of Clare Market landed fruit at the wharves in the parish and paid a toll of oranges and lemons to the church so they could cut through the churchyard.

This brings us to the connection with the church. Unfortunately, the rhyme does not specify which St Clement's said, 'Oranges and lemons'. Spare a thought for poor St Clement's (on Clement's Lane and King William Street) in Eastcheap, which has just as much claim to be the one in the rhyme as St Clement Danes, but was rudely elbowed aside in the 1920s when the latter decided to annexe the rhyme to themselves. They installed a carillon to play the tune every day, and inaugurated a special 'orange and lemon service', which still takes place on a weekday in late March each year, attended by the children of nearby St Clement Danes Primary School. At the end of the service, the congregation is given oranges and lemons.

SUSSEX GARDENS: ST JAMES'S CHURCH

Sunday 18 December
This day, according to annual custom, bread and cheese were thrown from Paddington steeple to the populace, agreeable to the will of two women, who were relieved there with bread and cheese when they were almost starved; and providence afterwards favouring them, they left an estate in that parish to continue the custom for ever on that day.

This brief report in the December 1737 edition of *London Magazine* describes a customary way of distributing food to the needy at Paddington.

It contains several traditional elements found in charity doles elsewhere in the country. Before the early nineteenth century, it was common practice for people to make provision in their wills to provide relief for the local poor. Sometimes the bequest comprised cash to be invested, but a safer way of ensuring perpetual funding was to designate particular pieces of land that could be rented out to generate the necessary finances. To ensure public accountability and continuity, a legal charity was created, usually administered by trustees such as the local clergyman, a magistrate, or dignitaries.

Charities existed to supply many things – blankets, coal, boots, and so on – but a particularly popular practice was to stipulate the distribution of bread and cheese on a particular day of the year, and the land set aside became traditionally known as the Bread and Cheese Lands. At Paddington, there were three parcels of agreed Bread and Cheese Land: Bayswater Field; a piece of ground on the south-west side of the Harrow Road at Westbourne Green; and another piece near Black Lion Lane. In 1838 the dole was abolished, and the money used for other charitable purposes. Over the next decades the land was gradually sold off or leased for building.

It is quite common for the details of older charities to have been lost over time, and at Paddington, even by the eighteenth century, neither the name of the original benefactor nor the original date was known. The story of two sisters who were kindly relieved with bread and cheese when passing through the parish was thus created to fill the void. The motif of 'two sisters' is also found in other doles, such as the most famous one at Biddenden in Kent, which is still distributed every year on Easter Monday.

Another traditional element was the throwing and scrambling. This was the favoured method of distribution in many doles up and down the country, and was probably regarded as the simplest way of ensuring no favouritism. At St Briavels, in Gloucestershire, they still scramble for their bread and cheese every Whitsun.

Paddington has had a number of parish churches. The first three were on Paddington Green – St Nicholas (*c.* 1222–1688), St James (1688–1787), and St Mary (1788–1845) – and the current one, St James, on Sussex Gardens, was built in 1845.

See also CHURCH ROAD, TWICKENHAM: ST MARY THE VIRGIN CHURCH, p. 369.

Vauxhall Bridge Road, Westminster

The notion of PLAGUE PITS (p. 120) is a real growth area in modern London folklore, with new and completely spurious pits appearing all over Greater London on an almost daily basis. But in the City of London and Westminster, a few places were indeed used as mass graves during the height of the plague, and occasionally one of these pits is disturbed, as reported in the *Annual Register* on 11 May 1827:

> Within these few weeks past a number of labourers have been employed in digging through the Vauxhall Bridge Road in order to form the great new common sewer from Westminster to the Thames. In the progress of this undertaking, it has been necessary to excavate to a very considerable depth; and as the excavators advanced from the fields called the Pest House Fields towards the pond, the soil in general became more sandy and soft, and in many places were found fragments of timber, old buckles and shoes, and the remains of wearing apparel, indicating that this place, during the Plague of 1664, had been the general cemetery for many hundreds of inhabitants of London. As the work proceeded, they met with human bones of every size and kind. The 'Pest House Fields' had in their centre a large building called the 'Pest House' to which all who could reach it before the malady had overpowered them, fled for succour. As fast as they died they were interred in the dykes dug for the purpose in the vicinity of the house, which has since been denominated the 'Five Chimnies'. Of this house, or mass of buildings, there are at present considerable remains, and the workmen, in cutting through one of the dykes, dug up a large box resembling a coffin, which contained the skeleton of five persons in a complete state. The teeth of three of them were perfect, and a solitary tuft of hair upon the head of one still remained. Upon the exposure of the bodies to the air, the bones crumbled into dust; and the skulls and some bones of three were purchased from the labourers by a surgeon of Vauxhall Bridge Road.

It is worth noting that even this grave was not the ad hoc plague pit of the local legend-maker, but was in the grounds of the local pest house, the official last resort for the very seriously ill.

VERE STREET

A court case was reported in *The Times* on 16 and 22 February and 2 March in 1854, in which a 'quack doctress', Jane Browning of Vere Street, was charged with assaulting Harriet Gunton, a coachman's wife of Lincoln's Inn Fields. She had been pretending to cure her of the 'worms' from which she was reputed to be suffering. Browning said she usually charged £5 for such a cure, but because Mrs Gunton was a poor woman, she would only charge £2. She sold her some medicine, and a few days later Harriet visited Browning's house for the 'operation', which took some hours, and, she claimed, gave her worse pain than childbirth. Fortunately, the newspaper does not go into full details of the procedure, but Browning kept declaring that she was trying to get hold of the worms, and they kept biting her fingers. Eventually, as Mrs Gunton testified:

> . . . she put her hand under the [bed]clothes. I felt something touch me like a cloth, and she drew away her hand, throwing something into the pan, which sounded with a heavy splash. She said she had been trying at it all night, and had got it away at last while I was asleep. She said it was half snake and half eel. I looked into the pan and saw the same thing there that is now in the jar produced in court. It was then alive, and moved. The prisoner said, 'It has just come from your body, and will soon die.' She said she would put it in a bottle for me with some stuff to preserve it, and afterwards she brought the bottle produced to me, charging 2s 8d for the bottle and stuff. She said that she had shown it to a doctor, who told her she was a very clever woman, and that it had been in my body at least 20 years. I was confined to my bed for a week owing to the pain I suffered, and I still feel that I am hurt inwardly.

When this bottle was first produced in court it 'occasioned roars of laughter, as the specimen preserved was evidently a common eel, of considerable dimensions'.

The jury found Browning guilty of 'unlawfully assaulting and beating and inflicting grievous bodily harm on Harriet Gunton', and:

> Mr Witham [the judge] remarked that it was perfectly marvellous to see the way in which people of this class were imposed upon, and the case was one requiring very severe punishment. He then sentenced the prisoner to one year's imprisonment with hard labour.

Plague Pits

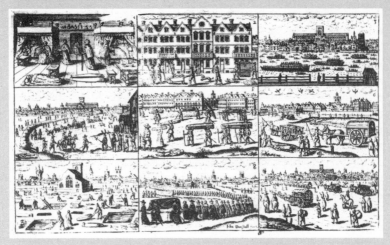

A seventeenth-century engraving showing the devastation caused by the Great Plague. Note the large graves being dug in the bottom left-hand corner.

The Great Plague of 1665–6 is one of the major landmarks in London history and engendered considerable folklore in its time, but although these traditions do not seem to have lasted, modern legend-makers remain fascinated by the subject and appear intent on introducing it into as many areas of modern life as possible. The first example of this tendency is the widespread idea that the children's rhyme 'Ring a Ring a Roses' is a relic of the plague, an idea that first emerged in the mid twentieth century when it became fashionable to invent ancient origins for traditional rhymes and games. It is almost certain that it was the use of the word *posies* in the rhyme that kick-started the theory, because people in plague times were supposed to have carried posies of flowers that they would hold to their noses to escape contagion and the smell of dead bodies, and from that starting point the whole erroneous explanation was built. There is no shred of evidence to link the rhyme, known only from late Victorian times, to the plague, but historically groundless as it may be, the theory is now so deeply entrenched in the British collective psyche that it has achieved the honorary status of being itself folklore.

However, the main sphere in which the plague still contributes strongly to modern lore is in the notion of plague pits. Any seemingly unused piece of land is likely to attract the story that it has been shunned by successive generations because it was a plague pit. In rural areas, small odd-shaped pieces of land at road junctions often acquire this reputation, although they may also suffer from the equally sinister idea that suicides were buried there. In urban areas, plague pits also feature increasingly as one of the standard explanations for ghostly manifestation in houses. 'My neighbour says it's because the house was built on a plague pit' is a standard explanation. Local Studies librarians in London are accustomed to dealing with people who have been told – and who believe – these stories, which seem to arise by a process akin to spontaneous combustion.

In one instance, in Croydon in the late 1990s, a young woman was genuinely worried about the 1950s house she was living in, as she had been told the plague-pit story by an older acquaintance. He had added the corroborative detail, 'that's why there are so many black birds around here'. This little incident demonstrates the inherent weakness of unromantic rational argument in such a situation. After being shown that her overspill estate was built on farmland and that there were no cemeteries for miles, the woman was still unconvinced, and she clearly chose to believe her friend rather than the librarian. 'Why would he lie to me?' was her parting comment.

Indeed, plague pit stories are multiplying rapidly, as can be seen from this article that appeared in the *Croydon Guardian* on 23 May 2007:

> Norbury residents are fighting plans to put storage containers on land used to bury victims of the seventeenth-century Great Plague of London ... Local opposition was so fierce the council is re-thinking the plan and considering alternative locations. Geoff Langham, of Semley Road, said: 'We all know this is a plague burial ground. We think of it like a cemetery.'

In fact, Norbury in the seventeenth century had only a handful of inhabitants, and no one is recorded as having died of the plague.

See also THE GREAT PLAGUE, p. 24; VAUXHALL BRIDGE ROAD, WESTMINSTER, p. 118.

This case has to be understood in the context of an extremely widespread belief that animals – particularly reptiles and insects – can invade and live inside the human body.

See also KENT STREET, SOUTHWARK, p. 335; KENTISH TOWN; p. 233; NEW MALDEN, p. 404; SILVERTOWN, p. 300.

VICTORIA EMBANKMENT: CLEOPATRA'S NEEDLE

It is a commonplace of British folklore that anything Egyptian must have a curse on it, but Cleopatra's Needle is a real disappointment in this respect. Admittedly, the voyage across from Egypt in 1877–8 had major problems, and six seamen died in a storm that nearly sank the Needle for good, but it has been quiet ever since. The Needle is a granite obelisk, over 60 feet tall and weighing about 186 tons. It dates from around 1475 BC and was first inscribed to Pharaoh Tuthmosis III; other inscriptions were added later. It was given to the British government in 1819, but no one was quite sure how to ship it over, until the plan to tow it in a specially made iron container was hatched in 1877, partly because the French already had an Egyptian obelisk in Paris and we could not be left behind. It was placed on Victoria Embankment, not far from Waterloo Bridge, with a time-capsule underneath.

As is so often the case when a supernatural angle is needed, ghost-hunter Elliott O'Donnell comes to the rescue, and this extract is taken from his 1957 book *Haunted Waters*:

> I have often felt when in near proximity to some rivers and pools as if the water possessed a strange, magnetic influence and attraction, as well as sensing the presence of a spirit, sometimes friendly and sometimes inimical . . . The spot where Cleopatra's Needle stands was well known to be haunted. None of the outcasts [homeless people living rough] would venture near it. Two of them told me that they saw one night a tall, nude, shadowy figure, with a peak-shaped head and a body covered with what looked like scales, suddenly appear by the Needle, wave a long arm at them and leap over the wall into the river. They said that they sometimes heard unearthly groans and hellish, mocking laughter in the river.

Samuel Pepys (1633–1703) recorded many London traditions and superstitions in his *Diary*, so it is fitting that there is now a custom that revolves around him – an annual memorial service in his parish church of St Olave's in Hart Street. The service includes seventeenth-century music and an address by an eminent scholar.

This life-size marble effigy of John Stow (1525–1605) can be found where he is buried, at St Andrew's Undershaft Church, Leadenhall Street. The son of a tailor, and apprenticed to that trade, Stow gave it up in favour of writing, and his 1598 *Survey of London* puts him at the forefront of the capital's historians. His quill is replaced during a memorial service every year.

This illustration from 1820 shows Doggett's boat race on the Thames – an event which has taken place every year since 1715, except during the Second World War. It was set up by the actor Thomas Doggett (c.1670–1721), in honour of George I and his new Hanoverian dynasty. Above, the winners are shown in the Lord Mayor's Day parade, sporting their prizes of bright red coats (originally orange, the symbolic colour of the Hanoverians) and large, ornate silver badges.

Framed by escalators in the Richard Rogers-designed Lloyd's of London building, the Lutine Bell was salvaged in 1859 from the shipwrecked boat *La Lutine* (the Sprite). It used to be rung whenever a maritime announcement was made – one stroke for bad news, two for good – which brought a hushed silence to the underwriting room. It is often erroneously cited as the basis for the twentieth-century superstition that one must stop a ringing glass 'to save a sailor from drowning'.

Every year, St Clement Danes church on the Strand holds an 'orange and lemon service', where the citrus fruits are distributed to local primary schoolchildren. Proud of its reputed association with the popular children's rhyme, the church has also installed a carillon to play the tune every day at noon.

The actor Robert Baddeley (1733–94) is depicted here in his most renowned role of Moses in Sheridan's *The School for Scandal*. The popular and benevolent actor left a bequest to help struggling actors and theatrical folk, as well as a small annual sum to supply drinks and cake every Twelfth Night to the cast of the current production at the Theatre Royal, Drury Lane.

Gainsborough's portrait shows Elizabeth Montagu (1720–1800), a well-known society leader and author, and also friend to chimney sweeps. Every May Day, London's sweeps would arrive on her doorstep – Montagu House on Portman Square – where she would provide a meal of roast beef and plum pudding.

'Cursed be he who removeth his neighbour's landmark – Whack it, boys, whack it!' cries the Chief Yeoman Warder, during the Tower of London's Beating of the Bounds ceremony. Every third Ascension Day, the group perambulates the Tower's boundaries, beating the markers with willow wands. Before detailed maps, the custom was a way of ensuring the boundaries were known and respected.

Whitehall's Cenotaph is the site of national commemoration for those who lost their lives in England's armed conflicts. On the second Sunday in November, the Queen and other members of the royal family, political and religious leaders, senior military figures, war veterans and civilians gather here to remember those who gave their lives in the nation's armed conflicts. The Queen lays the first wreath of poppies at the Cenotaph's foot and, by the end of the ceremony, Whitehall has become a sea of red.

The Chinese New Year celebrations are a fine example of the new customs that London embraces alongside its time-worn traditions. The festivities were first staged in Soho in 1973 and were designed to establish a Chinese presence in the wider community. The area continues to host the colourful processions, popular with tourists and Londoners alike.

The Lord Mayor's ornate horse-drawn coach dates from 1757 and is used during the Lord Mayor's Show – an annual event full of pomp and circumstance. Since 1215, the Lord Mayor's first official act must be to visit the Royal Courts of Justice and swear an oath of allegiance to the Crown. What was initially a simple journey has become increasingly grand over the years, and it now takes over an hour for the procession to pass one spot.

This Robert Cruikshank (1789–1856, brother of the more famous George) illustration shows the main characters from Pierce Egan's popular book *Life in London* (1820) visiting a fortune-teller. Such visits were rather in vogue among nineteenth-century ladies, who enjoyed the thrill of a brush with the occult. The fortune-teller here is practising cartomancy; other techniques included dice, astrology and the 'Bible and Key' method.

Students at Westminster School, Little Dean's Yard, like many others, have always been fond of engaging in pranks, especially ones that involved ghosts. Robert Cruikshank's 1826 illustration shows them scaring a passer-by with a model; another instance was reported in St James's Park twenty years earlier, when Westminster boys used a 'Phantasmagoria' device to create a ghostly figure, giving such a tremendous shock to two Coldstream Guards, that they required hospitalisation.

Today the Thames is straddled by several bridges, but until the eighteenth century, the only way to cross the river was by ferry or via London Bridge (shown here in its most recent incarnation, second from the top). Many customs and superstitions developed around the infamous bridge, ranging from the rhyme 'London Bridge is Falling Down', to the more gruesome tradition of displaying the severed heads of traitors on spikes at its entrance.

WELLINGTON STREET: LYCEUM

A theatre story that is less commonplace than usual – about a ghostless head rather than a headless ghost – can be found in J. A. Brooks's *Ghosts of London* (1991). The incident took place at the Lyceum in Wellington Street. Sometime in the 1880s, a couple were sitting in their box waiting for a performance to start, when they glanced down at the stalls and saw a woman calmly sitting there with a man's severed head in her lap. As the lights dimmed a few moments later, they were unable to verify what they had seen, and at the interval the woman was still there but had a shawl across her lap. After the performance, the couple could not catch up with her in the crowd, and were left to puzzle over their bizarre experience. Years later, however, on a visit to a great house in Yorkshire, the man was amazed to see a portrait that clearly bore the same face as the unfortunate head in the lady's lap. He was told that it was a picture of a man whose family had owned the Lyceum site, who was beheaded by the order of Oliver Cromwell.

Brooks points out that the theatre was built in 1772 on the grounds of Exeter House, and that at least two of its former owners had been executed, although centuries before Cromwell's time. But two questions remain unanswered. First, how did the man recognise a face seen from above for brief moments, years later? Surely a memorable distinguishing mark would have clinched the identification. And secondly, for the benefit of those visualising the story, how did the lady carry the head into and out of the theatre? Under her arm, grasped by the hair, or in a capacious handbag?

WESTMINSTER ABBEY

Long Meg of Westminster was first mentioned in publications of the 1580s and 1590s that have not survived, and by the early seventeenth century she was widely known, with several chapbooks devoted to her exploits. Victorian bibliophile Charles Hindley reprinted one, first published in London in 1635, in *The Old Book Collector's Miscellany* (1862). Its full title was *The Life of Long Meg of Westminster; containing the Mad Merry Prankes She Played in her Life Time, not onely in Performing Sundry Quarrels with*

Long Meg of Westminster was first mentioned in publications of the 1580s and '90s when she was described as a feisty woman who often dressed as a man. Some claim that an eleven-foot-long stone in the Abbey cloisters marks her final resting place.

Divers Ruffians about London, and it purports to tell her life story in eighteen short chapters.

According to this edition, Meg lived in the time of Henry VIII, and in the first chapter she accompanies some country girls going into service in London. When the carrier demands too much money, Meg belabours him with her cudgel, and the same pattern is repeated in most of the episodes, as braggarts, cheats, bullies, and French soldiers at the Battle of Boulogne are battered into submission. Meg often went about dressed as a man, and her victims are always male, but her proto-feminist credentials are marred, in Chapter 13 when she marries a 'proper tall man, and a soldier', who deliberately tries to provoke her by beating her with a stick, and she refuses to fight back on the grounds that a wife must submit to her husband.

These tales are highly formulaic, akin to the jest books of the period, and are thus of no value as real biography. There is a widespread but unlikely tradition that Meg was buried in Westminster Abbey, and a large black marble stone in the south walk of the cloisters, inscribed to Abbot Gervasius de Blois, who died in 1160, is often pointed out as her grave, presumably as it is almost eleven feet long. Whether or not any real Meg ever existed is debatable, and the question is confused because the name itself became proverbial. Any tall person could be nicknamed Long Meg, and even inanimate objects such as a cannon in the Tower of London could bear the name.

There are also indications of different traditions regarding her life. Correspondence in *Notes and Queries* (1850), for example, quotes early seventeenth-century publications which portray her as a brothel-keeper, including the following, from 1609: 'Long Meg of Westminster kept alwaies twenty courtizans in her house, whom, by their pictures, she sold to all commers.' There is perhaps more to be discovered about Long Meg.

A very different aspect of womanhood is celebrated at the Abbey when the annual Florence Nightingale Commemoration service takes place on or near her birthday, 12 May. It commemorates Florence and her life's work, and also celebrates the professions of nursing, midwifery, and other healthcare work, and is organised by the Florence Nightingale Foundation. Over 2,000 people attended the 2007 service. Echoing the popular image of 'the lady with the lamp', the proceedings include a procession to the altar in which a member of the Foundation, escorted by student nurses in their uniforms, carries a lamp and then passes it to another scholar, to symbolise the passing of knowledge from one to another. The Foundation was set up by public appeal on Florence's return from the Crimea, and has been active in promoting and supporting the nursing professions ever since, particularly in the field of education. There are other, smaller, commemorations in other parts of the country.

Florence Nightingale (1820–1910) also features prominently on the impressive Crimean War Memorial, by John Henry Foley and Arthur George Walker, which is situated at the junction of Lower Regent Street and Pall Mall. There is also a Florence Nightingale Museum at St Thomas's Hospital, Lambeth Palace Road.

One of the more intimate pieces of royal pageantry is the distribution of alms to pensioners on Maundy Thursday, the day before Good Friday. The sovereign, or occasionally his or her representative, presents a purse containing specially minted silver coins to selected recipients, whose number reflects the sovereign's age. So, in 2006, when the Queen was eighty years of age, there were eighty men and eighty women. The ceremony moves around different cathedrals, and the recipients are drawn from the relevant local community. Every ten years or so it returns to Westminster Abbey, and was held there in 1981, 1991, and 2001.

The ceremony is based on biblical precedent. The Gospel of John (13:4) describes how Jesus washed the feet of his disciples, immediately after the Last Supper, and then commanded them to love one another. The word translated as 'command' is *mandatum*, and Maundy is derived directly from this, and the notion of charity from the 'love one another' rubric.

The ceremony has a very long history indeed in England – the first known sovereign to take part was King John in 1210 – but it has changed a great deal over the years. Until the reign of James II, the sovereign really did wash the feet of the recipients, and until Elizabeth I's time, expensive clothes were handed out as well as food and money. In the past the people were chosen because they were really poor, but nowadays it is an honour bestowed upon pensioners in recognition of their service to the community. The coins are now given in special red or white purses, and they still bear the same image of the Queen as did the coins minted in 1953 at the start of her reign.

WESTMINSTER BRIDGE

There is no end to the lore surrounding the Whitechapel murders of 1888 and the theories about who 'Jack the Ripper' really was. One minor piece of the jigsaw is provided by Elliott O'Donnell in his *Ghosts of London* (1932):

> It was said that they terminated with the suicide of a man who was seen to leap from Westminster Bridge on the stroke of midnight, December 31, 1888. This man, so it was asserted, was a member of the medical profession, who had been suspected for some time by the police. When he realized the net was closing round him and arrest would probably take place very shortly, he took the fatal leap . . . I met several people, during my nocturnal rambles, who assured me Westminster Bridge was haunted by the ghost of a man who was, periodically, seen jumping from it, as Big Ben sounded midnight.

This might be a confused memory of the finding of the body of Montague John Druitt (1857–88), one of the main suspects in the murders, on 31 December 1888, although he had actually committed suicide some time earlier that month.

See also BUCKS ROW, WHITECHAPEL, p. 257.

WHITEHALL

From the moment he was executed in Whitehall on 30 January 1649, it was inevitable that Charles I would be regarded as a martyr by many in England, and once Charles II was restored to the throne, it was made official. The day of Charles's execution was included in the calendar of saints' days in the 1662 Anglican Prayer Book, and special prayers for the day provided. These were only removed in 1859.

The oldest of several societies with a specific interest in Charles I's life and legacy is the Society of King Charles the Martyr, founded in 1894 and still very active. They describe themselves as 'a Christian devotional society', and one of their aims is: 'The propagation of the true knowledge about the life and times of St Charles (and to win general recognition of the great debt the Church of England owes to him for his faithfulness unto death in defence of the Church and Her apostolic ministry).'

The Society has particularly close ties to the church of St Andrew-by-the-Wardrobe, Queen Victoria Street, EC4, where many of their meetings and events are held. The Society usually celebrates the day of Charles I's birthday (19 November) and the Restoration of Charles II (19 May), but their main commemorative event is a banquet, held every year since 1951, on or near 30 January, in the Banqueting Hall, Whitehall, the site of the execution. With a nice touch of irony, the Society's website records:

> In 1956 SKCM donated a bust of St Charles to St Margaret's, Westminster, where it was set up, most appropriately, facing the statue of Cromwell which stands outside Westminster Hall. A similar bust was later placed above the entrance to the Banqueting House, Whitehall.

Perhaps the most dramatic scene Whitehall has ever witnessed was the execution of Charles I on 30 January 1649. He was officially recognised as a martyr when his son Charles II returned to the English throne in 1660.

Two other organisations with an interest in Charles I's memory are the Royal Martyr Church Union and the Royal Stuart Society.

WHITEHALL: CENOTAPH

All over the country on the second Sunday in November, there are gatherings at war memorials and churches to commemorate local people who gave their lives in the nation's armed conflicts. It could be argued that it is these local events which properly exemplify remembrance, precisely because they are relatively low-key and personal in scope. But there must also be a national commemoration, and the official ceremony at the Cenotaph in Whitehall is designed to symbolise the gratitude and remembrance of the whole nation.

The group that gathers at the Cenotaph is an impressive one, and probably includes a higher percentage of our society's leaders than any other annual event. The Queen attends, along with other members of the royal family, political and religious leaders, senior military figures, Commonwealth High Commissioners, serving personnel from all branches of the armed forces, war veterans, and civilians.

The traditional two minutes' silence is followed by the playing of the Last Post. The Queen lays a wreath of poppies at the foot of the Cenotaph, and others do the same in turn. The veterans march past to pay their respects to their fallen comrades. By the end of the ceremony Whitehall is awash with wreaths of red poppies.

The way we conduct our rituals of remembrance was largely dictated by decisions made in the immediate aftermath of the First World War, a time of immense relief, emotional exhaustion, and widespread grief. Even before the war was over, there was much discussion in the press about the most appropriate way to commemorate the sacrifice of so many lives. A clear consensus was quickly reached that the tone of any commemoration should be one of solemn remembrance rather than the glorification of military victory or triumphing over vanquished enemies, and this feeling set the tone for national remembrance that still resonates today.

The original Armistice Day was placed on 11 November because that was the official day that hostilities ceased – on the eleventh hour of the eleventh day of the eleventh month. The day was renamed Remembrance Day after the

Second World War, and was moved to the nearest Sunday. This change of day was a sensible move, but it has been argued that the symbolism of the day was weakened and lost its edge. Certainly, as older folk still testify, there was something immensely impressive about the whole nation coming to a standstill for two minutes on a busy weekday. All traffic was halted, schools, offices, and factories fell silent; it is too easy to be silent on a Sunday, they say.

Thousands of war memorials were erected up and down the country, varying from simple plaques to large public monuments, while some communities dedicated practical projects, such a new hospital wing or village hall, to the memory of their lost generation. The government issued guidance on approved ways to proceed, but many communities ignored them and went their own way.

There is still some doubt about who first suggested the two-minute silence. A South African, Sir Percy Fitzpatrick, and an Australian journalist, Edward George Honey, are both credited with its invention, but it is quite possible that the idea occurred to more than one person at the same time. One minute and three minutes were considered, and it is said that King George V decided on two.

The Cenotaph in Whitehall was designed by Sir Edwin Lutyens (1869–1944), one of the leading architects of his generation, who had already been involved in work with the Imperial War Graves Commission, and who was also commissioned to design major memorials in Dublin, Leicester, Rochdale, and abroad. He was also responsible for the merchant navy memorial on Tower Hill, London. The deceptively simple Cenotaph is constructed of Portland stone, and its name derives from the Greek words for 'empty' and 'tomb'. A temporary version was constructed in time for the 1919 commemoration, and the real thing was in place the following year.

Poppies were already taking on a symbolic role during the war, and a poem written in 1915 by John Macrae, a Canadian forces doctor, entitled 'In Flanders Fields' was influential. It begins with the lines:

> In Flanders fields the poppies blow
> Between the crosses, row on row.

In 1921, the British Legion introduced the first artificial poppies and raised £106,000, a huge sum in those days. It was soon suggested that the poppies could be made by disabled veterans, and the Poppy Factory was established at Richmond, where they are still made today.

WEST LONDON

*The London Boroughs of Brent, Ealing,
Hammersmith & Fulham, Harrow, Hillingdon,
Hounslow and the Royal Borough of
Kensington & Chelsea*

ACTON

One of the many fascinating working-class superstitions from the time of
the First World War that Edward Lovett included in his *Magic in Modern
London* (1925) was the wearing of necklaces of blue beads to keep away
bronchitis. He obtained details from the Medical Inspector of Schools,
Urban District Council of Acton, which prompted him to start asking
around elsewhere in London:

> My first interview was with an old lady who keeps a 'marine store', and I
> told her that I had heard of these beads, and asked her if she knew of them.
> She seemed surprised that I did not appear to know anything about it, and
> told me that she wore a necklace herself, and that all her friends, especially
> the children, did the same. I said that I had never seen them worn,
> whereupon she replied that they were always worn beneath the neck or
> collar of the dress, and therefore were not visible. I then asked her if I might
> see her beads, whereupon she drew them above her dress, and I saw that
> they were the cheap blue beads of which I had heard.

Upon further enquiries, he discovered that they were put on the necks of
very young children and never taken off, not even when the wearers were
washed or bathed, and they were even left in situ after death. When a string
broke the beads were immediately re-threaded on a fresh string and
replaced round the neck. Although the colour sometimes varied, it was
almost always sky blue.

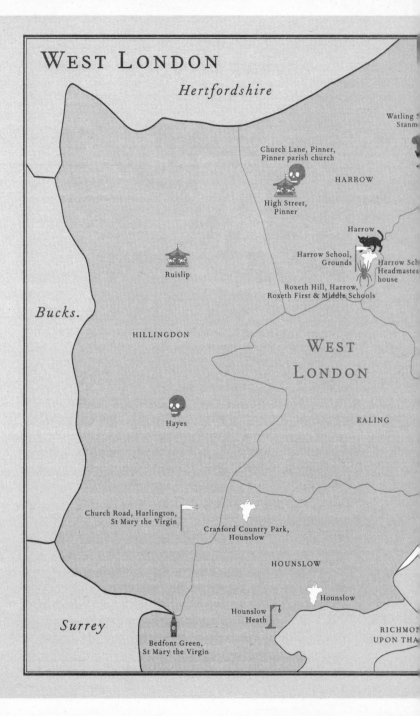

WEST LONDON

Hertfordshire

Watling S[...]
Stanm[...]

HARROW

Church Lane, Pinner,
Pinner parish church

High Street,
Pinner

Harrow

Harrow School,
Grounds

Harrow Sch[...]
Headmaster[...]
house

Ruislip

Roxeth Hill, Harrow,
Roxeth First & Middle Schools

Bucks.

HILLINGDON

WEST
LONDON

Hayes

EALING

Church Road, Harlington,
St Mary the Virgin

Cranford Country Park,
Hounslow

HOUNSLOW

Hounslow

Surrey

Hounslow
Heath

RICHMON[...]
UPON THA[...]

Bedfont Green,
St Mary the Virgin

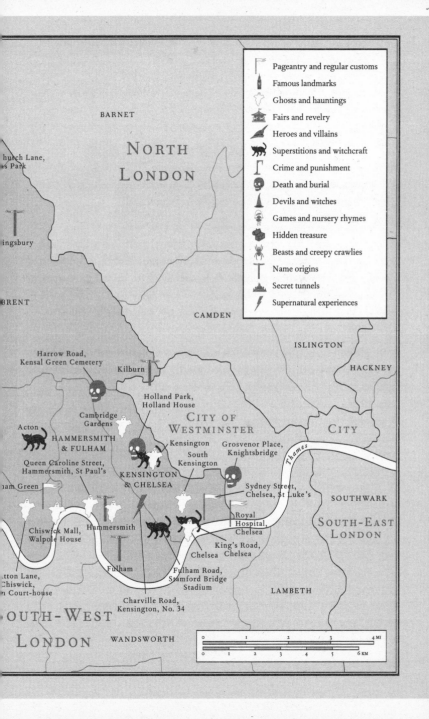

Legend

	Pageantry and regular customs
	Famous landmarks
	Ghosts and hauntings
	Fairs and revelry
	Heroes and villains
	Superstitions and witchcraft
	Crime and punishment
	Death and burial
	Devils and witches
	Games and nursery rhymes
	Hidden treasure
	Beasts and creepy crawlies
	Name origins
	Secret tunnels
	Supernatural experiences

BARNET

NORTH LONDON

hurch Lane,
's Park

ingsbury

BRENT

CAMDEN

ISLINGTON

HACKNEY

Harrow Road,
Kensal Green Cemetery

Kilburn

Holland Park,
Holland House

Cambridge
Gardens

CITY OF
WESTMINSTER

CITY

Acton

HAMMERSMITH
& FULHAM

Kensington
South
Kensington

Grosvenor Place,
Knightsbridge

Queen Caroline Street,
Hammersmith, St Paul's

KENSINGTON
& CHELSEA

Sydney Street,
Chelsea, St Luke's

am Green

Royal
Hospital,
Chelsea

SOUTHWARK

SOUTH-EAST
LONDON

Chiswick Mall,
Walpole House

Hammersmith

King's Road, Chelsea
Chelsea

tton Lane,
Chiswick,
n Court-house

Fulham

Fulham Road,
Stamford Bridge
Stadium

LAMBETH

OUTH-WEST
LONDON

WANDSWORTH

Charville Road,
Kensington, No. 34

Thames

| 0 | 1 | 2 | 3 | 4 MI |
| 0 | 1 | 2 | 3 | 4 | 5 | 6 KM |

They consisted, on an average, of thirty-four beads, each about the size of a large pea, or a grain of maize. They fastened at the back, and at the throat was a crude sort of heart-shaped pendant, a sort of 'locket' . . . I also ascertained that although mostly worn by women and girls, men, especially of the 'navvy' class, also wore them. Of the many enquiries I made I found that these men had a profound confidence in them as a cure for bronchitis.

In his systematic way, Lovett separated London into twenty-six districts and spent a day making enquiries at shops in each area, telling the shop-keeper that he knew a child suffering from bronchitis.

The shops where I made my enquiries were of two classes, viz.: A poor class shop where they sold cheap confectionery, buttons, tapes, pins, beads, and the bronchitis beads. The other was a better class shop of the Fancy species, where they also sold beads, of the fashionable sort . . . Every shop of the lower class recognised the blue beads as a cure for bronchitis, but not a single shop of the better class knew anything about it, or if they did would not admit it.

Blue beads were also reported in other parts of the country, but seem to have been particularly popular in London; however, no satisfactory explanation for their origin has been put forward. A set of the beads can be seen in the collection of Lovett's material at the Cuming Museum, Walworth Road, Southwark.

BEDFONT GREEN: ST MARY THE VIRGIN CHURCH

One of the most famous sights of Hounslow borough is the Bedfont peacocks: two highly impressive yew trees cut into the shape of sitting birds with fancy tails. They form an arch over the entrance to the parish church of St Mary the Virgin. There have been several explanations for the origin of these figures, and the dominant theme of many of them is that they represent two young women, usually presumed to be sisters, who were prideful and vain; the peacocks are therefore said to be a satirical jibe at the

The Bedfont peacocks, as they appeared in Victorian times. These two peacock-shaped yew trees stand at the entrance to St Mary the Virgin church in Hounslow and are traditionally said to represent two local and very vain women.

sisters' expense. The tale nowadays often assumes that the women were actually transformed into peacocks, as punishment for their habit of hanging around the churchyard gate every Sunday, to be admired in their finery while their modestly dressed fellow parishioners filed meekly into church. But another, more prosaic, version explains that their 'pride' consisted in turning down a local man who sought to marry them. According to earlier accounts, the initials J. H., J. G., and R. T were cut into the trees, and these were said to be those of the man and the two girls, which would seem to run against the idea that they were sisters as the surname initials are different. A much less well-known story is that the birds were meant to represent a pair of fighting cocks, to commemorate a local vicar who was particularly fond of that sport.

The transformation version is immortalised in Thomas Hood's poem 'The Two Peacocks of Bedfont', published in the *London Magazine* in October 1822, which most writers accept as the 'true' account of the birds' origin:

> Where erst two haughty maidens used to be,
> In pride of plume, where plumy Death hath trod,
> Trailing their gorgeous velvet wantonly,
> Most unmeet pall, over the holy sod:
> There, gentle stranger, thou may'st only see
> Two sombre peacocks. Age, with sapient nod
> Marking the spot, still tarries to declare
> How once they lived and wherefore they are there.

In a footnote, Hood claims that the date 1704 was cut into one of the trees, and this is now taken as the date at which the sculpting first took place and is now cut most prominently in the foliage of the left-hand tree.

Such fancifully shaped yews may seem weird today, but in the eighteenth century they would have been far from unusual. As Gilbert Burnett comments in his *Outlines of Botany* (1835):

> The yew is one of the most tonsile trees we have; and hence, when the formal systems of horticulture were in vogue, yew hedges and yew images were in great repute. Few vestiges of this perversion remain; between Henley and Oxford, however, there are two yew trees cut into the form of peacocks, and in Bedfont churchyard there are two others.

An engraving published in Edward Walford's *Greater London* (1883–4), which shows Harlington church in 1803, only three miles away from Bedfont, clearly shows a similarly sculpted tree. It is thus their survival that makes the Bedfont peacocks so special, and Burnett suggests that this longevity is not entirely accidental: 'there is no chance of escape for these metamorphosed trees, an annuity having been left by some eccentric person to keep these yews thus cut for ever.' Unfortunately there is no evidence of this annuity in the parish records.

CAMBRIDGE GARDENS, KENSINGTON

In a neat updating of the old 'phantom coach' type of tale, there is a story of a ghostly No.7 double-decker bus, in the livery of the General Omnibus Company (which was absorbed into London Transport in 1933), at the junction of Cambridge Gardens and St Mark's Road. The story reportedly came to light in June 1934, at the inquest of a driver who had been killed when he swerved violently for no apparent reason. Other drivers came forward to say that they had had to take similar evasive action at the same spot to avoid a bus tearing towards them, lights a-blazing, which promptly disappeared after it passed them.

People talking about a ghost bus at an official inquest must have been quite an event, and it would be interesting to follow it up. Jack Hallam seems to have been the first modern ghost-writer to print the story, in his *Ghosts of London* (1975), but in his usual fashion he gives no information about his source, or checkable details such as newspaper titles or even the name of the accident victim. Now that website compilers have got hold of Hallam's story, the number of witnesses who came forward at the time has grown to 'hundreds'. It would be useful if someone could come up with the coroner's report.

CHARVILLE ROAD, KENSINGTON: NO. 34

A wraith of someone on the point of death appearing to another person is a common enough motif in British ghost-lore, and there are several examples in this book. Meeting one's own double is much less common, although a famous example from HOLLAND HOUSE is detailed on p. 154. Perhaps related to these themes is another story from the same area, which is probably unique in that it is told by the person whose apparition appears to others, rather than the other way round, and seems to be an example of involuntary astral projection. It is included in A. W. M. Stirling's *Ghosts Vivisected* (1957), as told to her by the principal character, Mr Hamilton-Carson:

> On Good Friday, April 2nd 1926, about seven o'clock in the evening. I was sitting on a bench with my sister in a cemetery in Kensington . . .
>
> At the same time, about three-quarters of a mile away, at 34 Charville Road, Kensington, Mrs Wickham, the owner of the house, and a Mr Johnstone who also knew me, saw me standing in the doorway of the dining-room where they then were . . . I appeared quite solid and my usual self, and the clothes they saw me in were the clothes I was actually wearing that evening as I sat in the cemetery.

Both Mrs Wickham and Mr Johnstone at once greeted me . . . I made no reply, then *vanished*! Mr Johnstone immediately rushed out into the hall to look for me, and re-entered the room looking rather pale and upset; he then, on second thoughts, hurried out again to the front door of the house, opened it and gazed up the street. He saw no signs of me, but noticing a young lady at the window of the next house who also knew me, he inquired from her if she had seen me go out? She replied, 'No – but I saw him *go in* just now.'

My friends, in consequence of this strange occurrence, concluded that I had died, and that what they had seen was a ghost. Mr Johnstone decided to go round at once to ascertain what had happened; but as he was on his way, I met him in the street! . . . I did not myself know that I had paid this astral visit to my friend, and to my knowledge I did not use any effort to do so.

CHELSEA

Every place has to have at least one poltergeist, and Chelsea had its chance in December 1938. A woman, identified by the pseudonym of Miss Whalen, who lived in a '300-year old cottage in Chelsea', reported what she referred to as an 'invisible man', whose footsteps were heard. She also heard the door-knocker sounding of its own accord, and said that things had gone missing or were mysteriously moved. She phoned the top poltergeist-buster of the day, Dr Nandor Fodor, who came hot-foot from his success with the THORNTON HEATH poltergeist (*see* p. 365). Fodor was in the process of developing his psychological explanation of poltergeist activity, so instead of identifying and exorcising Miss Whalen's ghost, he confronted her:

> In view of Miss Whalen's condition, heroic measures were necessary to save her. I decided to ignore the dynamics of the reported happenings. I told her that, in my considered opinion, she was haunted by her own past: while she was successful in keeping some unhappy memories from entering into her consciousness, the bottling-up process had failed, her libido had side-slipped and walked out on her in the form of a ghost, and she had been wasting her own vitality in a vain attempt to convey a message, in the same way neurotic symptoms manifest themselves.

Miss Whalen was quite pleased with this diagnosis, and they set about practical remedies such as putting up a sign saying 'Please ring the bell' to stop the door-knocking, and subjecting her to intensive dream analysis. Miss Whalen's problem was, of course, mostly to do with sex, but she was only partially cured when Fodor had to leave for America, so we do not know the end of her story. Anyone interested in further details of the case can read about it in his *The Haunted Mind* (1959).

See also BRIMSDOWN, ENFIELD, p. 196; GROVE PARK: ALLOTMENTS, p. 333; PLAISTOW, p. 293; REVERDY ROAD, BERMONDSEY: NOS 56 AND 58, p. 342; STOCKWELL, p. 414; SUTTON LANE, CHISWICK: SUTTON COURT-HOUSE, p. 173.

CHISWICK MALL: WALPOLE HOUSE

Walpole House, one of the finest terraced houses in London, is said to be haunted by Barbara Villiers (1640–1709), Countess of Castlemaine and Duchess of Cleveland. Barbara was a serious beauty in her time, and between 1660 and 1670 was the pre-eminent mistress of Charles II. In old age she contracted dropsy, and was buried at St Nicholas's parish church. According to Peter Underwood's *Gazetteer of British Ghosts* (1971):

> She must have led a sad life here after the years of pleasure and probably often walked up and down the shallow stairs in the high heels she always wore, gazing wistfully out of the tall windows of the drawing room. It is said that she would raise her hands to the moon-lit sky on occasions, begging for the return of her lost beauty ... At certain times the rap-tap of her heels is said to be heard on the stairway and on stormy, moonlit nights, her form has been seen at the window of the drawing room, wringing her hands.

Underwood does not name his source of either the ghost story or the high-heels detail. On most ghost websites poor Barbara's ghost is said to have 'a heavy tread'.

CHURCH LANE, PINNER: PINNER PARISH CHURCH

In the churchyard of St John the Baptist in Pinner one can find a strange memorial erected by John Claudius Loudon in 1843, for his parents, William and Agnes. It is pyramid-shaped, with rounded open arches at the base, and halfway up one face is what looks like a protruding coffin. This protuberance has given rise to a local legend that the Loudons' remains are actually encased in a stone coffin inside the memorial. The story goes on to explain that a legacy was left to the church and will only continue to be paid as long as the Loudons are 'above ground'. In fact, John's parents are buried under the strange-shaped memorial, which it is now a Grade II listed building.

CHURCH ROAD, HARLINGTON: ST MARY THE VIRGIN CHURCH

The popularity of bell-ringing on 5 November is mentioned at BROADWAY, RAINHAM: CHURCH OF ST HELEN AND ST GILES (*see* p. 257). H. Edwards's *Collection of Old English Customs* (1842), quoting Charity Commissioners' Report vol. IX, reported that the ringers at Harlington were well provided for:

> It is stated in the register, under the date of 1683, that half an acre of land was given by some person, whose name was forgotten. It has always been understood, that this piece of land was given, for the benefit of the bellringers of the parish, to provide them with a leg of pork, for ringing on the 5th of November. It is called the Pork Acre. The ground is let by the parish officers at 50s a year, which is paid by them to the bellringers.

CRANFORD COUNTRY PARK, HOUNSLOW

In his autobiography, *My Life and Recollections* (1865), politician and sportsman Grantley F. Berkeley wrote of an incident that had occurred around the year 1820 at the family home, Cranford. The estate adjoined Hounslow

Heath, which at the time was an extremely remote and desolate area. Berkeley and his brother had stayed up late because they were going out in the hope of capturing some poachers who had been active in the area. All other occupants of the house were already in bed when the two boys opened the kitchen door to go out the back way. The room was well lit by the glowing embers in the great fireplace, and as they stood in the doorway they could see a tall woman, separated from them only by the width of the kitchen table.

> She was dressed, or seemed to be dressed, as a maid-servant, with a sort of poke bonnet on, and a large shawl drawn or pinned tightly across her breast. On my entrance she slowly turned her head to look at me, and as she did so, every feature ought to have stood forth in the light of the fire, but I at once saw that there was beneath the bonnet an indistinctness of outline not to be accounted for.

The boys locked the door behind them, but the figure moved.

> After I had thus locked the door, on turning round there was no woman to be seen, so I asked my brother whither she had gone. He instantly replied, 'Up the kitchen towards the screen.' 'Come on, then,' I cried, 'let's have some fun and catch her, to see who it is.' Our impression was that it was one of the maid-servants sitting up long after the usual hours, and we at once proceeded, each taking a separate corner of the screen, and meeting on the side next to the fire – but there was nothing there! Astonished at this, we then commenced a most minute search of the kitchen, looked up the chimney and beneath the table, into the oven and into the drawers – in short into every nook and corner that could have held a rat. But there was no living thing in the kitchen but ourselves.

The writer is at pains to point out that all the windows were closed, and too high to offer any exit, and both doors to the kitchen were locked.

In the same volume, Berkeley relates a story his father used to tell about the night he too saw a ghost – the figure of a man who descended to the cellar. Needless to say, there was no other exit, and no one could be found down there.

But this was not the last of the ghosts seen at Cranford. Two more were recorded in the *Middlesex Quarterly* of Winter 1955. The first was reported by Miss E. Turbayne, of Uxbridge, as having occurred to her mother and brother before the Second World War. They were out walking one wet October afternoon when they saw quite clearly a woman dressed in white, sitting on a stone seat on the other side of the River Crane. 'Somebody crazy; fancy sitting out in white on a day like this,' commented the mother. They looked round the church, and returning by the same route, the mother said, 'I wonder if that woman is still sitting on the wet seat?' But not only had the woman disappeared, but the seat had as well.

The writer of the article, A. Leonard Summers, added a strange tale from his own experience, which, like the one already cited, is fairly typical of many modern ghost sightings, in that the ghost appears to have no purpose, or to do anything particularly remarkable:

> On a bright sunny morning, September 25, 1948, in Cranford Park, I was walking through the most densely-wooded part towards Harlington, along a narrow path which ran almost parallel to another beside a high wall, when I noticed a tall man walking in the same direction. I only gave him a casual glance, so cannot describe him in detail, and the trees meeting overhead at this point made the light too dim and uncertain to recognise anyone clearly but I would say he wore a black or very dark suit and trilby hat. The two pathways were about 20 yards apart, converging and joining at the stile. My pace being rather quicker than that of the stranger (whose steps I plainly heard rustling the fallen leaves), I reached the exit first, hearing the man coming on behind, some 30 paces. At the stile I paused and looked back to ascertain if he was anyone I knew. To my intense surprise there was nobody to be seen – my companion had vanished.

FULHAM

See PUTNEY, p. 409 for a story about how Putney and Fulham got their names.

FULHAM ROAD: STAMFORD BRIDGE STADIUM

In the football violence crisis of the 1980s, Chelsea supporters were one of those groups who attracted a particularly bad reputation, so it is no surprise that they were the ones to star in a children's rumour-panic, called 'The

Chelsea Smilers'. This was an excellent example of the rumour-panic genre, which swept like proverbial wildfire across South London secondary schools in January/February 1989. School panics like this are not that unusual, and often come and go leaving little trace, with adults only briefly aware of them. But this one was particularly upsetting, and happened to take place when my daughter Kate was a thirteen-year-old at school in Croydon, and she recognised it as a legend and reported it to me. She had cousins and friends at other schools, so we immediately learned that it was widespread and were able to start documenting it from its beginning, or thereabouts. We thus have more detailed information than is usual in these cases, when a panic can be over before those interested can start collecting data.

The basic story was that there was a group of men called the Chelsea Smilers going round from school to school. They travelled in a van with smiley faces painted on the side. They would ask pupils questions about Chelsea Football Club, and if you got the answers wrong they would cut the corners of your mouth, then hit you hard to make you scream, so opening the wounds even further, leaving permanent 'smile-shaped' scars. There were many other details which varied – the weapon could be a knife, a razor, or even a credit or phone card; they put vinegar or salt in the wounds to make them worse. A recurrent feature was that they were at such-and-such a school yesterday and they are coming *here* today, and it was this immediacy that caused so much distress.

In the cold light of hindsight this seems a silly enough story, but it caused genuine panic in the lower years of the schools affected, although older pupils were dismissive. Many younger ones were in tears, some in hysterics, many refusing to go home till their parents came for them, and there were queues to use the public phones (this was before mobile phones, of course). The children talked of nothing else, and some parents kept children home the next day. Teachers were nonplussed, and were in the classic rumour bind of not knowing what had hit them and not having any clear information on which to act. Most phoned the police and other schools, but could get no clear answers. Some headteachers sent a note to all classes to scotch the rumours, others called an emergency assembly, and sometimes their actions made things worse. More than one headteacher arranged for the local police to be at the school gates at home-time to reassure the children, but many pupils took the police presence to be a confirmation of the story, and thought that the Smilers would simply wait until the police had gone.

On the evidence gathered at the time, the panic hit schools in Bexley first, about 31 January, and spread right across the South London boroughs, reaching Wandsworth, Merton and Sutton by the first week in March. There were some reports of the story north of the river, but it is not clear whether the panic accompanied it. Information from schools in Surrey, Kent, and further afield is also patchy but indicates that the story reached them soon afterwards, although the panic did not. In the South London schools, the panic seems to have subsided quickly, but the story entered the general repertoire of children's scary stories, albeit without the sense of immediate menace.

Looking at the wider picture, it is clear that this is one small instance of a range of panic stories, many of which involve similar motifs. In September and October 1991, for example, a panic swept through Glasgow schools about men dressed as clowns, driving a van, offering sweets to children outside the school gates and then kidnapping them. In 1995, a parent in Glasgow wrote to say that his six-year-old son had told him a story he heard from a classmate:

> There are these clowns who juggle fire and throw it at you. Afterwards they take off their suits. They have a blue van. When they ask what kind of face paint you want, if you say the name of a facepaint they carve a smile on you with a knife.

As far as antecedents are concerned, there are plenty of possibilities: the famous razor gangs of Glasgow in the 1950s; the Green Jackets gang in Liverpool in 1971, who played noughts and crosses on people's faces with knives; the Yellow Jackets in Yorkshire about 1979; the Britsea Estate Boot Boys in Bristol, who had spiked gloves that punched holes in people's faces; and so on. But why the Chelsea Smilers turned up in Bexley in January 1989 is anybody's guess.

GROSVENOR PLACE, KNIGHTSBRIDGE

Knightsbridge has the distinction of being the location of the last suicide in England to be buried by the roadside. According to local historian Henry Davis, in his *Memorials of the Hamlet of Knightsbridge* (1859):

At the intersection of the cross-roads at the end of Grosvenor Place, suicides were subjected to the revolting burial then awarded by the law. The last person on whom the law was carried out here was named Griffiths, the son of a colonel in the army, who had first murdered his father, and then destroyed himself. This took place on June 27th 1823.

See also SUICIDE BURIALS, p. 260.

HAMMERSMITH

A cute little story collected by folklorist John Emslie and published in *London Studies* (1974) explains the origin of the name 'Hammersmith':

> *24 Aug 1873*
> A policeman at Highhway Farm, Harefield, told me that King Charles, going through Hammersmith, heard the sound of blows upon an anvil; 'That's a hammer,' said he, 'it's a smith,' said a courtier; so the place was called Hammersmith.

As J. A. Brooks comments in his 1991 book *Ghosts of London*, Hammersmith seems to have been particularly rich in ghosts, although it would be more accurate to say particularly rich in ghost impostors. The first documented case dates from 1803–4, when local residents were troubled by a white-clad figure who would jump out and frighten them on dark nights. It was said that a pregnant woman had been so frightened by one encounter that she died within two days, and that a wagon carrying passengers only just avoided catastrophe when the driver ran off in fear, having seen the apparition. After visiting the White Hart pub one evening, Francis Smith, an exciseman, decided to do a spot of ghost-hunting, taking with him a loaded gun. A short time later a white figure did indeed approach him down the dark lane, and although Smith claimed later that he twice challenged the figure to identify itself, there was no reply, so he fired. The 'ghost' turned out to be 23-year-old Thomas Millwood, dressed in white jacket and trousers and covered in the dust of his trade.

Smith was tried and found guilty, and although the jury attempted to bring in a verdict of manslaughter, the judge declared that in the circumstances murder was the only option, and sentenced him to death. His sentence was, however, commuted to one year's imprisonment.

Meanwhile, in January 1804, the 'real' ghost was apprehended. One James Graham, a shoemaker, admitted to the magistrate that he had dressed up as a ghost on previous occasions in order, he claimed, to get revenge on his apprentices, who had frightened his children with ghost stories.

Two decades later, in 1824, the citizens of Hammersmith were again pestered by a ghost, but the perpetrator was soon caught, and turned out to be a local farmer called John Benjamin.

The next scare, eight years later, was less straightforward, and may have been fictitious. It was reported that a 'monster' was targeting women, and not just frightening them but also scratching and wounding them badly. It was erroneously claimed that he had been apprehended, and that when arrested he was wearing a large white dress, 'with long nails or claws, by which he was enabled to scale walls and hedges'. In a different account he was dressed in armour, and it was said that he had made a wager to strip the clothes off a certain number of females in a certain time, and only had a few more to go. This latter motif is uncannily similar to some of the stories that circulated about SPRING-HEELED JACK (p. 148) in the 1830s.

HARROW

Local journalists are not always known for their accuracy in reporting historical matters, but Jim Golland adopted an unusually sceptical mood in a piece in the *Harrow Observer* on 16 January 1992 where he listed many of the local legends that were patently *not* true. Among other things, he rightly pointed out that Henry VIII built as many hunting lodges as Queen Elizabeth had beds, and that local place-names easily engender spurious etymological notions. A street-name such as Monk's Walk, for example, will always conjure up a non-existent monastery, however recently the name was coined. He goes on:

> Mysterious underground tunnels are widely thought to exist. Similar stories circulate about one from the King's Head in Harrow to St Mary's, or from Headstone Farm to St Mary's. A shopkeeper in Harrow High Street assured

me that the tunnel leading from her cellars to Harrow Park was used by monks. Again, there is no trace of a monastery locally.

Golland also squashes the idea that Harrow schoolboys wear black ties to commemorate Queen Victoria's death, stating that they have been wearing them since about the time she came to the throne, not when she had just left it.

HARROW ROAD: KENSAL GREEN CEMETERY

Townshend & Ffoulkes's *True Ghost Stories* (1936) contains an effective story about L., a successful publisher who moved in moneyed and intellectual circles. Accidentally lost one day in Kensal Green Cemetery, he came across the neglected grave of an earlier girlfriend, Elsie, whom he had long left behind in his rise to fame and fortune. On a whim, he noted down the grave number while idly thinking he might pay for the grave to be cleaned up and renovated. Back at home, he was curiously unsettled by memories of Elsie and to take his mind off thoughts of mortality and death, decided to phone a friend to invite him round. To his horror he suddenly realised that he had asked to be connected to Kensal Green —, the number of Elsie's grave, and her voice answered:

A voice, at first muffled, then gradually becoming louder, said: 'Yes, who's calling?' L. gave his name. The person at the other end uttered a little gasp of delighted surprise. And L., with his blood turning to water, recognised the voice of Elsie. 'Why, it's never you, darling! Do you want me? Of course I'll come' (just as she had always answered his one-time calls). L. wanted to say, *No, no, no*, but speech was frozen, 'I won't be long,' continued the voice, 'but I was very far away, darling, when you rang up.' Panic fear seized L. He dropped the receiver.

Unsure whether to leave or stay, he finally decided to wait and see what would happen.

The front door opened noiselessly, then closed. Footsteps dragged a little, as if their owner's limbs had recently been cramped, came slowly down the passage, heralded by a current of icy air. L. did not meet the visitor. He fainted – and lay unconscious until early next morning when Bowden [his

Spring-Heeled Jack

A Victorian artist's impression of Spring-Heeled Jack, the subject of a major scare in the 1830s. He was reputed to have blazing red eyes, sharp talons and the ability to vomit blue flame.

The Spring-Heeled Jack affair started in the late 1830s and baffled the authorities of the time. Jack was reputedly superhuman or even supernatural, and he attacked people viciously. For a time many were frightened to walk the streets at night. Accounts of his appearance varied widely, and he has been described as a madman, a mass murderer, a ghost, a demon, or, in the late twentieth century, an alien visitor from outer space. Early stories claimed that he could leap over hedges and walls because he had springs in his boots, which is where the popular name came from. Other accounts, however, ignore this feature and focus on his horrific appearance: preternaturally tall with sharp talons, blazing red eyes, and the ability to vomit blue flame.

Our first knowledge of the affair comes from a letter printed in *The Times* on 9 January 1838 from 'A Resident of Peckham' to the Lord Mayor. The correspondent claimed that, on the strength of a bet, a wealthy young man was scaring people in the guises of a ghost, a bear, and a devil, and that seven ladies had been literally frightened out of their wits. Nothing had thus far appeared in the press, but the writer was convinced 'that they have the whole history at their finger ends, but, through interested motives, are induced to remain silent'. This has all the hallmarks of contemporary legend: the precise detail (*seven* women); the high jinks of wealthy young men (a popular motif of the period); and a conspiracy to hush it up. It appears that rumours had been circulating for some time, and were beginning to cause some panic. A reporter from the *Morning Herald* decided to visit the areas of West London where Jack was at large, but met with the classic legend response – every person he spoke to referred him to an alleged victim who in turn said, 'No, it wasn't me, it was so-and-so.' He found numerous stories but not one single person who had actually been attacked, had witnessed an attack or even seen the demon.

Nevertheless, on 22 February, *The Times* carried an alarming report under the headline 'Outrage on a Young Lady'. Jane Alsop, an eighteen-year-old living between Bow and Old Ford, answered a ringing at the gate and was confronted by a man wrapped in a cloak and claiming to be a policeman. He called out, 'For God's sake, bring me a light, for we have caught Spring-Heeled Jack here in the lane!' She fetched a candle, and he immediately:

> ... threw off his outer garment, and applying the lighted candle to his breast, presented a most hideous and frightful appearance, and vomited forth a quantity of blue and white flame from his mouth, and his eyes resembled red balls of fire ... he darted at her, and catching her partly by her dress and the back part of her neck, placed her head under one of his arms and commenced tearing her gown with his claws, which she was certain were of some metallic substance.

With the aid of her sisters, Jane fought him off, and he escaped. This incident is the first case to provide us with a date and place of attack. Given Jane and her family's testimony to the police, it appears that some form of assault did indeed take place. And even though the perpetrator was never named, the testimony shows that the name Spring-Heeled Jack was already in circulation. A deluge of reports of other attacks in the London area then followed – a few sensible but most patently fanciful – and despite attempts by the authorities to solve the mystery, no one was ever convicted, and the panic gradually died down. Spring-Heeled Jack became a staple of the 'penny dreadfuls', and at least one writer turned him into something of a superhero.

One hundred and seventy years later, it is difficult to make sense of what was going on. By far the best, and fullest, modern account is Mike Dash's article in the journal *Fortean Studies* (1996), which brings together a wealth of contemporary information. But the fundamental problem is that the evidence is partial, and based largely on official sources, whereas folklore on the ground is by its very nature chaotic and largely unrecorded. What seems clear is that the whole affair is best viewed as a particularly potent example of a contemporary legend. The most likely scenario is that a legend, or group of them, circulated and created a moral panic. One or more people may have started to imitate the stories, which in turn bred more rumours and more imitations, but it is most probable that the vast majority of reported sightings and attacks never actually happened.

valet] discovered him. 'And, believe me, or believe me not,' said Bowden, when discussing L.'s unaccountable seizure, 'bits of wet clay were sticking to the carpet, and some was on his dinner jacket. Beats me how it got there. As for the hall mat, it was all messed up. Why can't people wipe their feet like Christians?'

Surprisingly L. did not waste away, but he did gain two quirks of character – he would never use the phone, or go to funerals.

HARROW SCHOOL: GROUNDS

Something of the rough and dangerous character of 5 November celebrations in the nineteenth century is indicated in *Recollections of School Days at Harrow* (1890), the autobiography of H. J. Torre, who was at Harrow School from 1832 to 1838.

> I must not omit to mention the 5th of November, on which day most of the boys went after dark to the cricket ground and after letting off a few Roman candles and small catherine wheels, the real object of our assembling began, viz: One boy crept quietly up to another, and the unperceived noiselessly lighted a squib and fizzed it off as close as possible to the part of the body used in sitting. Boys with coat tails were not eligible to be operated on, but there were enough without tails to make it a good time for the Harrow tailors, as the singeing of the boys' clothes was very noticeable the next day. This squibbing and putting lighted crackers into boys' pockets was the sport of the evening, till every boy became more or less suspicious of any other boy approaching him.

Squibs were the standard cheap fireworks, closely akin to what became known to later generations as 'bangers'.

A somewhat less alarming game was also recalled by Torre, and he comments that neither this nor the firework pastime was sanctioned by the school authorities:

> Among other after-dark amusements, Jack o' Lantern should be mentioned. This was a game for the very darkest, foggiest night, when about twenty boys, having selected one sharp fellow to carry a lantern, set out to find their way to the fields. This boy with the lantern having had a start given

In the nineteenth century the cricket ground at Harrow School was the setting for some wild celebrations on Guy Fawkes Night.

him, was to hide the light and shew it again at intervals, like a real will-o'-the-wisp, running over the wettest ditches and hedges he could find. The other boys tried to catch him in the dark. This was very exciting, and in a few hours the boys returned covered with mud and often soaked with water, which added to the amusement.

See also GUY FAWKES NIGHT, p. 338.

HARROW SCHOOL: HEADMASTER'S HOUSE

Augustus Hare (1834–1903) was a prolific writer, and published six volumes of autobiography under the title *The Story of My Life* (1896–1900), based heavily on his journals and letters. Hare was quite fond of ghost stories and other strange anecdotes, and the following is his record of what a visitor, Herman Merivale, told him in November 1871:

He was staying at Harrow, and very late at night was summoned to London. Exactly as the clock struck twelve he passed the headmaster's door in a fly. Both he and a friend who was with him were at that moment attracted by seeing a hackney-coach at the door – a most unusual sight at that time of night, and a male figure wrapped in black, descend from it and glide into the house, without, apparently, ringing, or any door being opened. He spoke of it to his friend, and they both agreed that it was equally mysterious and inexplicable. The next day, the circumstances so dwelt on Mr Merivale's mind, that he returned to Harrow, and going to the house, asked if the headmaster, Dr Butler, was at home. 'No,' said the servant. Then he asked who had come at twelve o'clock the night before. No one had come, no one had been heard of, and no carriage had been seen; but Dr Butler's father had died at just that moment in a distant county.

This is an interesting variant on the 'point-of-death wraith' story, because it is unusual for strangers to see the apparition rather than a family member. It is also worth asking why a ghost that can walk through doors needs a ghostly hackney-cab to get from place to place.

HAYES

In an interesting article on local ghosts in the Winter 1955 issue of the *Middlesex Quarterly*, the writer presents a number of stories that are not found elsewhere, including the following, which he claims is factual, the people involved being well known to him. In the late 1940s, a highly respected couple were living quietly in a house in the Hayes area. A 'gentleman from the north of England' who was staying with a friend of theirs, further up the road, suddenly asked about the couple's house and said:

> 'Is the lady big and very tall?' He was duly informed that she was rather a small woman of medium height. He looked perturbed and gravely remarked, 'Then I fear those unfortunate people are in for some serious trouble.'

He went on to explain that as he was passing their house he saw 'a very tall woman with a halo round her head', hurrying along the garden path towards the couple's front door. Within a few days both the occupants of the house were dead.

HIGH STREET, PINNER

One of the fairs to the west of London whose reputation spread beyond local boundaries was Pinner Fair, held traditionally at Whitsun, and nowadays on the Wednesday after the Spring Bank Holiday. The founding charter dates from the time of Edward III, 1336, and despite several attempts in the past to shut the fair down, it has survived to the present day and is very popular with local folk. It also attracts some 40,000 visitors each year. Uniquely in the region, the fair is held in the streets in the centre of town, with High Street and Bridge Street closed to traffic for the duration, and is proudly labelled the 'last surviving street fair in Middlesex'.

In his autobiography, *Recollections of School Days at Harrow* (1890), the Revd. Henry Torre wrote of his visits to the fair in the 1830s:

> We used to go across the fields about four miles to Pinner. There were booths and stalls in a small way. The chief attractions were roundabouts, swinging-boats, single-sticks and boxing matches; among the labourers, jumping in sacks, climbing a greased pole for a leg of mutton or a hat on the top, and last but not least in importance a dance at a public house.

For young people, one of the most popular attractions of a fair was dancing. At some there were booths where couples could dance for a small entrance fee, or so much per dance, while at others a local publican would take advantage of the gathered crowds and organise a dance in one of his rooms. These were not, of course, grand or sedate affairs, but were a rare chance for working people to let their hair down. Torre gives a sense of the ambiance:

> The dancing was in a small room, and the atmosphere, impregnated with the smell of beer and tobacco, and the noise of dancing in chaw-boots, etc., to a merry fiddle were something indescribable. Dancing continued till about midnight, when we walked back to Harrow. I remember day dawning on us before we got to our respective houses.

In a small place like Pinner, even the arrival of the fair people was exciting, and everyone would gather on the Tuesday evening before the fair to witness the 'rush-in'. A six o'clock, the police sergeant would blow his whistle and all the fair people would rush in to the High Street from the side roads and try to claim the best spots by putting a pole down in the gutter.

A contributor to a Pinner Local History Society booklet of memories, *When I was a Child* (1984), remembered one of the attractions of the inter-war fairs:

> I have clear memories of the pressure gas lamps burning with a hissing noise in the dark. We used to stay and gaze at the men and women making the humbug toffee, which was dark brown and dirty yellow. This was done by pulling a large chunk of sticky toffee into a thick snake, which was then thrown over a hook, and they pulled it down again and kept pulling it down and throwing it over the hook. We were never allowed to have any because my mother always said it was dirty, as the men before they'd do it always used to spit on their hands to stop them sticking to the toffee.

HOLLAND PARK: HOLLAND HOUSE

The public space of Holland Park was developed around the grounds of Holland House, the magnificent Jacobean mansion unfortunately largely destroyed by enemy action in the Second World War. Like any respectable building of its age, Holland House boasted a resident ghost and also a family omen in the shape of a death warning. Likable but gullible John Aubrey first reported the latter, in his book of *Miscellanies* (1696):

> The beautiful Lady Diana Rich, daughter to the Earl of Holland, as she was walking in her father's garden at Kensington, to take the fresh air before dinner, about eleven o'clock, being then very well, met with her own apparition, habit, and every thing, as in a looking-glass. About a month after, she died of the small-pox. And it is said that her sister, the Lady Isabella Thynne, saw the like of herself also, before she died. This account I had from a person of honour.

Princess Marie Liechtenstein, who wrote a history of Holland House, added a further detail, and summed it up in characteristically romantic fashion:

> A third sister, Mary, was married to the first Earl of Breadalbane, and it has been recorded that she, also, not long after her marriage, had some such warning of her approaching dissolution. And so the old tradition has remained – and who would wish to remove it? Belonging to past times, it

Holland House boasted both a resident ghost and a wraith that served as a family death warning. A magnificent Jacobean mansion, as this Victorian view shows, the house was destroyed by bombing during the Second World War.

should be respected. But whether we respect tradition or not, it is as a received fact, that whenever the mistress of Holland House meets herself, Death is hovering about her.

In English folklore, apparitions of the living, or wraiths, occur quite frequently, but they are almost always the likenesses of friends of family members who appear to loved ones as they are dying, some distance away. As modern folklorists Jennifer Westwood and Jacqueline Simpson point out in their *Lore of the Land* (2005), meeting one's own double is relatively rare in English lore, although it is better known in Ireland and Scotland. The exception, however, is in the practice of porch-watching. It was a widespread idea that if you place yourself in the church porch at midnight on a certain day of the year (which varies from version to version), you will see the wraiths of all your fellow parishioners pass before you going into church and then returning, most of them, a few minutes later. The wraiths of those who will die during the year do not come out of the church. In some versions, if the watcher sees himself, he will sicken and die within a few days.

The Holland House ghost story is also told by Princess Marie:

> And so the brilliant medal has its reverse: for now, in spite of being still sometimes filled by a joyous, laughing crowd, the Gilt Room is said to be tenanted by the solitary ghost of its first lord, who, according to tradition, issues forth at midnight from behind a secret door, and walks slowly through the scenes of former triumphs with his head in his hand. To add to this mystery, there is a tale of three spots of blood on the side of the recess whence he issues, three spots of blood which can never be effaced.

No doubt the actions of the Luftwaffe have effaced them now. The ghost is presumably that of Henry Rich, first Earl of Holland, who managed to offend both sides in the Civil War and was executed in March 1649. The story seems to have been generally known, as folklorist John Emslie's notebooks include the following note:

> *May 1875*
> Mr England, a student at Heatherley's Academy, told me that Holland House, Kensington, is said to be haunted. A Lord Holland was beheaded, and his ghost is seen walking about at night with his head carried under his arm.

HOUNSLOW

Local historian G. E. Bate included two lesser-known stories in his 1948 book *And So Make a City Here*. His informant, 'a well-known local gentleman', made the important point that ghosts, if they exist, are not necessarily terrifying creatures rattling their chains and threatening to drag mortals off to their graves, but may have lingered on earth for other perfectly reasonable motives.

The first story the gentleman told was from personal experience. He was alone one summer night in his large old house not far from Hounslow, as his family were away on holiday. The night was hot, and so he slept in a little-used bedroom on the cooler side of the house:

> About two in the morning I was curiously moved to wake and sit up in bed, then I saw someone looking at me over the foot of the bedstead. 'This is

very strange,' I thought, 'here is a ghost, a visitor to the old house, maybe, I must take all this in.' There stood the figure in a green velvet jacket, with bright buttons, a cutaway collar and white cravat. One hand was grasping the bedstead, and the face was turned towards me as if to say, 'Did you call me?' It was a finely cut face with well-chiselled features. It possessed little hair and that was white. As the face turned towards me I noticed that the eyes were missing. In the surprise of the moment I made some remark, and the figure vanished. Why did I speak? Surely if I had kept quiet something more might have been observed.

The second story was told to the gentleman by a retired policeman, and is set in a very old house on the west side of Heston and Isleworth. The house was standing empty, but being cleaned ready for new tenants, and the officer was passing by when a chimney sweep rushed out of the house and begged his help. The sweep said that he was about to sweep a chimney in a particular room when he heard a voice say, 'Don't sweep this flue.' He looked into adjoining rooms to see who had spoken, but he was alone in the house and put it down to his imagination. He started to get his brushes ready again, when the command came again: 'Don't sweep this flue.' Seriously rattled, he rushed out and met the policeman. Together they searched the house, including cupboards and cellars, but no one was there. The constable laughed at the sweep and left him to carry on, but he made sure not to sweep that particular chimney.

One other story included by Bate is a well-developed ghost tale, nicely told. It was related to him by a friend who had moved into the remaining part of a much larger establishment, built in early Tudor times, near Hounslow. In the back of the premises was an old door, fastened with a wooden bar that

Chimney sweeps figure prominently in English folklore. In one story, told about an old house in Hounslow, a sweep becomes seriously alarmed when a spectral voice addresses him from a chimney flue.

fitted into slots on either side. Each night the new owner fastened the door, and each morning it was found unlocked. A local shopkeeper informed him that the house was reputed to be haunted, and a previous caretaker had mentioned having similar problems with the same door. They had taken on a young country girl as a servant, and returning home one evening found her standing in front of the house, too frightened to go in because of the 'man in black, who had come across the garden from the summer house'. Bate writes:

> One evening, the wife went into the garden with the dog. The dog generally bounded round the garden but this evening it stopped short, and ran behind her whining, its tail down and hair bristling. She turned and spoke to it, and as she did so she heard a slight rustling like the sound of dry leaves being moved by the wind. Looking up she saw a figure gliding across the lawn. It was dressed in a black cassock and had a black pointed hood drawn over its face so that no features were visible . . .

The figure was seen again, taking the same route, and neighbours confirmed that they too had encountered it in the past. Ghostly footsteps were also heard in the house, and the dog often showed signs of fear and distress. The house has now been demolished, and the ghost has not been seen since.

HOUNSLOW HEATH

Like many other places on the key routes out of London, Hounslow owed its prosperity in the eighteenth century to the carriage trade, but travellers to and from the west had to cross the extensive wild country between Hounslow and Staines, known as Hounslow Heath, which was originally part of the extensive Forest of Staines. The Heath comprised over 4,000 acres of wild country, and became legendary as the haunt of highwaymen and was lined with gibbets, on which the bodies of executed criminals were left to rot. As early as the mid sixteenth century, Henry Machyn noted in his diary:

> *The 21st day of December* [1552]
> Rode to Tyburn to be hanged for a robbery done on Hounslow Heath, 3 tall men and a lacquey.

The danger of crossing the heath was not exaggerated, but the exploits and characters of the individual highwaymen certainly were, and conformed to the prevalent notion of them as 'gentlemen of the road', as perpetuated in countless chapbooks and popular novels. The roll-call of well-known robbers who frequented the heath included pickpocket-turned-highwayman John Cottington, who specialised in robbing Roundheads, as he was a staunch Royalist; the cross-dressing Mary Frith, or Moll Cutpurse, as she was more famously called; Captain Dick Dudley; and Claude Duval, who reputedly danced a coranto with a lady whose carriage his gang had held up.

The highwaymen did not always have everything their own way, and there were several tales and ballads that tell of highwaymen being outwitted. One, given in Patrick Pringle's history of highwaymen, *Stand and Deliver* (1991), concerns a tailor who was challenged to hand over his money while crossing the heath. The tailor replied, 'I'll do that with pleasure, but suppose you do me a favour in return? My friends would laugh at me were I to go home and tell them I was robbed with as much patience as a lamb; suppose you fire your two bull-dogs through the crown of my hat and it will then look like a show of resistance.' The request seemed reasonable enough, and the highwayman fired both his pistols at the tailor's hat. Whereupon the tailor promptly produced a pistol of his own, and the highwayman rode off without making any further demands.

Where there is a heath, there must be DICK TURPIN (p. 162), and there are many unsubstantiated stories of his activities, as for example a local tradition recorded by Middlesex folklorist John Emslie in 1874:

> It is said that in the grounds of the powder mills at Mount Corner, Hounslow, there used to be a cave in which Dick Turpin often hid himself.

Indeed, even in Turpin's own lifetime (1705?–1739) people were aware of his legendary status, as a newspaper report from 1737, quoted by James Sharpe in his biography of Turpin, makes clear:

> On Tuesday 10 May, a single highwayman robbed four coaches and several passengers at different times on Hounslow Heath and they gave out it was Turpin, but that fellow having done so much mischief of late, runs in everybody's head.

It was taken for granted that the keepers of the many inns and taverns that served the area were in league with the highwaymen and kept them

One of the notorious highwaymen of Hounslow Heath.

informed of travellers' plans. The Green Man at Hatton, for example, was reputed to have a secret hiding place behind the fireplace in the parlour, and the landlord also provided safe-storage for valuables.

Numerous other stories are told of the highwaymen of Hounslow, many of which have legendary characteristics or connections. An excellent source of this type of material is Gordon Maxwell's *Highwayman's Heath* (1935), from which the following three pieces are taken. The first he gathered from 'an anonymous writer in an old magazine'. At some distance from the main road across the heath stood an old farmhouse or inn, which was reputed to have been a highwayman's hideout, and to have a resident highwayman-ghost:

> When it was demolished, cunningly placed behind the panelling was a cavity wall, which, when opened, showed a gruesome sight. Propped up against the wall, half sitting, half kneeling, was the skeleton of a man dressed in the riding attire of about 1780, with a pistol in his belt and another on the floor by him. The latter had been discharged, and part of the man's skull was blown away. Fallen from the pocket of his now rotten coat were two gold watches, some rings, and a score of guineas dated 1776.

Maxwell's next story is based on a news report from 1766, concerning the Bath–London stage. Two heavily veiled females had taken outside places, and as they climbed aboard were observed to be wearing men's boots and britches underneath their dresses. Taken into custody, they explained that far from being criminals in disguise, they were travellers carrying large sums of money, and thought that their clothes would fool any highwaymen into thinking they were simply poor women.

Maxwell quotes the third story from F. E. Baines's *On the Track of the Mail Coach* (1895):

A man who bought a horse cheap in London. When he was returning home over Hounslow Heath all went well until he observed another horseman approaching. His horse at once sidled up to the newcomer as though he would ride him down, and behaved in so menacing a way that the stranger promptly produced his purse. Explanations and apologies followed. Soon a post-chaise drew near; again the sidling process was gone through. Now, however, blunderbusses were thrust through the window and threats were used that if the alarmed robber did not draw off the inmates would fire at him. At Colnbrook the rider sold the horse, not wishing further to own a steed so well acquainted with the habits of the knights of the road.

These last two tales seem to be forerunners of modern contemporary legends, which often have motifs of men disguised as women, and of second-hand motor cars bought cheaply because they have some nefarious history.

KENSINGTON

C. G. Harper relates a neat ghost story in his *Haunted Houses* (1924), which he claims had been a cause célèbre in December 1913, and he adds the delicious comment that it is 'probably the first appearance of a taxicab as a spectral adjunct'.

> The vicar of a Kensington church was leaving the church after choir practice when a lady stepped out of the aisle and asked him in agitated tones to come with her at once to an address near by. 'A gentleman is dying there,' she said. 'He is extremely concerned about the state of his soul and anxious to see you before he dies.'

They went to the house in the taxicab she had waiting, and the vicar knocked on the door. The butler who answered denied that there was anyone ill in the house.

'But this lady,' exclaimed the vicar, as he turned round, and then an expression of blank astonishment came over him. *The taxicab and the lady had completely vanished.*

Dick Turpin

Of all the historical figures who have achieved lasting fame in traditional legends, Dick Turpin is easily the most popular. Numerous places around London boast cottages and inns where he hid from the authorities, or places where he plied his trade, or toll-gates over which Black Bess leapt so valiantly on the way to York.

The real Turpin was born in Hempstead, Essex, probably in 1705, and started out as a butcher's apprentice. By 1735 he was involved in deer-stealing in Epping Forest, and two years later was committing highway robbery and horse theft. Turpin took up with fellow highwayman Matthew King, and their meeting itself became part of the legend. According to the chapbook *The Life and Adventures of Dick Turpin*, printed by James Catnach around 1820:

> King, the highwayman, as he was returning ... to London, being well dressed and mounted, Turpin seeing him have the appearance of a substantial gentleman ... bid him stand and deliver, and therewith producing his pistols, King fell a-laughing at him, and said, 'What dog rob dog! Come, come brother Turpin, if you don't know me, I know you, and should be glad of your company.'

Their joint career was short-lived, and they were ambushed by the authorities at the Red Lion in Whitechapel. In the resulting fracas, King was mortally wounded, and again the chapbook describes a heroic moment:

> ... before King could get fairly seated [on his horse] he was seized by one of the party, and called on Dick to fire. Turpin replied, 'If I do, I shall hit you.' 'Fire, if you are my friend,' said King, but the ill-fated ball took fatal effect in King's breast. Dick stood a moment in grief but self-preservation made him urge his mare forward to elude his pursuers.

Turpin was by that time too well known to operate around London, and he was next heard of in Yorkshire, under the name of Samuel Palmer.

The final act in this real-life drama is anything but heroic, and shows him to be either too confident or just plain stupid. Returning from a hunt, presumably the worse for drink, he shot a neighbour's cockerel and threatened to shoot the man too. Arrested for disturbing the peace, he refused to provide sureties for future good behaviour and was therefore kept in custody, where he was soon identified and then tried. He was executed at York on 7 April 1739.

As was common for well-known criminals, his execution was attended by a vast crowd, and they were pleased that he died a 'valiant death'. His life was

Real-life criminal Dick Turpin was a favourite of nineteenth-century chapbooks, particularly following the publication in 1834 of *Rookwood* by William Harrison Ainsworth, a novel that romanticised the life of highwaymen, styling them as 'gentlemen of the road'.

soon written up by chapbook printers, but it would be nearly another century before he became the most famous highwayman of all time, with the publication of the historical novel *Rookwood*, by William Harrison Ainsworth, in 1834. Ainsworth also wrote the life of another celebrity criminal, *Jack Sheppard* (1839), and these 'Newgate novels' were immensely popular, but came in for great criticism for romanticising dangerous outlaws.

In *Rookwood*, Ainsworth provided the central escapade of the Turpin legend: the exciting ride to York and the pathos of the death of the ever-faithful Black Bess, which proved so popular that it was turned into innumerable circus acts, pantomimes, children's books, and so on. In Thomas Hardy's *Far from the Madding Crowd* (1874), for example, two of his countryfolk characters, Jan Coggan and Joseph Poorgrass, enjoy a spirited performance of 'The Royal Hippodrome Performance of Turpin's Ride to York and the Death of Black Bess', in a tent at their local sheep fair.

In fact, the story of the prodigious ride to York had previously been attached to several other highwaymen, most notably William Nevison (d. 1684). It was Ainsworth who set not only the legend for Turpin himself, but also the romanticised template for all sorts of highwaymen that is still current today. Instead of the ruthless, violent criminals that the real men were, Ainsworth's highwaymen were 'gentlemen of the road'.

See also HOUNSLOW HEATH, p. 158; PARLIAMENT SQUARE, p. 97; SPANIARDS ROAD, CAMDEN: THE SPANIARDS PUB, p. 247; WANSTEAD PLACE: ST MARY'S CHURCH, p. 304.

The man in question then came to door, and invited the vicar inside. He said that he was not ill, but strangely enough he had lately been struggling with spiritual questions and had been contemplating calling in some aid. The vicar stayed and they enjoyed a fruitful discussion, agreeing to continue the following day. When the man failed to attend church the next day, the vicar returned to the house, where the butler sadly explained that his master had died a mere ten minutes after the vicar had left the night before.

> They went upstairs to the bedroom where the dead man lay, and on a table in the middle of the room stood a portrait of the lady who had brought the clergyman in the cab from the church. 'Who is that?' asked the astonished clergyman. 'That, sir,' replied the butler, 'is my master's wife, who died fifteen years ago.'

Kensington inhabitants – and ghosts – may often be well-heeled enough to have butlers and ride in taxicabs, but they are not above the odd superstition. Two interesting examples of superstitions to do with houses were noted in Kensington and submitted to the journal *Folk-Lore* in 1928:

> In the block of flats where I live, in Kensington, the numbers run from twelve to fourteen, thirteen being eliminated. I find both respectable, intelligent hall-porters very unwilling to answer any questions about this, or to allude to the subject in any way. In a well-known street in Knightsbridge my cousins tried for more than a year to dispose of a desirable flat, numbered 13. A friend advised them to change the number to 12a. This was done; enquiries followed almost immediately, and the flat found a new tenant within months . . . I was going down the lowest stairs in this block (in Kensington) when a girl, who had turned in quickly from the street and begun to come up, suddenly jumped back and stood at the foot of the stairs. I thanked her in passing, and suggested that there might have been room for us both, but she replied, 'Yes! But it is unlucky to cross another on the stairs.'

Both of these superstitions are still current.

KILBURN

On 26 January 1873, London folklorist John Emslie collected the following astonishing piece of folk etymology:

> Kilburn received its name because the Catholics used to kill and burn so many people there. The Priory was held by 200 Protestants against a large number of Catholics; a Catholic gentlemen had a house at Kingsbury, the Catholics assembled there, and fought all the way from there to Kilburn, where they were beaten in an attempt to storm the place. There was a battle fought at Mary-le-bone.

Needless to say, the derivation of Kilburn is not so exciting as this, although the *Place-Names of Middlesex* (1942) cannot quite decide between 'royal stream', or 'Cylla's stream'.

Kilburn was home to John Pocock, who was born in 1814, and kept a diary for a short time, which includes a number of references to local folklore:

1 May 1828
Chimney sweepers day, plenty of Jacks in the Green like myself

2 May 1828
Sweepers drumming all over town today

Not only do these references show that the Jack-in-the-Green was active in the Kilburn area at the time, but that there was more than one team around. His comment 'like myself' is explained by the entry for 8 March 1828: 'Clerks gave me the name of "Jack in the Green" from my dashing green surtout.'

The previous year he had written:

27 March 1827
Dreamed last night I shall not live a week, arose in good spirits at so good an omen.

It has long been a widely held superstition that dreams 'go by opposites'. And finally:

4 September 1828
... continued along the river until we came up to the Grand Junction Canal

... and I do not remember seeing anything so dark and terrible as the water just here. Like my mother, who, it is prophesied, will be drowned, I also have an instinctive horror of water.

John Pocock's fascinating diary was finally published as *Travels of a London Schoolboy 1826–1830*.

See also MAY DAY IN LONDON, p. 318.

KING'S ROAD, CHELSEA

One of the best evocations of growing up poor in London in the 1920s is Rose Gamble's *Chelsea Child* (1979). Rose lived in a street between the King's Road and the Embankment, and her superb eye for detail, excellent memory, and affectionate humour make the whole account a joy to read. The chapter on superstitions, in particular, reveals a small corner of the world of traditional lore that surrounded most working-class children of the time:

> We were intensely superstitious, and it is hardly surprising that much of the nonsense in which we unquestionably believed was concerned with sickness, dying, death, misfortune, and downright disaster. It was not a rare occurrence, particularly near the stall at the top of our street or in the Fulham Market, to see a cut flower lying on the ground, and if one of the younger children went to touch it, the rest of us dragged him back gasping, 'Pick up a flower, pick up a fever!' On the other hand, if something edible was similarly abandoned and you had the good fortune to pounce on it before anyone else, you could justifiably eat it as long as you first said the protective words, 'Waste not, want not, pick it up and eat it.'
>
> To tread deliberately on the cracks between paving stones would bring an accident and should two knives lie in a crossed position there would certainly be a row. A dropped spoon meant bad news or an unwelcome visitor, and at the first sign of a thunderstorm, Mum had taught us to cover up the looking-glass and the water jug with cloths. Bad luck and tragedies had to be tidied up for Mum by running in threes ... If we saw an ambulance or even heard its distant bell ring, we clawed dramatically at our throats, licked our fingers, and touched the ground, gabbling, 'Touch collar, never swaller, never get the fever.'

According to one resident of Kilburn in the early nineteenth century, May Day was marked locally by celebrations that included appearances by teams of 'Jacks-in-the-Green' – a Jack-in-the-Green being a person (often a chimney sweep) covered in leaves.

None of these can be said to be London superstitions in that they were exclusive to the area, and in fact they were all quite well known elsewhere in the country, but they are typical of what was said all over the city at that time. No one has come up with a genuine reason to explain why children dreaded picking up a flower, although it has been suggested that for urban working-class children, the only cut flowers they saw were at hospitals or in graveyards. Similarly, the reasoning behind 'don't step on the cracks' is elusive, although it is still current among some children. The symbolism of crossed knives (i.e. swords) is quite obvious; and dropped cutlery was usually taken to mean an unexpected visitor – some said a dropped knife meant a man, a fork a woman, and a spoon a child. It was widely thought that any shiny surface attracted lightning, so mirrors, silver utensils, and so on would be covered up to protect the house in a storm. Bad luck coming in threes is still regularly quoted, and some people, on breaking something, will deliberately destroy two other worthless items to break the spell. The 'touch collar' belief was also said about funerals, and it is possible that the gesture was in imitation of the adult custom of taking off the hat and holding it across the chest as a mark of respect when a funeral went by.

A little later in the book, Rose and her brother are in hospital, and Rose's life is ''angin' by a fread'. Older sister Lu was sent each day to get news. Sitting in the waiting room gazing at a bizarre tableau of stuffed birds illustrating the rhyme 'Who Killed Cock Robin', Lu did what many people do in a situation of worry: she made up her own, temporary, superstition:

> She counted the birds again this time with intent. 'If it's the same number,' she said to herself, 'they're still all right. If there's more birds, they're better, and if there's less, they're worse.' She counted and only numbered thirty. 'They are going to be worse. I'll count again.' She did so, searching the leafless bushes for an extra bird. 'Twenty-nine, thirty, thirty-one. It's all right! They'll be all right, an' I didn't cheat.'

And they were.

KINGSBURY

Explanations of the origins of place-names are often very literal, so it is not surprising that the belief that kings were buried at Kingsbury has circulated for some time.

John Emslie, collecting in the area in the early 1870s, found that the idea of kings being buried at Kingsbury was widespread, along with other seemingly connected traditions:

> *17 December 1871*
> Some youths told me of the existence, before the memory of any living person, of houses around Kingsbury Church. One man told me that 'they say' that three or four kings were buried at Kingsbury. A monument (he was doubtful whether of one of these kings) was formerly in the floor of the church, and is now set up in its wall; it is said that there are very few older churches in England.

> *31 December 1871*
> I was talking to a man at Bush Farm, Kingsbury; he confirmed what I had heard on December 17th, and said that there were many houses at Kingsbury; kings had been buried there, 'that's why it's called Kingsbury'; a battle had been fought there in olden time, but he knew nothing about it.

31 August 1873

Seven kings were buried in one day at Kingsbury; in the time when there was a king in every parish, or county. A king is buried at Belmont.

7 September 1873

An old man at Kingsbury Green told me how to lay a ghost. Twelve persons and one priest meet at a certain time, and sit round a table in the room that it haunted; they wait until the spirit comes, and they then draw a 'circuit' round it; the spirit cannot get out of this, and it is then banished to some particular spot, a cupboard, for instance, from whence it can never issue. The same men supposed that the seven kings buried at Kingsbury were probably 'kings of counties' in the reign of William the Conqueror, that fought in one of the many battles that have been fought here, and were all killed together.

These extracts were published in *London Studies* (1974). Traditions about the origins of a place-name are almost always very wide of the mark, because they are based on the modern version of the name, rather than the earliest known forms. It is obvious here that the original was 'King's Burgh', or manor, and has nothing to do with being *buried*.

QUEEN CAROLINE STREET, HAMMERSMITH: ST PAUL'S CHURCHYARD

In July 1955, a reporter with the *West London Observer* claimed that there was a ghost that appeared in St Paul's churchyard every fifty years, and it had last been seen in 1905. He declared his intention of spending the night in the churchyard, but this unfortunately brought a few hundred spectators to the spot, whom the police had trouble controlling. When nothing happened at midnight, most of the crowd drifted away, but the ghost was clearly unaware of British Summer Time, because an hour later a bright white figure duly appeared and floated from the church porch to a particular tomb, into which it vanished. Several witnesses confirmed the story.

ROYAL HOSPITAL, CHELSEA

The Royal Hospital, Chelsea, was founded in 1682 by Charles II, 'for the relief of such land soldiers as are, or shall be, old, lame, or infirm in the service of the crown'. In *Old & New London* (1877), Edward Walford and Walter Thornbury write:

> According to popular tradition, the first idea of converting it into an asylum for broken-down soldiers sprang from the charitable heart of Nell Gwynne, the frail actress, with whom, for all her frailties, the English people can never be angry. As the story goes, a wounded and destitute soldier hobbled up to Nellie's coach-window to ask alms, and the kind-hearted woman was so pained to see a man who had fought for his country begging his bread in the street that she prevailed upon Charles II to establish at Chelsea a permanent home for military invalids.

However, the more prosaic explanation is that Charles was probably inspired by the Hotel des Invalides in Paris, founded by Louis XIV in 1670. The legend of Nell Gwynne was already in circulation when Daniel Lysons published his *Environs of London* in 1795, and he noted that a nearby pub had her portrait as its sign and an inscription detailing the story.

In modern times, the Chelsea Pensioners add to the pageantry of London when they attend events in their bright red coats and tricorn hats. This is their dress uniform, based on the army uniform of the early eighteenth century, and it is worn on special occasions and also if venturing more than a mile from the Hospital.

But their own major celebration is the Founder's Day parade on 29 May (or thereabouts), which was Charles II's birthday and also the day on which he returned to London to take up the throne at the Restoration. Declared a day of celebration in his honour, 29 May became part of the traditional English calendar, known as Royal Oak Day, or Oak Apple Day, to commemorate the tradition that Charles had escaped from Parliamentary forces after the Battle of Worcester in 1651 by hiding in an oak tree.

The day's accepted symbol is, unsurprisingly, an oak leaf, and on Founder's Day the pensioners and guests wear sprigs of these leaves, and the impressive statue of Charles is wreathed in oak branches. A visiting dignitary, sometimes a member of the royal family, stands under the statue

According to popular tradition, the idea of setting up a hospital for old or infirm soldiers in Chelsea came from Charles II's mistress Nell Gwynne, who was moved by the plight of a wounded and destitute soldier she encountered.

to review the pensioners who march smartly past, and they give three cheers for 'our pious founder' and for the reigning monarch.

ROXETH HILL, HARROW: ROXETH FIRST AND MIDDLE SCHOOLS

Harrow seems to specialise in ghosts of domestic animals, if the feature published in the *Harrow Observer* on 12 September 1980 is anything to go by. At Roxeth First and Middle Schools, Roxeth Hill, for example, a former teacher at the school, Mrs Jennifer May, reported an incident that had occurred there in the mid 1960s:

'There was a little house attached to the infants' section which used to be the mistress' house,' said Mrs May. 'At this time it was used as a staff building.

Both the secretary and the welfare worker said they had seen a ginger cat there. The cat was supposed to be the ghost of a teacher who lived there a long time before. Mr Yates, who was then headmaster, said it was all nonsense, and quite untrue. Then, one day, he saw the cat shoot up the stairs. He said it was a very dilapidated looking animal. Mr Yates tore up after it, and when it went into the stock room, he followed and closed the door. He hunted and hunted, but couldn't find it. After that he felt convinced it was a ghost.'

The other animal is a ghost dog in Bentley Priory, an eighteenth-century house at Stanmore. The building also has a lady ghost in a green dress, but in 1976 a dog was heard barking in the dining room, even though there were no animals in the house. It has been claimed that this is the ghost of an Alsatian who died in the house during the Second World War, but no evidence is given for this.

Psychic researcher Dr Nandor Fodor was quite convinced that animal spirits have existed and he quotes several examples, including one from his own experience, in his *Between Two Worlds* (1964). He also maintained that telepathic links between loved pets and owners is quite common.

RUISLIP

Walter Druett includes a passing reference to Ruislip in his book *Harrow Through the Ages* (1956), although unfortunately he does not name his source:

It is recorded in 1576 that the citizens of Ruislip assembled 'with unknown malefactors and unlawfully played a game called footeball by reason of which there arose among them a great affray, likely to result in homicides and serious accidents'.

'Football' in the sixteenth century bore little resemblance to the organised game we know today. It was played in the streets of towns, or in neighbouring fields, and anyone could join in. The 'goals' could literally be miles apart. There were few, if any, rules, the ball could be kicked, thrown, carried, or even hidden, and there was usually very little restriction on how much violence players could inflict on each other.

See also KINGSTON-UPON-THAMES, p. 393.

South Kensington

A story that appeared in the article 'Is it Possible?' in the magazine *All the Year Round* on 22 June 1867 took place 'in one of the large and fashionable mansions in the district of South Kensington':

> On the first night of their occupation, the lady of the house, while arranging her hair at the glass, saw in the latter the reflection of the figure of a man. He was old, of strange appearance, and was seated in an arm-chair, that stood near her bed. He wore a grey coat with a cape, and had spectacles. The lady possessed strong nerves, and after the first moment of surprise, finding that the spectre did not disappear, came to the conclusion that her vision was affected by some disarrangement in the system. Resolved to test it, she turned calmly round, walked straight to the mysterious object, and sat down upon its very knees! She found herself alone in the chair.

The next morning she related the story to her doctor, who listened with seriousness rather than the mirth she expected. He claimed that her description of the ghostly figure identified him as a close neighbour who had been found dead, probably murdered, the night before.

Sutton Lane, Chiswick: Sutton Court-house

Like many places in London, Chiswick has seen a poltergeist disturbance, as reported in *The Times* on 16 September 1841:

> Singular occurrence at Chiswick: Since Saturday last the family and establishment of a lady named Churton, residing at Sutton Court-house, Sutton Lane, Chiswick, leading to the banks of the Thames at Strand-on-the-Green, have been in a continued state of alarm and excitement by the windows of the mansion being continually broken by some unknown agent, every method adopted for detecting the party guilty of the outrage failing in its object. The mansion in question is a detached one, with extensive grounds around it, the whole of which are encircled with high walls, so that the roof alone is visible from the outside. On the opposite side of the lane is also another high wall, which surrounds the domain of the Duke of Devonshire, so that no other

building overlooks the premises. The breaking of the windows first commenced on Saturday last, and in consequence of the continuance of the outrage application was made to the police. Since then two constables of the T division have been placed on duty in the house and premises night and day, and with the assistance of the gardener, coachman, butler, and other male servants, a continued watch has been kept up, but without preventing the outrage, or obtaining any clue as to the perpetrators thereof. From half past 12 to 1 o'clock yesterday morning several were broken, and from the fact of their being broken at the front as well as the back of the house, the matter has become more mysterious. It is to be hoped for the quiet of the neighbourhood that the police will detect the perpetrators of the outrage, and that they will receive the punishment they deserve.

See also BEVERSTONE ROAD, THORNTON HEATH, p. 174; BRIMSDOWN, ENFIELD, p. 196; CHELSEA, p. 138; GROVE PARK: ALLOTMENTS, p. 333; PLAISTOW, p. 293; REVERDY ROAD, BERMONDSEY: NOS 56 AND 58, p. 342; STOCKWELL, p. 414.

SYDNEY STREET, CHELSEA: ST LUKE'S CHURCH

Indications of Chelsea's village past are included in extracts of the churchwardens' accounts of St Luke's parish church, published in Daniel Lysons' *Environs of London: Middlesex* (1795):

1606 Of the good wives their hocking money 53 shillings
1607 Of the women that went a hocking 45 shillings
1611 Received of Robert Munden that the men did get by hocking 10 shillings

Hocktide is the Monday and Tuesday after Easter, a time when people went 'hocking' or 'binding', which was a way of collecting money for the church . On one of the days, the women would capture with ropes any men they met in the street, and only release them on payment of a small fine. On the other day, the men would capture the women.

1670 Spent at the perambulation dinner £3 10s
Given to the boys that were whipped 4s
Paid for points for the boys 2s

The 'perambulation' was the annual BEATING THE BOUNDS (p. 370), in which local officials and parishioners walked around the parish boundary to ensure that no one had interfered with boundary markers, encroached upon parish land, or erected any building without permission. A gala day was made of the event, with feasting, drinking, and sermons and hymns at key points. Before the era of reliable maps, it was essential that young people in the parish were made to remember where the boundary markers were situated, and various traditional methods were adopted to ensure this. Boys were 'bumped' on stones, turned upside down and 'whipped' with flexible willow rods. In many cases, it was the markers that were thrashed with the rods. 'Points' were decorative laces given to the boys as mementoes.

TURNHAM GREEN

One of the most widespread of traditional calendar customs across Britain was the mumming play, with something like 2,000 different places known to have had their own team at some time between 1800 and 1939. The mummers' natural habitat seems to have been the country village, although many towns also had teams and, as mummers were peripatetic and covered a wide circle around their homes each year, it is quite possible that some of them penetrated inner London. The nearest documented sighting to the centre is in Hammersmith, but there were plenty of teams on the Middlesex side of Greater London, and a handful in the metropolitan areas of the other neighbouring counties, such as Barnet and Croydon.

In other parts of the country, plays were performed at Easter, Hallowe'en or Plough Monday (the first Monday after Twelfth Day, 6 January), but in the South-east it was invariably a Christmas custom, usually taking place over the whole season, and most teams spent several days tramping the neighbourhood. Performances were given at 'big houses' (by appointment), but also in pubs and sometimes in the open air in the street or on the village green, and the motives of the performers were to provide entertainment and be paid – in money, food or drink, or preferably all three.

Of the thousands of examples documented in Britain, no two were exactly the same, and each team would have its own particular version of text, costume, and performance, although there were definite regional patterns, and it must be said that the similarities across the country were far more striking than the differences.

The men dressed in strange costumes, often made of colourful strips of paper, ribbon, or rag, which completely covered their bodies from head to foot. Standard characters were Father Christmas, King or St George, a Turkish knight, a doctor, and a number of supernumeraries, such as Little Johnny Jack or Beelzebub, who contributed little or nothing to the action. Because the individual characters were not distinguished by costume, they had to rely on their spoken words to identify themselves; each one introducing himself with a line such as 'In comes I, King George', and often ending by introducing the next, 'Step in Turkish Knight and clear the way'. In the core of the action, two or more 'knights' have a sword fight, and one is killed or wounded. The doctor is called, who, with some topsy-turvy humour, cures the knight, and the men then appeal to their audience for money, or Christmas fare.

> Roast beef, plum pudding and mince pie
> Who likes that any better than I?

Most teams would also entertain the onlookers with a song or two after the play.

Traditional mumming performances unlike anything seen today. They were not performed like a pantomime or melodrama with audience participation, nor were they played for laughs or full of ad-libbed jokes, but were taken quite seriously, if somewhat perfunctorily. For most of the play, the performers remained rigidly upright, and their movements were highly stylised, almost wooden, with a great deal of pacing backwards and forwards. Even the sword fight was underplayed and could be little more than a few clashes of wooden swords after which one man would fall, or even simply drop to one knee. The text is couched in rhymed mock-heroic couplets, and was declaimed in a similarly stilted and non-realistic manner.

The origins of the mumming plays are still unclear, but it is now well established that some form of 'literary' play of the mid-eighteenth century is at their root, rather than an ancient pagan ritual.

G. W. Septimus Piesse contributed the following to *Notes and Queries* in December 1860:

The Mummers

About this time every year the inhabitants of Chiswick, Turnham Green, and the neighbourhood are entertained (?) with a queer sort of performance by a set of boys calling themselves 'the Mummers'. They dress in masks, and bedizen themselves in coloured ribbon and paper, then go from shop to tavern reciting the following jumble. I can remember it as an annual festival gradually degenerating for twenty years past, and the oldest inhabitants of Chiswick say, 'It's nothing now to what it used to be.'

> *Enter Girl, with a broom*
> A room! a room! pray guard us all
> Give us room to rise and fall
> We come here to show you activity
>
> *Enter Boy*
> In comes I, Swiff Swash and Swagger
> With my gold-laced hat and dagger
> Once I courted a damsel
> She's often in my mind
> But now, alas! she's proved unkind.
>
> *Enter Second Boy*
> In comes I, King George, with my spear
> Once I gained three golden crowns
> As true as I was drawn through the slaughter
> I also won the King of Egypt's daughter.
>
> *Enter Third Boy*
> I plainly see you are a king
> My sword it points, Alonso unto thee
> A battle! a battle! between you and I
> Let's see which on the earth shall lie.
>
> *They fight and the king is slain. They all shout*
> A doctor! A doctor!
>
> *Enter a Doctor*
> Is there a doctor to be found
> To cure this man bleeding on the ground?
> Oh! yes, there is a doctor to be found
> And I am he, can cure him safe and sound.

They all shout
What can you cure?

Doctor
I can cure the hitch, the stitch, the palsy, and the gout
Pains within and pains without
Bring me an old woman that's been dead ten years
And nine years in her grave
If she can crack me one of my pills between her nose and chin
I'll forfeit two thousand pounds if I don't bring her to life again.

The Doctor then administers to the king, saying
I'll give him a drop of my triple distill
I'll warrant he'll soon fight again.

The king rises. Enter Lord Grubb
In comes Lord Grubb
On my shoulder I carry my club
Under my chin my dripping pan
Now don't you think I'm a handsome man

Finale: music and dancing.

One or two points should be made about this interesting version. Piesse uses the word 'boys', although it is quite possible that the performers were youths, as was common elsewhere. In Lancashire, and neighbouring counties, there was a strong tradition of children's teams, but this was not the norm in the South-east. Similarly, he mentions a girl; it was virtually unheard of for females to take part in mummers' plays (again, except for the children's teams in Lancashire), and it is likely that this character was actually a 'man-woman', that is, a male dressed as a female, which was a very common practice.

In comparison to other versions, this text is cut down almost to its bare bones, and bears signs of words and sections being misunderstood, which again is not uncommon. Lord Grubb, for example, speaks the lines usually associated with the character called Beelzebub. It is interesting to note that another correspondent to *Notes and Queries*, in 1874, wrote of seeing a party of mummers in Hammersmith and Chiswick, and provided another verse, spoken at the end of the performance:

Here comes Old Father Christmas
Who has but a short time to stay
I hope you'll think of Old Father Christmas
Before he goes away.

WATLING STREET, STANMORE

In the north of the borough of Harrow, around Stanmore, there are various traditions concerning Romans and Britons. According to earlier writers, for example, there is a lost Roman city, full of treasure, somewhere along Watling Street, the Roman road that runs direct from London to St Albans. Some believe that it was sited at Brockley Hill and use the nearby Sulloniacae settlement, just on the east side of the street, to back up this claim. A short distance to the west is Stanmore Common, the site of a battle between Caesar's forces and those of the Catuvellauni in 54 BC, and which still boasts a 'Caesar's Pond'. The common is also claimed by some as the place where Boudicca's final defeat took place, and a mound in the grounds of nearby Lime's House is a reputed Boudicca's grave.

See also BOUDICCA'S GRAVES, p. 180.

WHITCHURCH LANE, CANONS PARK

Folklorist John Emslie noted the following from a labouring man in January 1873, later published in *London Studies* (1974). The man stated that the ability to see ghosts depended on a person's time of birth, or his having an intimate connection with the deceased.

> He had never seen a ghost until about two months back, when, passing along the lane from Kenton to Whitchurch, he heard a sound like footsteps, and, looking to the right, at a distance of about two yards, distinctly saw a friend of his, a faint light showed him, all around was dark; he knew that his friend was ill, and far away; and next morning received a letter announcing the death of his friend in the night.

Boudicca's Graves

Little is known about Boudicca's life, which perhaps explains why she is constantly reinvented in British folklore. This seventeenth-century engraving shows her in heroic mode, defending not only her country but also her daughter's honour.

Little is known of Boudicca's real life. She was the wife of Prasutagus, King of the Iceni, the British tribe that occupied what is now Norfolk and parts of Cambridgeshire and Suffolk. She led a rebellion against Roman rule in AD 60/61, which was briefly successful before she was defeated by Suetonius' troops. Following the rout, she probably committed suicide by poison. Most of what we know of these events has been supplied by two Roman writers, Tacitus and Cassius Dio, but if history is written by the victors, legend is at the service of the vanquished, and it is often the case that legends provide the more memorable stories. Boudicca survives in British folklore as the Warrior Queen, and one of the most persistent strands of her legacy is the ongoing speculation about where her last battle took place and where her grave is to be found.

In late Victorian times, there was a strong tradition that she was buried in a round barrow on Parliament Hill. The site was investigated by Charles H. Read for the London County Council and his findings were written up in the *Proceedings of the Society of Antiquaries* (1894). He was able to show that the mound, though man-made, long pre-dated Boudicca's time and so could not have been her grave. He also argued persuasively that it was most unlikely that the Romans would have allowed such a splendid grave to have been built for a despised rebel leader, particularly so close to the city she had destroyed.

Another persistent rumour arose in the 1940s and maintains that her grave lies beneath Platform 10 of King's Cross Station. This idea comes from the fact that the station is built on the site of a hamlet called Battle Bridge, which because of its name has been assumed to be the site of Boudicca's last stand. An investigation of the place-name, however, shows that the earliest known reference to 'Battle Bridge' is as late as 1559, and it seems to have been a simple corruption of the earlier form 'Bradford Bridge', which derives from a 'broad ford'.

As we know so little of the real Boudicca, she can be easily remodelled to suit the fashions of each age. She was all the rage in Elizabeth I's time, out of favour in the male-dominated Commonwealth, romantically popular after the publication of William Cowper's 'Boadicea: An Ode' in 1782, and again captured the public imagination during Victoria's reign, to the extent that in 1902 an impressive statue by Thomas Thorneycroft was erected to her memory on the Victoria Embankment by Westminster Bridge. The suffragettes held her up as an example and in the later twentieth century she again became a feminist icon, while at the same time being effortlessly incorporated into the largely spurious Celtophilia of New Age writers.

But it helps to have a selective memory when choosing national heroes from the remote past, and Boudicca's history is not untainted. As a rebel leader her initial success was brief and against relatively ill-prepared troops. If the Roman writers are to be believed, her people were particularly barbaric, slaughtering not just the Roman 'invaders' but also Britons by the tens of thousands. The Iceni looted and burned down the commercial and cultural centres of Colchester, St Albans, and London. In their one battle with the enemy, they lost ignominiously, despite their vast numerical supremacy, and in direct consequence of these actions, tribal lands were laid waste by the victors, and the tribe 'enslaved' to a much higher degree than ever before. Not much glory there.

Yet for some it is enough that she stood for 'British liberty' against a foreign tyrant. Writing in his book *Legendary London* (1937), for example, Lewis Spence stands in reverence before Boudicca's statue:

> For centuries to come men of chivalrous and patriotic sentiment will stand in worship before the statue of 'the British warrior queen'. Our homage to the heroic figures of the more distant past burns all too dimly, yet here, in the very heart of our Empire, is surely an altar of patriotism unsullied. Boudicca is said to signify 'Victorious', and victorious it has been indeed against the insults of time as it was against those of tyranny.

See PARLIAMENT SQUARE, p. 97; WATLING STREET: STANMORE, p. 179.

The idea of the time of birth affecting sensitivity to the supernatural was widespread in Britain in the nineteenth century, and probably earlier. Many people thought that only those born at night would be able to see ghosts, while others believed that those born at the 'chime hours' would be particularly gifted. There was disagreement about what constituted the 'chime hours': most people thought they were three, six, nine and twelve o'clock, but a few believed them to be four, eight and twelve. Either way, midnight was by far the most powerful in this respect, and midnight on certain key days – Christmas Eve, New Year's Eve, Hallowe'en, for example – was doubly effective. Similarly, it was a widely held idea that the spirit of a dying person could appear to family members or a particularly close friend.

NORTH LONDON

*The London Boroughs of Barnet, Camden,
Enfield, Haringey and Islington*

Alexandra Palace, Wood Green

The 'People's Palace' opened in 1873, but within three weeks it had burnt to the ground. Rebuilt and reopened in 1875, it never quite succeeded in matching the Crystal Palace in South London (which itself burnt down in 1936), but it has been a popular venue for North Londoners for many years, although it was again severely damaged by fire in July 1980. Mike Hall in his *Haunted Places of Middlesex* (2004), puts forward the following explanation for this:

> When this grotesque structure was built in the 1860s a group of gypsies was forcibly removed from their encampment on the top of the hill. Enraged, they put a curse on the place: 'May death and destruction befall this place and everything associated with it!'

Barnet Hill, High Barnet

Barnet Fair was founded by charter in 1588, and in its heyday was widely famous for the sale of livestock, as confirmed by Edward Walford's *Greater London* (1883–4):

> The horse and cattle fair held yearly, in September, has made the name of Barnet known not only throughout the kingdom, but even abroad. It is held in the fields surrounding the railway station at High Barnet, and many thousand head of cattle from the Highlands change hands here. Even Cossacks from the neighbourhood of the Don, in Russia, have been known to attend the fair, clothed in the costume of their native country.

NORTH LONDON

Whitewebbs Lan[e]
Enfield, King & T[own]

ENF[IELD]

Enfie[ld]
Chas[e]

NORTH
LONDON

BARNET

Barnet Hill,
High Barnet

East End Road,
East Finchley

Alexandra Palace,
Wood Green

HARINGE[Y]

Hornsey

High Street,
Highgate

Highgate
Green

Spaniards Road,
Camden,
The Spaniards

Woodstock Road,
Finsbury
Park

Highgate
Hill

Hampstead
Heath

Highgate
Cemetery

WEST
BRENT
LONDON

Hampstead,
55 Glannet Road

Dartmouth Park

Seven Sisters
Road

Hampstead
Sewers

Kentish
Town

CAMDEN

ISLINGTON

Mil[e]
St[reet]
Can[onbury]

Chalk Farm
Road, Camden

Camden
Town

Barnsbury Park,
Islington,
Belitha Villas

SEE INSET MAP

Camden High Street,
Old Mother Redcap pub

KENSINGTON
& CHELSEA

CITY OF
WESTMINSTER

CIT[Y]

EALING

HAMMERSMITH
& FULHAM

| 0 | 1 | 2 | 3 | 4 MI |

| 0 | 1 | 2 | 3 | 4 | 5 | 6 KM |

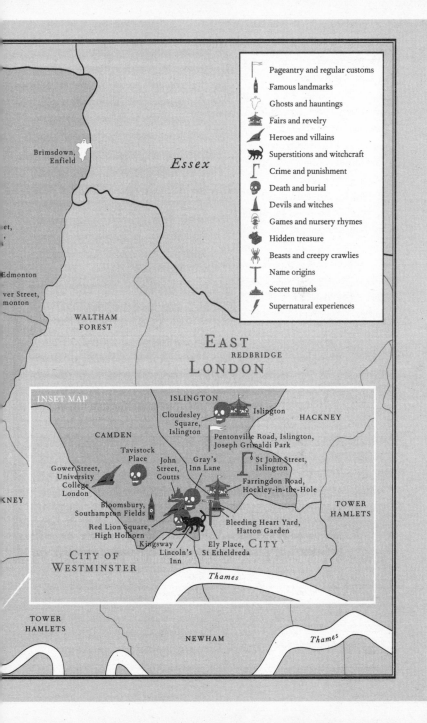

Brimsdown,
Enfield

Essex

Edmonton

ver Street,
monton

WALTHAM
FOREST

EAST
REDBRIDGE
LONDON

Legend

- Pageantry and regular customs
- Famous landmarks
- Ghosts and hauntings
- Fairs and revelry
- Heroes and villains
- Superstitions and witchcraft
- Crime and punishment
- Death and burial
- Devils and witches
- Games and nursery rhymes
- Hidden treasure
- Beasts and creepy crawlies
- Name origins
- Secret tunnels
- Supernatural experiences

INSET MAP

ISLINGTON

HACKNEY

CAMDEN

Cloudesley
Square,
Islington

Islington

Pentonville Road, Islington,
Joseph Grimaldi Park

Tavistock
Place

John
Street,
Coutts

Gray's
Inn Lane

St John Street,
Islington

Gower Street,
University
College
London

Farringdon Road,
Hockley-in-the-Hole

Bloomsbury,
Southampton Fields

TOWER
HAMLETS

KNEY

Red Lion Square,
High Holborn

Kingsway

Bleeding Heart Yard,
Hatton Garden

Lincoln's
Inn

Ely Place, CITY
St Etheldreda

CITY OF
WESTMINSTER

Thames

TOWER
HAMLETS

NEWHAM

Thames

The horse fair naturally attracted the Gypsy fraternity, and there was also a pleasure fair, which was so popular with street traders from all over North and East London that it became known as the Costers' Carnival. The latter took great pride in their horse and carts, which were brightly decorated for the day, and in their own dress. The procession of horse-drawn vehicles, of all shapes and sizes, was a popular and entertaining sight for onlookers every September, and once at the fair there were plenty of attractions to suit every taste.

Costermongers, such as this one, used to throng to Barnet Fair in such numbers that it became known as the Costers' Carnival.

James Greenwood, a journalist who specialised in writing about life at the lower end of the social scale, wrote several pieces on fairs, including the following, which is extracted from his *Low Life Deeps* (1876). It is purportedly in the very words of one of the visiting costermongers, but it has clearly been reshaped by Greenwood's pen:

> Then there's the shows. Barnet sets an example in that line sich as other places of public amoosement might get a wrinkle out of. Women's tastes ain't like men's; their ideas of enjoyment being natarally more delikit. At Barnet they manages to suit all parties, and gives em a opportunity of pairin' off so as to suit their tastes. For instance, while the missus went to the wax work, me and Simmonds was in the next tent having a game at skittles; then we took a turn in Sluggers' sparrin'-booth, while the ladies passed a pleasant 'arf-hour in the Star Ghost carawan and got their blood froze for a penny, which, considerin the 'eat of the afternoon, wasn't dear. After that, by way of restorin' their sperits, they went to see the four-legged duck and the big-headed child and the livin' skellington; Bill and me meanwhile enjoyin' ourselves in a van where there was a Kaffir eating live rats; by which time we was ready for tea and a relish with it.

The fair was still a lively event in the early years of the twentieth century, as Sidney Day, who was born in Highgate in 1912, recorded in his book *London Born* (2006):

Barnet Fair was one of the best fairs in the world. It had everything – you name it, it was there. There was a horse fair and dog shows. They sold sausages and fish and chips, hot pies, jellied eels and mash. There was Siamese twins in a tent and a five-legged cow – I seen it with me own eyes. There was rides like roundabouts, swings and all that sort of thing. I didn't like the rides meself – always seemed to make me sick and give me a headache . . . There was fortune tellers sat in a tiny tent, and if you paid yer money they would tell you a load of old cobblers. There was plenty of bartering and selling at the fair, too. The biggest money spinner was the horses. Everybody brought horses – sometimes there was two or three hundred of them for sale. I would get paid a tanner to get the horse and run him up the field, perhaps a half mile, then fetch him back. Then somebody might say, 'Right, I'll have him.' It was a dangerous job cause a lot of them was wild bleeding horses.

By the late nineteenth century the fair was suffering greatly from the encroachment of building development, and it was forced to move sites frequently from year to year. By the second half of the twentieth century it was a mere shadow of its former self, but the Horse Fair still just about manages to survive, and you can contact Barnet Council for details.

The fair was not the only famous connection between Barnet and horses, as the place was also well known for its flat racing. The *Victoria County History of Hertfordshire* (Vol. 1, 1902), taking its information from the *Sporting Magazine* (1794), gives something of the flavour of the sport 200 years ago:

The Barnet race meeting was one of the first held in the county. It was discontinued for several years, but reinstituted in 1793. In the next year the meeting there appears to have been rowdy beyond description. One man for a bet walked out of an upstairs window and was killed, and his widow claimed the money. Another man for a bet galloped on a horse up High Street with his hands tied behind his back, and had his brains dashed out against a lamp-post. The accidents that occurred to drunken men on their return from the races were of course numerous, and cock fighting was freely indulged in when nothing else was going on.

The last Barnet race meeting was held in September 1870, and High Barnet railway station was built on the site in 1872.

Barnsbury Park, Islington: Belitha Villas

A classic 'point-of-death' appearance, one of the regular motifs in British ghost-lore, was included by F. G. Lee in his *Glimpses in the Twilight* (1885), as written down by 'a lady'. While her husband was away, the narrator took the opportunity to hold a children's party in their house in Belitha Villas, Barnsbury Park. Hearing footsteps in the hall, she went to greet the newcomer, but:

> Instead of the expected guest, I found standing on the door-mat a very old friend of my husband's, Mr G— S—, who, in the earlier days of our married life, had been welcome to our house almost as a brother. Unfortunately his career became, from some unexplained cause, one which we could not approve, and we no longer received him under our roof. How and why, then, should he, after a lapse of seven years, be standing there on that door-mat, looking not one bit older, just as handsome, just as carefully attired, as in the early days of our friendship?

In her amazement she turned to call a friend who was in the other room, but when she turned back, the figure had disappeared.

> No sign, no indication of any kind, of the so recent visitation. Not a sound was heard, not a door had moved. He had been, and he was gone; but how and wherefore? For a moment I stood aghast; then, with an indescribable feeling, which I tried in vain to dispel, I descended to the breakfast-room, to entertain my little party.

Shortly afterwards, a servant brought in another visitor:

> 'I am George's cousin and namesake,' he said. 'Remembering your husband's great kindness and friendship, I am come to ask advice and assistance about the funeral. I feel assured you will grieve to hear that George expired about an hour ago.'

BLEEDING HEART YARD, HATTON GARDEN

Bleeding Heart Yard is off Greville Street, in Hatton Garden. Any place with such a mysterious name is likely to attract a legend, and a well-known tale was told of this locality. The story has attached itself to a historical figure, Lady Elizabeth, wife of Sir William Hatton, who was a favourite of Elizabeth I and Chancellor of England. The Hattons took over the house and gardens of Ely Place from the Bishops of Ely, whose London home it had been for some time. The Bishops were none too happy about this arrangement, but the Hattons had the Queen's blessing. Sir William built Hatton House on the site about 1576, and the area became known as Hatton Garden.

The Hattons achieved considerable social and political success, and the legend grew up that this was by the simple expedient of Lady Elizabeth's selling her soul to the Devil. His Satanic Majesty chose to foreclose on the deal on the very night of one of the Hattons' most lavish parties, and he grabbed Lady Elizabeth in full view of her terrified guests, tore her limb from limb, and carried her off, leaving only a still-bleeding, still-beating heart behind on the ground.

Later writers have often assumed that this story goes back to the time in which it is set, but there is as yet no evidence that it is any older than the 1820s. Nevertheless, its early history is sufficiently cloudy to allow for an earlier provenance, which may well be turned up by further research.

As with several other seemingly historical legends, the key figure in the story's development and dissemination is Richard Harris Barham, one of the great early Victorian purveyors of literary legends. In the fictional guise of 'Thomas Ingoldsby', Barham wrote a number of mostly humorous stories, in poetry and prose, which were published in various periodicals of the time, and then in book form as *The Ingoldsby Legends* (in three series: 1840, 1842, and 1847).

Barham's winning formula was to take existing tales, sometimes little-known, and often macabre, and to retell them in semi-comic form. He was not at all averse to adding new elements to the stories to make them fit for his purpose, and his popularity ensured that his 'retold' legends were repeated uncritically by subsequent writers, becoming the generally accepted versions for later generations. The public lapped them up, and there is evidence that many people found the contents of some of the legends quite shocking and alarming, despite their jocular tone. There is no doubt also that many people actually believed the stories. But *The Ingoldsby Legends* have not weathered well, and few modern readers appreciate the poetic style or the laboured punning humour.

Barham's version of the Hatton House legend was entitled 'The House-Warming! A Legend of Bleedingheart Yard' and was first published in the *New Monthly Magazine* in 1843, and in book form, posthumously, in 1847. It is clear, however, that Barham did not write the story from scratch, but was following his established pattern of recasting a tale that was already in circulation. Evidence for this conclusion comes from a fascinating passage in Charles Mackay's *Extraordinary Popular Delusions and the Madness of Crowds* (1841), which is worth quoting in full because it demonstrates not only that the legend was already in active circulation, but that it was sufficiently powerful to influence people's beliefs and actions:

> Many houses are still to be found in England with the horse-shoe (the grand preservative against witchcraft) nailed against the threshold. If any over-wise philosopher should attempt to remove them, the chances are that he would have more broken bones than thanks for his interference. Let any man walk into Cross Street, Hatton Garden, and from thence into Bleeding-Heart Yard, and learn the tales still told and believed of one house in that neighbourhood, and he will ask himself in astonishment if such things can be in the nineteenth century. The witchcraft of Lady Hatton, the wife of the famous Sir Christopher, so renowned for his elegant dancing in the days of Elizabeth, is as devoutly believed in as the Gospels. The room is to be seen where the devil seized her after the expiration of the contract he had made with her, and bore her away bodily to the pit of Tophet: the pump against which he dashed her is still pointed out, and the spot where her heart was found after he had torn it out of her bosom with his iron claws, has received the name of Bleeding-Heart Yard, in confirmation of the story.

Mackay's intermingling of the bleeding-heart story and the horseshoe may simply have been because both are in the same locality, or there may have been a connecting element that has been lost to us. If so, it was clearly an important element in the story:

> Whether the horse-shoe still remains upon the door of the haunted house, to keep away other witches, is uncertain. A former inmate relates that, 'about twenty years ago, more than one old woman begged for admittance

repeatedly, to satisfy themselves that it was in its proper place. One poor creature, apparently insane, and clothed in rags, came to the door with a tremendous double-knock, as loud as that of a fashionable footman, and walked straight along the passage to the horse-shoe. Great was the wonderment of the inmates, especially when the woman spat upon the horse-shoe, and expressed her sorrow that she could do no harm while it remained there. After spitting upon, and kicking it again and again, she coolly turned round and left the house, without saying a word to anybody. This poor creature perhaps intended a joke, but the probability is that she imagined herself a witch. In Saffron Hill, where she resided, her ignorant neighbours gave her that character, and looked upon her with no little fear and aversion.

The bleeding-heart story clearly lived on, and acquired other elements not published by Barham. The London folklore collector John Emslie, for example, wrote in his notebook on 30 September 1872:

An errand-boy, in Bleeding Heart Yard, told me that Lady Hatton, having sold her soul to the devil, knocked out her brains on the pump in that yard, and that since then blood will flow out of the spout if any one will work the pump at midnight. He also showed me the mark of her hand on a door step at the corner of Kirby Street; the mark was an Ordnance Survey broad-arrow; to convince me he applied his hand to it.

An integral part of the way that such legends function is the implication that the place is named after the story, but this is invariably incorrect. In nearly all such cases, the legend has been invented to explain the name, and in this instance, the name can be perfectly easily explained without the aid of the supernatural. From the Middle Ages onwards the heart was regularly represented graphically as the symbol of the Virgin Mary. It appeared in many contexts – the broken heart, the wounded heart, the bleeding heart of the sorrowing mother, and, in one common version, the heart pierced with five swords as a representation of the five sorrowful mysteries of the rosary. Bleeding Heart Yard was thus named after a tavern, situated there, which displayed on its sign Mary and her bleeding heart.

BLOOMSBURY: SOUTHAMPTON FIELDS

The area to the north of the British Museum, and east of Gower Street, was open land and called Southampton Fields until the early nineteenth century, at which point Russell Square, Tavistock Square, and Gordon Square were developed. Before being built on, the area enjoyed a very unsavoury reputation for robberies and murders, and also, slightly more romantically, a reputation for being the place where duels took place. It was a supposed duel that gave the area its most enduring legend, often referred to as 'The Brothers' Steps', and this led to the area being called the 'Field of the Forty Footsteps'.

The basic tale is rather simple. Sometime in the late seventeenth century, two brothers fought a duel over a woman, and both were killed. The grass will never grow in their footprints or where they fell.

For such an undeveloped story, the legend proved remarkably popular and enduring, partly because it was seen as evidence of God's hand. Indeed, the earliest full account appeared in the *Arminian Magazine* in 1781, which was in effect the house journal of the nascent Methodist church. Strangely enough, the journal is a wonderful source for the folklore and traditional beliefs of the period, as its pages are full of stories of prophetic dreams, apparitions, poltergeists, and amazing occurrences. The early Methodists believed that a denial of the spirit world was a denial of God's existence.

There is much confusion in the literature of this legend, with a long history of misquotation, and the original piece should therefore be given in full:

AN ACCOUNT OF THE BROTHERS' STEPS

Last summer I received a letter from a friend, wherein were these words. 'I think it would be worth your while to take a view of those wonderful marks of the Lord's hatred to duelling, called *The Brothers' Steps*. They are in the fields, about a third of a mile northward from Montague-House. And the awful tradition concerning them is, that two brothers quarrelled about a worthless woman, and according to the fashion of those days, fought with sword and pistol. The prints of their feet are about the depth of three inches, and nothing will vegetate, so much as to disfigure them. The number is only eighty three; but probably some are at present filled up. For I think there were formerly more in the centre, where each unhappy combatant wounded the other to death. And a bank on which the first who fell, died, retains the form of his agonizing couch, by the curse of barrenness, while grass flourishes all about it. Mr George Hall, who was the Librarian of Lincoln's-Inn, first showed me those steps, twenty eight years ago, when, I think, they were not quite so deep as now. He remembered them about thirty years, and the man who first shewed them him, about thirty more; which goes back to the year 1692; but I suppose they originated in King Charles the Second's reign. My mother well remembered their being ploughed up, and corn sown to deface them about fifty years ago. But all was labour in vain; for the prints returned in a while to their pristine form; as probably will those that are now filled up. Indeed I think an account of them in your magazine should be a pious memorial of their lasting reality. These hints are only offered as a small token of my goodwill to yourself, and the work, by Your Son and Brother in the Gospel, JOHN WALSH.'

The journal clearly took this very seriously. While similar letters were printed without comment, in this case the editor added the result of his own commentary:

This journal seemed to me so very extraordinary, that I knew not what to think of it. I knew Mr Walsh to be a person of good understanding and real piety. And he testified what he had seen with his own eyes; but still I wanted more witnesses; till a while ago, being at Mr Cary's, in Copthal Buildings, I occasionally mentioned The Brothers' Footsteps, and asked the company if they had heard any thing of them? 'Sir,' said Mr Cary, 'sixteen years ago, I saw and counted them myself.' Another added, 'And I saw them four years ago.' I could then no longer doubt, but they had been. And a week or two after, I went with Mr Cary and another person to seek them.

We sought for nearly half an hour in vain. We could find no steps at all, within a quarter of a mile, no nor half a mile, north of Montague House. We were almost out of hope, when an honest man, who was at work, directed us to the next ground, adjoining to a pond. There we found what we fought for, about three-quarters of a mile north of Montague-House, and about five hundred yards east of Tottenham-Court-Road. The steps answer Mr Walsh's description. They are of the size of a large human foot, about three inches deep, and lie nearly from north-east to south-west. We counted only seventy-six; but we were not exact in counting. The place where one or both the brothers are supposed to have fallen, is still bare of grass. The labourer shewed us also the bank, where (the tradition is) the wretched woman sat to see the combat.

Then he tried hard to fit such mysteries into his religious worldview:

What shall we say to these things? Why, to atheists or infidels of any kind, I would not say one word about them. For if they hear not Moses and the Prophets, they will not regard any thing of this kind. But to men of candour, who believe the Bible to be of God, I would say, is not this an astonishing instance, held forth to all the inhabitants of London, of the justice and power of God? Does not the curse he has denounced upon this ground bear some little resemblance to that of our Lord on the barren figtree, *Henceforth let no fruit grow upon thee for ever!* I see no reason or pretence for any rational man to doubt the truth of the story; since it has been confirmed by these open visible tokens for more than a hundred years successively.

Problems in the literature start immediately. The next airing of the story is in the *Gentleman's Magazine* in 1804, and purports to be a letter from William Herbert, dated 1778, i.e. before the *Arminian Magazine*, but is clearly copied in large part from the latter. These two pieces are the ultimate sources of almost every subsequent telling, but because they were both written in letter form in the first person singular, each time an author reprints or copies their words it is implied that a new person is speaking about his or her own time. This has happened most notably with the poet Robert Southey, who copied the piece into his *Commonplace Book* (1849), which later writers have taken as evidence of his personal investigation, and to mean that the 'footsteps' were still visible in his time.

Nevertheless, another description exists which seems to be independent of the versions in the *Arminian Magazine* and the *Gentleman's Magazine*. It was included by John Thomas Smith in his highly entertaining *A Book for a Rainy Day*, published in 1845, twelve years after his death. Smith was born in 1766, and he describes the site in the entry for the year 1773, which, if accurate, would make it the earliest reference to the legend. Unfortunately, though, his mention of a novel written in 1828 proves that he actually wrote the piece rather later. Nevertheless, Smith's evidence is valuable, because it is clearly a first-hand account:

The whole of the ground north from Capper's farm, at the back of the British Museum, so often mentioned as being frequented by duellists, was in irregular patches, many fields with turnstiles . . . [People went there to gather] watercresses, which grew in great abundance and perfection, or to visit the 'Brother's Steps', well known to Londoners . . . I have frequently passed over them; they were in a field on the site of Mr Martin's chapel, or very nearly so, and not on the spot as communicated to Miss Potter, who has written an entertaining novel on the subject.

The site was already being obliterated at the turn of the nineteenth century, as an extract from the commonplace book of Joseph Moser published in *Notes and Queries* (1850) makes clear:

16 June 1800
Went into the fields at the back of Montague House, and there saw, for the last time, the *forty footsteps*; the building materials are there ready to cover them from the sight of man. I counted more than forty, but they might be the footprints of the workmen.

Two nineteenth-century literary productions took the basic legend and used it as background: Jane and Anna Maria Potter's novel *Coming Out* (1828); and a melodrama, *The Field of Forty Footsteps*, by Percy Farren (1830). And as if to show that you cannot keep a good title down, two more recent historical novels, by Geoffrey Trease (1977) and Phyllis Hastings (1978), were entitled *The Field of Forty Steps*, but their plots have nothing to do with the legend.

It seems fairly well attested that some sort of bare patches existed in Southampton Fields, but it is impossible to know what they were. All that can be said now is that it is a curiously unsatisfactory sort of legend, in that we are not told who these brothers were, or the exact nature of their relationship with the 'worthless woman', who is also anonymous, and how they came to be so cross with each other. The motif of plants refusing to grow where something terrible has happened is common enough in British tradition.

A completely different legend concerning Southampton Fields was recorded by the pioneering antiquarian John Aubrey, in his *Miscellanies* (1696):

The last summer, on the day of St John the Baptist, 1694, I accidentally was walking in the pasture behind Montague house, it was 12 o'clock. I saw there about two or three and twenty young women, most of them well habited, on their knees very busy, as if they had been weeding. I could not precisely learn what the matter was; at last a young man told me, that they were looking for a coal under the root of a plantain, to put under their head that night, and they should dream who would be their husbands. It was to be sought for that day and hour.

This has the feel of a localised version of a contemporary legend of the day, and the basic idea was certainly not new. Similar stories had been published in the years before Aubrey's time, including one in Thomas Lupton's *A Thousand Notable Things* (1579). Lupton writes of a coal to be found on Midsummer Eve, under the root of a mugwort, which, if carried, protects the bearer from 'plague, carbuncle, lightning, the quartain ague, and from burning', and even he was quoting an earlier work by the sixteenth-century French physician and astrologer Mizaldus (Antoine Mizauld).

BRIMSDOWN, ENFIELD

In August 1977, a family in Enfield started to be troubled with poltergeist activity, and the case is described in Alan Baker's *Ghosts and Spirits* (1998). The occurrences were all stereotypical poltergeist mischief: furniture moved, doors opened by themselves, small objects were thrown (or threw themselves), and loud knocks could be heard. The mother was naturally worried, and called, in turn, the neighbours, the police, the *Daily Mirror*, and then the Society for Psychical Research. The representatives of the SPR investigated thoroughly, but their findings were inconclusive, partly because their equipment always 'malfunctioned' at the crucial moment. But they did discover that when they asked the poltergeist questions, it would answer with knocks. Presumably, the poltergeist was a sentient being who spoke English. After a sequence of experts had investigated, the poltergeist simply faded away, as they always do; perhaps they have a low boredom threshold. Some SPR members were critical of the investigations, and at least one declared that it was the children playing pranks, a verdict that Baker regarded as 'depressing'. Others might rather be comforted that people are at risk from children's tricks rather than malevolent supernatural spirits. The SPR's investigator, Guy Lyon Playfair, tells his side of the story in his book *This House is Haunted* (1980).

This is not the first time that Enfield has been troubled by such events. A note in John Emslie's collection of London folklore, published in *London Studies* (1974), records the following:

1872

A middle-aged man said that there was an old house at Turkey Street, Enfield, in which people could get no rest of a night on account of knocking and scratching noises heard in it; but the noises have not been heard recently.

See also BEVERSTONE ROAD, THORNTON HEATH, p. 365; CHELSEA, p. 138; GROVE PARK: ALLOTMENTS, p. 333; PLAISTOW, p. 293; REVERDY ROAD, BERMONDSEY: NOS 56 AND 58, p. 342; STOCKWELL, p. 414; SUTTON LANE, CHISWICK: SUTTON COURT-HOUSE, p. 173.

CAMDEN HIGH STREET: OLD MOTHER REDCAP PUB

The Old Mother Redcap pub (now called the World's End) in Camden High Street has been a well-known landmark for centuries. It is shown, for example, in splendid isolation on John Rocque's 1745 map of London, long before Camden Town was thought of, and is in the centre of Camden Town on Edward Stanford's map of 'London and its Suburbs' in 1861. But any attempt to explain its name and history is fraught with complexity.

Samuel Pepys, on his way home from his parents' house at Brampton, Huntingdon, wrote:

24 September 1661

So we rode easily through and only drinking at Halloway at the sign of a woman with cakes in one hand and a pot of ale in the other, which did give good occasion of mirth, resembling her to the maid that served us.

In published editions of the diary, this is usually glossed as the Mother Redcap, although the picture on the sign sounds a little jollier than the usual image conjured up by the name, but this is presumably not the one at Camden. According to George Daniel, in his *Merrie England in the Olden Time* (1842); there were two 'ancient' Mother Redcap inns – one on the Hampstead Road, near Kentish Town, and one at Holloway. In this context, Kentish Town is synonymous with Camden.

MOTHER DAMNABLE, *the remarkable* SHREW, *of* KENTISH TOWN, *the person who gave rise to the Sign of* Mother Red Cap, *on the Hampstead Road, near London. An. Dom. 1676.*

'Mother Damnable of Kentish Town' as depicted in a seventeenth-century pamphlet. The original engraving was accompanied by a verse which claimed that, when vexed, she would put the ale-cellar key into her pocket so that no one could have any beer.

There is a standard explanation of who Mother Redcap was, which derives from that published by Samuel Palmer in his *History of St Pancras* (1870). Unfortunately, Palmer does not make it clear where he got his information, but more than halfway through his long piece he writes, 'The extraordinary death of this singular character is given in an old pamphlet', leaving us to guess if the rest is from the same source. He identifies a real person, Jinney Bingham, who lived at the time of the English Civil War, and who was sometimes called the Shrew of Kentish Town, sometimes Mother Damnable, and sometimes Mother Red Cap.

According to Palmer, Jinney was the daughter of a brickmaker, Jacob Bingham, and a Scots pedlar's daughter. Her parents were later 'carried before the justices for practising the black art, and therewith causing the death of a maiden, for which they were both hung'. When she was sixteen, she had a child by 'Gipsy George' Coulter, with whom she lived until he was hanged for sheep-stealing. She then lived with a drunkard named Darby, who disappeared, then with a man Pitcher, who was found burnt to a cinder in the oven. A neighbour testified that he 'often got into the oven to hide himself from her tongue'. Jinney became something of a recluse, but during the Commonwealth a man with money came to lodge with her, and when he died there were rumours that she had poisoned him. She became old and ugly, and was regularly attacked by the mob as a witch, although she was also consulted as a fortune-teller and healer. When she died:

Hundreds of men, women and children were witnesses of the devil entering her house in his very appearance and state, and that, although his return was narrowly watched for, he was not seen again; and that Mother Damnable was found dead on the following morning, sitting before the fireplace, holding a crutch over it, with a tea-pot full of herbs, drugs, and liquid, part of which being given to the cat, the hair fell off in two hours, and the cat soon died.

This is a good story, but it introduces two problems: firstly, it implies that there was only one individual who gave rise to the name Old Mother Redcap; and secondly, it treats Old Mother Redcap as synonymous with Old Mother Damnable and 'the Shrew of Kentish Town', although there is evidence that they were two or three different fictional characters who later got confused.

The name Mother Redcap had already been in circulation long before the Commonwealth, as it appears in the title of a jest-book of 1595 and a play of 1598, and again in a publication of 1631, where it is used simply to indicate a pub landlady. None of these gives any clue to the bad reputation Palmer describes.

On the other hand, Mother Damnable appears a little later, with a flurry of mentions in the mid seventeenth century. A ballad called 'Mother Damnable's Ordinary' was registered on 30 July 1656, but unfortunately no copy seems to have survived. However, one broadside that has survived, albeit in a single copy only, is simply headed *Mother Damnable* and dated 1676, and this provides an engraving of the person in question, which is the picture most later authorities print as Mother Redcap.

The picture shows a suitably ugly old woman, wearing a shawl with black patches, crouched before the fire, with a crutch in one hand and jugs and mugs scattered around. The 22-line verse accompanying the picture refers to her as 'Mother Damnable of Kentish Town', but bears no apparent relationship to the stories told by Palmer above. She might be described in the following rather unflattering way:

> Unmatched by Mackbeth's Wayward-Womens Ring
> For cursing, Scolding, Fuming, flinging Fire
> Ith' Face of Madam, Lord, Knight, Gent, Cit, Squire,

However, the worst thing she is accused of is, when vexed, putting the ale-cellar key into her pocket so that no one can get any beer. Later printings of this engraving include the statement that Mothers Damnable and Redcap were the same person.

Mother Redcap had clearly become a figure of fun by the mid nineteenth century, as, for example, in the pantomime *Harlequin and Beauty and the Beast*, performed at Sadler's Wells on 28 December 1857. In the first scene, Mother Bunch, Mother Goose, Mother Redcap, and Mother Hubbard are discovered with brooms stirring up the contents of a huge cauldron inscribed, 'Mother Bunch's Infant Food'.

There is clearly a lot more to be discovered about Old Mother Redcap. For example, pantomimes, and English popular culture generally, abound with female characters called 'Old Mother —' or just 'Mother —', sometimes referring to a witch, sometimes to a more benign character – Old Mother Shipton, Old Mother Hubbard, Mother Bunch, Mother Goose, Mother Needham, and so on – and this thread could be followed up. 'Mother Damnable' also has been used many times in history, either to indicate a witch or a 'madam' of a brothel. In another direction, we can see that there are, or were, Mother Redcap pubs in Wallasey, Bradway (Sheffield), Blackburn, Luton, Accrington, Oswaldtwistle (Rossendale), as well as a market of the same name in Dublin.

CAMDEN TOWN

The following extracts about children's games in Camden Town are from Edwin Pugh's *The City of the World*, which bears the subtitle *A Book About London and the Londoner* (*c*.1912). Pugh uses a device commonly employed in this type of book: a conversation in which one knowledgeable adult talks to another, and explains what is going on before them. In this case, they are watching London children at play in the street on a Saturday evening, and the description successfully conjures up the organised chaos of unsupervised poor children at play in a setting that hardly ever occurs today. Pugh begins with a well-observed and delightful detail about child-centred language, when one boy says to another, 'Are you out?', by which he does not mean simply 'Are you here outside your house?', but more importantly, 'Are you engaged on some vexatious errand for your mother or your father, or are you at liberty to join in any fun that may crop up?' The narrator continues:

Look at those boys over there now. See that one crawling about on the pavement, all heaped up with jackets and hanging on to the end of a rope that another boy is holding by the other end – for all the world like a dog on a chain. And all those others with their hats tied on to pieces of string, waiting to fetch the crawling boy a welt. They're playing *Ugly Bear*. Watch 'em and listen! The boys circle round the crawling figure and the holder of the rope. And they cry: 'Who brought this Ugly Bear to market?' The rope-holder replies: 'Such a man as I.' They ask, 'What's his name?', and he answers, 'John Bull.' 'How many whacks for a shilling?' they inquire. 'As many as you can get,' says he, and dashes after them to the length of his rope. They dodge him and aim blows at the crawling figure, until one of them is caught and forced to take the crawling figure's place.

Other boys are playing Horny Winkles. One group of boys bends over to make a bridge of backs that stretches across the pavement from the wall to the kerb, while others vault upon their backs and ride them astride to a thrice-repeated chorus of 'Charley Knackers, one, two, three. Off – off – fee!' or until the backs collapse helplessly under their weight.

But there are girls playing there too, and it is they who 'bring a spice of poetry into the games of the street':

> Take *Hopscotch* for instance. No boy or man has ever really arrived at the true inwardness of Hopscotch. And is there any mystery so fascinating? Why, it's just female nature. They do something with chalk and a bit of china on the pavement. And if they don't do it right they go on all the same. And if they do do it right they're about as pleased as a cat in the fender. Though it doesn't seem to make any difference at all.

Girls also play Gobs or Five Stones, sitting on a doorstep, but their 'love games' take up much of their time:

> Poor Jenny is a-weeping, a-weeping, a-weeping
> Poor Jenny is a-weeping, on a bright summer's day
> On the carpet you shall kneel
> While the grass grows in the field
> Stand up, stand up upon your feet
> Choose the one you love so sweet
> Choose once, choose twice, choose three times over!

There is a pause. Now a little boy and a big girl stand demurely, with linked hands, in the middle of the ring of dancing children. They circle round, singing

Now you're married I wish you joy
First a girl and then a boy
Seven years after son and daughter
Pray and cuddle and kiss together!
Kiss her once, kiss her twice, kiss her three times over!

The boy and girl embrace shyly. The girl kisses the boy on the cheek.

CHALK FARM ROAD, CAMDEN

Those who remember the twentieth-century 'penny for the guy' custom, whereby children made 'guys' and stood on street corners soliciting coppers from passers-by, probably regard the practice as either a quaint old custom now sadly gone, or even, perhaps, an example of licensed begging that we can do without. But the predominant Guy Fawkes custom in urban areas in the nineteenth century was very different, and far more rough and ready. Children did make 'guys', but the most prominent ones were constructed by youths, who paraded the streets in force, carrying their effigies, letting off fireworks, and collecting money in a more direct manner from pedestrians and shop-keepers than simply asking for a 'penny for the guy'. Violence was never far below the surface on these occasions. Added to this was a simmering religious resentment, with Catholics objecting to the open anti-popery sentiments of the celebrations, which sometimes broke out into confrontation. On 6 November 1838, for example, *The Times* reported a fracas on the border between the City and Tower Hamlets, when a group of Irish workers and schoolboys took umbrage at the cries of 'no popery', attacked the bonfire boys, and carried off the guy in triumph. Six years later, on 9 November 1844, the same paper reported an incident in Camden:

> A mob of about 200 persons, comprising some of the greatest vagabonds in London, paraded the northern part of the metropolis, with a donkey in the midst of them, on which was an effigy of Guy Fawkes. They had some discordant musical instruments, and every description of firework, which they exploded in the public streets . . . They went up to the Chalk [Farm] Road where they were attacked by a party of Irish labourers, who pelted them with stones; and a scuffle ensued, in which the musical instruments were broken, the fireworks thrown in the water, and the effigy smashed to atoms.

Guy Fawkes Night was celebrated with great gusto in the nineteenth century. Because of its strongly anti-Catholic nature, it was often the occasion for fights with local Irish communities, as an incident that occurred in Chalk Farm Road in 1844 confirms.

These mass processions, accompanied by fireworks, bonfires, blazing tar barrels, and other rough behaviour, continued to dominate the streets on 5 November in many areas of London until the 1860s and 1870s, when local authorities began attempts to ban them, and used the police to break them up. For a few years there were annual pitched battles between the police and the 'bonfire boys', but the former won in the end, and Guy Fawkes celebrations moved into family back gardens and organised displays.

See also GUY FAWKES NIGHT, p. 338.

CHURCH STREET, EDMONTON: ALL SAINTS' CHURCH

The churchyard of All Saints' church at Edmonton is the scene of a couple of contrasting ghost stories. The first was recorded in the *Middlesex Quarterly* of Winter 1956:

A more gentle pair of ghosts are those of Charles and Mary Lamb, buried in All Saints Church. They only make very occasional appearances. One 'medium' friend of mine told me some years back that she visited the district where the Lambs lived so happily for very many years, and suddenly saw 'such a nice old couple in the distance. He was thin and kindly-looking and she was stoutish and pleasant-looking. They were smiling so happily at each other, too.' It was only when they suddenly vanished completely that my friend realised with a shock that they had no corporeal existence. Seeing pictures of the pair later, she maintained this was the answer to her personal puzzle – she had seen the ghosts of Charles and Mary, still walking their beloved Edmonton, in spite of its changed appearance. Whether the solution was right or wrong, it is pleasant to think of a happy pair still getting enjoyment of this harmless type.

A second story is told in a much briefer report, in Mike Hall's *Haunted Places of Middlesex* (2004). It states that 'several people have seen a phantom white dog in the churchyard but, so long as you ignore it, they say it is quite harmless.'

CLOUDESLEY SQUARE, ISLINGTON

Some ghosts have the distinction of being referred to as *the —— Ghost*, such as the Hammersmith Ghost (*see* p. 145) and the Stockwell Ghost (*see* p. 414). This is often because they are the best-known, or even the only, supernatural being in the neighbourhood, but it may simply be that someone used this honorific title in a publication, and it stuck. So it appears to be with the Islington Ghost, which is the title of an anonymous pamphlet published in Clerkenwell in 1842. The ghost in question is that of Richard Cloudesley, who died in 1517. He is remembered as a major benefactor of the parish of Islington, and was buried in St Mary's churchyard, but in 1813 his remains were moved into the church as a mark of respect, and a new tomb erected. However, the pamphlet claims, on the 'testimony of a respectable writer', who is not named, that poor Richard's body was actually buried a nearby field:

As to the same heavings, or *tremblements de terre*, it is said that in a certain field, near unto the parish church of Islington, in like manner did take place a wondrous commotion in various parts, the earth swelling, and turning up every side towards the midst of the said field, and by tradition of this, it is observed that one Richard Cloudesley lay buried in or near that place, and that his body being restless, on the score of some sin by him peradventure committed, did shew, or seem to signify, that religious observance should there take place, to quiet his departed spirit; whereupon certain exorcisers (if we may so term them) did at the dead of night, nothing loth, using diverse exercises at torch light, set at rest the unruly spirit of the said Cloudesley, and the earth did return near to its pristine shape, never more commotion proceeding therefrom to this day, and this I know of a very certainty.

The real Richard Cloudesley is also commemorated in a stained-glass window in the former Holy Trinity church (built 1826–9), now the Celestial Church of Christ, which is situated on land he left to the parish, now appropriately called Cloudesley Square.

DARTMOUTH PARK

Sidney Day grew up in Highgate after the First World War, and published his memoirs under the title *London Born* in 2006. A passage from them describes a survival of the widespread fondness that London people had for caged birds:

> Nearly everybody who went to the Brookfield [pub] on a Sunday took a bird in a little carrying cage. Me dad took his cage wrapped up in a red and white spotted navvy's handkerchief so his bird wouldn't be afraid. He would put the cage underneath his arm and take off the cloth when he got to the pub. Every man put his bird up on the shelf that ran right the way along the bar. The bar was filled with birds fluttering and singing. Me dad had dozens of different birds: finches, linnets, thrushes, blackbirds. There weren't a type of bird that breathed that me dad didn't have at some time. We caught them by going bush bashing. Me dad made eight foot by three foot double layered nets out of black cotton. We would loop a net in between two trees in Kenwood and then bash the bushes with sticks to scare the birds towards it. When a bird flew through the net it was trapped in a pocket.

Singing birds were immensely popular in the nineteenth century, and thousands were sold each year to working-class buyers all over town. Henry Mayhew included a section on the trade in his *London Labour and the*

London Poor (1861), and he demonstrated that while many made a regular living at bird-catching in the more rural suburbs to supply the London market, there were thousands of amateurs who, like Sydney Day, took part for the sake of the sport, and for pocket money.

EAST END ROAD, EAST FINCHLEY

In East Finchley cemetery is the grave of Henry Croft (1862–1930), generally acknowledged as the originator, in around 1880, of the 'pearly king' costume. Croft was an orphan brought up in the local children's home, and for his whole working life he was employed as a municipal road-sweeper for St Pancras Council, but a great many sentimental legends have accumulated around the story of his life and the foundation of the pearly fashion.

It is claimed that he grew up in an orphanage, where he was taught to use a needle and thread, and that upon leaving he was determined to fulfil his promise to do something to help the other orphans. It is also suggested that he never grew to be taller than five foot and had something of an inferiority complex, but was fascinated by the local costermongers, with their flash clothes, ready wit, and independent spirit. Sadly, though, they are said to have ignored and derided him, perhaps because he did such a humble job. It is even said that a shipwrecked cargo ship flooded the market with cheap mother-of-pearl buttons just at the right moment. Earlier costermonger dress certainly included some shiny buttons, but Croft decided to take this to excess, covering a whole suit of clothes with the things, and, the legend states, he was instantly acclaimed by the costers, and declared their 'king'. However, as none of the writings of the principal perpetrators of the legend contains an acknowledgement of a source, it is impossible to sort fact from fiction.

Until about ten years ago, his tomb was graced with a life-sized statue of him in his famous pearled suit and top hat, which appears to have been added to the tomb four years after Croft's death. On 12 September 1933, an Australian tourist, A. M. Reeves, reported the responses he had received to his question in *The Times* about pearly kings:

> I was offered a life-size stone statue of Croft wearing [his] marvellous costume. The statue was ordered some years ago from a Tottenham stone-mason, who had it sculptured in Italy, but could not collect the payment (£200).

Someone must have taken notice, because *The Times* of 1 June 1934 carried the following piece:

> The Rev A. D. Belton, of Whitefields Central Mission, Tottenham Court Road, unveiled yesterday in St Pancras Cemetery a statue of Henry Croft, the 'pearly king' who died four years ago, and who collected over £4000 for charity. The statue represents Mr Croft in his 'pearly king' clothes with top hat. Hundreds of people gathered to watch a procession of 'pearlies' who had come from all parts of the country and gathered round the statue.

Unfortunately, in the late 1990s the statue proved just too tempting a target for vandals, and was repeatedly damaged. It has now been replaced by a marble slab, bearing a photograph of the statue, and the original figure is safe in the crypt of St Martin in the Fields, Trafalgar Square.

Henry's original suit also has its own tale to tell. According to a report in the *Evening Standard* on 10 April 1974, it was dramatically unearthed in an attic in Romford. An article by Mary Braid called 'The War of the Pearly Kings' that appeared in the *Independent* on 7 July 2001 details the strained relations between different factions in the pearly world and mentions 'twenty-five antique suits', including Croft's, which had been stored at a secret address, 'for their safety'.

See also PEARLY KINGS AND QUEENS, p. 208.

EDMONTON

It is not clear why, but two well-known seventeenth-century dramas use Edmonton as the setting for supernatural occurrences. *The Merry Devil of Edmonton*, a romantic comedy, was first published anonymously in 1608, although there have been various unsuccessful attempts to assign it to known authors, including Shakespeare. The title refers to Peter Fabel of Edmonton, a magician whose powers stem from a pact with the Devil, but there is little magic in the plot, which mainly concerns young lovers who must overcome the machinations of their parents to keep them apart.

A chapbook entitled *The Merry Devil of Edmonton*, printed in London in 1631 (and reprinted in 1819), was clearly designed to capitalise on the brand name. As is common with this type of production, it comprises a series of short humorous pieces, reminiscent of the earlier jest-book tradition. In the

Pearly Kings and Queens

A Pearly King in the 1920s wearing a costume adorned with buttons. This style of dress was initially inspired by the clothing of costermongers.

Internationally known and recognised as attractive symbols of old London, pearly kings and queens appear in almost as many tourist brochures as red buses and Big Ben. Their unique costume is a godsend to photographers, and this is exactly as it should be. Ask any pearly why they dress up as they do, and they will say that they exist to collect money for charity, and the more publicity they can get the better. They will say that this is why the pearlies were started, and they will proudly claim a hundred-year-old tradition of good work, and that vast sums have been collected to support hospitals and other charities over that time.

As far as it goes, this is perfectly true, but the story of the pearlies is not quite as straightforward as it seems, and it is clear that legend plays as large a part as verifiable history in their tradition. Despite several books on the subject, the definitive history still waits to be compiled.

It is generally accepted that the first person who decided to sew rows and rows of pearly buttons on his clothes was Henry Croft (1862–1930), municipal road-sweeper for St Pancras Council, who was an admirer of the style of dress adopted by the costermongers of the day. He took their relatively subdued liking for rows of shiny buttons to an almost absurd conclusion, and covered his whole suit with them some time in the early 1880s. Some claim that even at this early stage he knew that he wanted to dress up in order to collect money for charity, but it is hard to find any real evidence for this.

Legend has it that Croft called himself 'King of the Costers' or something similar, but it is unclear when the term *pearly king* was coined. A photograph of Croft as 'the Pearlie [*sic*] King of Somers Town' was contributed by a reader to the *Strand Magazine* in 1902 and is the earliest reference to the term so far located in print. The word *pearlies*, however, pre-dates it: the *OED* quotes an article in the *Daily News* from 27 January 1897 that refers to 'a sharp-looking urchin wearing a complete set of coster "pearlies"'.

However the term originated, one consequence of the 'royal' terminology has been the idea that pearly status is hereditary, i.e. that there can also be pearly princes and princesses, and only a limited number of people have the right to call themselves 'proper' pearlies. In one account the tradition takes an almost biblical turn, with proper pearly families being described as the descendants of Croft's original helpers. One wonders if there were twelve of them. Yet another explanation maintains that there should be a 'pearly king and queen' for each borough, and that they are 'elected', though it never says by whom.

Modern pearlies continue to do excellent work on the charity front and do not overly concern themselves with the niceties of historical research, but are content with an essentially oral tradition. Many pearly families now live outside London, and estimates of their number vary considerably, but perhaps forty families are still active to some degree. They still appear at many London events such as the LORD MAYOR'S SHOW (p. 10), and at three harvest festivals in September or October: at St Mary-le-Bow in Cheapside, and at St Martin-in-the-Fields and St Paul's church in Covent Garden. The Museum of London has several pearly costumes, including a splendid example from Herbert (Dick) Lyon, a chimney sweep who became pearly king of Shoreditch in 1925.

See EAST END ROAD, EAST FINCHLEY, p. 206.

first two tales, Peter Fabel outwits the Devil, and in the third he plays a trick on a lascivious friar. But in the other seventeen tales the hero is Smug, Fabel's drunken friend, and it details the tricks he plays on a variety of people.

A much more interesting treatment of the supernatural appears in *The Witch of Edmonton*, a tragi-comedy written by Thomas Dekker, John Ford, and William Rowley, which was probably first performed in 1623, although not published until 1658. The main plot concerns a man who marries two women and murders one of them to escape the consequences, and is eventually executed for his crimes. The secondary plot, however, concerns the witch of the title, and provides a very useful synopsis of witchcraft beliefs of the time.

Mother Sawyer, an old woman from Edmonton, is persecuted and abused by her neighbours, and is presumed to be a witch, primarily because she is old and ugly.

> That my bad tongue – by their bad usage made so –
> Forspeaks their cattle, doth bewitch their corn
> Themselves, their servants, and their babes at nurse

In order to prove her a witch, and to summon her, they burn a piece of her thatched roof. She decides to wreak vengeance on them and summons up the Devil, who appears in the form of a black dog and agrees to do her bidding, in return for her soul. The Devil thus attacks the villagers' crops and animals, and their wives and servants, but he eventually deserts Mother Sawyer at the crucial moment and leaves her to be executed. Another sub-plot involves the preparations of a troupe of morris dancers, and the play's description of them provides useful information about the form of the dance in the early seventeenth century.

ELY PLACE: ST ETHELDREDA'S CHURCH

St Etheldreda's church, in Ely Place, was built as the town chapel of the Bishops of Ely in about 1290, and according to their website is the oldest Catholic church in England. It is named after the best-known female Anglo-Saxon saint, a daughter of King Anna of the East Angles, who lived from AD 630 to 679. One of the miracles associated with her was that when her remains were exhumed and moved to the new Ely Cathedral, 450 years

St Etheldreda's church, in Ely Place, is the setting for the annual 'blessing the throats' ceremony that takes place on St Blaise's day, 3 February.

after her death, her body was found to be in a perfect state of preservation, a story told of many saints. She is also known for the story, first published by the Venerable Bede (*c.* 673–735), that she died from a tumour in her throat, which she piously accepted as just retribution for her habit of wearing necklaces in her youth.

Etheldreda's name is sometimes modernised as *Audrey*, and it is often stated that the modern word *tawdry* is derived from the custom of wearing necklaces in her honour, which were bought at St Audrey's fairs. These necklaces were so cheaply and badly made, it is said, that the term *tawdry* took on its modern meaning of shoddy finery. This theory, however, is at best only half-proven, and does not quite fit the known facts. It is certainly the case that in the sixteenth and seventeenth centuries a tawdry lace, in various spellings, was the name of a popular women's neck adornment, usually described as made of fine silk. It was believed at the time that the garment was named after St Audrey, and the tumour legend was quoted as the reason for the connection. But the leap from fine silk to shoddy necklace is too great to be taken on faith. The derogatory connotation of the word is first documented later in the seventeenth century, and there seems to be no evidence to connect it to fairground trinkets; it is possible, but equally unproven, that it was coined by disapproving Puritans, who were always so quick to accuse females of bad things.

Given her legend, it is appropriate that St Etheldreda's church is also connected with another throat story, that of the 'blessing the throats' ceremony, carried out each year on St Blaise's Day, 3 February. St Blaise (or Blaze, or Blaize, and often referred to as Bishop Blaise) was formerly very popular in England, and is one of the many saints whose 'lives' are so little documented that they can be said to exist almost entirely in later legend, but he is believed to have been an Armenian bishop in the fourth century. His legend has two components that contributed to his popularity in the Middle Ages. It tells that he was martyred by being torn to death with iron combs, and this made him an ideal choice as the patron saint of the woolcombers – a numerous and important group in the wool trade in medieval and early modern times. Every year, on 3 February, the woolcombers staged spectacular processions and pageants, held feasts, and generally celebrated hard. Machines now do the work of the woolcombers and they are largely forgotten.

But the other part of his legend lives on in Ely Place, and elsewhere. While hiding from his pursuers in a cave, the good Bishop carried out various miraculous cures, and in particular he saved the life of a boy who had a fishbone stuck in his throat. This has resulted in his name being invoked in cures for throat problems. Every year on his day, any visitor to St Etheldreda's can kneel before the priest to have two holy candles held in the shape of a cross at their throat, while he intones a blessing in the name of St Blaise.

ENFIELD CHASE

A story told by T. Westwood in *Notes and Queries* (1873), but quoting an unnamed friend, has become something of a classic. He relates how it occurred in an old house on the edge of Enfield Chase, the home of two elderly sisters, to which he had been invited for dinner; and he calls his story 'The Shudder'.

Having some changes to make in my attire, a servant led the way to an upper chamber, and left me. No sooner was he gone than I became conscious of a peculiar sound in the room – a sort of shuddering sound, as of suppressed dread. It seemed close to me. I gave little heed to it at first, setting it down for the wind in the chimney, or a draught from the half open door; but, moving about the room, I perceived that the sound moved with me. Whichever way I turned it followed me. I went to the furthest extremity of the chamber – it was there also. Beginning to feel uneasy, and being quite unable to account for the singularity, I completed my toilet in haste, and descended to the drawing-room, hoping I should thus leave the uncomfortable sound behind me – but not so. It was on the landing, on the stair; it went down with me – always the same sound of shuddering horror, faint, but audible, and always close at hand. Even at the dinner table, when the conversation flagged, I heard it unmistakably several times, and so near, that if there were an entity connected with it, *we were two on one chair*. It seemed to be noticed by nobody else, but it ended by harassing and distressing me, and I was relieved to think I had not to sleep in the house that night.

The narrator was much relieved when the party broke up early, and he could escape the oppressive house. The sound disappeared as soon as he reached the fresh air.

When I met my hosts again, it was under another and unhaunted roof. On my telling them what had occurred to me, they smiled, and said it was perfectly true; but added, they were so used to the sound it had ceased to perturb them. Sometimes, they said, it would be quiet for weeks, at others it followed them from room to room, from floor to floor, pertinaciously, as it had followed me. They could give no explanation of the phenomenon. It was a sound, no more, and quite harmless. Perhaps so, but of what strange horror, not ended with life, but perpetuated in the limbo of invisible things, was that sound the exponent?

FARRINGDON ROAD: HOCKLEY-IN-THE-HOLE

Hockley-in-the-Hole stood in the area to the east of Farringdon Road and north of the current Clerkenwell Road. From about the 1680s to the turn of the nineteenth century, Hockley was the best-known venue in London for blood sports such as bear- and bull-baiting, dog-fighting, and also the

Hockley-in-the-Hole was, up until the turn of the nineteenth century, a popular venue for blood sports such as bear- and bull-baiting and dog-fighting. This later, Victorian engraving shows a strangely romanticised view of these rather brutal sports.

'gladiatorial' pastimes of prize-fighting, sword-play, cudgel-fighting, and so on. It succeeded BEAR GARDENS, BANKSIDE (p. 314) as the prime venue for these events, but went much further in its provision of certain forms of 'entertainment', and there were houses that specialised in 'naked women wrestlers', in addition to normal brothels and shady drinking establishments. William Boulton, in *The Amusements of Old London* (1901), described the scene:

> Hockley in the Hole was a tumble-down affair even in its prime. It was surrounded by ruinous houses inhabited by very shady characters; by low taverns and raffish institutions for the training of bull and fighting dogs, and the whole vicinage was subject to periodical overflowings of the adjacent Fleet ditch, upon whose banks indeed Hockley was built . . . There was an atmosphere of blackguardism about the place and its entertainments from the first; there were, for example rumours of dark

passages to the banks of the Fleet for the convenience of gentry who attended its diversions and had particular reasons for avoiding constables and Bow Street officers . . .

It was very usual during the early years of the eighteenth century to encounter in the streets of the city of London a band of men marching in a kind of military order to the beat of kettle-drums, with colours flying and drawn swords, and followed by a numerous retinue distributing handbills to passers-by. The handbills contained particulars of surprising entertainments to be enjoyed at Hockley.

In their heyday, blood sports at Hockley were extremely popular with all sections of the population, although it must be said that the upper and middle classes gradually turned against them in the later eighteenth century. The movement to ban animal cruelty made slow progress until the 1820s, but then gradually succeeded in changing both the laws of the country and public opinion.

Hockley-in-the-Hole disappeared in the development of Farringdon Road in the 1850s.

GOWER STREET: UNIVERSITY COLLEGE LONDON

If you enter University College London through the South Cloisters, you will come upon the body of Jeremy Bentham (1748–1832), founder of the college and a social philosopher and reformer of some considerable repute. It was Bentham's wish that his 'auto-icon', or self-image, be displayed in perpetuity, and the seated figure is displayed in a glass-fronted box.

Bentham was a staunch utilitarian, and his notion that even his own dead body could have a use seemed to be the logical conclusion of his beliefs. He was one of the leading sponsors of the Anatomy Act of 1832, which sought to regularise the supply of dead bodies for doctors and surgeons to dissect and learn from. Before the Act, the only bodies that anatomists could legally claim were those of executed criminals, and this supply was not sufficient to satisfy the needs of the growing profession. The gap was infamously filled by the services of resurrectionists and grave-robbers, some of whom started to resort to murdering their victims to shorten the supply chain.

The 1832 Anatomy Act destroyed the market for body-snatching at a stroke, but it had other unfortunate social consequences. It stipulated that surgeons could claim the bodies of those who had died destitute, and made the poor even more terrified of dying in the workhouse or on parish relief than before. It was argued, with much justification, that the surgeons were given licence to practise on the poor to acquire the skills to cure the rich.

The Act was passed just after Bentham's death, and, according to the terms of his will, his body passed to his friend and colleague T. Southwood Smith, for dissection and then preservation. Smith delivered a public lecture on anatomy and the 'structure and functions of the human frame', over his friend's body, and the occasion was not without its own Gothic drama, as recorded by Ruth Richardson and Brian Hurwitz in 1987:

> While he was speaking a thunderstorm broke, which shook the building. With a face 'as white as that of the dead philosopher before him' he continued in a 'clear unfaltering voice'. Bentham, he said, wished to set an example to others to rise above their prejudice. Between flashes of lightning, Southwood Smith turned full on his audience, among whom were leading political and intellectual figures, some of whom had steered the Anatomy Bill through Parliament.

Bentham's skeleton was carefully wired back together, and a 'body' made with straw and other materials, and dressed in Bentham's best clothes. The head proved a bit of a problem, as they could not preserve it in a presentable state, so a wax likeness was made. The original skull was at first placed within the ribcage, then in a box at his feet, and it is now in the vaults of University College.

It is perhaps inevitable that such a bizarre tale would engender the odd ghost story, and it has been said that Bentham's figure has been seen by staff and students wandering the halls of the college, while others have heard the characteristic tap, tap, tap of his walking stick, which is in the glass case with him. One story says that he taps on the glass to demand a proper burial, but this is most unlikely considering the great pains he took in life to have his remains preserved overground.

According to Jack Hallam's *Ghosts of London* (1975), another famous ghost of the Gower Street area is nurse Lizzie Church, who frequents University College Hospital. She apparently worked there at the turn of the twentieth century, and accidentally administered a fatal overdose of morphine to her fiancé, who was also her patient. She likes to appear, sad-faced at the bedside, when injections are given.

Gray's Inn Lane

One of the most regular motifs in ghost-lore over the years is that at the point of someone's death their wraith appears to family or close friends many miles away. The following story was published in the *Burlington Magazine* (1915) under the heading 'Fragments of the Autobiography of Thomas Gosse', and appears to be an example of this belief, although the wraith seems a little premature:

> [In November 1788] Mother now coming to lodge with me in Acton Street, at the top of Gray's Inn Lane. But soon poor mother took to her bed, and, 'I shall die' she says to our landlady, 'I shall die, Mrs Ingle!' One morning Mrs Ingle came to tell me that, tho' my mother could not leave her bed, yet had she just seen her standing at a window and gazing out at the green fields, so plainly that she could discern the grey hairs over her forehead. This was by second sight, for I went immediately upstairs and found mother speechless in her bed, nor did she speak again, but once lifted up her hand with a melancholy movement, and so expired.

Hampstead: 55 Glannet Road

Elliott O'Donnell's *Haunted People* (1950) tells a gripping story, quoting an article in *Reynolds News* that appeared on 23 September 1923. As is usual for O'Donnell, he deliberately gives false names and addresses, but maintains that the story is true.

The tale involves a Mr Haglet who buys 55 Glannet Road, despite its dilapidated state, knowing that it had stood empty for a while. In the process of moving in, and having reached the point where some furniture had already arrived, Mr Haglet decided to rest and smoke his pipe:

> He went into the little room on the ground floor which he intended using for his study, and sat down. Immediately he did so an armchair opposite him gave a loud creak, and he saw the seat suddenly sink in as if depressed by a heavy weight.

A little later:

He got up, shunting his chair a little as he did so. Almost immediately, the seat of the chair opposite him rose with a spring, while the chair itself moved, as if someone was pushing it.

Going up the stairs, he heard footsteps following him, pausing as he paused, and so on. Only slightly unnerved, Haglet continued to move into the house.

A few days later he met a friend, who was aghast that he had bought No. 55 and predicted that he would be out within six months, and from then on things got much worse. Haglet's niece Ethel, who was staying with him, started sensing and seeing things, as did Hannah, the cook, who distinctly saw a woman, dressed in late Victorian clothes, carefully choosing a knife in the kitchen and walking out with it. Apparitions continued to appear, getting more and more grotesque, including evil faces in mirrors. Haglet finally gave the house up and moved out.

Meeting his friend again, Haglet asked what he knew, and he explained that a man had committed suicide in the house, by cutting his throat, about forty years before. Now the sequence of events made sense, and Haglet understood that, rather than seeing a suicide, they had been watching scenes being played out and ending in a foul murder.

HAMPSTEAD HEATH

Hampstead Heath was the scene for the annual Guy Fawkes celebrations in the late nineteenth century. These were not, however, the tumultuous rowdy street celebrations that were being suppressed in other places about this time, but excellent examples of the new, controlled, and well-behaved affairs that local authorities were keen to promote in their communities. *The Times* commented approvingly on the Hampstead example almost every year from 1882 onwards.

The event was organised by a committee, financed by subscription, and supported by the local tradesmen. Each year, the High Street was illuminated with Chinese lanterns and other carnival decorations. The torch-lit procession featured marching bands (in 1883 one band was dressed in night-caps and night-shirts), elaborate floats with themes such as 'Britannia', banners, and various groups and individuals in fancy dress.

An illustration from *The Illustrated London News* of 4 November 1848 showing Guy Fawkes celebrations on Hampstead Heath.

They all processed to the heath for an immense bonfire, and the affair regularly attracted in excess of 50,000 visitors.

This was indeed a far cry from the pitched battles between the police and the 'bonfire boys' that were taking place in other towns, but all was not sweetness and light even in Hampstead, as an article in *The Times* from 6 November 1886 shows:

> The dangerous practice of discharging fireworks in the streets was also freely carried on by some bystanders awaiting the arrival of the procession, a perfect fusilade going on in some quarters.

HAMPSTEAD SEWERS

In Henry Mayhew's extensive research for his *London Labour and the London Poor*, which was published in parts in the early 1850s, and in book form in 1861, he talked to representatives of a huge range of occupations, many of which were hardly known at all outside the immediate community in which they were situated. One of the least known were the shore-men, or 'toshers', who made a living searching the sewers of London for lost items such as money, jewellery, scrap metal, and so on. As with other out-of-the-way occupational groups, they proved to have their own skills and language, and also their own traditions:

There is a strange tale in existence among the shore-workers, of a race of wild hogs inhabiting the sewers in the neighbourhood of Hampstead. The story runs, that a sow in young, by some accident got down the sewer through an opening, and, wandering away from the spot, littered and reared her offspring in the drain, feeding on the offal and garbage washed into it continually. Here, it is alleged, this breed multiplied exceedingly, and have become almost as ferocious as they are numerous. This story, apocryphal as it seems, has nevertheless its believers, and it is ingeniously argued, that the reason why none of the subterranean animals have been able to make their way to the light of day, is that they could only do so by reaching the mouth of the sewer at the river-side, while, in order to arrive at that point they must necessarily encounter the Fleet ditch, which runs towards the river with great rapidity, and as it is the obstinate nature of a pig to swim against the stream, the wild hogs of the sewers invariably work their way back to their original quarters, and are thus never to be seen.

There must have been many thousands of contemporary legends such as this that came and went without our knowledge because they did not achieve the status of being written down for posterity. But the Hampstead hogs are referred to once again, this time in the *Daily Telegraph* on 10 October 1859:

It has been said that beasts of the chase still roam in verdant fastness of Grosvenor Square, that there are undiscovered patches of primeval forest in Hyde Park, and that Hampstead sewers shelter a monstrous breed of black swine, which have propagated and run wild among the slimy feculence, and whose ferocious snouts will one day uproot Highgate archway; while they make Highgate intolerable with their grunting.

We do not know, of course, whether the *Telegraph* writer was remembering Mayhew's article, or had heard the legend from an independent source, but one or two new details in his piece imply that the story had entered the 'oral tradition' and was therefore subject to development.

A few other traditions can be teased out of Mayhew's conversations with the shore-men. It is perhaps surprising that they did not report many tales about rats, although they mentioned them quite often. They stressed that the rats normally kept out of the way of the humans, but occasionally things went wrong:

> I knows a chap as the rats tackled in the sewers; they bit him hawfully; you must have heard on it, it was him as the water-men went in arter when they heard him a shouting as they was a rowin' by. Only for the watermen, the rats would ha' done for him, safe enough. Do you recollect hearing on the man as was found in the sewers about twelve years ago? Oh you must – the rats eat every bit of him, and left nothink but his bones. I knowed him well, he was a reg'lar shore-worker.

A 'tosher' at work, searching the sewers of Victorian London for lost money, jewellery and scrap metal. The dangerous nature of work in the sewers gave rise to various superstitions and beliefs, including the story that wild hogs lived in the Hampstead sewers.

There were stories of isolated pockets of bad air in the sewers, which would cause instantaneous death if breathed in, but the men also maintained that the general air in their underground habitat was actually beneficial, and kept them healthy. This ties in with a particularly widespread notion that particular 'airs' are good for the lungs, and for curing respiratory problems. The air in question is often industrial – gas works, boiling tar, and so on – but at other times is natural, such as the breath of a donkey, the smell of a flock of sheep, or a pile of manure.

High Street, Highgate

Two hundred years ago, Highgate was nationally famous for a custom called 'swearing on the horns'. Standing as it does on one of the major northern routes into the capital, Highgate was well placed to play an important part in the coaching trade, and dozens of coaches stopped at inns in the village every day, on their way to and from London. At each of these inns, any passenger who had not been through Highgate before could be asked to undergo the swearing ceremony, which would of course involve paying a fee or providing a round of drinks.

The landlord would don a black gown and a wig to act as judge, accompanied by a 'clerk', and would bring out a pair of animal horns (the species varied) mounted upon a pole about five feet tall, which was presented to the applicant while an oath was read out. Several writers stress that all classes of people were thus 'sworn at Highgate', and although it seems all and sundry enjoyed the joke, it is most likely that the ceremony was altered to suit the company. The exact details of the oath also varied from place to place, but were usually on similar lines, such as the following quoted in William Hone's *Every-Day Book* in 1825:

> Upstanding and uncovered: Silence. Take notice what I now say to you, for that is the first word of the oath, mind that! You must acknowledge me to be your adopted father, and I must acknowledge you to be my adopted son. If you do not call me father, you forfeit a bottle of wine; if I do not call you son, I forfeit the same. And now, my good son, if you are travelling through this village of Highgate, and you have no money in your pocket, go call for a bottle of wine at any house you may think proper to enter, and book it to your father's score. If you have any friends with you, you may treat them as well . . .

> If at any time you are going through the hamlet and want to rest yourself, and you see a pig lying in a ditch, you are quite at liberty to kick her out and take her place; but if you see three lying together you must only kick the middle one and lie between the two . . .

The ceremony always ended with the applicant kissing the horns:

> So now, my son, God bless you; kiss the horns, or a pretty girl if you see one here, which you like best, and so be free of Highgate.

A recurrent motif in the proceedings took the following form:

> You must not eat brown bread while you can get white, except you like the
> brown the best; you must not drink small beer while you can get strong,
> except you like the small the best. You must not kiss the maid while you
> can kiss the mistress, except you like the maid the best, but sooner than lose
> a good chance you may kiss them both.

This jocular theme of 'going for the best' in any situation is clearly what
the ceremony was famous for, and Francis Grose included the phrase 'He
has been sworn at Highgate' as a proverb applied to a 'knowing fellow
who is well acquainted with the good things', in his *Classical Dictionary of
the Vulgar Tongue* (1785). Another little trick was to test people who had
previously been sworn by asking them what the first word of the oath was,
and to fine them if they got it wrong. The answer to the question is *that*.

The custom was already widely known in the mid eighteenth century,
and lasted well into the nineteenth, but then declined as the coaching trade
was destroyed by the railways. Nevertheless, there have been regular
short-lived revivals, and it still takes place on occasion in some local pubs.

Various suggestions of origin have been made, but the only one that
makes any sense is that it was originally a drovers' custom. In addition to
the coaching trade, Highgate was also on the road for animals brought in
on the hoof to the London markets, and the ceremony may have been a
jocular initiation rite for the men who drove them. There is no reason to
believe that it was ever anything more serious.

HIGHGATE CEMETERY

While it is inevitable that cemeteries will attract a fair amount of traditional
lore – ghost stories, superstitions, tales of grave-robbers and other dark
deeds – it is the unfortunate fate of Highgate Cemetery to have attracted
the notice of those strange people who genuinely believe in vampires. Since
the 1970s, there has been continuous interest in Highgate from the
vampire-hunting brigade, and now that the Internet has given the notion
perpetual life, there is little hope of it ever being forgotten.

Highgate was opened in 1839 as one of seven new private cemeteries in
the Greater London area, in response to concerns about widespread

overcrowding and malpractice in the city's older churchyards. The new cemetery was extended when the eastern section was opened in 1854, giving a total area of 37 acres, and more than 168,000 people were eventually interred there. The older section in particular became famous for its extravagant tombs in a wonderful mixture of styles, mock-Egyptian, classical and Gothic all vying for attention, and many impressive angels and other life-size sculptures bear witness to the way Victorians viewed and celebrated death.

But Highgate inevitably suffered from the problems of all privately owned cemeteries – in particular, how to make a profit once it was full. Between the wars, it was woefully neglected and was allowed to become completely overgrown, with the grand tombs left to decay and fall apart. Nevertheless, this neglected state added significantly to the cemetery's Gothic appearance, and it is clear that local adolescents were in the habit of using it as a 'scary place' to visit, with 'schoolboys climbing on graves at night as a dare', as one cemetery caretaker complained in 1970. But this was a minor irritant compared with what was about to hit the area.

On 6 February 1970, the *Hampstead and Highgate Express* published a letter from one David Farrant, entitled 'Ghostly Walks in Highgate', in which the writer related his supernatural experiences in the cemetery: 'On three occasions I have seen what appeared to be a ghost-like figure inside the gates at the top of Swains Lane.' A number of people wrote in response to this letter, telling of their own spooky experiences in the vicinity of the cemetery, but they all told different stories and they were all about vague sightings and scary feelings. As often happens with such local ghost-lore, there was no coherent pattern of narrative in these letters or subsequent publications, but it is quite possible that such stories had previously existed in the local community without being recorded.

And so it would have been left had two things not happened. Firstly, an 'expert' on the occult declared that these were not any ordinary ghosts but were in fact sightings of a vampire which was terrorising the neighbourhood, and secondly, the media picked up on this story. The rapid escalation of media coverage, from local press to national press to national television, turned a small local event into a major flap, and it was the TV coverage that did the real damage, by airing reports with a spurious 'let the viewer decide' angle, and giving some very silly ideas a national platform. The immediate result was scores of mostly young people descending on Highgate, many armed with home-made stakes and crucifixes. While most of them were content to mill about outside the cemetery gates, some got inside in order to search for the undead. Over the next months there were reports of tombs being broken open and vandalised, and in a few cases some graves were desecrated, with corpses being manhandled and mutilated.

It is difficult to piece together exactly what happened over the next few months, as several things were clearly occurring at roughly the same time. The cemetery became fair game for a potent mix of hoaxes, publicity stunts, vandals, and bored or excitable young people. There were, for example, persistent panics about satanists using the cemetery for black magic rites, and numerous reported finds of incriminating evidence of blood and feathers, candles, burnt offerings, or remains of sacrificed animals, prompting the thought that devil-worshippers really should learn to clear up after themselves. This is classic territory for rumour and legend. Nobody actually stumbled across a black mass in operation, or bumped into a coach party of satanists on their way to or from their AGM at the nearest tomb, but lots of people reported that 'so-and-so' had found 'such-and-such', which 'must have' been used in a black mass, and there was always an 'expert' on hand to confirm it to the media.

As is often the case with fringe societies and organisations, the leaders of the vampire scare, who were the ones always quoted by the media, soon fell out, and each publicly condemned the others as rank amateurs and posers. But at least one of them still insists that he did battle with and destroyed two or three vampires in the Highgate area, with the aid of wooden stakes, crucifixes, garlic, and Latin incantations. If he did save the world from the unspeakable evil of the undead, we should certainly be grateful to him.

Most available descriptions of the Highgate phenomenon have been written by the those whose main intent is to prove the existence of vampires, but by far the best serious analysis is 'The Highgate Cemetery Vampire Hunt', published in the journal *Folklore* in 1993, by American folklorist Bill Ellis, and his subsequent book, *Raising the Devil* (2000). This author sets the Highgate events into the wider folkloric context of rumours, scares, moral panics, and adolescent belief and behaviour, in Britain and America. He draws parallels with previous local events, such as children invading local churchyards in Glasgow in the 1930s and 1950s searching for 'the monster with iron teeth', and also the genuinely disturbing gullibility of some local authorities, which led to accusations of satanic child abuse in

Highgate Cemetery shortly after it opened in 1839. Neglected and overgrown by the 1970s, it became a focal point for vampire sightings.

certain British communities. He also identifies a common genre of local adolescent tradition called the 'legend-trip', where the 'trip' to a local site – usually somewhere scary like a churchyard – is undertaken and talked about by adolescent groups, which fulfils a similar role to local legends. Another factor is the phenomenon that folklorists call 'ostension', whereby people (usually, but not always, adolescents) begin to 'act out' the rumours and legends circulating in their community. This can be potent enough on a small-scale local level, but can have serious repercussions if given the oxygen of publicity by the mass media.

As a footnote to this account, it should be pointed out that, contrary to widespread assumption, vampires are not a widespread feature in British tradition, and are, in fact, relatively recent intruders, apart from the apparently isolated tales recorded by William Newburgh in his *Historia Rerum Anglicarum* in the late twelfth century. The word *vampire* is not found in English before the 1730s, and blood-sucking living-dead creatures only became well known in this country with the publication of popular Gothic novels such as *Varney the Vampire* (1845–7) and Bram Stoker's *Dracula* (1897). But it is abundantly clear that the ideas about vampires and how to vanquish them that were current in Highgate in the 1970s and 1980s were entirely gleaned from the immensely popular series of vampire films made by Hammer Films, starting with *Dracula* in 1958. There is little doubt that panics such as the Highgate story will occur again in the future, and it will be interesting to see if those involved will have forgotten the Hammer films and instead be influenced by popular TV series such as *Buffy the Vampire Slayer*.

Since 1981, the cemetery has been under the control of the Friends of Highgate Cemetery, a charitable trust, whose largely volunteer workforce has worked miracles in beating back nature and returning the site to its former glory. It is now not only a working cemetery again, but also a major heritage site, with guided tours. But there is no stopping the story of the Highgate Vampire, which now features on innumerable websites as one of the 'proven' vampire infestations of the modern age.

HIGHGATE GREEN

The modern image conjured up by a 'fair' is of flashy rides, shows, and stalls, but in earlier days fair-goers could enjoy the simpler pleasures of races, contests, and stunts. An advertisement for Highgate Fair in the mid eighteenth century, reprinted in George Daniel's *Merrie England in the Olden Time* (1842), gives a flavour of these events:

2 July 1744
This is to give notice that Highgate Fair will be kept on Wednesday, Thursday, and Friday next, in a pleasant shady walk in the middle of the town. On Wednesday a pig will be turned loose, and he that takes it up by the tail and throws it over his head, shall have it. To pay two-pence entrance, and no less than twelve to enter. On Thursday a match will be run by two men, a hundred yards in two sacks, for a large sum. And, to encourage the sport, the landlord of the Mitre will give a pair of gloves, to be run for by six men, the winner to have them. And on Friday a hat, value ten shillings, will be run for by men twelve times round the Green; to pay one shilling entrance: no less than four to start; as many as will enter, and the second man to have all the money above four.

These events are quite typical of fairs of the day, although in many cases the pig would have been 'greased' to make it harder to catch.

Dick Whittington

Dick Whittington with his cat, from an eighteenth-century chapbook.

Perennial pantomime classic *Dick Whittington* is about a poor orphan from Gloucester who made his way to London because he had heard that the streets were paved with gold. Finding work as a lowly servant in the kitchen of a wealthy merchant called Fitzwarren, Dick had a miserable time and was mistreated and bullied, particularly by the cook in whose charge he was placed. His only possession was the cat he had bought for a penny, to help keep down the vermin in the garret where he slept.

As was the custom in those days, when Fitzwarren had a ship ready to sail on a trading mission, he asked if anyone would like to purchase a stake in the venture, and as Dick had nothing else to contribute, he sent his cat. Some time later, wearying of his unhappy life as scullion, Dick decided to leave and set off on the long walk home, but sat down to rest by a milestone on Highgate Hill. As he sat, he heard the bells of Bow church ringing, and they seemed to be saying, 'Turn again, Whittington, thrice Lord Mayor of London.' He took the hint, and returned to his post in the merchant's kitchen. Meanwhile, unknown to him, Fitzwarren's ship had reached Barbary and docked in a country which had never seen a cat and whose royal court was overrun with rats and mice. The wealthy ruler of this land was so pleased with the performance of Dick's cat as vermin catcher that he immediately paid a huge sum for it, as well as buying the whole of the ship's cargo, and when the ship returned to England Dick found he was a very rich man. He duly married Fitzwarren's daughter, and rose to be Lord Mayor, not once, but three times.

As has long been generally accepted, there was indeed a Richard Whittington (*c*.1350–1423) from Gloucestershire, who was three and a half times Lord Mayor. This came about because although he was elected Mayor three times (1397, 1406 and 1419), he had already served for some months when appointed by Richard II to complete the term of a mayor who died in office. But his biography includes no hint as to why the well-known story became attached to his name. Far from being a poor boy, the real Whittington was a wealthy mercer who supplied members of the royal family and other court nobles with expensive clothes, and was rich enough to lend considerable sums to successive monarchs. He died childless and left most of his estate to be laid out in philanthropic causes.

The rags-to-riches story of Dick Whittington, with cat motif, was widely disseminated in plays, ballads, and prose chapbooks from at least the early seventeenth century. The earliest record is in February 1605, when a play was registered at Stationer's Hall under the title *The History of Richard Whittington, of his lowe birthe, his great fortune, as yt was played by the Prynces Servants*, but it is clear that the story was already well known at the time, as indicated by a line in the play *Eastward Ho!* written by Ben Jonson, George Chapman and John Marston in the same year: 'when the famous fable of Whittington and his pusse shal be forgotten'.

Throughout the eighteenth and nineteenth centuries, the story continued to be circulated in chapbooks aimed at children, and it received a new lease of life when pantomime writers picked up on the story and made it one of their staple productions. The earliest known in this genre was *Harlequin Whittington, or the Lord Mayor of London*, performed in 1814 at Covent Garden.

There are many memorials to Dick Whittington all over London, including the milestone at the foot of HIGHGATE HILL (p. 230) and St Michael Paternoster church in COLLEGE HILL (p. 18). A famous stained-glass window depicting him, in the Guildhall, was destroyed in the Blitz, but a new one by Douglas Strachan was later erected, and there is a memorial statue outside the same building.

HIGHGATE HILL

Perhaps the best-known memorial to DICK WHITTINGTON (p. 228), one of the most popular figures in London folklore, is the stone on Highgate Hill that claims to mark the place where he heard the bells advising him to return: 'Turn again, Whittington, thrice Lord Mayor of London!' The current stone, which is at least the third on the site (or nearby), is topped by a life-size figure of a cat, added in 1964. The earliest known stone was the base of a wayside cross (not a milestone as is often claimed), which was removed in 1795 and, following a public outcry, replaced by a new stone.

The oft-repeated story of Dick Whittington tells how he was persuaded by the ringing of Bow bells to return to his life of drudgery as a kitchen hand. Shortly after his return, though, he discovered that his one possession – his cat – had brought him great wealth because his merchant employer had sold it to the royal court of Barbary to keep the vermin infestation under control.

The motif of a fortune made by a cat is truly international, and has been recorded in more than twenty different countries, with the earliest versions pre-dating the historical Dick Whittington. One example, reported in *The Times* on 21 September 1874, was told by the famous solar scholar Max Müller to a gathering of the International Congress of Orientalists, in the presence of the then Lord Mayor. Müller was quoting a Persian historian named Wassif who lived at the beginning of the fourteenth century, from an original manuscript in the Imperial Library at Vienna:

> There was in Siraf a noble merchant prince of the name of Kaisar. When he died he left three sons, who very soon squandered the paternal fortune, and left their poor old mother to starve alone with her cat. Now, it is the habit in Eastern countries, when a merchant sails from port, to ask poor people for a small present and their blessing, and to promise to bring them back some present in return. The poor widow, when asked for a present, had nothing to give but her cat, and that cat she gave to the sailor, though with a sad heart. The sailor came to India and was invited to dine with the King, and while they sat at dinner he saw a man with a club standing by the King and killing the mice, with which the palace was swarming. The sailor fetched his cat, the cat killed the mice, and the King bought the cat for a fabulous sum. The honest sailor, returning, handed over the money to the poor widow, and she, good soul and kind mother as she was, gave all the money to her sons.

'Turn again, Whittington, thrice Lord Mayor of London.' A romanticised nineteenth-century view of Highgate Hill and the story of Dick Whittington.

There have been many theories to explain the appearance of the cat in the Whittington legend, including a number which argue that the origin should be sought in etymological mistakes or misreadings. So, for example, it has been stated that *cate* was an Old English word for 'provisions'; that *achat* was a Norman English word meaning 'purchases'; that a *scat* was the bundle of possessions carried on a stick over the shoulder; and that a *cat* was a type of sailing ship on the east coast of England. But none of these is convincing.

It is doubtful that the connection between Whittington and the cat will ever now be severed. A report in *The Times* on 18 July 1929 shows how deep it goes:

> At the Justice Room, Guildhall, yesterday, there was a defendant named Dick Whittington, and his case was heard in the presence of the official cat 'Donald'. Mr Whittington of the Hampton Court Hotel, was fined 20s. for causing an obstruction with his motor car in Great Swan Alley on June 28. The official tabby is generally in seclusion while the Court is sitting, but at the moment the name 'Dick Whittington' was called, Donald sprang on to the front of the dock and settled down as though prepared to hear the case out. One of the officials, however, restored him to his proper place.

It is unlikely that the defendant was amused; anyone with the name Richard Whittington must get very fed up with cat jokes.

HORNSEY

According to A. R. Wright and T. E. Lones's classic work *British Calendar Customs* (1940), Hornsey children constructed grottoes each August in the

1890s, as elsewhere in London. When asking for money from passers-by they would chant the following rhyme:

> Please remember the grotto
> Father's gone to sea
> Mother's gone to fetch him home
> Please remember me.

See also GROTTOES AND SPRING GARDENS, p. 402.

ISLINGTON

In 1893, the writer Robert Cope specifically referred to 'Islington lands' as 'a famous ducking land', and by this he was referring to the sport of duck-hunting. Joseph Strutt's classic work *Sports and Pastimes* (1833 edn) gives more details of what he calls a 'barbarous pastime':

> For the performance it is necessary to have recourse to a pond of water sufficiently extensive to give the duck plenty of room for making her escape from the dogs when she is closely pursued; which she does by diving as often as any of them come near her. Duck-hunting was much practised in the neighbourhood of London about thirty or forty years ago; but of late it is gone out of fashion; yet I cannot help thinking that the deficiency, at present, of places proper for the purpose, has done more towards the abolishment of this sport than any amendment in the nature and inclinations of the populace.

The dogs involved were often spaniels, and there were duck ponds in various parts of London. Pubs called the Dog and Duck often commemorate the sport. But far more barbarous was another version of 'duck-hunting', in which a live owl was strapped to the back of a live duck. The owl's noise and frantic movements frightened the duck into diving. When it re-surfaced, if the owl was still alive the cycle would begin all over again. The audience thought this very amusing.

See also MAYFAIR, p. 94.

John Street: Coutts

In his *Banker Tells All* (1956), R. Thurston Hopkins describes a visit to the extensive vaults of the former Coutts Bank in John Street, which had been taken over by a firm of wine merchants:

> I met a journalist, Arthur Machen, whose newspaper, the *Evening News*, had sent him to spend an inquisitive midnight hour in the haunted vault. He said: 'I wouldn't spend a night alone in those wine cellars for a fortune. There's something very odd about the place. I walked along one of the passages with a powerful electric torch I had borrowed from a cinema doorkeeper – and, do you know, a damn great black cat flew at my face, snarling and scratching like the devil. It shot between my legs and made for a wine cellar which had no exit. But when I flashed my torch to the end of the tunnel, there was nothing there. The cat did not come out again, I can swear. And when I asked the cellar foreman, he said they had not a cat of any kind down in the wine vaults. Nobody in the neighbourhood had a black cat. But, he added, if a stranger came into the cellars, the phantom cat seemed to resent it, and out he jumped.'

Arthur Machen, incidentally, was the writer who claimed to have started the Angel of Mons legend, the story of how the British forces, when retreating from Mons in 1914, were heartened by visions of English bowmen in the sky.

Kentish Town

A widespread international motif found in folklore, and the science fiction and horror genres, is the idea that animals can get inside humans and can live, thrive, and maybe even breed there. In British folk tradition, the creatures are usually reptiles – snakes, frogs, newts, eels, worms – which live in the stomach and digestive tracts; or insects, which can be anywhere inside the body, or just under the skin. The creatures are said to find their way in there in various ways, for example when we eat unwashed vegetables or over-ripe fruit, drink contaminated water, or sleep out in the open. Sometimes it is said that the parasite has been ingested by accident and just happens to live and grow, while others deliberately seek out humans in which to live and breed. In some contemporary legends, foreign insects lay their eggs in their bites, and the young then burrow inwards, or suddenly appear when the swelling bursts. Earwigs, of course, crawl into your ears.

Some examples, noted in Kentish Town, were submitted to the journal *Folk-Lore* in 1926:

> In 1905 a girl employed in an East-end factory (London born) was telling me how careful she was to avoid eating over-ripe fruit. 'There was a young girl in our street ate a whole pound of plums, I think it was, and there was maggots in them. And they grew inside her. They took her to the hospital but they couldn't do nothing for her: they had to get consent to smother her!' In 1926 I heard the story again from a very superior and refined young woman (Liverpool born) in Kentish Town. She expressed a horror of 'blackbeetles', and said that she dreaded them particularly on account of her little boy. She could never forget a case of which her mother had told her: a child was allowed to crawl on the kitchen floor, 'and he must have picked up a blackbeetle and swallowed it. They had a nurse in to look after him, because he was ill and they didn't know what was the matter; and she found it out. One day she turned out the light and waited about ten minutes, and turned the light on suddenly; and there was a great blackbeetle just coming out of the child's ear! I think mother said they had it smothered, and there was an inquest, and they found it simply swarming with beetles inside.' In each case the story was told with full gravity and conviction of its truth, and the 'smothering' was mentioned without indignation or even emphasis, as what would naturally be done in the circumstances.
>
> With this may be compared the widely held belief that doctors 'do away with' abnormal children at birth. A middle-aged woman in Kentish Town said that her mother, having been frightened by a monkey which clawed her skirt, gave birth to a monkey-headed child. 'Of course the doctor done away with it. Mother didn't see it, but she always used to tell us what it was like.'
>
> In July 1909, a London charwoman told my wife that people often swallowed frogs or beetles when eating watercress or drinking; these creatures bred and caused trouble. She knew herself a young woman who was ill in bed, and had a glass of milk left on the floor at night by the bedside. She drank it and must have drunk some beetles with it, for 'when she died, the doctors opened her and found her full of holes and blackbeetles.'

It is surprising how seriously these stories were taken – indeed, still are taken, in some circumstances. There were also many ancillary beliefs, such as the idea mentioned above that in extreme cases of infestation the only thing to do was to smother the patient, and that this was perfectly legal if the authorities obtained permission from the King. In other instances, the condition could be cured by tricking the animal out. So, for example, the patient was made to fast or take no drink for days, so that the animal could be tempted out by holding food or a glass of milk to the sufferer's mouth. But of course one has to be very quick to catch the creature when it makes an appearance.

On a broader scale, there are definite connections between these stories and vernacular ideas about illness being a parasite or a malevolent animal, as well as with notions of infestations by devils in witchcraft or fundamentalist religion, as folklorist Gillian Bennett explored in her book *Bodies: Sex, Violence, Disease and Death in Contemporary Legend* (2005).

See also KENT ST, SOUTHWARK, p. 335; NEW MALDEN, p. 404; SILVERTOWN, p. 300; VERE STREET, p. 119.

KINGSWAY

There are several episodes in A. W. M. Stirling's book of miscellaneous pieces, *The Merry Wives of Battersea* (1956), that, by implication, she thought were genuine 'unexplained' mysteries. One had apparently appeared in the press at some point, but she gives no date or other details:

> A girl was walking along Kingsway after her luncheon, when, to her horror, she suddenly saw what appeared to be the body of a woman come hurtling down from the window of a high building and fall with a crash at her feet. The shock of this dreadful sight was so great that the girl collapsed on the pavement and was picked up by two men and half carried into a nearby pharmacy. When she revived, she explained the cause of her collapse, but to her amazement was assured that nothing of what she described had taken place, the accident, or the suicide, which she believed she had witnessed had been a figment of her imagination. Later, however, she learnt that the whole thing had actually taken place, as she saw it, in the exact locality and at the precise hour, 3 p.m., when she had visualised it, but *eighteen months previously*.

See also BLACKFRIARS BRIDGE, p. 6.

LINCOLN'S INN

For those who wished to undertake some 'offensive' witchcraft, designed to cause harm to others, there were certain methods that anyone could employ, given the knowledge of the right procedures and words. But there were also professionals (cunning men, conjurers, and so on) who professed to have powers, or arcane knowledge, beyond the capabilities of ordinary folk, and from which they made a living.

One of the commonest forms of ill-wishing was 'image magic', which involved sticking pins into a small effigy of the intended victim, but a less well-known form of cursing is explored in an article by W. Paley Baildon, published in the *Proceedings of the Society of Antiquaries* in 1900. The article describes a lead tablet, about 4? by 3? inches in size, which had been dug up the previous year in Lincoln's Inn. One face of the tablet had been divided into squares, nine across and nine down, and in each square a number of one or two digits had been crudely etched. The other face bore the words 'That nothinge maye prosper Nor goe forward that Raufe Scrope takethe in hande', together with the names Hasmodai, Schedbarschemoth, and

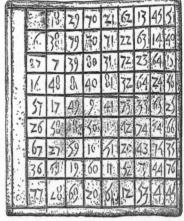

A contemporary engraving of a lead cursing square found at Lincoln's Inn in 1899. The main inscription reads, 'That nothinge maye prosper Nor goe forward that Raufe Scrope taketh in hande'. Documentary evidence shows that a Ralph Scrope was associated with the place between 1543 and 1572.

Schartatan, and three astrological symbols. Ralph Scrope was associated with Lincoln's Inn, in various capacities, from 1543 to 1572, but it is not known who owed him such spite, or why.

As Baildon points out, however, this is not the only surviving example of a lead cursing square, and a fair amount is known about their purpose and use. He quotes from *Three Books of Occult Philosophy*, written by Henry Cornelius Agrippa in 1533, translated into English and published in 1651. This work goes into great detail about how and when such squares should be used, stressing in particular the effect of the action on each different day of the moon's phase. The paragraph most relevant to this case seems to be the following:

> And if it be an unfortunate moon in a plate of lead, wherever it shall be buried, it makes that place unfortunate, and the inhabitants thereabouts, as also ships, rivers, fountains, mills, and it makes every man unfortunate against which it shall be directly done, making him fly from his country, and that place of his abode where it shall be buried, and it hinders physicians, and orators, and all men whatsoever in their office against whom it shall be made.

There is also a great deal of mumbo-jumbo about planets, and it gives the peculiar names found on the tablet at Lincoln's Inn as those of spirits. Clearly, the curse did not work very well, as Scrope ended his days as one of the Inn's governors, but its lack of effectiveness may be put down to a simple error in the mathematics. In theory, in a nine-by-nine square like this one, the numbers in the horizontal and vertical lines should each add up to 369, but whoever cut this tablet made two errors, using 45 and 64 twice, and missing out 54 and 55, so perhaps it is no wonder it did not work. It is interesting to note that Agrippa made exactly the same mistakes in his published versions.

See also WITCH BOTTLES p. 238.

MILDMAY STREET, CANONBURY

Writing in the collection of memoirs published as *Growing Up in the Twenties* (1993), Bob Rutty, of Mildmay Street, listed the games he remembered playing, with descriptions in his own words:

Witch Bottles

A typical witch bottle made out of a bellarmine, a German stoneware jug decorated with a bearded face. Like the one that was dug out of the Thames mud near Paul's Pier Wharf, it was found with a heart-shaped piece of cloth pierced with pins inside it.

Past practices such as popular witchcraft, however widespread in their day, often leave no trace, and hard evidence is difficult to come by. But one physical item that still turns up from time to time in old houses or buried in the ground is the so-called witch bottle. Ralph Merrifield's study of *The Archaeology of Ritual and Magic* (1987) includes several interesting examples of these bottles, dating from the seventeenth and eighteenth centuries, which have been found in various locations in London as well as in country areas. One was discovered in the Thames mud about nine feet from the bottom of the steps at Paul's Pier Wharf in the City, and included a piece of felt cut into the shape of a heart, pierced with five brass pins. Another bottle, unearthed at the corner of Great College and Tufton Street in 1904, contained a similarly shaped piece of cloth, together with pins, human hair, and nail parings. Other examples were found in Duke's Place, Aldgate; Pennington Street, Stepney; and Plaisterers' Hall, Noble Street in the City of London. A particularly popular vessel for this kind of operation was a bellarmine, a German stoneware jug or bottle, which bore a relief figure of a bearded face.

The contents of the bottles are always very similar: sharp things such as pins, nails, and thorns; personal items such as hair or nail clippings; liquid, often urine; and something to represent the victim's heart or other body parts. The sharp objects were designed to cause pain to the victim of the spell, especially if the bottle was heated and its contents agitated. Interestingly, however, these bottles were not necessarily *offensive* witchcraft, but quite often *defensive*.

There is a basic premise in popular witchcraft that in casting a malevolent spell, or even simply wishing someone ill, a sort of invisible thread of influence or sympathy is created which links the ill-wisher to the victim, and allows the evil intention to be passed along. However, this 'thread' functions in both directions, and once the victim realises what is happening, the 'thread' can be used to mount a counter-attack. These bottles might therefore have been used as counter-spells, aimed at causing the original ill-wisher enough pain to be forced to remove the original spell.

A similar effect was thought to be achieved by piercing an animal's heart, as in this example included by Edward Lovett in his *Magic in Modern London*, published in 1925:

> I was rather surprised to come across a genuine case of this form of magic in the north-east district of London, about the year 1902. A cowkeeper, who was one of the old school and who originally came from Devonshire, had the misfortune to incur the intense wrath of a man of very vindictive temper. He threatened to bewitch the poor man's cows, and two of them died. The cowkeeper thereupon took the heart of one of the dead animals, stuck it all over with pins and nails and hung it up in the chimney of his house. Steps were taken to let the man who had done the mischief know of all this, and such action is supposed to be of such a serious nature that it brought about an arrangement of a more or less satisfactory character.

See WAPPING, p. 304.

Release

Two sides. One side (being chased) was given a specific area in which could run and hide; they had to endeavour to get back to base without being caught, but even on arriving back they were not caught until their hands clasped over the heads had been pulled asunder.

Jimmy-Jimmy-Knacko

Two sides. One side had a stalwart with his back to the wall, and maybe two or three of his mates bent with their body horizontal from the waist, with the first man's head against the stalwart, and so on. The others ran and leapt on to the back of the benders until they gave way. Also known as weak horses.

Three Sticks

Three sticks against a wall with a horizontal stick balanced on top. You stood several feet away and threw your ball at them, to knock them down. Similarly with stones within a chalked ring.

Rope Strings

Ropes tied to the protruding arms of the lamp-post, or tied just below it. It was either swung backwards or forwards or round and round. Generally a girls' game. The householders used to dislodge you if they caught you.

A Pin a Pick

Why a pin I don't know. Various oddments, like postcards or cigarette cards, were placed within the pages of a large book and you inserted the pin where you thought the item might be, winning it as a prize if you discovered it, but giving up the pin.

Cigarette cards

Collecting and swapping, and playing a game of trying to flick your card onto a master card for a prize of so many cards. Or flicking them all one after another and collecting any card that your own one settled upon.

PENTONVILLE ROAD, ISLINGTON:
JOSEPH GRIMALDI PARK

See BEECHWOOD ROAD, DALSTON: HOLY TRINITY CHURCH, p. 256.

RED LION SQUARE, HIGH HOLBORN

The Red Lion, in High Holborn, was for a long time the largest and most popular inn in the neighbourhood, and stood next to a paddock until around 1698, when the square named after it was built. The central space of the square was allowed to lapse into dereliction, but then residents took it in hand in the 1720s and laid it out as a formal garden, with a watchtower at each corner and an obelisk in the centre. It was laid out as a public space in 1885, and was acquired by the London County Council in 1894.

It is claimed that the modern square is haunted by three cloaked figures who walk diagonally across it, ignoring modern pathways, apparently deep in conversation, and they all have their heads in place. This last detail is important, because it is generally believed that they are the ghosts of Cromwell and his two fellow regicides, Ireton and Bradshaw, who might, or might not, have been secretly buried in the square, before or after their heads were chopped off. It is not clear when the three ghosts were first seen, and they are probably of relatively recent invention, but they are mentioned by Christina Hole in her *Haunted England* (1940).

Most historians have rejected this secret burial idea, but it refuses to go away, and as with all good legends there are enough circumstantial details to keep it in play. As is well known, Charles II ordered the exhumation of the three bodies from their Westminster Abbey tombs. They were taken to Tyburn, hung for a day like common criminals, cut down, decapitated, and their bodies buried at the foot of the gallows.

John Evelyn, the diarist, was pleased:

30th January 1661
This day (O the stupendous and inscrutable judgments of God!) were the carcasses of those arch-rebels, Cromwell, Bradshaw (the judge who condemned his majesty), and Ireton (son-in-law to the Usurper), dragged out of their superb tombs in Westminster among the kings, to Tyburn and hanged on the gallows, there from nine in the morning till six at night, and then buried under that fatal and ignominious monument in a deep pit; thousands of people who had seen them in all their pride being spectators.

Their heads were displayed on spikes on the roof of Westminster Hall.

Nevertheless, at least one contemporary states that after exhumation the bodies were taken to the Red Lion inn, kept overnight, and taken to

Tyburn the next day. It has never been clear why this inn was chosen. It is not on the route from Westminster Abbey to Tyburn, and there were plenty of other suitable places. Some have argued that the answer is simple: people at the time used 'Tyburn' as a generic term for 'gallows' (which is true), and there was a gallows near the Red Lion. It is therefore argued that the actual hanging took place at the Red Lion, but this is most unlikely. If this were the case, at least one of the eyewitness and contemporary accounts would have casually mentioned the location as the Red Lion, or Holborn, but none do so.

More convincingly, it is said that they were taken there as part of a plot to switch them for other bodies, and the real ones were quietly buried in the paddock at the back of the inn, at the spot where the obelisk was later erected. It is not clear when this story was first circulated, but it was already well known in the late eighteenth century, over a century after the event, and the obelisk itself was not installed until sixty years after the supposed burial. The presence of an obelisk always seems to invite a legend, usually of either a battle or a burial. This one had no observable purpose, and was graced by an inscription that no one seems to have been able to decipher; given in Edward Walford and Walter Thornbury's *Old and New London* (1878), as:

OBTUSUM OBTUSIORIS INGENII MONUMENTUM. QUID ME RESPICIS, VIATOR? VADE.

There are many holes in the official version of events – not least, as pointed out by Frederick Varley in 1939, that Ireton had died of the plague in Ireland and was almost certainly buried there. There are therefore many supporters of the secret-burial theory, and not only on the fringe of conspiracy theorists. H. F. McMains's *The Death of Oliver Cromwell* (2000), for example, dismisses the official version of Cromwell's death and burials, presenting plenty of 'evidence' to support the Red Lion site as his final resting place, and even posits the theory that he did not die of ill health, but was poisoned. Somebody certainly needs to dig up Red Lion Square to find out.

Leaving Cromwell and friends to their own devices, there are two other reports of ghosts in Red Lion Square, both recorded by Elliott O'Donnell, from his own experience. The first is in his *Haunted Places in England* (1919), and tells of a time he was visiting a friend in Sloane Square. He found himself impressed by a chair that stood by the fire in the house, and his friend claimed it came from a haunted house in Red Lion Square and that people who sat in it had very strange experiences. O'Donnell was curious and took the chair home to try it out. First of all, his cat would not go near it. Then, during the night, he could hear it moving, groaning, and rocking furiously, but sitting in it produced no supernatural experience, until one Friday night he tried again.

> Then by degrees, quite imperceptibly, I lost cognisance of all these things [in the room]; and, intuitively, I began to feel the presence of something strange and wholly novel . . . I felt it steal forth from a piece of dark and ancient tapestry my wife had hung on the wall. It was merely a shadow, an undefined shadow, a shadow such as the moon, when very low in the heavens might possibly fashion from the figure of a man.

The shadow bent over him, placed its hands on his eyes, and then he became completely numb. At characteristically great length O'Donnell describes his sensations, but finally he became aware of a scene playing out before him like, it must be said, a very bad play. He claims to have seen two men in eighteenth-century costume in, perhaps, a tavern. They had previously been rivals for the hand of a woman; the one who had won her had mistreated her, and she was now dead. The one who had not married her claimed that she had often come to him, in spirit, in his house in Red Lion Square. The scene changed, and the two men were in that house, talking of spirits and hauntings. One said that the house was too recent to have a history, and without a history there could be no hauntings:

> 'True. So far this house has no history. No history whatever. But it will have one, Wilfred. It will.' And baring the blade of his formidable weapon, he crouched low and crept forward . . .

O'Donnell took the chair back to his friend, who confirmed that others had had similar experiences with it. The friend added:

> 'I wonder if a murder did actually take place in that house? I shouldn't be at all surprised. There is an old stain on the floor of one of the rooms on the second landing, and they say that, despite the most vigorous washing, it still retains its colour – red, blood-red.'

As with many of O'Donnell's stories, this is far too contrived to be anything but an invention on his part, but his other Red Lion story is slightly more believable. It appears in his *Ghosts of London* (1932). He and his wife were living on the third and fourth floor of a house in the square in the early years of the First World War. One Saturday afternoon, when he was alone in the house, he heard heavy ponderous footsteps slowly ascending the stairs. They reached his landing and stopped, then started to descend. He followed them down, but could see nobody, and on the ground floor the house door opened and closed by itself. Mentioning the experience to others in the house, he learned that they too had heard the footsteps and that the house was well known in the square for being haunted. Another time, his wife heard a heavy object fall on the stairs, but could see nothing. The caretaker's daughter reported seeing an old man with a white beard on several occasions. There were rumours of some accident or tragedy, but nothing was resolved, and the O'Donnells moved on.

See also PARLIAMENT SQUARE, p. 97.

St John Street, Islington

Islington hardly sounds like the back of beyond, but even in the eighteenth century it was still sufficiently remote from London to be a dangerous place to travel to and from. According to Edward Walford and Walter Thornbury's *Old and New London* (1878):

In 1739 the roads and footpaths of Islington seem to have been infested by highwaymen and footpads, the hornets and mosquitoes of those days. In the year above mentioned, the Islington Vestry agreed to pay a reward of £10 to any person who apprehended a robber. It was customary at this time for persons walking from the City to Islington after dark to wait at the end of St John Street till a sufficient number had collected, and then to be escorted by an armed patrol.

In 1771 the inhabitants of Islington subscribed a sum of money for rewarding persons apprehending robbers, as many dwellings had been broken open, and the Islington stage was frequently stopped. In 1780, in consequence of riots and depredations, the inhabitants furnished themselves with arms and equipments, and formed a military society for general protection . . .

SEVEN SISTERS ROAD

The name Seven Sisters is a very popular one. Among many others, it appears as the name of the famous chalk cliffs in East Sussex; a locality in Neath; a star cluster (the Pleiades), with attendant classical myths of the seven daughters of Atlas and Pleione; seven liberal arts women's colleges in north-eastern USA; seven Stalinist skyscrapers in Moscow (built 1947–53); and the title of at least five different novels in the last eighty years, and one farce comedy.

But most Londoners will connect the name with the long Seven Sisters Road, laid out in the early 1830s, running from Holloway, through Finsbury Park, to Tottenham, with Seven Sisters station at the latter end. As Walford and Thornbury point out, it gets its name from a circle of trees:

> The 'Seven Sisters' was the sign of an old public house at Tottenham, in front of which were planted seven elms in a circle, with a walnut-tree in the middle . . . The trees were more recently to be seen at the entrance of the village from Page Green; and when they died off, a few years ago, they were replaced by others.

The first evidence of their existence is on the Dorset Survey map of 1619, which shows a clump of trees at Page Green, and eleven years later, in 1630, William Bedwell mentions them as one of the 'three wonders of Tottenham':

> A walnut tree standing in the midst of a tuft of elms set in the manner of a circle beneath the Hermitage on the end of Page Green by the middle Stone bridge. This tree hath these many years stood there, and it is observed yearly to live and bear leaves, and yet to stand at a stay; that is to grow neither greater nor higher. The people do commonly tell the reason to be, for that there was one burnt upon that place for the profession of the gospel, but who it was, and when it should be done, they cannot tell; and I find no such thing in our stories upon record, and therefore I do not tell this for a truth.

It is particularly odd that Bedwell, vicar of the parish, does not mention the number of trees, or give them any name, and it is clear that the legendary basis of the clump resided in his time in the walnut tree and its religious martyr. Nevertheless, a hundred years later, in 1732, we have the first solid reference to the name Seven Sisters, and from then on their presence is more widely known, and their number fixed.

Along with the name came a new origin legend, which is mentioned by numerous writers, but is relatively vague and undeveloped. The core motif is that they were planted by seven sisters when parting to go their separate ways. Some add that one of the sisters was disabled, so her tree grew crookedly, others that as each sister died her tree died also, but no other details are given to enable us to grasp the full story.

This has left the field open for more fanciful origin stories, and ones that seem to rely on invented connections going backwards in time. One theory is that they were planted by the family of Robert the Bruce, who lived in the thirteenth century at nearby Bruce Castle, and who, it is said, had seven daughters. Another supposed origin story is even more audacious, relying on at best dubious assumptions and at worst false reasoning. Because the trees stand at the edge of Page Green, which is very close in name to 'Pagan's Green', some have tried to find a Celtic origin story. It is known that ancient Britons worshipped in groves of trees, so some theorise that the Seven Sisters must have been the site of Druid worship. However, walnut trees are not indigenous to England, but were introduced by the Romans. Rather than admit that this reasoning is therefore flawed, some claim that the Druid worship must have taken place after the Romans had incorporated it into their religion.

Trees do not last for ever, of course, and have to be replaced from time to time, and it is inevitable that in more recent times this has taken on an air of a publicity event. The central walnut seems to have been forgotten, but seven trees were planted by the McRae sisters in 1852, by the Hibbert sisters in 1886, and on 31 December 1955, seven sisters by the name of Basten were filmed by the BBC as each one planted a Lombardy poplar. The current seven hornbeams were planted in 1996.

SILVER STREET, EDMONTON

In John Emslie's folklore notebooks, published in *London Studies* (1974), one can find brief references to hauntings at Wire Hall that would bear further investigation:

11 January 1874
At Wire Hall, Edmonton, once upon a time, the butler murdered the cook,

and the room in which the murder was committed became haunted, was closed, and never re-opened until the house was pulled down about fifty years ago. The neighbourhood of the house also became haunted, people passing the spot have been unable to see anything, but have felt a form rush against them and suddenly leap on to their shoulders, and waggons have often been mysteriously overturned. One gentleman told me he had heard inklings of superstitious tales about Wire Hall, had often passed it at night: 'Didn't you see anything?' asked his neighbours. 'No.' 'Ah! you would then a few years back.' The spectres here seem to have disappeared

25 January 1874
A young man told me that people going near Wire Hall used to hear mysterious sounds, but could never see anything.

There were two houses called Wire Hall in Silver Street, both long gone now that the area has been redeveloped. These stories presumably refer to the earlier one, dating from Tudor times or even the late medieval period and home of the Leak and Huxley families, which was demolished in 1818. A Victorian house called Wire Hall, on the opposite side of the street, but built on an old moated site, was gone by the 1930s.

SPANIARDS ROAD, CAMDEN: THE SPANIARDS PUB

The Spaniards, Spaniards Road, is reputed to date from 1585, and is situated on the road from Highgate to Hampstead, on the edge of Hampstead Heath, right on the boundary between the boroughs of Camden and Barnet. It is not clear how the pub got its name, but the two main theories are that a Spanish ambassador used to live there or, more excitingly, that it was owned by two Spanish brothers, Francesco and Juan Porero, who both died fighting a duel over a woman. Some say that only Juan died, and he was then buried in the garden.

But heaths always give rise to highwaymen stories, and highwaymen stories inevitably lead to DICK TURPIN (p. 162). And in the Dick Turpin industry, the Spaniards is at the forefront, with claims to house the ghost of the man himself, a secret tunnel to the stables where Black Bess was lodged, and, until they were stolen, a pair of Dick's pistols. Not only is Turpin claimed as a regular visitor, but it is often confidently stated that he was born

An nineteenth-century woodcut of Dick Turpin in classic pose, escaping from the forces of law. The Spaniards on Hampstead Heath claims the ghost of the man himself.

in the pub because his father was the landlord. This is strange, because it is well known that Turpin was born in Essex. But all becomes clear when it is realised that Turpin's father was indeed a publican (of the Blue Bell Inn) in Hempstead, Essex, and that Dick was born there – a simple case of mistaking Hampstead for Hempstead.

Other ghosts are reported in and around the building: a lady in white wanders the gardens, and drinkers sometimes feel someone tugging at their sleeve. There was a flurry of interest in the pub's ghosts in the 1970s, when the current landlord reported to the press that Dick Turpin's ghost was definitely haunting the place. But even Jack Hallam, not one to play down the slightest hint of an apparition, seemed disappointed, in his *Ghosts of London* (1975), that the landlord could report nothing but a few strange noises.

Tavistock Place

An example of a story in which someone's wraith appears to others just as he is dying was published by Jessie Middleton in her *White Ghost Book* (1916), quoting the *Daily Telegraph* (1881). It was contributed by Surgeon-Major Armand Leslie, who was walking home one autumn night in 1878 when . . .

. . . a man suddenly appeared, striding up Tavistock Place, coming towards me in a direction opposite to mine. When first seen he was standing exactly in front of my own door (in Tavistock Place). Young and ghastly pale, he was dressed in evening clothes, evidently made by a foreign tailor. Tall and slim, he walked with long, measured strides, noiselessly. A tall white hat, covered thickly with black crape, and an eyeglass completed the costume of this strange form.

The moonbeams falling on the corpse-like features revealed a face well-known to me – that of a friend and relative. The sole and only person in the street beyond myself and this strange being was [a woman] . . . She stopped abruptly, as if spellbound; then, rushing towards the man, she gazed intently and with horror unmistakable on his face, which was now turned to the heavens and smiling horribly . . . She ran away with a terrific shriek and yell.

A week after this event, news of this very friend's death reached me. It occurred on the morning in question. From the family I learned that, according to the rites of the Greek Church and the custom of the country he resided in, he was buried in his evening clothes, made abroad by a foreign tailor . . . When in England, he lived in Tavistock Place and occupied my rooms during my absence.

Whitewebbs Lane, Enfield: King and Tinker pub

A fairly well-known ballad relates a meeting between King James I and a tinker. The story goes that the King was out hunting deer on day when 'in hope of some pastime', he left his entire retinue behind, went to an alehouse, and sat down next to a tinker. They drank and joked together, and then the tinker let slip that he had heard the King was in the neighbourhood, and was hoping to see him. The King laughed and told the tinker to jump up behind on his horse so that they could go and find him. Upon seeing all the nobles, the tinker asked which one was the King, and was told that the King was the only one with his hat on (the others had all removed theirs). The tinker then fell to his knees and begged forgiveness, but the King knighted him on the spot:

> Sir John of the Dale he has land, he has fee
> At the court of the king who so happy as he
> Yet still in his hall hangs the tinker's old sack
> And the budget of tools which he bore at his back.

The text does not say where this took place, and several places claim the story as their own. From internal evidence it is often assumed that it is a Scottish border legend, and in *Ancient Poems* (1846) ballad editor James Henry Dixon mentions Norwood in Surrey as one of the claimants. Enfield Chase is also a traditional candidate, and there is a well-known pub called King and Tinker in Whitewebbs Lane, just outside Enfield. The pub has borne this name since at least 1716, although it sometimes appears in the records as the Bull or the Black Bull. The building is even older, dating from late medieval or early Tudor times.

None of the early printings of the ballad is given a date, but it is usually assumed to have been composed in the mid seventeenth century.

The idea that a king is human enough to hob-nob with the lowest of his subjects is a popular one. Indeed, the doyen of ballad research, Professor Francis James Child, whose *The English and Scottish Popular Ballads* (1884–98) still provides the bedrock of the subject, commented, 'Next to adventures of Robin Hood and his men, the most favourite topic in English popular poetry is the chance-encounter of a king, unrecognised as such, with one of his humbler subjects.' Child includes several other ballads on similar topics in his collection, including 'King Edward the Fourth and a Tanner of Tamworth' and 'King Henry the Second and the Miller of Mansfield', but he does not give our 'King and Tinker' his stamp of approval by including it in his canon. He discusses all the main 'king and subject' ballads in Volume 5 of his seminal work, under the heading of ballad No. 273.

WOODSTOCK ROAD, FINSBURY PARK

C. H. Rolph lived in Finsbury Park from 1910–14 and he collected his childhood memories into a book called *London Particulars* (1982). It is particularly interesting to read of the medical superstitions that were current at that time. Some would seem strange to modern sensibilities, such as the custom of staving off whooping cough in young children by wheeling them around the gasworks to inhale the fumes until they vomited:

> Some mothers did this day after day for weeks, the children strained horribly in their attempts to vomit, and I don't doubt that this had much to do with the high proportion of cross-eyed children among my contemporaries.

But this belief in the curative properties of certain 'airs', such as those of the gasworks, was extremely common at the time (for example at HAMPSTEAD SEWERS, p. 219).

As well as whooping cough, there was a great fear of 'catching the fever', and rumours circulated about the various sources:

> . . . privet leaves, putting an iron key in your mouth; passing a smelly drain without a handkerchief to clap over your mouth and nose . . . sitting on damp grass (this led to something called rheumatic fever); eating wild mushrooms; wasp and bee stings; and trading with the 'rag, iron or bone' man.

Children were also well aware that certain illnesses, such as scarlet fever, meant immediate removal to an isolation hospital:

> There were in fact special ambulances for 'fever patients', and we always regarded them with pity and horror, as if their occupants were victims of the Black Death. The children at Finsbury Park . . . would grasp their coat collars on seeing an ambulance of any kind and call out something like, 'Grab your collar, don't swaller, never catch the fever', or, 'There goes the fever van, never touch the mealy-man' . . . There was also a superstition that, having seen an ambulance in the street, you must hold your breath and pinch your nose until you saw a black or brown dog.

All of these superstitions were widespread at the beginning of the twentieth century, and Rose Gamble's memories of her Chelsea childhood, recorded under KING'S ROAD, CHELSEA (p. 166) also included the 'Grab your collar' rubric.

EAST LONDON

The London Boroughs of Barking & Dagenham,
Hackney, Havering, Newham, Redbridge,
Tower Hamlets and Waltham Forest

ALBERT ROAD, NEWHAM: ROYAL VICTORIA GARDENS

Any tragedy is likely to engender legends and tales, and one that still has resonance in the local community is the sinking of the paddle-steamer *Princess Alice*, carrying hundreds of day-trippers, on 3 September 1878. She was literally cut in two in a collision with a collier, and sank within minutes. The speed with which the tragedy took place, the lack of emergency provision, and the fact that few of the victims knew how to swim and that the clothes of the period were particularly encumbering all contributed to the death toll, and even though they were only a few hundred yards from the shore, well over 600 people lost their lives, and only 100 survived. To add insult to injury, the collision took place at one of the worst polluted points in a notoriously badly polluted area, just where the main East London sewers discharged tons of untreated sewerage straight into the river.

According to Melanie McGrath, who wrote about local traditions in her 2002 book *Silvertown*:

> The Gardens had a sinister reputation and there were rumours that they were haunted after dark by the souls of those who drowned nearby when the Princess Alice went down at Gallions Reach thirty years before . . . They were buried in Woolwich Old Cemetery but it was said that their ghosts still inhabited the waters at Gallions Reach and cast curses and spells on Silvertown and all those who had failed to save them.

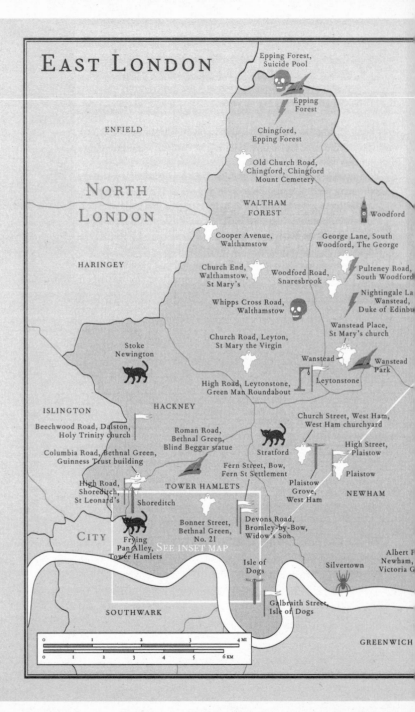

EAST LONDON

ENFIELD

NORTH
LONDON

HARINGEY

Epping Forest,
Suicide Pool

Epping
Forest

Chingford,
Epping Forest

Old Church Road,
Chingford, Chingford
Mount Cemetery

WALTHAM
FOREST

Woodford

Cooper Avenue,
Walthamstow

George Lane, South
Woodford, The George

Church End,
Walthamstow,
St Mary's

Woodford Road,
Snaresbrook

Pulteney Road,
South Woodford

Nightingale La
Wanstead,
Duke of Edinbu

Whipps Cross Road,
Walthamstow

Wanstead Place,
St Mary's church

Stoke
Newington

Church Road, Leyton,
St Mary the Virgin

Wanstead

Wanstead
Park

Leytonstone

ISLINGTON

HACKNEY

High Road, Leytonstone,
Green Man Roundabout

Beechwood Road, Dalston,
Holy Trinity church

Roman Road,
Bethnal Green,
Blind Beggar statue

Church Street, West Ham,
West Ham churchyard

Columbia Road, Bethnal Green,
Guinness Trust building

Stratford

High Street,
Plaistow

Fern Street, Bow,
Fern St Settlement

Plaistow

High Road,
Shoreditch,
St Leonard's

TOWER HAMLETS

Plaistow
Grove,
West Ham

NEWHAM

Shoreditch

CITY

Bonner Street,
Bethnal Green,
No. 21

Devons Road,
Bromley-by-Bow,
Widow's Son

Frying
Pan Alley,
Tower Hamlets

SEE INSET MAP

Isle of
Dogs

Silvertown

Albert F
Newham,
Victoria G

Galbraith Street,
Isle of Dogs

SOUTHWARK

GREENWICH

| 0 | 1 | 2 | 3 | 4 MI |

| 0 | 1 | 2 | 3 | 4 | 5 | 6 KM |

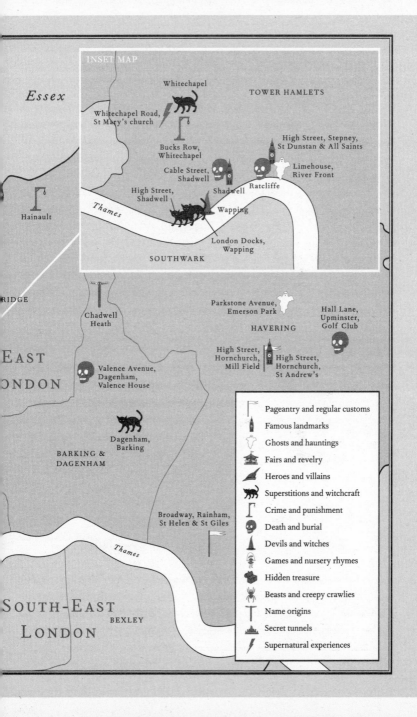

INSET MAP

Essex

Whitechapel

TOWER HAMLETS

Whitechapel Road,
St Mary's church

Bucks Row,
Whitechapel

High Street, Stepney,
St Dunstan & All Saints

Cable Street,
Shadwell

Limehouse,
River Front

High Street,
Shadwell

Shadwell

Ratcliffe

Hainault

Thames

Wapping

London Docks,
Wapping

SOUTHWARK

RIDGE

Chadwell
Heath

Parkstone Avenue,
Emerson Park

Hall Lane,
Upminster,
Golf Club

HAVERING

EAST
ONDON

High Street,
Hornchurch,
Mill Field

High Street,
Hornchurch,
St Andrew's

Valence Avenue,
Dagenham,
Valence House

BARKING &
DAGENHAM

Dagenham,
Barking

Broadway, Rainham,
St Helen & St Giles

Thames

SOUTH-EAST
LONDON

BEXLEY

Pageantry and regular customs

Famous landmarks

Ghosts and hauntings

Fairs and revelry

Heroes and villains

Superstitions and witchcraft

Crime and punishment

Death and burial

Devils and witches

Games and nursery rhymes

Hidden treasure

Beasts and creepy crawlies

Name origins

Secret tunnels

Supernatural experiences

Beechwood Road, Dalston:
Holy Trinity church

On the first Sunday in February, Holy Trinity church hosts the annual Clowns' Service, organised by Clowns International. Clowns, both amateur and professional, don their most colourful costumes and gather from all parts to celebrate their craft and honour the memory of comedian Joseph Grimaldi (1779–1837). 'Joey', who lived in Clerkenwell, was an immensely popular stage performer in his time, and his act laid the foundations for the modern clown tradition, including its traditional costume. Grimaldi was buried at St James's, Pentonville Road, and although that church was demolished in the late 1950s, the area which includes his grave has been made into a public park, named in his memory, and his tomb can still be seen there. The annual commemoration service started informally at St James's in 1946, moved to Holy Trinity in 1956, and from 1967 the clowns have been allowed to attend in costume. During the service, clowns read the lessons, and the congregation recites:

> Dear Lord, I thank you for calling me to share with others your most precious gift of laughter. May I never forget that it is your gift and my privilege. As your children are rebuked in their self-importance and cheered in their sadness, help me to remember that your foolishness is wiser than men's wisdom.

After the service there is a free clowns' show at a nearby school. Clown enthusiasts can also visit the Clowns International Gallery and Archives at the All Saints Centre, Haggerston Road, Hackney.

Bonner Street, Bethnal Green: No. 21

No. 21 Bonner Street used to be a pub known as the Bonner Arms and, more recently, the Bishop Bonner. It was named after Edmund Bonner, who had a house in Bethnal Green and was consecrated Bishop of London in 1539. He led a chequered career under successive monarchs, and gained an evil reputation as 'bloody Bonner' by his zealous prosecution of 'heretics' during Mary's brief restoration of Catholicism. He died while in prison in 1569.

In the past, church bells were rung on a whole range of occasions. The church-wardens' accounts for Rainham in 1760, for example, show that the bells were rung on Guy Fawkes Night.

His coach is said to be one of the ghostly attractions of Victoria Park on moonlit nights, pulled by four black horses, and, according to a report in the *East London Advertiser* on 10 July 1992, he may also have haunted the pub named after him.

BROADWAY, RAINHAM: CHURCH OF ST HELEN AND ST GILES

When most villages had an active team of bell-ringers there were certain days when by long custom they were expected to perform, in addition to the regular Sunday ringing, weddings, funerals, and so on. During the eighteenth century, these 'ringing nights', as they were called, included Christmas Eve, New Year's Eve, Royal Oak Day (29 May), and, very popular indeed, 5 November. In the churchwardens' accounts for Rainham in 1760, for example, one can find the entry: 'Paid for ringing on gunpowder treason 3s 0d.'

See also CHURCH ROAD, HARLINGTON: ST MARY THE VIRGIN CHURCH, p. 140.

BUCKS ROW, WHITECHAPEL

The horrible Whitechapel murders of 1888, when, in four short months, five or six women were killed by 'Jack the Ripper' in the back streets of East London, constitute the most famous unsolved case in Britain, and possibly the world. As with all such cases, the events generated a large number of legends and rumours at the time, and a perusal of the extensive Ripper literature shows no shortage of theories put forward ever since. One of the most persistent legends feeds our need for conspiracy theories by maintaining that the perpetrator was a member of the upper class, perhaps even of the royal family, and that is why his identity has never been revealed.

Considering the huge interest the case engendered at the time, and the veritable industry of Ripper-related books, articles, films, television programmes, and other media productions, it is surprising how few related ghosts stories are in circulation. Prolific ghost-writer Elliot O'Donnell tells a story about Jack himself jumping from WESTMINSTER BRIDGE (p. 125) every New Year's Eve, but the other ghost writers of the last fifty years have only recycled one rather vague story, also from O'Donnell, who had been a schoolboy in Bristol at the time of the murders. In his *Haunted Britain* (1948), he tells his tale:

> In 1895, when staying in London, I visited Whitechapel and had interesting conversations about the murders with several inhabitants of the district. They told me that in the streets where the murders had been committed appalling screams and groans uttered by no living human being were sometimes heard at night, and that in Bucks Row, a huddled up figure, like that of a woman, emitting from all over it a ghostly light, was frequently to be seen lying in the gutter. None of the people with whom I conversed believed the murders were the work of one man only. 'Had they been,' they told me, 'someone would have given him away.'

The logic of that last sentence is a little suspect. One would have thought that the more people involved, the more likely someone would have been discovered.

CABLE STREET, SHADWELL

William Kent published the following piece from *The Citizen* of August 1886 in his compilation of *London in the News* (1954). It concerns the usual way in which the bodies of suicides were treated in the past:

> In excavating a trench for a main for the Commercial Gas Company, the workmen of Messrs. John Aird and Sons made a remarkable discovery a

few days ago at a point where Cannon Street Road and Cable Street, in St George's-in-the-East, cross one another, and at a depth of six feet below the surface, they discovered the skeleton of a man with a stake driven through it, and some portions of a chain were lying near the bones. It is believed that the skeleton is that of a man who murdered a Mr and Mrs Marr, their infant child and a young apprentice in their house in Ratcliff Highway in 1811 . . . He hanged himself while under remand in Coldbath Fields Prison. A Coroner's Jury having brought in a verdict of *felo de se*, the murderer was buried in accordance with the custom of the time.

See also SUICIDE BURIALS, p. 260.

CHADWELL HEATH

There is some confusion over the derivation of the name Chadwell Heath, in Barking (and Chadwell St Mary, in Essex). It is very often assumed that the name commemorates a holy well – possibly a healing one – named after St Chad, who died in AD 672. Like many early saints, his sanctity was proved by miracles occurring around his tomb, and in Chad's case there were many stories of miraculous cures. The Venerable Bede (*c.* 673–735) describes Chad's tomb in his *History of the English Church and People*:

> Chad's burial place is covered by a wooden tomb made in the form of a little house with an aperture in the wall through which those who visit it out of devotion may insert their hand and take out some of the dust. They mix this in water and give it to sick men or beasts to drink, by which means their ailment is quickly relieved and they are restored to the longed-for joys of health.

The truth, though, is that the name Chadwell derives not from miraculous healing waters but from 'Cold Well', and the places that bear those names have no holy connotations, apart from those tacked on at a later date, when people started to act upon their etymological misinterpretations. Typical of these were the late nineteenth-century High Church antiquarians, whose enthusiasm often exceeded their erudition, and St Chad was one of their favourite saints to find in unlikely places. When the new church was consecrated at Chadwell Heath in 1886, it seemed logical to call it St Chad's.

Suicide Burials

A suicide burial was designed to be a complete antithesis of a Christian one, taking place at night, in an unmarked grave by the roadside – often at a crossroads – and with a wooden stake driven through the body.

Until the passing of the Burial of Suicide Act in 1823, the bodies of those found to have died *felo de se* (by their own hand) were deliberately treated with religious barbarism, not only to punish the perpetrator, but also to demonstrate to everyone else the horror with which such a crime should be regarded. Suicides were buried at night, by the roadside (not necessarily at a crossroads), without a service, with a wooden stake driven through the body and sometimes with chains around it. This treatment was clearly designed to be a complete antithesis of a normal Christian burial, and each element underlines the fact. The ground is unconsecrated and no prayers are said, no mourners are present and the grave is unmarked, the idea being that the person will soon be forgotten.

Two unwarranted assumptions about these proceedings are often made by modern writers. It is routinely suggested that the stake through the body was designed to stop the suicide's ghost walking or even becoming a vampire, but there is no evidence that this was the case at the time. Britain had no popular tradition of vampires, let alone methods of preventing them, until they were introduced in the nineteenth-century penny dreadfuls. It is far more likely that the stake was a further piece of official spite in that it was designed to impede the resurrection of the body on the Day of Judgement, either literally or symbolically. The second assumption is that the burial took place at a crossroads in order to confuse any ghost, should it decide to walk, but again this is unlikely. The point of a roadside burial is another reversal of normal Christian behaviour, and one of contempt. Whereas people respect normal graves and try not to tread on them, numerous people will pass by or even walk over the suicide's grave without a thought for its occupant.

Burial with a stake was already being carried out by the sixteenth century, and was accepted by coroners up and down the country as the legal requirement for dealing with suicides, but its origins are something of a mystery. It has proved impossible so far to identify any actual law dictating this treatment – or indeed any other for suicides. Knightsbridge has the distinction of being the location of the last suicide in England to be buried by the roadside, although apparently without the stake, in June 1823, only days before the Act came into force.

The 1823 Act specifically forbade the stake and the roadside burial, but dictated that the burial be undertaken between nine and twelve at night, without benefit of a burial service. In most places an unpopular or unfrequented part of the churchyard was chosen; to the north of the church, for example, or in a far corner by the wall. This Act was in turn repealed in 1882.

A number of superstitions and traditions grew up around suicides and their graves in the nineteenth and twentieth centuries. In some places, a misshapen or eerie tree by the roadside was reputed to have grown from the stake, or a ghost's presence would be simply explained by a presumed grave nearby. There was a widespread notion that a suicide's body would not start to decompose until the 'natural', God-ordained time for his or her death, and it was thought extremely unlucky to touch a suicide's corpse. People often refused to cut a hanging body down, or pull a corpse out of the water, and would leave them to someone in authority to deal with.

See BLACKFRIARS BRIDGE, p. 6; CABLE STREET, SHADWELL, p. 258; EPPING FOREST: SUICIDE POOL, p. 269; FENCHURCH STREET: STAR ALLEY, p. 21; GROSVENOR PLACE, KNIGHTSBRIDGE, p. 144; KINGSWAY, p. 235.

A letter published in *Essex Countryside* in 1959 shows that the assumption had also achieved 'official plaque' status:

> From my bedroom window I have a fine view of the remainder of Chadwell Heath, a part of which is a lane by the name of Billet Road. Along this lane is a tablet which reads as follows: 'St Chad's Well, from which the name Chadwell Heath was derived.'

CHINGFORD, EPPING FOREST

High Beech Hill in Epping Forest is the setting for an eerie story included in Elliott O'Donnell's 1957 book, *Haunted Waters*. The story concerns twin sisters who grew up in Chingford and played in the forest. They were particularly fond of visiting a pond, which they nicknamed the Nymph's Pool, at High Beech. The sisters grew up and went their separate ways, and one, Delphine, married and lived abroad. Sadly, her marriage did not work out, and she finally left her husband and cabled her sister to say that she was coming home from South America. On the day before Delphine's arrival in England, her sister was visiting the old family home at Chingford:

> I suddenly experienced a sensation of intense coldness. I glanced at the door to see if it was open, but it was shut; the window was open at the top, as the weather was very close. A longing came over me to see the Nymph's Pool . . . and I set off at once to High Beech Hill . . . I kept thinking about Delphine, wishing it was the next day when I should hear from her and wondering if I should see any change in her. When I came within sight of the Nymph's Pool, I saw someone standing by it. It was a woman in dark clothes, and on drawing near to her I saw, to my utter amazement, that it was Delphine. I was distressed to see she was very pale and did not look at all well, so thin and wan, not a bit like her old self. 'Delphine!' I cried joyfully. 'What a gorgeous surprise! What bliss to see you again.' She smiled and held out her arms, and I was running to embrace her when she vanished. There was no Delphine, only the Nymph Tree . . . The following morning I received a telegram saying Delphine had died suddenly the previous evening . . . She had died at about the time I had seen her apparition.

See also EPPING FOREST: SUICIDE POOL, p. 269.

The churchyard of St Mary's, Walthamstow. Not long ago, local children would place a coin on one of the tombstones here and then dance around in the hope of conjuring up a ghost.

CHURCH END, WALTHAMSTOW: ST MARY'S CHURCHYARD

A tradition concerning the Turner tomb in St Mary's churchyard was recorded by witchcraft and ghost expert Eric Maple in the *Waltham Forest Guardian* on 20 December 1974. He explained that children used to say that if you put sixpence on the stone, and dance around it seven times, a ghost would appear, but by the point at which he was writing the sum had gone up to ten pence and the number of circuits to twelve. The children also spoke of one lad who had tried to raise the ghost without laying the coin down:

> The spectre leapt from the grave with a terrifying shriek, clutched the boy in its arms and dragged him into the bowels of the earth.

Similar stories are told by children about other graves all over the country. Another story, from the same churchyard, reveals that in 1972 a girl was startled by the sight of a man in Victorian clothes:

> She was frightened by his extremely sinister appearance. He had strange bushy eyebrows and there was something horrible about one of his hands.

His clothes seemed to be composed of air and swirled in the wind. Then he slowly vanished as if drawn towards the graves. The girl was with her mother at the time. The parent did not see the spectre.

Another interesting feature of the churchyard is a memorial to mark the grave of Joseph Wilton (died 1803), which was used in the early nineteenth century as a convenient shelter for those guarding the cemetery against body-snatchers.

CHURCH ROAD, LEYTON: ST MARY THE VIRGIN CHURCH

On 12 January 1935, the *West Ham and Stratford Express* ran a story under the title 'Laying the Leyton Church Ghosts'. Its subject was some recent articles in the national newspapers concerning Leyton parish church and the reaction of its vicar, the Revd Robert Bren. We can be sure that the Reverend himself approved of the article, because he had cut it out and pasted it into his copy of a local history book (now held in Waltham Forest Local Studies Library). The article runs as follows:

> The strangest story of the week comes from Leyton. It concerns the vicar, the Rev Robert Bren MA, and two ghostly figures he is alleged to have seen, dressed in grey, kneeling at prayer in the front pew of his church. On Sunday special articles appeared in a section of the press describing eerie events in the old church, which, it was alleged, were keeping parishioners away; about a young man in mediaeval clothes, who walked through a wall and vanished; and about members of the congregation, and even church officers, who were afraid to venture into the building after dark. The articles were given great prominence and heavy type headlines.

The *Express* reporter had contacted the Revd Bren, and had interviewed him about the articles in the national press, finding a very different story indeed. The Reverend was incensed by the totally inaccurate reporting of the national papers, and was at pains to point out that although there were indeed one or two ghost stories about his church, there had been no recent panic, and nor were parishioners staying away for fear, or any other reason:

When I came to Leyton some seven years ago, I heard the story of a gentleman, clad in a cape, with a sword tucked under his arm, and carrying a hat with a large feather, who appeared and walked down through the middle of the pews, where are the pillars of the north aisle, and disappeared at the reading desk. There the figure would end, and it was the hypothesis of some of the older inhabitants that he was a ghostly visitant walking down what had been the old aisle of the church. I have never been able to find anybody who has seen this cavalier, although quite a number were then familiar with the story.

Corpses were always buried in a white shroud, which perhaps led to the stereotypical image of ghosts wrapped in white sheets as depicted in this woodcut. This idea was frequently abused by pranksters and hoaxers, as happened in West Ham in the mid nineteenth century.

The Revd Bren went on to point out that early records show that there had never been an aisle in that position. He also mentioned that several journalists had attended services at Leyton as a result of the coverage in the national papers, and had been disappointed to discover that the congregation was full. But they printed the story about people staying away just the same.

CHURCH STREET, WEST HAM: WEST HAM CHURCHYARD

A West Ham resident, Mr Holbrook, appeared in the *East Ham and Stratford Express* on 27 October 1894 relating a tale about a supposed 'haunting' in West Ham churchyard, which he remembered from the middle of the nineteenth century. Local residents had gathered around the edge of the churchyard, perturbed by the sight of a white-clad figure slipping around the gravestones. But one local, more cynical than the rest, decided to wrap himself in his white tablecloth and start chasing the first 'ghost', who apparently thought the newcomer was a real spirit and fled in terror. Realising the hoax, the locals pursued the first 'ghost', caught him, and, as Mr Holbrook commented: 'They nearly made a ghost of him, I think, before they'd done with him.'

The idea of someone dressed as a ghost with a white sheet over their heads is nowadays such a worn cliché that it is more or less confined to children dressing up at Hallowe'en. It may therefore seem strange that grown people in the past could be fooled by such an obvious ruse, and it has to be said that a lot of people seem to have been more gullible and less openly sceptical than they are now. But in mitigation it should also be understood that corpses were always buried in a white shroud, and it was quite common in illustrations to depict ghosts as being wrapped in a white cloth.

COLUMBIA ROAD, BETHNAL GREEN: GUINNESS TRUST BUILDING

In September 1924, a flurry of interest was caused when a face was reportedly seen at the window of the Guinness Trust building in Columbia Road, Bethnal Green. For several nights following, large crowds gathered outside and had to be controlled by local police. But the newspapers blamed the overactive imaginations of some boys who had seen *The Haunted House*, a Buster Keaton film, at the cinema nearby. Two young men were arrested inside the buildings, claiming they had come to 'see about this ghost business'.

COOPER AVENUE, WALTHAMSTOW

According to a report in the *Walthamstow Guardian* on 31 October 1969, a couple living in an ordinary three-bedroomed council house in Cooper Avenue were so troubled by a supernatural presence that they asked to be rehoused. A few weeks after they moved in, their four-year-old son, Paul, started talking about the 'white lady' who kept appearing in his room and talking to him. Paul was obviously disturbed by her presence and started refusing to sleep in the room. He told his parents that the lady kept telling him to go downstairs. On at least one occasion, his mother was in the room when Paul talked to the lady, but she could see nothing, though the family dog also shunned the bedroom. A previous tenant reported that she too had seen a strange apparition, earlier that year, soon after her husband died, and also told the newspaper reporter about an evil woman with white hair, a violent temper, and a hatred of children, who used to occupy Paul's room before she moved to Stroud, and died there. 'But if the White Lady is her, trying to get back to her room, then I think the little boy is in danger there,' she said.

DAGENHAM, BARKING

William Book of Dagenham died in 1433 and left a particular provision in his will:

> Item I bequeath a sheep to be driven before my body on the day of burial in the name of a foredrove.

According to Miss Angela Green, writing in the *Essex Review* in 1957, this was a fairly common practice in Essex. An animal such as a sheep or ewe, a bullock or cow, or occasionally a horse, would be led before the body in the funeral procession. Sometimes the animal was even offered as a payment to the church at death.

A further example of this custom can be seen in another edition of the *Essex Review* where it is recorded that Robert Sweete, of Chalkwell Hall in the Island of Foulness, 'had on the island more than three hundred sheep, of which three, known locally as the "foredrove", were driven before the corpse at his funeral, in accordance with his will'.

DEVONS ROAD, BROMLEY-BY-BOW: WIDOW'S SON PUB

A unique custom takes place at the Widow's Son pub, 75 Devons Road, Bromley-by-Bow, every Good Friday. The pub has a mass of blackened and dusty hot-cross buns hanging from its ceiling, and every year a sailor adds a new one. It is not clear how long this bun-hanging has been going on, but the pub has been called the Widow's Son since at least 1851, and the legend attached to the custom claims that it pre-dates the pub. A poor widow, whose son was away at sea, was said to have lived in a cottage on the site. Expecting him home for Easter, she baked him a hot-cross bun, but he did not arrive. The following year, and every year afterwards until her death, she baked another, until she had quite a collection, hanging from a beam in her kitchen. When the widow's cottage was demolished, and the pub built on its site, the landlords decided to continue the custom, and named their new establishment accordingly.

In 1943, folklorist Christina Hole claimed that there were already 173 buns, which, she added, 'during air-raids, are taken to a place of safety along with the other valuables of the house'. That number of buns, at one a year, would mean that the custom began in the 1770s, which is most unlikely.

It is not clear whether the story was invented to explain the pub's name, or the pub was named after an existing story, but although the story of the widow is probably fictitious, the hanging of bread or buns from the ceiling was not an unusual occurrence in days gone by. From at least the mid eighteenth century, and possibly much earlier, it was very widely believed in Britain that bread baked on Good Friday had miraculous powers. It was claimed that it would never grow mouldy, and that its presence in the house was lucky and protective, and the bread itself had a wide range of medicinal uses. It was traditional to hang such bread on a string from the kitchen ceiling, and to leave it there ready for use. Pieces were then broken off, or grated, and given to sick people in the house. Hanging it up in this way ensured that it stayed dry and hard.

EPPING FOREST

Until well into the twentieth century, the Epping Forest, and the villages around, were widely known as one of the main Gypsy haunts in the outer London area. Relations between the travellers and the settled population were often strained and stormy, but it is also clear that in many respects a peaceful symbiotic relationship could exist. Although priding themselves on their independence and self-sufficiency, many nineteenth-century Gypsies made almost all their living from catering to the villagers – as migrant farm workers, buying or selling to the settled population, or providing entertainment and services such as fortune-telling and herbal cures. Writing of the Gypsies around Hainault in *Essex: Its Forest, Folk and Folklore* (1928), Charlotte Mason tells of behaviour that may have seemed intimidating:

> A lady tells me that when a small child she was taken in a family party for a picnic to the Forest. No sooner was a white cloth spread on the ground, and the dinner laid out, than they were entirely surrounded by Gipsies, who took up sitting positions and hemmed them in.

This behaviour, however, is cast in a less threatening light by a similar piece from a 1900 edition of *Surrey Magazine* that relates to the Gypsies of Norwood :

> A number of gentry would come into the woods for a picnic . . . A cloth would be laid on the grass in some open field, and a hearty meal would be partaken of. That done the question would arise, 'What shall we do next?' This was the gypsies' chance. They would gather round them from all sides, begging, telling fortunes and selling trinkets . . . A good business was made out of this sort of thing, and they rarely did anything else for a living.

See also ANERLEY WOOD, p. 309; NORWOOD, p. 405.

EPPING FOREST: SUICIDE POOL

There is reputed to be a 'Suicide Pool' in Epping Forest, and a letter in the *Essex Countryside* in 1959 requested information on its whereabouts. In the next volume of the journal a correspondent suggested that Wake Valley Pond may have acquired this reputation, but another writer, Mrs Piggins, poured scorn on this suggestion. She claimed to know where the Suicide Pool was situated but refused to describe its exact location, on the grounds that it was too evil and dangerous a place to direct people to:

> The Suicide Pool is deep in the heart of the forest, far from any road. Birds are never heard there; squirrels and deer shun its vicinity; no one fishes there for there are no fish. It is dank, evil and malignant, with an atmosphere unpleasant beyond description. I doubt if the sunshine ever penetrates through the surrounding trees; if it did it would never lighten the black waters.

Mrs Piggins stated that those who visit the pool, however sceptical they may be about the supernatural, always come running away after a short time, unless they end up dead in its waters, as many mysteriously do. She claimed that these tragedies happened before the Second World War, and cited Elliott O'Donnell's *Haunted Britain* (1948) as containing further information.

The presence of spirits and other supernatural forces in places such as ponds and trees is one of the regular themes of O'Donnell's books, and in this case he claimed first-hand experience of the Suicide Pool:

> The pool, which is ten feet deep and very weedy in places, has been the scene of many mysterious tragedies, whence it derives its name. People who have been thought by their most intimate friends to have had no inclination to commit suicide have been found drowned in the pool . . . I have done several nocturnal vigils by the pool and although I visualized no ghost, I more than once sensed a mixture of influences in the atmosphere and the near proximity of unearthly presences, some very miserable, and others definitely evil.

Unfortunately, it has so far proved impossible to find any further references that would help pin down the exact location of this evil pond, and none of the current forest rangers has even heard of it.

Another Epping Forest pond story is given by Eric Maple in his 1977 book *Supernatural England*. He claims it is thought to be at least 300 years old. A young couple used to meet secretly at a forest pool that was graced with a willow tree. The girl's father discovered their secret, and killed her in his rage. The murdered girl appeared at her usual place under the tree, but as her lover embraced her she 'melted away in his arms'. As Maple says, 'This area of forest was long shunned by courting couples as a place of unmitigated doom.'

See also CHINGFORD, EPPING FOREST, p. 262; HYDE PARK, p. 84.

FERN STREET, BOW: FERN STREET SETTLEMENT

The settlement movement was one of the great Victorian socio-religious experiments in which young middle- and upper-class people were encouraged to live in the poorest areas of Britain's cities in an effort to improve the lot of the families who lived there in severe deprivation. Settlement workers offered practical help running soup kitchens, clothing clubs, youth clubs, evening classes, and talks on hygiene and how to cook on a limited budget, among other things. But most of all it was hoped that their very presence would raise local standards by setting a good example and offering moral and spiritual support. Some have dismissed these people as interfering do-gooders with condescending attitudes to the working classes that betray their own social ignorance and arrogance. However, when one considers the appalling conditions in which many of the poorest families lived, and that at that time the state took little responsibility for social care and welfare, it is hard to criticise those who made a genuine effort to help.

The Fern Street Settlement was founded in 1907 by Clara Grant, who came from Somerset and had been appointed headteacher of the Devons Road School on Bow Common. Grant and her supporters were soon heavily involved in a wide range of imaginative philanthropic initiatives including classes for sewing and home hygiene, schemes to help people buy necessary items from fireguards to spectacles, and campaigns to promote handkerchiefs and toothbrushes. One of the settlement's small initiatives that achieved wider fame was the weekly distribution of 'farthing bundles' to local children. These bundles contained an eclectic range of items – pieces of ribbon or coloured material, pencils, crayons, chalk, cut-out pictures, broken dolls, tops, used Christmas cards, blank paper, shells, beads, cotton reels – anything that might fire the imagination or provide a little colour for children who were deprived of the kind of treasures those from wealthier families could take for granted.

Every Saturday morning, whatever the weather, hundreds of children would join the bundle queue, each clutching a farthing tightly in their hand. The scheme was enormously popular: over 14,000 were distributed in 1914 alone. In order to make sure the bundles went to the younger children, the settlement decided to select by height, and from 1913 onwards the children were asked to walk under a low wooden arch without stooping, to prove they were small enough. On two occasions over the years the height of the arch has had to be raised, as improved health among the children has meant they have become, on average, much taller for their age. The arch bears the motto: 'Enter all ye children small. None can come who are too tall.'

The weekly bundles were finally discontinued in 1984, but they are still distributed on special occasions, such as the settlement's centenary celebrations in May 2007.

London Speech

'Sixpence a pottle, scarlet strawberries' would have been this street-seller's cry in nineteenth-century London. Although the language of an educated Londoner, such as the gentleman on the left, has long been respected as the basic model for 'Standard English', the speech of ordinary London folk has, until quite recently, been almost universally derided.

It is not easy to pin down one accent or dialect that is typically 'London', perhaps because there have always been several of them in the capital. East Londoners have certainly had a identifiable accent for many years, as have people from areas of North and South London. In the past, long-term residents of what are now the outer London boroughs usually spoke with a version of the relevant county accent – Kent for Bromley, Surrey for Mitcham, Essex for Barking, Middlesex for Hounslow, and so on – and in some cases they still do.

While the mode of speech of the educated Londoner has long been privileged as the basic model for Standard English, the language spoken by ordinary Londoners has been almost universally derided, as can be seen in this extract from the *Report of the Conference on the Teaching of English in London Elementary Schools* (1909):

> The Cockney mode of speech, with its unpleasant twang, is a modern corruption without legitimate credentials, and is unworthy of being the speech of any person in the capital city of the Empire.

Writing in 1938, William Matthews made an impassioned plea for the recognition of London speech as a valid dialect of English. He noted how regional country speech, and even the indigenous language of major towns such as Glasgow and Birmingham, has been accorded the status of a dialect and lovingly collected, published and studied by experts, but London had been denied this recognition.

We mere Londoners, who humbly suffer the gibes of even Glaswegians at our dialect, are always impressed by the self-regard of the many societies of —shire men who gather year by year to hymn in reassumed dialects the praise of reassumed beverages. We may wonder why their gatherings are held in London – *dulcior dissipere in loco!* – but we are profoundly impressed. There is no Society of Cockneys. Not even in the outposts of Empire do Londoners meet together to renew formally the delights of four-ale and spring onions or to admire the speech of Bethnal Green and Peckham Rye.

Perhaps one reason for this is that in areas with recognisable regional accents, the better-educated members of the community have usually retained at least some of the traits of the regional speech, so that in addition to, say, broad Birmingham speech, there has also been 'posh' Birmingham speech. But in London, it is argued, the language of the upper reaches of society has simply been accepted as 'Standard English', so there is no 'posh cockney'. This is a simplistic notion, but contains some small truths.

Language Expert David Crystal commented in *The Stories of English* (2004) that signs of the rise of London language were detectable fifty years ago:

> As early as 1949, in one of his BBC talks, Daniel Jones had commented that 'it seems quite likely that in the future our present English will develop in the direction of Cockney unless special influences come in to counteract this tendency'.

Nevertheless, the astonishing rise of 'Estuary English', first recognised and labelled in 1984, but really taking off in the 1990s in the mouths of celebrities, media presenters and politicians, took many people by surprise. It was as if the East End boys of the Thatcher era money markets were now giving lessons to the linguistic trendsetters of the day. Estuary English is heavily influenced by older London speech, using forms such as glottal stops, *vv* instead of *th* (muvver, faaver) and so on, and has spread like wildfire into the Greater London area and across the country, so that David Crystal, among others, has suggested that the label is too narrow. But, following Matthews' thesis of the long-term neglect of London dialect, we can see Estuary English as the Londoners' revenge on the rest of the country. 'No longer will we tolerate your derision; we will show you, in short order, what our "dialect" can do – it can wipe out yours at a stroke!'

See also RHYMING SLANG, p. 290.

Despite huge changes in the area, the settlement still continues its philanthropic work, although its main focus now is as a community centre for the elderly. Its founder's name was officially commemorated when Devons Road school was renamed the Clara Grant School in 1993.

FRYING PAN ALLEY, TOWER HAMLETS

A court case heard at the Old Bailey shines a light on the practice of FORTUNE-TELLING (p. 78). Frying Pan Alley was just off Middlesex Street, the official name of Petticoat Lane at the time. On 18 September 1816, Elizabeth Shunshine claimed that a tablespoon, a teaspoon, and four dessert spoons had gone missing from her father's house. She tackled her niece, Charlotte Anthony, about them, who admitted that she had taken them to a woman named Harriet Garva who lived on Frying Pan Alley, Petticoat Lane. She earned a living making bonnets and telling fortunes. Under the pretence of wanting her fortune told, Shunshine then visited Garva, who had the nerve to tell her that she had lost some valuable items and then to describe Anthony as the thief. Garva was convicted of receiving stolen property and transported for fourteen years.

GALBRAITH STREET, ISLE OF DOGS

On Good Friday, there was often a tension between the official religious line for the day and what the people themselves wanted to do. For the religious, Good Friday was a day of sombre reflection and fasting, but for many people it was one of the few days of holiday, and it was spring, so they were determined to enjoy themselves. While many staid middle-aged people worked on their gardens or allotments, others would flock to fairs and other gatherings, or indulge in a variety of traditional games, such as skipping. It is not clear why skipping became a regular feature of Good Friday (some communities did it on Shrove Tuesday instead), but in various parts of the country the long ropes came out and the whole community joined in. In a typescript volume entitled *Please to Remember*, housed in Tower Hamlets

Local Studies Library, Ellen Morris (born in Galbraith Street in 1913) recalls her childhood on the Isle of Dogs:

> Good Friday brought the skipping . . . it began early in the day. Ropes were brought out from hidden places to be stretched and pulled to remove the kinks of storage. They reached from pavement to pavement across the roads. Every street would have several being turned slowly to become pliant and straight.
>
> Almost everyone joined in. Those who could not skip took a turn at the end of the rope, sometimes sitting on chairs carried out from kitchens. Children adored the game, jumping and twisting as the ropes swung, showing how it should be done. Soon the streets would be full of people pushing each other into the skipping. 'Follow my leader', in one side of the rope and out the other. 'Over the waves', many a trip up with that one. Those too young to skip were caught up in strong arms and borne along, squealing with delight. Neighbours who may not have spoken for months found themselves moving together, quarrels forgotten for that day at least. Even the sick and bed-ridden tried to watch from the windows above the streets.
>
> It would come to a halt when the procession from the church came through the streets . . . As soon as the last flicker of lace had vanished the ropes appeared again. On would go the game as before. 'Blue bells, cockle shells, eevie ivy over.' The older ones would be dropping out now, tired and aching. We grew weary too but determined to keep the fun going as long as we could.

GEORGE LANE, SOUTH WOODFORD: THE GEORGE

The George, on the corner of George Lane and Woodford High Road, is one of the buildings in the area that are reputed to be haunted. An article on the pub, published in the *Redbridge Guardian* on 30 March 1995, quotes relatives of previous tenants who claimed to have experienced, or heard about, ghostly occurrences, including a Mrs Browne, whose parents ran the pub in the 1950s and 1960s. At the age of eleven or twelve, she claimed, she had become conscious of 'something' in the attic, and of a child or children being involved. 'I was sure there was a ghost there,' she said. 'It was at the top of the stairs to my bedroom at the back.'

Another informant, Mrs Doreen Oaks, explained that in the late nineteenth century the landlord's alcoholic father had locked a child in a dark cupboard, where it had died of fright.

HAINAULT

According to a report the *Ilford Recorder* on 30 January 1977, an ordinary two-bedroomed house in Hainault was so badly troubled by spirits that the owners were forced to move out. The worst of it was that their three-year-old daughter woke screaming at night because of the people shouting and arguing in her bedroom, and the sounds of breaking glass and other violence. A neighbour (there is always a neighbour ready with a story) explained that a man had been killed in the house more than forty years previously. He had been a wife-beater, and was stabbed to death by his own twin sons, who were not convicted of murder because they claimed self-defence. Unsurprisingly, the couple were rather upset that they had not been told of this problem when they bought the house.

HALL LANE, UPMINSTER: GOLF CLUB

The clubhouse of Upminster Golf Club has a resident ghost, with a well-developed melodramatic legend to explain its presence. Jack Hallam included it in his *Ghosts of London* in 1975, but characteristically did not reveal the source of his information or the date to which it referred. He wrote that the clubhouse was previously a great manor house, built in the seventeenth century, known as Havering Hall. At some point in its history, the owner became obsessed with the daughter of one of the local gentry, but she refused him. Enraged, he kidnapped her, bricked her up in a tiny room and left her to die. The sealed room has never been found, but it is said to be situated within the thick walls of the club lounge. The ghost of a young woman in a white gown has apparently been seen around the building by various club-members.

HIGH ROAD, LEYTONSTONE:
GREEN MAN ROUNDABOUT

The Green Man Inn had been a widely known landmark in Leytonstone since at least 1668. It is now called O'Neills, but the old name lives on in the name of the roundabout on which the pub stands. Writing in the *Essex Review* in 1905, Z. Moon summed up the romantic reputation of the inn, and managed to combine three of our favourite legendary themes – highwaymen, secret tunnels, and ghosts – in one story. He was writing just before the inn was completely rebuilt:

> There is to this day a room known as 'The Dick Turpin Chamber', in which formerly stood an enormous chest, so large that three or four men could have concealed themselves therein. A few years ago this was removed to an outer passage (where it may still be seen), when underneath where the chest stood was discovered a spring flap which afforded means of escape to a room beneath, in the floor of which was a trap-door, giving access to a cave whence a subterranean passage led far away to some outlet in the denseness of the Forest. This outlet is, of course, now bricked up, but a portion of the aperture from the rooms above still remains.
>
> It was no unusual thing in those days of superstition for persons who wished to avoid pursuit to trump up a ghost story, and comfortably ensconce themselves in the 'haunted chamber', secure from pursuit by their credulous followers; needless to say the Green Man Inn had its haunted room, and though there appears to be no authentic record of any spectre, goblin, wraith, fairy or pixy having been seen there, so firm was the belief in the story that even in recent years no servant was willing to enter the room alone.

HIGH ROAD, SHOREDITCH: ST LEONARD'S CHURCH

Thomas Fairchild, a gardener, lived in the parish of Shoreditch between 1667 and 1729, and had a vineyard at Hoxton. He was a knowledgeable botanist, member of the Royal Society, and author of the influential book *The City Gardener* (1722). When he died in 1729 his will included a sum of money to fund an annual lecture, to be delivered at St Leonard's every Whit Tuesday, on the theme of 'The Wonderful works of God in the

Creation' or 'The Certainty of the resurrection of the dead, proved by the certain changes of the animal and vegetable parts of the creation'. Officially, it is called the Fairchild Lecture, but the themes have given rise to the nicknames the 'Botanical Lecture' and the 'Vegetable Lecture'. Many eminent botanists and horticulturalists have given the lecture over the years, which is still delivered annually, but it moves from church to church for convenience.

See also LEADENHALL STREET: ST KATHARINE CREE CHURCH, p. 34.

HIGH STREET, HORNCHURCH: ST ANDREW'S CHURCH

St Andrew's church at Hornchurch is a Grade I listed thirteenth-century building that was substantially altered in the fifteenth century and again in 1802 and about 1870. Its north wall contains many bottles within the masonry, some with necks facing outwards and others with bases foremost, and a weathered stone figure of a bishop in the turret is believed to represent the church's major benefactor, William of Wykeham. But the most unusual feature of the building is the stone bull's head, with its splendid pair of metal horns, that adorns the outside face of the east wall of the chancel.

The first definite reference to head and horns is in 1824, when they were made of copper, but a 1610 source mentions 'points of lead fashioned like horns'. Centuries earlier, in 1222, the building was already being referred to as the *monasterium cornutum* (horned church or monastery). These pre-nineteenth-century references are tantalising because they do not mention the bull's head, and it is possible that the church simply had horn-shaped gables, which gave it the name Hornchurch, and some playful mason added the bull's head to complete the picture. In the absence of positive dating, it is not even clear whether the place is named after the church, or vice versa. *The Victoria County History for Essex* (Vol. 7, 1978) points out that the seal of the Prior of Hornchurch in 1384/5 includes a bull's head, and puts forward the possibility that the horns on the church are a symbol of the local tanning industry. But the truth is that, at present, nobody can tell for sure.

Various other stories have grown up to explain them, for example the one recorded by seventeenth-century antiquarian John Aubrey, which even suggests that the horns may not always have been from a bull:

Horn-church in Essex hath its denomination from the horns of a hart that happened to be killed by the King's dogs near the church as it was building; and the horns were put in the wall of the church; Mr Estcot, a gentleman commoner 1647 of Trinity College, Oxon, went to school there and said that the stumps of the horns were extant in his time.

But more recent local stories have claimed other origins, from the mildly miraculous – a prior was on his way to church when a bull began to charge him, but a herd of cows averted the attack by surrounding him – to the prosaic: a bull got loose from its master and somehow got its head stuck between the railings of the church and could not be released, so its head had to be chopped off.

HIGH STREET, HORNCHURCH: MILL FIELD

In William Hone's *Every-Day Book* (1825), an annual custom is briefly described:

> On Christmas Day, the following custom has been observed at Hornchurch, in Essex, from time immemorial. The lessee of the tithes, which belong to New College, Oxford, supplies a boar's head dressed, and garnished with bay-leaves, etc. In the afternoon, it is carried in procession into the Mill Field, adjoining the churchyard, where it is wrestled for; and it is afterwards feasted upon, at one of the public-houses, by the rustic conqueror and his friends, with all the merriment peculiar to the season.

One explanation, printed in *Notes and Queries* in 1852, was that the boar's head gift was stipulated by an ancient charter, though as yet no evidence has been found to support this. According to Charles Perfect's book of local history *Ye Olde Village of Hornchurch* (1917):

> One of our oldest inhabitants, who witnessed many of the bouts for the boar's head, tells us that it was cooked at Hornchurch Hall, where the first slice was always cut off. It was then brought into the Millfield on a pitchfork, bedecked with ribbons and holly, and with an orange in its mouth. Often as many as twenty wrestlers competed for the prize.

In its later years the wrestling match was between the men of Hornchurch and the men of Romford, but because of increasing rowdiness the event was held for the last time in 1868. Initial enquiries at the New College archives have brought no further information, but further digging may do so.

Although this custom seems to be unique as it stands, each of its constituent elements is found elsewhere. It is not strange to find a boar's head associated with an Oxford college at Christmas, and even the contest for such a prize is echoed in other places, such as at Ebernoe Horn Fair in Sussex, where they hold an annual cricket match and the best player receives the head and horns of the ram that has been roasted and eaten on the day.

HIGH STREET, PLAISTOW

'Penny for the guy' was a custom in which children took part all over London, but the following evocative story is told by Ken Kimberley, who grew up in Plaistow in the 1930s, and is taken from his book of memories, *Oi Jimmy Knacker* (1998). He remembers planning with his friends, Alf and Charlie, to take Charlie's guy up to the High Street one evening:

> His guy sat in a barrow that his elder brother had made, its long legs hanging over the edge. A scruffy bowler hat was perched on top of a Guy Fawkes mask, and two fat arms with gloves tied to the ends clutched a notice that read 'Please spare a copper for the guy'. We admired Charlie's handiwork, helped him push the barrow to the top and found the best spot opposite the tram and bus stop. Next door was the tobacconist's. It was a very good time as all the grown-ups were coming home from work. It wasn't long before we were busy asking, 'Please spare a copper for the guy, mister.'

They did a brisk trade, although they were a bit put out to see Albie Gibbs begging for coppers across the road, on the strength of their guy:

> 'Blooming cheek', exclaimed Charlie. 'He ain't got a guy. He's using ours!' Seeing us and our guy, he hurried over. 'It's all right if I use yours, is it? Cos I couldn't find any old clothes this year to make one.' Alf said with a laugh, 'Just stand there, Albie, 'cos you'll do as you are!'

Asking for a 'penny for the guy' could be quite lucrative. Local tradition in Plaistow dictated that the person who made the guy kept half the takings, the rest being split between his helpers.

When the crowds thinned, and the shops started closing, they reckoned up their takings, which, including Albie's, amounted to two shillings and sixpence. Local code of practice dictated that Charlie got half, because it was his guy, so the rest got five pence each. Not bad for a few hours' work.

See also GUY FAWKES NIGHT, p. 338.

HIGH STREET, SHADWELL

The following report of a case that was heard at the Old Bailey in October 1834 provides a great deal of information about the widespread belief in FORTUNE-TELLING (p. 78), and the antics of those who preyed on the gullibility of the believers. Catherine Padley Mather, the twenty-year-old daughter of a hosier in the High Street, Shadwell, claimed that Ellen Morgan came into their shop and first asked if they had any broken glass to sell, and then offered to tell fortunes. 'My charge is a shilling piece, but I will tell two fortunes for a shilling.' Catherine said no, but Morgan launched into her rigmarole and, worried that her father would catch them telling fortunes in the shop, Catherine told her persistent visitor to go into the kitchen.

> She then asked me for the largest piece of silver I had, which was half-a-crown, and I was to cross my hand three times with it – she took the half-crown and said she was to put it on the planet – she then asked me for three more of the largest pieces of silver I had; they were shillings; she told me to cross my hand three times with them, and she took them; they were to go to the planet; she was to return them to me in the evening.

Morgan left, but returned half an hour later asking for clothes, and took away a pair of stockings, a silk handkerchief, and a shirt, and came back a few days later demanding another ten shillings 'to make up the planet'. Needless to say, no money or clothes were ever returned.

Several extra details emerged in the cross-examination following this deposition. Far from being the stereotypical old woman, this fortune-teller was only nineteen, and younger than her 'victim'. Less surprisingly, it seems that the whole business of 'fortunes' was primarily concerned with the prediction of marriage prospects:

> MORGAN: Did not you ask me whether I could tell your fortune, and say you would give me a shilling to tell yours and the servant's?
> MATHER: No, I did not; I did not say I should like to have my fortune told, as I was deeply in love with a young man.
> MORGAN: She said she would give me any thing if I would tell her the young man she was to be married to.

Morgan was found guilty, and transported for seven years.

Other trials of fortune-tellers in London in the period reveal a similar pattern. The request for money is naturally the most common element, and although the money was sometimes simply taken away, it was occasionally substituted for worthless metal by sleight of hand. The detail of putting the money 'on a planet' is a common one in such cases, but of obscure meaning. It clearly represents some sort of astrological mumbo-jumbo, but it is never made clear quite what.

HIGH STREET, STEPNEY:
CHURCH OF ST DUNSTAN AND ALL SAINTS

Against the west wall of St Dunstan and All Saints, on Stepney High Street, is a monument to Dame Rebecca Berry, wife of Thomas Elton, of Stratford Bow, who died in 1696. Commonly called the 'Fish and Ring' monument, a coat of arms including these items is emblazoned on it. Their appearance has fuelled a tradition that Dame Rebecca was the heroine of a ballad entitled 'The Cruel Knight; or, Fortunate Farmer's Daughter'. This ballad was popular as a broadside around the turn of the nineteenth century, and has a rather long and involved story.

Near York, there was a farmer and his wife who had fallen on hard times. They had just given birth to their seventh child – a girl – when a noble knight rode by. Being skilled in astrology he took out his 'book' to see the fate of this new baby girl, and found to his astonishment that she was destined to be his wife. He was not pleased with this, so he persuaded the farmer and his wife to give the baby to him by promising to bring her up as a rich lady. They reluctantly agreed, so he went off with the baby, and tossed her in the river to get rid of her. As luck would have it, the tide took her downstream to a childless fisherman, who took her home to his wife. When she was eleven, and already a stunning beauty, she happened to call at the inn where her adoptive father, the fisherman, was drinking with some other men, prompting him to explain to them how he came to have such a lovely daughter. Unfortunately, the cruel knight was at the inn, and heard the whole story. This time, he persuaded the fisherman to let him take the girl and he sent her, with a servant, to his brother, bearing a sealed letter asking him to kill her immediately. On the journey, the girl and her servant stopped at an inn, and a thief attempted to rob them during the night. Finding nothing worth stealing, the thief read the letter, and, presumably on a whim, altered it to instruct the brother to take care of the girl and bring her up as a rich lady. Some years later, the knight visited his brother and was annoyed to discover that the girl was still alive. He took her to the seashore to throw her in, but she managed to persuade him to spare her life by promising not to contact him. He showed her a ring and threw it in the sea, saying, 'Never contact me unless you can bring that very ring with you.' She then got a job as a kitchen maid at a nobleman's house, and while preparing dinner cut open a cod and found the ring inside.

The nobleman's wife had noticed the girl, who seemed to her too beautiful and accomplished to remain a maid, so she dressed her up to be her companion. The cruel knight then came to visit and was incensed to find her there. He upbraided her, but she produced the ring, provoking in him a sudden change of heart that led him to ask her forgiveness and her hand in marriage. She agreed and they lived happily ever after.

Only in folktales would her marriage to a man twice her age who has tried to murder her several times be considered a happy ending. The legend of the Stepney memorial prompted a three-volume novel by Elizabeth Isabella Spence, entitled *Dame Rebecca Berry, or Court Scenes in the Reign of Charles II* (1827), and a prose version of the story, from Yorkshire, was published in William Henderson's *Folk-Lore of the Northern Counties of England* (1866). This has a very similar plot to the broadside, but gets round the awkwardness of the ending by making the knight find out at the beginning that it is his *son*'s fate to marry the girl.

The motif of things being lost or thrown away and then being recovered in a fish is very old and extremely widespread, with versions being found in many different cultures. In some, the tale is simply one of magic, but in many accounts it is the work of fate or destiny, as in the oldest version, from Herodotus' *Histories* (about 450 BC):

Polycrates had seized power in Samos, and was expanding his dominion all around. All his campaigns were victorious, his every venture a success, and his luck became the talk of Ionia and the rest of Greece. His ally, Amasis, King of Egypt, wrote to him, saying, 'It is a pleasure to hear of a friend and ally doing well, but, as I know that the gods are jealous of success, I cannot rejoice at the excess of your prosperity.' Amasis suggested that Polycrates decide on the most precious thing in his possession, and that he deliberately get rid of it, so that he can claim some misfortune to balance his excessive luck. Polycrates chose a signet ring, which was particularly precious to him, had himself rowed out to sea, and threw it overboard, and then went home to lament its loss. A few days later a fisherman caught a particularly large and fine fish, and presented it to Polycrates to eat at a coming feast. But the ring was found inside the fish, and Polycrates realised that man cannot cheat destiny. Hearing the story, Amasis immediately cancelled his pact with Polycrates, because he knew that he must be heading for a fall. It was not long before he was tricked into going to see Oroetes, who had him murdered.

In Christian narrative, fate becomes the hand of God, and the legends of, among others, St Kentigern, St Arnold, St Lupus, and St Verena, include lost rings found in fish. Two other legends in England, given in Jennifer Westwood and Jacqueline Simpson's *Lore of the Land* (2005), have connections with this tale: one from Newcastle-upon-Tyne, dating from 1627, involves a lost ring found in a fish; and another from Ribbesford in Worcestershire is a version of the 'lucky shot' story, in which a hunter fires an arrow at his quarry and a salmon, with the ring inside it, happens to leap out of the river at exactly the right moment and is impaled as it blocks the shot.

ISLE OF DOGS

The derivation of the Isle of Dogs, the name given to the area enclosed within the U-bend of the Thames containing Millwall and Cubitt Town, is uncertain. The earliest known reference to dogs is on a map of 1588, and various suggestions have been made, including that it was the place where Henry VIII (or Edward III) kept his hunting dogs, which is possible but unfortunately not backed up with any evidence. Another unsupported suggestion is that it was previously known as Isle of Ducks, because its marshy land was ideal for wildfowl. But the best etymology so far recorded – in terms of narrative interest if not plausibility – is a story that was told by a Poplar man, to his daughter Jane, before the First World War, as reported in *Silvertown* (2002), Melanie McGrath's memoir of an East End family:

Jane Fulcher's favourite story, one her father often tells, concerns two mastiffs and a cow. The cow had been left to graze on the marsh south of Poplar in the loop of the Thames. The dogs, whose job it was to protect the cow from hungry poachers, were chained to the animal's feet. Every week a marshman came along and left meat for the dogs and between times they dug for worms and pounced on any small thing that crossed their path. But a mist came down as mists often did in the marsh and the cow, wandering about and unable to see its feet, stumbled on its chains and fell into a nearby bog, catapulting its unfortunate protectors into the quicksand. After a struggle the cows sank into the slime and died, but, being lighter, the dogs remained on the surface for a while longer. For four days and nights the residents of Poplar heard a terrible wailing, but were too frightened to go down to the bog and see what was afoot. Rumours rushed around that the devil had landed in the marsh and was taunting them before making his move. When the marshman eventually returned to check on his charge he found two mastiff heads preserved in the marshy brine, their jaws open as if in a long, last howl of injustice. And that is how, [her father] says, the Isle of Dogs got its name.

LEYTONSTONE

One of the most common children's customs in nineteenth- and twentieth-century London was to build a grotto in the street in late summer, and beg coins from passers-by. An unusually detailed description of the custom, as seen in Leytonstone, appeared in *Folk-Lore* in 1905:

During the past grotto season (1904) I invited several of the older boys into the garden and watched them construct one of their edifices. The *size* varies; roughly perhaps it is some two feet across, eighteen inches deep, and eighteen inches high. The *structure* consists of a floor, back, side-walls and roof; the front is left partly open. The roof is formed by placing sticks across the walls and then piling stones upon them, the general form of the roof being that of a dome. *Flowers*: The outside of the structure is ornamented with flowers pushed in between the crevices. *Materials*: If possible, shells – oyster shells for choice – are procured, but generally, as a matter of fact, the clinkers and stones are used. *Candle*: the first halfpenny given by the passer-by is spent in purchasing a candle, which is put in the grotto and lighted. The *date* for making these grottoes did not seem to them clear. 'It is grotto time now,' said one, 'we see others building them'; 'we keep a note-book with the time for the peg-tops, leap-frog and grotto time,' said others. *Reason for building*: None of them knew of any reason for their erection; no one had ever seen it elsewhere; they had done it at school, having seen others.

See also GROTTOES AND SPRING GARDENS, p. 402.

LIMEHOUSE: RIVER FRONT

A famous ghost who haunted the river front at Limehouse was known as the vicar of Ratcliffe Cross, and was said to have run a seamen's hostel some 200 years ago. He was in the habit of murdering some of his unsuspecting guests for their money, and throwing their bodies into the river. The vicar's ghost was reputedly well known to local dock-workers, who avoided the area after dark, and he was seen as recently as 1971. This is what an entry in *Man, Myth and Magic*, an extremely influential part-work publication published weekly in 1970–72, claims, and the article quotes several named people who had recently seen the vicar's apparition, and gives the dates and circumstances of the sightings, along with their reactions. The piece does not look at all out of place among the supernatural fare in which the publication specialised, but it was later admitted that the story of the vicar's ghost was a deliberate hoax, composed by Frank Smyth, one of the staff writers on the project. In an article printed in the *Sunday Times* on 24 August 1975, Smyth admitted his forgery, commenting:

> Twentieth-century ghosts had fallen into such a sad decline, I decided to create one of the old school. The majority of them didn't even take the trouble to frighten anyone, preferring to tramp invisibly up and down the stairs of council houses in the middle of the afternoon.

Whatever his motives at the time, many readers took the story at face value, and his admission came too late to prevent the story turning up in several books of London ghosts in the early 1970s, including some by the most reputable writers in the field, who presumably were not amused by Smyth's joke.

No author can afford to crow about others caught out by hoaxes such as this one. We all spend our time reading other works on our chosen subject, and we recycle what we need, but the affair shines a harsh spotlight on the nature of research into ghost-lore, and also brings useful questions of evidence and belief into sharp relief. By their very nature, stories of ghost sightings are largely unsupported by testable evidence, and the ghost writer routinely relies on what in the common-sense world would be dismissed as hearsay. But it is difficult to imagine any other field of research where serious writers would unquestioningly believe such a popular, unprovenanced, frankly low-grade publication as *Man, Myth and Magic*,

Limehouse, supposedly the setting for the 'Vicar of Ratcliffe Cross' ghost story.

and would repeat its assertions without even a hint of reserve or revealing their source. It certainly appears to be a classic example of how 'willingness to believe' so easily becomes 'desire to believe'.

In one sense, however, Frank Smyth has simply created another piece of folklore, and if his story is a good one it is likely to be repeated and therefore become 'true' in the folkloric sense. As he himself said in the *Sunday Times* article:

> I met a lighter-man in Islington who said he heard about the phantom vicar from his grandfather. I told him that was impossible, I'd invented him entirely. He wouldn't have that. 'There's a phantom vicar there all right. That's why they used to close the docks there at five every night. No one would work there after dark.'

But there is yet another interesting twist to this saga, by which we can see that even a fake ghost can be used to support a belief in the supernatural. By slightly altering the chronology of the events, at least two writers have claimed that this lighter-man spoke to Smyth *before* his story was published, and it can therefore be argued that although the latter thought he invented the story from scratch, he was really being informed, or even manipulated, by spirit forces beyond his control, and that the vicar's ghost really does exist.

LONDON DOCKS, WAPPING

A popular sight on Good Friday in the nineteenth century, for those who lived near the docks, was the custom of 'flogging Judas' on board any Portuguese or South American ships that happened to be berthed there on the day, and a description appeared in *The Times* on 4 April 1874. In the early morning, a figure intended to represent Judas was made of wood or straw and dressed as a sailor. It was hoisted to the yardarm, where it remained suspended while the sailors attended Mass. The effigy was then lowered overboard and dipped in the water three times, before being hauled across the deck and bound to the capstan. The crew then attacked it with ropes, quite literally lashing it to pieces. Custom then dictated that the remains be burnt, but as fires were not allowed in the docks, Judas was dumped ignominiously overboard. The whole proceedings took about three hours, and were accompanied by the sailors vociferously cursing and swearing at Judas for his treachery. The custom was particularly popular with the crew because they were given extra rations of grog.

There is no evidence that this custom was adopted by the locals in London, but it certainly was in Liverpool, where a Good Friday children's custom called 'burning Judas', similar to burning the guy on Guy Fawkes Night, lasted until at least the 1950s. An engraving of the custom on a Portuguese ship was printed in the *Graphic* on 15 April 1876.

A very different piece of dockland lore is given in a story printed by Elliott O'Donnell in his *Haunted Waters* (1957), although he gives no source for his information. In the summer of 1803, the *Result*, which sailed mainly between Australia and Britain, was docked in the Port of London and its cargo being unloaded. The work suddenly came to a halt, however, as one of the gang spotted an apparent stowaway standing between the crates. The men called to the stranger to get ashore before he was detected, but he took no notice, and several attempts to get his attention were met with no response at all. When they finally cleared a way to get to him, they found not a live stowaway, but a mummified corpse, kept upright by being wedged between the boxes. The body was never identified, nor the circumstances of his journey discovered.

Rhyming Slang

The first page of Duncan Anglicus's *The Vulgar Tongue* (1857). It is interesting to note that many of the words and phrases listed here would be familiar to users of cockney rhyming slang today.

Rhyming slang is one of the most famous products of the London working class, although it has had a few outposts elsewhere, most notably in Australia. The documentary record shows that it sprang into being in the mid nineteenth century; its early history and development are relatively clear, but its origin is not. It is often assumed that it was an extension of the flash language, or thieves' cant, of earlier years, which inevitably led to the notion that rhyming slang was designed to be a way of disguising the meaning of conversation from potential victims or those in authority. But this is most unlikely, as a disguise that drops such heavy hints to its hidden meaning is quite ineffectual for long-term camouflage. Flash language is itself quite well documented and shows little sign of the exuberance of rhyming slang. It is much more likely to have been simply a result of the love of word-play and wit for which costermongers and other working groups in London were already becoming well known in Victorian times.

The earliest reference to the term *rhyming slang* is in James Camden Hotten's *Slang Dictionary* of 1859, and he notes that it had been introduced about ten or twelve years previously. This assertion is supported by Henry Mayhew's comment in his *London Labour and the London Poor*, in 1851, that 'the new style of cadger's cant is done all on the rhyming principle'. One of the first authors to offer examples was Ducange Anglicus, in *The Vulgar Tongue* (1857), and it is interesting to note that of the sixty-two phrases quoted by him, many have remained in the core repertoire – apples and pears, mince pies, Barnet fair, and so on. But it is also clear that the new slang was only just becoming well known in the early 1850s. Charles Dickens, for example, in an article on London slang in his *Household Words* published 24 September 1853, does not even mention it.

Rhyming slang's heyday had passed by the early years of the twentieth century, and it was seemingly on its last legs by the 1930s. Writing of his childhood in Stepney, Jim Wolveridge (born 1920) commented:

> Rhyming slang had been used a lot at one time mostly by costermongers but by the thirties it had almost died out and might have vanished entirely if it hadn't been taken up by the professional Cockney comedians on the stage and radio. Quite suddenly it regained its popularity, and it was also taken up by the middle classes and it's not really ours any more. Today it's thought of as purely a humorous thing, but it wasn't originally, it was spoken in a natural fashion without any stress or emphasis. I don't know why all this fuss is made about it.

In corroboration, George Orwell, in his *Down and Out in Paris and London* (1933), claimed that 'it is almost extinct'. But since the Second World War it has undergone something of a renaissance, led perhaps by the tourist trade – although, like all living slang, in the wrong mouth it can sound false and silly, especially if the accent clashes with the words being said. And the worst that the budding rhyming slanger can do is not know when to shorten the phrase to the first word (nearly always), and when to say the whole thing. Occasionally, you must say more than half, as in 'he's a bit mutton' ('Mutt and Jeff' = deaf). Only the native speaker can get it right. New terms are still being coined, but the tendency these days is to use celebrity names as the model; you can buy a round of 'Britneys' at the pub, for example.

Several terms that started as rhyming slang have now entered the general language, albeit not at the posh end of the spectrum. It is not uncommon to hear the verb *to rabbit* (from *rabbit and pork*), meaning to talk a lot, or for someone to say, 'Let's have a butcher's at that', or 'That's a load of old cobblers'. There are many people who say 'He's a right berk', or 'He's a proper Charlie', without realising that the words originated as contractions of Berkshire Hunt and Charlie Hunt.

See CHEAPSIDE: ST MARY-LE-BOW, p. 9.

NIGHTINGALE LANE, WANSTEAD:
DUKE OF EDINBURGH PUB

Problems apparently started in this pub in the mid 1970s. The disturbances are the standard pub-haunting fare of lights turning on and off, beer taps mysteriously being left on, and the feeling that one is not alone in the cellars. A different detail was supplied by landlords Mr and Mrs Cairns in the *Essex Pictorial* on 22 September 1976:

'We have tried to install umpteen grandfather clocks but they just keep stopping. In the shop they are working but as soon as we bring them into the pub they stop for no reason at all.'

OLD CHURCH ROAD, CHINGFORD:
CHINGFORD MOUNT CEMETERY

If anywhere has a right to be haunted, it is a graveyard, and Chingford Mount Cemetery made the local press in 1969 with its own ghost story. According to an article in the *Leytonstone Independent* on 14 November, Mr Gradley, the new superintendent, who had been living at the Lodge with his family for five months, had experienced numerous unexplained occurrences:

Something always wakes me up. The house has an atmosphere upstairs. It gives you a creepy feeling. A whining noise sometimes echoes around the house and there are the inevitable things that go bang in the night. On one occasion I searched the house from top to bottom with a truncheon, after my wife heard noises in the kitchen. But I found nothing.

Atmospheres and strange noises are all very well, but one day he was in the grounds with his four-year-old son, when the boy pointed across the empty cemetery and asked, 'Who is that funny man on the black horse?'

Parkstone Avenue, Emerson Park

Jessie Payne's *A Ghost-Hunter's Guide to Essex* (1987) includes the following nice little story:

> One afternoon, in October 1984, Mr K. O. James woke from a doze he had been enjoying in an armchair in a 1897 house in Parkstone Avenue, Emerson Park, Hornchurch, to see a little girl in Edwardian costume, who said, 'Can I have my ball back, please?' He rubbed his eyes and she had gone. What Mr Jones did not know was that his son-in-law had found a painted rubber ball under the floorboards in an upstairs room three days earlier.

Plaistow

In a small pamphlet, entitled *Strange and Fearfull Newes from Plaisto, in the Parish of West-Ham, neere Bow, foure miles from London, in the house of Paul Fox a Silke-Weaver* (printed in London in 1645), an early version of a poltergeist was described, as happening to 'a man of honest life and conversation'. Firstly, a sword that hung in the chamber 'in a sudden came flourishing about the room, flying up and down; no hand touching it'. Then a walking cane, which was in the kitchen, came hopping up the stairs and into the room where the sword was performing. The sword remained still while the cane danced around, and then they lay down together. Later that evening came a 'strange kind of rapping at the door', and when Fox demanded who was there he was answered by a spirit that spoke with 'a soft hollow voice [and] commanded him to open the door, saying, he must dwell there'. Fearing that it was an evil spirit, Fox refused to let it in, but this seemed to anger it, for the next day when they were weaving their silk was cut to pieces before their eyes, and tiles, brickbats, oyster shells, pieces of bread, and so on came flying through the windows, smashing the glass. Even a large stone, weighing half a hundredweight, which lay in the yard, came up the stairs and into the house, and when taken out, made its way back.

> I should be too tedious to relate every particular that hath happened here within the space of this month, how Fox, his son and his men are sometimes

pulled by the hair, lugged by the ears, knockt on the head, pinched in their sleep, pulled out of their beds, troubled with many noises . . . What the event may be we know not, but it continues to this day, and there be thousands that have been eye witnesses to the truth thereof . . .

See also BEVERSTONE ROAD, THORNTON HEATH, p. 365; BRIMSDOWN, ENFIELD, p. 196; CHELSEA, p. 138; GROVE PARK: ALLOTMENTS, p. 333; REVERDY ROAD, BERMONDSEY: NOS 56 AND 58, p. 342; STOCKWELL, p. 414; SUTTON LANE, CHISWICK: SUTTON COURT-HOUSE, p. 173.

PLAISTOW GROVE, WEST HAM

A fascinating article was published in the *East Ham and Stratford Express* on 27 October 1894 as part of a series based on the reminiscences of older inhabitants of the area. The article uncovers an interesting story about a local landmark:

The fields at the back of the Polly Memorial Schools used to be called 'Ladywell Fields'. The well was just where you now turn into Plaistow Grove. A lady is said to have drowned herself in that well – that was how it got its name – and this lady, so the tale went, used to rise up every night at twelve o'clock. I've known people who have declared they had seen her.'

'You never saw her yourself?'

'No, nor any other ghost, but people used to say there were a good many of them about West Ham in those days.'

PULTENEY ROAD, SOUTH WOODFORD

On 5 October 1979, the *Redbridge Guardian* reported a ghostly occurrence in a warehouse belonging at the time to Emess Lighting in Pulteney Road. The staff described ghostly footsteps, doors opening and closing, and a figure glimpsed when no one else was there. One worker added:

'About half an hour later it went very quiet. I could sense something – some force – sliding all over me. I couldn't lift my arm up. I had goose-pimples and I felt very ill.'

One theory of the origin of the haunting is that the premises back on to the railway line. More than thirty years previously, a man had been killed by a passing train after his wife, standing on the footbridge, had warned him to be careful crossing the line.

RATCLIFFE

A tradition regarding a house in Ratcliffe was included by Walter Besant in his *East London* (1901). This house, which was beside the church (then the vicarage), and built about the end of the seventeenth century, was remarkable for the Italian landscapes painted on its dining-room walls. A rich London merchant had reputedly owned the house, and had engaged a young Italian artist to decorate the rooms. Inevitably, the young artist formed an attachment with the merchant's daughter, but they were discovered, and the Italian was ordered to pack up his things and leave the house within half an hour. When the merchant went up to the young man's room to find out why he had not yet departed, he found him hanging from the canopy of the bed. The room was believed to be haunted for a while, and servants refused to stay in it, but a redoubtable vicar's wife slept in the room and declared she had heard and seen nothing. The ghost's credibility being thus severely damaged, he departed immediately.

ROMAN ROAD, BETHNAL GREEN:
BLIND BEGGAR STATUE

On the Cranbrook estate one can find a bronze statue by Dame Elizabeth Frinks commemorating the Blind Beggar of Bethnal Green, a story that has been known across the English-speaking world, in one form or another, since the early seventeenth century.

It was a blind beggar that long lost his sight,
He had a fair daughter, most pleasant and bright,
And many a gallant brave suitor had she,
For none was so comely as pretty Bessee.

So runs the first verse of a broadside from about 1685, which takes over 250 lines to tell the story of the blind beggar and his beautiful daughter Bessy. Leaving home to seek her fortune, Bessy finds work at the King's Arms in Romford. She becomes popular with the young men there and receives proposals from a knight, a merchant, a gentleman, and her master's own son. When they learn who her father is ('The silly blind beggar of Bednal Green'), three of her suitors withdraw in disgust, but, despite his family's objection, the knight continues his suit ('I weigh not true love by the weight of the purse'). They travel to meet Bessy's father, who challenges the knight to declare his wealth, and the latter throws down £3,000 in gold, which the beggar counters by throwing down twice as much, plus 'a hundred pounds more to buy her a gown'. They have an expensive wedding. Part 2 of the song explains that the beggar's real name is Monford and he lost his sight

A chapbook illustration of scenes from the life of the Blind Beggar of Bethnal Green. The lower part of the illustration depicts the part of the story where the Blind Beggar reveals his hidden wealth to a knight who wishes to marry the beggar's daughter.

fighting for the King in France, but was found on the battlefield and nursed back to life by a young woman, whom he later married, before assuming the disguise of a beggar.

Most ballad scholars assume that the song was composed in the reign of Elizabeth I, which is feasible but as yet unproven. Extant broadsides date from the late seventeenth century, and the famous manuscript on which Bishop Percy based the version published in his *Reliques of Ancient English Poetry*, is usually dated about 1650. But other sources show that a ballad, 'The Blind Beggar', was licensed by the Company of Stationers in London in 1624, and a play entitled

The Blind Beggar of Bethnal Green was acted by 'The Admiral's Men' in 1600.

The ballad was printed on a number of different broadsides from the late seventeenth century onwards, and the story also appeared in prose chapbooks. But around the turn of the nineteenth century a severely curtailed text of ten or twelve verses appeared on broadsides, and this version was picked up by traditional singers in Britain and North America and was still being sung widely when folksong enthusiasts noted it down in the twentieth century.

Parallel to this 'traditional' life, the ballad has been regularly reprinted and discussed in collections of early poetry and literature, and it is here that a simple error has crept in. In his usual cavalier approach to the texts he edited, Percy interpolated verses of his own composition naming Simon de Montfort as the man behind the beggar's identity, and the Battle of Evesham (1265) as the place he was wounded, thereby lending a fake historicity to the ballad which has lasted ever since.

Bethnal Green is very proud of its Blind Beggar, and his story is also commemorated in the area's coat of arms, in a stained-glass window from 1923 in the local library, and in a relief on the wall of the old town hall in Patriot Square erected in 1938.

SHADWELL

It is sometimes assumed that the district gets its name from a well dedicated to St Chad, but earliest written forms show that it derives from words meaning 'shallow well'. Nevertheless, the area was known for a while for its waters, as recorded by Daniel Lysons in his *Environs of London: Middlesex* (1795):

> About fifty years ago, a mineral water of a very powerful nature (now called Shadwell Spa) was discovered by Walter Berry, Esq., in sinking a well in Sun-tavern fields. It is said to be impregnated with sulphur, vitriol, steel, and antimony. A pamphlet, published by D. W. Linden MD in 1749, written as a puff for the water, extols it as an approved cure for almost every disorder incident to the human frame, either by drinking or bathing. I understand that it has been found very serviceable as an antiscorbutic, and in all cutaneous

disorders. Of late, the water has been principally used for the purpose of extracting salts, and for preparing a liquor with which the calico printers fix their colours. The present proprietor intends to use it solely for medicinal purposes. There is another mineral spring in the parish, of a quality resembling that of the postern waters on Tower-hill.

SHOREDITCH

A false derivation of the name Shoreditch has been around since at least the mid seventeenth century. The claim is that the area is named after Jane Shore, Edward IV's most famous mistress, who died in poverty there, in a ditch. Elizabeth Jane Shore was real enough (she died around 1526), and she certainly was a royal mistress, but there is little evidence she died penniless, and the area was known as some variation of Shoreditch at least 400 years before her time. Unfortunately the place-name experts have not yet agreed on its exact origin. It was at one time suggested that it means 'ditch leading to the shore [of the Thames]', but this has since been discredited.

After her time, Jane Shore became a popular character in ballads and plays, including Thomas Heywood's *King Edward IV* (1599), Nicholas Rowe's *Tragedy of Jane Shore* (1714), and several broadsides, but it is not clear why she became regarded as the proverbial courtesan. She apparently had fewer faults than others of her ilk, and the Chancellor and leading courtier of the day, Thomas More, for example, was positively complimentary: 'a proper wit had she, and could read well and write, merry in company, ready and quick of answer, neither mute nor full of babble, sometime taunting without displeasure and not without disport.' Nevertheless, she had something of a rocky road after Edward's death, and had trouble with Richard III, and it is this aspect that the playwrights and ballad-mongers concentrated on. It is interesting to note that the false derivation is no mere modern fallacy, but was already current in the mid seventeenth century, and it is not clear whether this was the root of the other stereotype of Shoreditch's reputation, or vice versa. In his 1891 book entitled *London Past and Present*, Henry Wheatley notes that:

> Shoreditch was formerly notorious for the easy character of its women. 'To die in Shoreditch' was not a mere metaphorical term for dying in a sewer.

The Chelsea Pensioners' Founder's Day parade occurs around 29 May every year, commemorating the birthday and restoration of Charles II. A popular story claims that the King set up the Royal Hospital in Chelsea for military invalids at the request of his mistress, Nell Gwynne.

The signature many-buttoned attire of pearly kings and queens is thought to have been invented by a road-sweeper named Henry Croft (1862–1930). Croft was inspired by the way costers decorated their clothes with buttons, and took it to this ornate extreme.

Smithfield's Bartholomew Fair was a popular annual occasion, which sadly did not survive past the mid-nineteenth century. Originally designed as a trade fair and for many years the most important event for the cloth industry, it was also renowned for its large theatrical booths, where spectators could watch anything from Shakespeare to the latest farce.

The Cathedral and Collegiate Church of St Saviour and St Mary Overie is now commonly known as Southwark Cathedral. Although 'Overie' simply meant 'over the river', people have always been fond of a more colourful explanation, involving John Overs, the legendary 'rich ferryman of Southwark' and his daughter 'Mary'.

In late August, show-people used to move straight from Bartholomew to Southwark Fair. The raucous and bawdy atmosphere, captured by Hogarth's 1733 painting, goes some way to explaining why so many fairs came to be perceived as public nuisances and were eventually proscribed – in Southwark's case, less than thirty years after this painting.

'Penny for the guy' is a children's Guy Fawkes Night tradition that has been popular for centuries. Although somewhat superseded by Hallowe'en festivities, Guy Fawkes Night, with its bonfires, guys and fireworks, remains an entertaining annual event.

Every year clowns gather at the Holy Trinity Church, Dalston, to take part in a service in memory of Joseph Grimaldi (1779–1837). The comedian from Clerkenwell laid the foundations for the modern clown tradition, including the costume that is so familiar today.

A great beauty, Barbara Villiers (1640–1709) was one of Charles II's mistresses. She contracted dropsy, a swelling disease, when she grew older and her melancholy footsteps are said to be heard upon the staircase of her former abode, Walpole House in Chiswick.

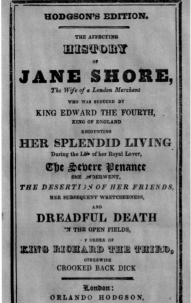

This nineteenth-century chapbook tells the sad tale of Jane Shore, Edward IV's mistress, who reputedly came to a miserable end. The story claims that after her benefactor's death she descended into poverty and eventually died in a ditch, giving her name to the area known as Shoreditch.

A cat on top of the Whittington Stone marks the spot on Highgate Hill where Dick Whittington, according to legend, heard the Bow Bells telling him to 'turn again, Whittington, thrice Lord Mayor of London'.

The Fleet sewer runs from Hampstead to the Thames, which it reaches just below Blackfriars Bridge. In the mid-nineteenth century, 'toshers', who scoured the sewers for any lost property that might be of value, believed it was inhabited by a race of ferocious wild hogs.

This eighteenth-century window of St Mary's Church, Lambeth, depicts the 'Lambeth Pedlar'. One of many stories surrounding this legendary figure is that he left money and land to the parish, so long as his dog could be buried in the churchyard.

In addition to serving food and drink, Battersea's Red House inn had an enclosed four-acre ground for bird-shooting, which attracted members of the nobility and working classes alike and enhanced the area's raffish reputation. The inn was closed down in 1852, two years after it was portrayed in this illustration.

An illustration from an eighteenth-century chapbook relating the life of Edward IV's mistress Jane Shore, who supposedly died in a ditch in a part of London that consequently became known as Shoreditch.

Numerous websites still state that Shoreditch is named after Jane Shore's dying in a ditch.

Folklorist Edward Lovett (1852–1933) was fascinated by the superstitions of working-class Londoners, and an avid collector of lucky charms, mascots, and talismans. Many of the objects he collected can be seen in the Cuming Museum, Walworth Road, Southwark. One of the things he soon learned was that any abnormal forms of natural objects were candidates for 'lucky' status, and the following piece, entitled 'The Luck of the "Left-handed" Whelk Shell', is taken from his book *Magic in Modern London* (1925):

> One of my interesting friends is 'Old Charlie', who keeps a whelk and oyster stall not very far from Shoreditch . . . One day during the war he told me that three of his chums went out to the front together. To use his own words: 'I had two of them lucky left-handed whelks which I gave to my two best chums, but I hadn't any to give to the other man! Well, guv'nor, p'raps you won't believe it, but them two I gave the shells to come home without a scratch! As for that other poor chap; nobody ever saw him again. He was blowed up in a dump, he was! I wish I'd had another o' them whelks for him.'

See also STOKE NEWINGTON, p. 300.

SILVERTOWN

Melanie McGrath, in her 2002 memoir of East London life, *Silvertown*, mentions a small example of a widespread tradition of beliefs and fears about animals and insects infesting the human body. In a paragraph on different types of dock-workers, based on her father's experiences (*c.* 1912), she writes:

> He'll tell about the sugar porters whose flesh is so raw from the sharpness of their cargo that the bluebottles get in underneath their skin and lay their eggs. How on a summer's day you can tell a sugar porter by the clouds of tiny flies bursting from his limbs.

See also KENT STREET, SOUTHWARK, p. 335; KENTISH TOWN, p. 233; NEW MALDEN, p. 404; VERE STREET, p. 119.

STOKE NEWINGTON

According to indefatigable curio collector Edward Lovett, lucky mascots were particularly popular with Londoners during the First World War. As he comments in his *Magic in Modern London* (1925):

> The following is worth recording if only for the reason that it upsets the usual theory of the mental aspect of a belief in the efficacy of amulets. It comes from somewhere not far from Stoke Newington. During the Great War a woman had an only son who was called up and sent to the front. The old lady, who was very much upset, wanted her son to take a mascot, but he, being very opposed to such things, declined. The mother, unknown to her son, took the mascot, which was a small pendant of Carnelian, and sewed it very carefully inside the lining of his tunic. I was afterwards told that her son returned without a scratch.

See also SHOREDITCH, p. 298.

STRATFORD

One of the intriguing vignettes of East London life included in Edward Lovett's *Magic in Modern London* (1925) concerns the use of tormentil:

> The root of *Potentilla tormentilla* is an ordinary herbal remedy. One of my many herbalist friends once informed me that two Stratford-by-Bow girls came into his shop one day and asked for a 'pennorth of tormentil'. A week later both girls returned for more, so he asked them what they wanted it for. The girls hesitated, when the younger said to the other, who had asked for the stuff: 'Oh, tell him, Jess; I don't mind.' The older girl then told the herbalist that her sister had been 'chucked' by her 'young man'. Whereupon she consulted an old woman who was 'wise' and that this old woman had told her to get some 'tormentil' root and to burn it at midnight on a Friday; this would so torment and worry the young man that he would soon return to his lone sweetheart. My herbalist friend told me that the girls came for three successive weeks and then stopped. My friend did not hear if the girls succeeded in their venture, or gave it up as a bad job – but he rather thought that they had won.

VALENCE AVENUE, DAGENHAM: VALENCE HOUSE

This former manor house is now home to Dagenham's museum and library, and instead of standing in extensive and well-tended grounds, as it would have done in times past, it is now surrounded by a huge council housing estate. An article written by a former occupant that was published in the February 1961 issue of *Essex Countryside*, claimed that Agnes, a member of the family that had owned the house in the fourteenth century, 'was said to have been murdered and to haunt the lawns. Her ghost was seen by a gardener who approached it, mistaking the apparition for one of the daughters of the house.' The story was supported by the discovery of an old dagger in the moat.

In July 1966 Leslie Cannon, the Deputy Borough Librarian, wrote a humorous piece debunking this legend for Barking council's magazine, the *Barking Record*. He included a spoof photograph of a ghostly 'Agnes' pointing into the moat where the dagger was discovered. Mr Cannon soon learned, however, that you cannot keep a good ghost story down, and he found that descriptions from people who claimed to have seen the ghost now matched the spoof photo suspiciously closely, and his attempt to debunk the story had simply given it an added dimension. The original *Essex Countryside* article also claimed that the cedar trees in the grounds were originally grown from saplings brought back from the Holy Land by a crusader; a legend also found elsewhere and presumably arising simply from the tree's popular name, Cedar of Lebanon.

By the late 1990s, however, a completely different figure was being talked about, one set fair to become Barking's 'official ghost in residence'. This is the ghost of Eliza Luxmoore, who lived in the house from 1878 until her death in 1913. Her figure has reputedly been seen since soon after her death, so she must have rubbed shoulders with Agnes. Far from attempting to debunk the story, the current staff adopted it (presumably on the lines of 'if you've got it, flaunt it'). Staff members now dress up as Eliza and use her character as a way of teaching history to visiting school-parties. They were famously visited by some TV programme ghost-hunters, along with a professional medium, who naturally confirmed Eliza's existence and found many other spirits hanging around the building, although she did not mention poor Agnes.

However, another Valence House story shows that fact is sometimes far more distressing than fiction. In April 1981, according to the newspapers of the time, a young local woman named Sandra Killington became convinced, with the help of a Ouija board, that she was the lover and soulmate of Thomas Fanshaw, a seventeenth-century figure whose portrait hangs in Valence House. She used to visit the house regularly to gaze at, and even talk to, the painting. Suffering from this delusion, she decided that the only way to join him was to die, and so she lay down in front of a train, clutching her four-year-old daughter. Sadly, Sandra was killed, but miraculously her daughter survived unhurt.

WANSTEAD

If regular reports in the local papers from the 1970s onwards are to be believed, Wanstead has more than its fair share of ghosts. But it is probably just a coincidence that long-term researcher and writer Eric Maple, who described himself as Britain's 'one and only full-time demonologist', lived there at that time. An example of one story appeared in the *Redbridge Guardian* on 4 January 1974:

> The ghost of a nun was said to haunt the upper floor of Wanstead Hospital, which had at one time been a convent. She is supposed to have committed suicide by jumping from an upstairs window.

One oft-repeated tradition focuses on the George pub in Wanstead High Street. Since at least the late 1960s, staff have complained of unexplained noises from upstairs rooms, including the creaking of a baby's cradle as it is rocked to and fro, and the faint cries of a woman and sometimes a baby. They have dubbed their ghost 'Mad Mollie', and the story is that she had given birth to an illegitimate child in the house, and murdered it by putting in on to the fire. She then went mad and for years never left the room, until she hanged herself, and her body vanished. A corroborative rumour states that a child's skeleton was dug up in the grounds. An apparently unrelated tradition agrees that there is a female ghost, but maintains that she is a previous landlady who was murdered by a labourer from Leyton when she rebuffed his advances.

WANSTEAD PARK

Wanstead Park, the site of Wanstead House, which was demolished in 1824, has a phantom coach carrying no less a person than Queen Elizabeth I, and also boasts the ghost of Lady Catherine Tylney-Long (died 1825), 'the last heiress of Wanstead', who wanders around the ornamental pond on some nights. She was fabulously wealthy, but her husband gambled and womanised all her money away until eventually they were declared bankrupt. She died of shame and a broken heart only eighteen months later. The husband, the Hon. William Pole-Tylney-Long-Wellesley, lived until 1857, and his obituary in the *Morning Chronicle* pulls no punches:

> A spendthrift, a profligate, and a gambler in his youth, he became a debaucher in his manhood. Redeemed by no single virtue, adorned by no single grace, his life has gone out even without a flicker of repentance.

If there was any justice in the netherworld, it would be he who restlessly walks this earth, not his poor wife.

WANSTEAD PLACE: ST MARY'S CHURCH

This church has a rather mild poltergeist who moves things such as flower vases when nobody is looking, but its churchyard must be one of the busiest in the land at night. For a start there is the unusual spectre of a skeleton who pushes a cart through the churchyard, apparently in search of his wife, who might have been stolen by grave-robbers. Then there is a grey lady, who was married in the church, but her husband was lost at sea, and she is especially restless each year on 13 September, her wedding anniversary. And even DICK TURPIN (p. 162) is reputed to visit the churchyard to pay respects to the grave of another of the same name.

WAPPING

A pamphlet entitled *The Witch of Wapping*, printed in London in 1652, tells the story of Joan Peterson. It claims she cured a man who was 'grievously troubled with the headache' simply by giving him something to drink; and she cured a cow that had been bewitched by boiling the cow-keeper's urine, which 'shewed her the face of the woman which the cow-keeper's wife suspected to have bewitched it'. But her nemesis came when she undertook to cure one Christopher Wilson, who was 'very sick and weak' of an unspecified illness. Her cure was successful, but when Wilson refused to pay her the agreed amount she threatened to make him 'ten times worse' than he was before, and from then on he fell into fits, began to 'walk up and down like a mere changeling', and 'then he fell very sick, and at this instant (if he be not dead) languisheth away, and rots as he lies'.

After this, a neighbour's young child, who was 'strangely tormented' and suffering from fits, was being watched by two women when:

A great black cat come to the cradle's side, and rock the cradle, whereupon one of the women took up the fire-fork to strike at it, and it immediately vanished. About an hour after the cat came again to the cradle side, whereupon the other woman kicked at it, but it presently vanished, and that leg she kicked with, began to swell and be very sore.

A neighbouring baker claimed that he had seen a great black cat 'that had so frighted him, that his hair stood on end'. An ex-servant of Peterson's then claimed that she had a squirrel familiar which she talked to. According to the pamphlet, 'these and other things being proved against her, she was condemn'd to be hanged at Tyburn on Monday the 12th of April, 1652.'

One of the interesting things about the pamphlet is that it shows that while 'cunning men and women', or those who professed to have skills in occult fields, were routinely used in a community to treat illness and to counteract malicious witchcraft, they also ran the constant risk of being accused of witchcraft themselves.

Whipps Cross Road, Walthamstow

A piece of land, about three miles long and fifty yards wide, was at one time situated in Leyton parish, but belonged to Walthamstow. The piece ran roughly north-east from the site of the present Whipps Cross Hospital, across Whipps Cross Road and the boating lake, until it reached the parish boundary just south of Snaresbrook Road. It was called the Walthamstow Slip, and existed in this form until the 1870s, when it was absorbed into Leyton.

Two slightly different tales have been told to explain the anomaly. The first tells of how a dead body was found on the banks of the River Lea in Leyton. The people of Leyton refused to bury it, and so the inhabitants of Walthamstow carried out the task. It was the legal custom at that time that in such cases the burying parish could claim all the land over which the body was carried.

A different tradition maintained that any land over which a funeral party passed became a public right of way for ever. In the case of the Walthamstow Slip, the mourners were said to have deliberately walked eleven abreast, at arms' length, which explains the unusual width of the piece of land.

The first story has been told in exactly the same form in various places in the country, to explain detached portions of parishes or oddly shaped boundaries, and the second was also an extremely widespread and deeply held belief. There are several recorded instances of funerals being refused access to land, or being prevented from crossing bridges, because the

According to tradition, when a body was found on the river Lea's banks in Leyton, the people of Leyton refused to bury it, so the inhabitants of Walthamstow undertook the task and then claimed all the land over which they carried the body – an area now known as the Walthamstow Slip.

owners believed they would be ceding public access, but no real basis in law can be found. It has been suggested, however, that the notion dates back to the time when the baulks, or raised walkways, between the strips of land in pre-enclosure open fields had to be wide enough to accommodate a funeral procession.

In fact, there are several parishes with detached portions in the area, and there was also a 'Wanstead Slip' in Leyton. It is not known for sure how the Walthamstow anomaly came about, but it was presumably caused by the buying or swapping of estate land in manorial times.

See also TOOTING, p. 416.

WHITECHAPEL

An example of East London herbal magic from Edward Lovett's *Magic in Modern London* (1925) that was designed to be effective in girls' love lives is given on p. 301. But another extract is concerned with the very different field of infant teething:

> Orris root – This is the root of *Iris florentina* which, in addition to other uses, seems to have some magical qualities. In Whitechapel I found that many of the Jewish inhabitants use it to rub the gums of their children when teething. For this purpose they always select a piece of the root bearing a fancied resemblance to the human figure, both male and female forms being selected. The male or 'he root' is used to rub the gums of girl babies, whilst the 'she root' is used for boys. I obtained confirmation of this custom at Shoreditch, Barking, and Bow. In non-Jewish localities I found no trace of this sexual distinction, but traced the use of the same root shaped like a child's coral.

WHITECHAPEL ROAD: ST MARY'S CHURCH

An article in the *East London Observer* on 17 September 1864 reported that a rumour of a ghost in Whitechapel parish church graveyard had resulted in considerable crowds of onlookers gathering to catch a sight of the alleged spirit. The local reporter was admirably sceptical about the whole affair:

> As chroniclers of local events, it is our duty to record the fact, with all its attendant circumstances. We must perforce, however, ask our readers to be satisfied with the fact only. Of the attendant circumstances we can say nothing, as our reporter was not favoured with a sight of the spectre, nor have we met with anybody who has. Whether, therefore, it be a spirit of health or goblin damned, bringing with it airs from heaven, or blasts from the opposite quarter – points upon which the reader may entertain a very natural curiosity – we are altogether unable to say.

Nevertheless, he made the serious point that these unfounded rumours were increasing in frequency, and that the consequent crowds occasioned the need for police action to control them. He also recorded another recent incident:

Bethnal Green Road Independent Chapel was the last spot favoured, and it required at length a strong police force to dispel the idle crowds which it collected. That spectre was traced ultimately to a reflection from a cabinet-maker's workshop.

WOODFORD

Although there is now some doubt about their exact location, Woodford was for a short time famous for its wells, which were reputed to be effective as a purgative and good for many illnesses. One, at least, had genuine chalybeate, or iron-bearing, properties, and Woodford's heyday as a spa was from about 1711 through the 1720s, a time when it could cash in on the huge popularity of the spas at Bath and Tunbridge Wells. A later writer, William Addison, captures the romantically genteel aura the spa proprietors hoped to engender, in his *English Spas* (1951):

> Woodford was an easy ride from the City, and what could have been pleasanter than a stroll on the Green, with its wide prospects across the Roding valley, after breakfasting in the manner of the day, on almond cheesecakes, tarts, seed or plum cakes, baked with fresh Epping butter?

WOODFORD ROAD, SNARESBROOK

The ghostly rider of Snaresbrook rides along the Woodford Road, an area in which highway robbery was rife in times past. According to a report in the *Redbridge Guardian* on 3 January 1975, the ghost was reputed to be that of local dignitary Sir Caesar Child (died 1753), who was stopped and robbed on this spot in 1735. It is not clear why the ghost of Sir Caesar would wish to return to this particular incident in his life. He was not killed or even hurt in the fracas, as far as we know, although his coachman did have the end of his nose shot off.

SOUTH-EAST LONDON

The London Boroughs of Bexley, Bromley,
Greenwich, Lewisham and Southwark

ANERLEY WOOD

The Norwood Gypsies were famed far and wide for at least 200 years. The area of Norwood is where five different London boroughs meet, and the following story was told by a Croydon man, about a Lambeth doctor, though the action takes place on the Bromley side of the border in Anerley and Penge woods. The story is from Thomas Frost's *Reminiscences of a Country Journalist* (1886), and concerns a Dr Gardiner, who lived in a white house facing Streatham Common. One evening, he was called out with some urgency by 'a wiry-looking gipsy, with black elf locks dangling about his bronzed countenance'. The Gypsy begged him to come to see his wife, who was in the throes of childbirth in their camp in Anerley Wood.

> For a moment the doctor hesitated. The night would be dark, and Anerley Wood was a place of evil repute. Where the briars and brambles grew the thickest amongst the hazels there was a hollow which bore the ominous names of Thieves' Den . . .

But he put his fears aside, put on his hat, and accompanied the man out into the night.

> It was growing dark when they reached the lane which intersected the wood, the gipsy striding on in advance, and looking over his shoulder from time to time to assure himself that the doctor was following. They descended into the valley through which the railway now runs, and then the gipsy paused, waiting with evident impatience until the doctor came up with him.

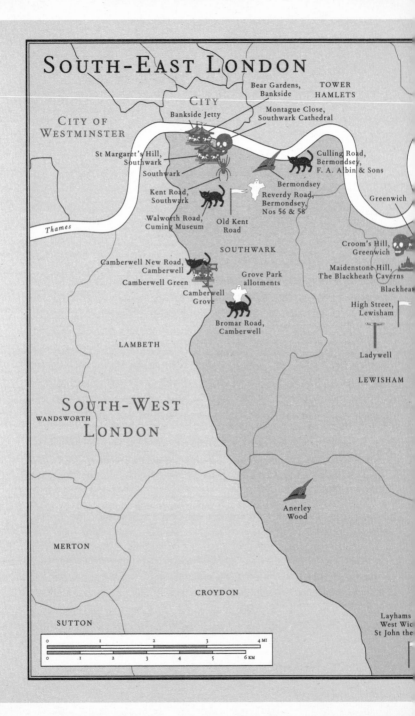

SOUTH-EAST LONDON

TOWER HAMLETS

CITY

Bear Gardens, Bankside

CITY OF WESTMINSTER

Bankside Jetty

Montague Close, Southwark Cathedral

St Margaret's Hill, Southwark

Southwark

Culling Road, Bermondsey, F. A. Albin & Sons

Greenwich

Kent Road, Southwark

Bermondsey
Reverdy Road, Bermondsey, Nos 56 & 58

Thames

Walworth Road, Cuming Museum

Old Kent Road

SOUTHWARK

Croom's Hill, Greenwich

Camberwell New Road, Camberwell

Camberwell Green

Maidenstone Hill, The Blackheath Caverns

Grove Park allotments

Blackheath

Camberwell Grove

High Street, Lewisham

Bromar Road, Camberwell

LAMBETH

Ladywell

LEWISHAM

SOUTH-WEST LONDON

WANDSWORTH

Anerley Wood

MERTON

CROYDON

SUTTON

Layhams
West Wic
St John the

0   1   2   3   4 MI

0   1   2   3   4   5   6 KM

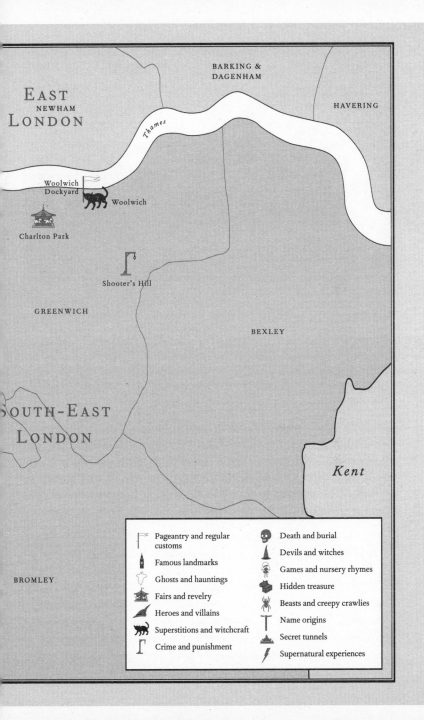

EAST
NEWHAM
LONDON

BARKING &
DAGENHAM

HAVERING

Thames

Woolwich
Dockyard

Woolwich

Charlton Park

Shooter's Hill

GREENWICH

BEXLEY

SOUTH-EAST
LONDON

Kent

BROMLEY

	Pageantry and regular customs		Death and burial
	Famous landmarks		Devils and witches
	Ghosts and hauntings		Games and nursery rhymes
	Fairs and revelry		Hidden treasure
	Heroes and villains		Beasts and creepy crawlies
	Superstitions and witchcraft		Name origins
	Crime and punishment		Secret tunnels
			Supernatural experiences

Anerley Wood and the surrounding Norwood area were famous for their much-feared gypsy inhabitants.

'Give me your handkerchief,' said he in a tone that sounded imperative, notwithstanding the respectfulness of his manner. 'You must not know the way to our tents. There are reasons for it. It will be only for a few minutes,' he added, on observing that the doctor hesitated.

Stumbling blindly through the undergrowth, holding on to the tail of the Gypsy's jacket, the doctor finally found himself in a candle-lit dome tent, where the man's wife lay on a bed of freshly cut bracken. An hour later, the Gypsy had a baby son, and the doctor was blindfolded and taken back to civilisation, by a different route. The Gypsy pulled out a guinea, but the doctor refused it:

'No, no,' said the doctor, declining the proffered fee. 'You are a poor man – I hope an honest one, give it to your wife, and let her do as she likes with it.' 'She won't want a guinea while I have got one,' returned the gipsy, as he dropped the coin back into the bag, which he thrust into his pocket. 'But if you won't have it, all I can say is, that I hope I may find an opportunity of paying the debt in another way. If you ever come into contact with any of our people in an unpleasant kind of way, you must say you are a friend of mine, or ask if Ned Righteous is in the camp, and you'll find the mention of that name very much to your advantage.'

Over a year later, Dr Gardiner was riding home from visiting a patient at Beckenham, when his horse's bridle was suddenly seized by two ruffians, who demanded his money. In desperation, the doctor remembered his previous encounter.

'You will not rob a friend of Ned Righteous?' he observed . . . 'The friends of Ned Righteous are our friends,' said one of the robbers, in an altered tone, but without loosing his hold of the doctor's bridle, 'but how are we to know that you are a friend of his?' 'If the man I mention is anywhere near here, he will answer for me,' said the doctor. 'Come on then,' returned one of the gipsies. 'We'll introduce you to Righteous in less time than it would take you to reach the "Jolly Sailor"'.'

They led him down a narrow path that meandered through Penge Wood, and uttered a strange cry, something like the hooting of an owl, which was answered from nearby, and a man soon appeared through the undergrowth.

'Here's a broadcloth cove as claims to be a friend of yours, Ned,' said one of the gipsies. 'You haven't many friends among the house-dwellers, have you?' 'You know me, Righteous?' said the doctor. 'Dr Gardiner!' exclaimed the gipsy, his face brightening with gratification. 'Dr Gardiner!' echoed one of the footpads, instantly loosing his hold of the doctor's bridle, which example was followed by his companion. 'Why, if we had knowed it was you, sir, or you had only jest told us your name, that would have been enough. You saved Righteous his child, and perhaps his wife, taking no gold for it, and your named is remembered for that in all the tents of the Romany.'

The good doctor enquired after the man's wife and child, and then went on his way, hoping that he would never again need to call on the help of Ned Righteous.

See also EPPING FOREST, p. 268; NORWOOD, p. 405.

BANKSIDE JETTY

Southwark was famous for centuries for its blood sports and loose women. The latter worked in the 'stews' that were lined up along Bankside facing the river, and so most of their customers were ferried across from the north bank. 'Stews' were originally heated bath-houses, but the name came to mean a brothel or 'house of ill repute', and they had been on this same site since at least 1161, when they were licensed by the Bishop of Winchester. They often had an uneasy relationship with the authorities, and were closed down and reopened at various times, but for most of their existence were closely regulated, and paid official rents and taxes. By custom, the stews were painted white, and as John Stow explained in his 1598 *Survey of London*, they had signs like pubs:

> Next on this bank was sometime the bordello, or stews, a place so-called of certain stew-houses privileged there, for the repair of incontinent men to the like women; these allowed stew-houses had signs on their fronts, towards the Thames, not hanged out, but painted on the walls, as a Boar's Head, the Cross Keys, the Gun, the Castle, the Crane, the Cardinal's Hat, the Bell, the Swan etc. I have heard of ancient men, of good credit, report that these single women were forbidden the rites of the church so long as they continued that sinful life, and were excluded from Christian burial if they were not reconciled before their death. And therefore there was a plot of ground called the Single Woman's Churchyard, appointed for them far from the parish church.

BEAR GARDENS, BANKSIDE

From Tudor times, Bankside was well known for animal sports. Baiting was immensely popular all over the country, and especially in London, and any kind of animal could be involved. Bulls, bears, horses, and badgers were common, but exotic beasts such as lions and leopards were offered when the organisers could get them. There were also dog-fights, cock-fights, and any other 'sport' that pitted animals against each other.

Both John Evelyn and Samuel Pepys recorded visits to the Bear Gardens in their diaries, and neither was very impressed:

14 August 1666
[Pepys] And after dinner with my wife and Mercer to the bear-garden, where I have not been I think of many years, and saw some good sport of the bull's tossing of the dogs – one into the very boxes. But it is a very rude and nasty pleasure. We had a great many hectors in the same box with us

and one, very fine, went into the pit and played his dog for a wager, which was a strange sport for a gentleman.

16 June 1670

[Evelyn] I was forced to accompany some friends to the Bear-garden: where was cock-fighting, bear, dog-fighting, bear and bull baiting, it being a famous day for all these butcherly sports, or rather barbarous cruelties; the bulls did exceedingly well but the Irish Wolf dog exceeded, which was a tall greyhound, a stately creature indeed, who beat a cruel mastiff. One of the bulls tossed a dog into a lady's lap, as she sat in one of the boxes at a considerable height from the arena. There were two poor dogs killed; and so all ended with the ape on horseback, and I most heartily weary of the rude and dirty pastime, which I had not seen I think twenty years before.

These entertainments were finally moved to HOCKLEY-IN-THE-HOLE (p. 213) in about 1682.

BERMONDSEY

In the Folklore Society's newsletter, *FLS News*, in 1995, Liz Thompson wrote about some traditional stories of the 'toshers' of Bermondsey, which had been passed down in her family. Toshers were men who worked in the sewers of London, collecting saleable items that had been washed down there – notably scrap metal, coins, and other valuables.

Just before he died, Ms Thompson's great-great-grandfather had spoken of his liaison, in the mid 1840s, with a 'rat-woman', and revealed some fascinating traditions about rats in the sewers. The story goes that there was a Queen Rat who would secretly listen to the men talking, and deduce what kind of woman each man particularly liked. If she fancied one, she would appear to him in the form of his dream girl and sleep with him. If she was pleased with him, she would bestow great luck on him, and he would be particularly successful in finding things in the sewers. There was, however, a strict condition: that he never spoke of their liaison. If he did, his luck would disappear and he would lead a wretched life from then on. The details given showed that the toshers' lore included well-developed legends, which had lasted several generations. One detail was that the Queen would give any favoured lover a bite on the neck, which functioned to warn other rats not to

As this eighteenth-century engraving shows, dancing around a maypole on May Day has a long history. An account from Bermondsey shows that it was still taking place in built-up areas as recently as the 1920s.

harm him. The toshers' human wives and girlfriends were careful not to give their men love-bites on the neck, in case these were misunderstood.

A great deal of information about toshers and their work in the mid nineteenth century was published by Henry Mayhew in his seminal book, *London Labour and the London Poor* (1861), but he included little about rats and nothing approaching the stories collected by Liz Thompson.

A completely different view of Bermondsey lore, but one that also shows how poor the inhabitants of the area were, was included in an anonymous piece called 'May Day Lost and Found' published in the *Evening Standard* on 1 May 1928, which revealed some interesting details of a May Day survival in South London. After a rather laboured piece about going to various parts of London asking people if they knew it was May Day, our intrepid writer continues:

An hour later, wandering gloomily through Bermondsey, I found what I had been seeking. From a patch of waste ground came the sound of young laughter and the wheezing of a mouth organ. A dozen small children were moving solemnly in a circle, each grasping in a grubby hand a piece of string about four feet long, the other end of which was tied to the top of a broomstick, the latter embedded a few inches in the earth. The broomstick was crowned with a piece of faded ribbon. I approached the children; asked them what they were doing. They stared at me in silence for a moment, then one little girl, pointing to the broomstick said, 'Why, this is our maypole. It's May Day today. Didn't you know?'

See also: HAMPSTEAD SEWERS, p. 219; MAY DAY IN LONDON, p. 318.

Blackheath

Blackheath Fair was one of the many fairs in Greater London that drew in London crowds as well as the local population, but whereas the early chartered fairs had started as markets for produce and livestock, and gradually became pleasure fairs, later ones were often openly associated with local publicans, and organised as much for their benefit as for any other reason. John Evelyn certainly thought this of Blackheath, as he noted in his diary:

> *1 May 1683*
> I went to Blackheath, to see the new fair, being the first procured by the Lord Dartmouth. This was the first day, pretended for the sale of cattle, but I think in truth to enrich the new tavern at the bowling-green, erected by Snape, his Majesty's farrier, a man full of projects. There appeared nothing but an innumerable assembly of drinking people from London, pedlars, etc. and I suppose it too near London to be of any great use to the country.

Among the swings, roundabouts, and gingerbread stalls, fairs on the outer fringes of London were particularly known for their 'monsters' or 'freak shows'. An advertisement dated 13 March 1741, reprinted in George Daniel's *Merrie England in Olden Time* (1842), gives a flavour of the occasion:

> This is to give notice to all gentlemen, ladies and others, that there is to be seen from eight in the morning till nine at night, at the end of the great booth at Blackheath, a west of England woman 38 years of age alive, with two heads, one above the other; having no hands, fingers, nor toes, yet can she dress and undress, knit, sew, read, sing.

After the change of calendar in 1752, Blackheath Fair took place on 12 May and 11 October and survived as what James Thorne's *Handbook to the Environs of London* (1876) calls dismissively a 'hog and pleasure fair' until 1872, when it was suppressed by order of the Home Secretary.

May Day in London

On every May Day from the seventeenth to the early nineteenth century, the milkmaids of London would dance in front of the houses they supplied with milk in the hope of winning an extra bonus from their customers.

Despite the fact that May Day is associated in the modern mind with rural pastimes and entertainment, it was a very popular day for traditional street performances in London and other urban areas, second only to Guy Fawkes Night. At different periods, from the seventeenth to the early twentieth century, the city streets played host to parties as diverse as pretty milkmaids, soot-black burlesque chimney sweeps, Jack-in-the-Greens, and children carrying garlands and portable maypoles.

First mentioned in 1630, and a regular sight until the early nineteenth century, the milkmaids of the town would dance in front of the houses to which they supplied milk, in the hope of an extra bonus from their customers. It seems that the custom, in its first manifestations, was relatively simple. The maids were dressed in their best clothes and carried their milk-pails, decorated with spring flowers and ribbons, on their heads as they danced to the sound of an accompanying fiddler. But at some later point the girls started decorating their pails with 'plate', i.e., silver domestic utensils, the shinier the better, either borrowed from their customers or even hired for the day. The 'garland' thus became so heavy and unwieldy that it was carried by an attendant male, or between two men on a litter, while the girls danced.

From at least the 1740s they were joined by celebrating chimney sweeps, who gradually came to monopolise the May Day streets. They too would dance, beating time with brushes and shovels, the symbols of their trade. Some would dress in fancy costumes; lords and ladies were popular, as were clowns. A character at first accompanying the sweeps, but later appearing in his own right, was the Jack-in-the-Green – a man inside a wicker-work frame, up to eight feet tall, completely covered with greenery, ribbons and other decoration. He was accompanied by the same clowns and man-ladies as the sweeps, and danced to a fiddle and drum. The Jack lasted in some areas until about the time of the First World War.

These were all adult customs, but in the nineteenth and early twentieth centuries May Day was also one of the key days for children's activities. Across the whole of the southern half of England, one of the most common sights on a May Day morning was children carrying their May garlands and singing their May song. The children either went from house to house round their neighbourhood, or stopped passers-by, sang their song and hoped that their audience would 'remember the garland' and give them money, which would be spent on sweets or a celebratory tea for themselves. The garlands themselves varied enormously in size, shape, and degree of complexity. Some were bell-shaped, others like crowns, or two circles at right angles. Many were big enough to be carried on a pole between two of the stronger children, and often had a doll suspended in the middle, called something like 'My Lady', which was treated with great respect. Sometimes two children dressed as a lord and a lady, and sometimes one was a May queen. In some areas, however, the garlands were much smaller – more like decorated sticks – and the children would hold one in each hand.

Lady Alice Bertha Gomme noted some details in her *Traditional Games of England, Scotland and Ireland* (1894):

> I remember one May Day in London, when the 'May girls' came with a garland and short sticks decorated with green and bunches of flowers, they sang:
>
> > Knots of May we've brought you,
> > Before your door it stands;
> > It is but a sprout, but it's well budded out,
> > By the work of the Lord's hands,
>
> and a Miss Spencer, who lived near Hampton (Middlesex), told me that she well remembered the May girls singing the first verse of this carol, using 'knots' instead of the more usual word 'branch' or 'bunch' and that she knew the small bunch of May blossom by the name of 'knots' of May, 'bringing in knots of May' being a usual expression of children.

See BERMONDSEY, p. 315; HIGH STREET, LEWISHAM, p. 334; KILBURN, p. 165; ST ANDREW'S UNDERSHAFT CHURCH, p. 32; PORTMAN SQUARE: MONTAGU HOUSE, p. 100.

Bromar Road, Camberwell

John Emslie, a Victorian collector of London folklore, noted a local example of a widespread belief in the 1870s that was subsequently published in *London Studies* in 1974:

> Telling Mr and Mrs Woolley that I should move into my lodgings in their house in Bromar Road, Camberwell, Mrs Woolley asked me not to come in on a Friday as it was such an unlucky day. I said, 'I don't believe that'; she said, 'Well, of course it's superstition; still, as many do believe it, it's as well to choose some other day.' I said, 'My father considered that Friday was a lucky day, not generally, but for himself'; she said, 'Ah yes, they say that when it's lucky for anybody, then it's very lucky indeed.' I told this to my servant, Annie Eames, and she said, 'Perhaps Mrs Woolley meant that the moving on Friday might bring bad luck into her house. And they say that when you move you should always take with you a piece of coal; and a piece of salt, as they will give you luck.'

Camberwell Green

Camberwell Fair was one of the best known in the area, and drew crowds from all the neighbouring parishes. It took place nominally for three days in August, but usually stretched to three weeks, from 9 August to 1 September (Feast of St Giles). It was widely believed to be a 'charter fair', founded in 1297, but no evidence can be found to support this idea, and it survived until the mid 1850s, when its reputation had severely deteriorated. As with other local fairs, in its heyday it had been a time of magic and fun and a temporary freedom from hard work, poor living conditions, and strict social conventions.

Hood's Magazine & Comical Miscellany, edited by Thomas Hood, includes a long and unusually sympathetic description of 'Camberwell Fair Towards Midnight' in its 1844 volume. The piece has been written in a nostalgic mood, the writer transported back to childhood, and it was probably penned by Hood himself, who was born in London in 1799 and went to school in Camberwell:

The roadside, even at this distance from the fair, was lined with stalls – where oysters, 'wilks', 'trotters', pickled salmon, fried plaice, and halfpenny toys, were offered for sale with eager vociferation. Their candles shaded with coloured paper – white, green and red – shed a softened and not unpleasing ray; edging the footpath with a line of glimmering light.

I found myself opposite the entrance of the principal avenue – a canvas-covered passage between two rows of gingerbread booths. I stood for a moment looking down the brilliant vista. How vividly the old childish admiration recurred to my memory, as I gazed on those

Oyster-sellers were among the many traders to be found at Camberwell Fair, which survived up until the 1850s.

glittering ranks of golden Kings and Queens, receding range above range, in blazing banks of splendour! all, too, with their little red ribbons round their necks, just as they used to be! and the enormous tin canisters standing on the ground, five or six in front of each booth – inexhaustible I used to think them – deep pits of spicy pleasure – quarries of endless cake – gingerbread for generations.

He describes the rides – a roundabout with painted horses, giant swings, and the 'up-and-down':

> . . . a great vertical wheel, revolving like a windmill, with four boat-like cars which are alternately carried up thirty feet into the air, and whirled down again to within a foot of the ground.

He sits in a weighing machine mounted on a tripod, attends a performance at Richardson's theatre, sees performing monkeys and a crocodile, and ends up in a dancing booth. One other incident, which he describes in detail, is worth recording:

> Whrrrrrr-r-r-r! a sudden galvanic shock ran down my spine accompanied by a horrid rattling croak, which made my flesh creep and shook my nerves

like Tetanus. I sprang convulsively into the air, turning instinctively in my descent, to face my unseen assailant. 'All's fair at fair-time' cried a girl, bursting with laughter. 'Did you never feel a back-scratcher before?' I made haste to procure one of these implements, and found it resembled a diminutive watchman's rattle . . . It was of wood, and cost a penny, and it seemed a favourite weapon – especially among the women.

The same craze was recorded at Greenwich fair by Nathaniel Hawthorne in his *Our Old Home* (1863).

Nevertheless, as the nineteenth century progressed, there was a growing chorus of complaints about the noise and overcrowding, the drinking, dancing, and debauchery, lack of respect for property, entertainment on a Sunday, and the criminal elements attracted to the area. The following report that appeared in *The Times* on 21 August 1801 typifies the sort of behaviour people were complaining about:

> Wednesday morning, about four o'clock, a middle-aged decent dressed man was discovered in a ditch, leading from Camberwell to Kennington, in appearance almost dead; two labouring men going to work with some difficulty got him out of the ditch, quite helpless, and with other assistance they took him to the nearest public house, where in almost an hour he recovered, and stated that having on Tuesday been at Camberwell Fair with several acquaintances, and after spending the evening with them they separated; that he met with a female, who pretended to know him, and would accompany him home, and going across the fields they were overtaken by a man, who demanded his money; on refusing to deliver it, he was knocked down, when the woman assisted in rifling his pockets of his silver watch, and about two guineas, after which they threw him into a ditch, where it is supposed he had been nearly three hours.

Camberwell did seem to attract pickpockets and petty thieves in particularly large numbers. On 22 August 1854, for example, *The Times* reported that on one day the local magistrates spent three hours dealing with cases arising from the fair, including numerous children, as young as nine or ten, who were charged with pickpocketing.

Camberwell was a classic case of a reasonably well-controlled village fair which had served a useful purpose for many generations, but which became a serious nuisance when urban development and population growth altered the balance of the local community. Worst of all, improvements in transport brought the fair within reach of hordes of strangers in holiday mood. Several attempts were made to suppress it, but it was not until 1856 that the reformers were successful. In that year, a number of local objectors formed an abolition committee, which promptly bought the rights to the fair from the owner, and closed it down.

CAMBERWELL GROVE

In the second half of the eighteenth century, and the first half of the nineteenth, the story of George Barnwell was known to everybody in Britain, and many on the Continent as well. The reason for this widespread familiarity was George Lillo's play *The London Merchant, or the History of George Barnwell*, first produced at Drury Lane in 1731. Lillo is hardly a household name nowadays, and little is known of his life, but his place in the annals of theatrical history is assured because this relatively modest play changed the face of drama. It was the first successful 'domestic tragedy', with seemingly real-life characters in recognisable settings, rather than

Eighteenth-century chapbook illustrations of George Barnwell, a young apprentice, and Sarah Millwood, a woman of ill-repute who led him into a life of crime. Barnwell murdered his uncle, who is thought to have lived in Camberwell Grove.

nobles and statesmen in the rarefied milieu of the royal court, and it became immensely popular. It was rapidly translated into French, German, and Dutch, and the great drama historian Allardyce Nicoll called it a 'landmark in the history, not only of English drama, but of European drama'.

The basic story was not new, but had been published many times in ballad form since at least the middle of the seventeenth century. The ballad tells the story of George Barnwell, a young honest apprentice to a London merchant who was sufficiently trustworthy to collect substantial amounts of money from customers. He caught the eye of Sarah Milwood, a classy woman of ill-repute, who used her many charms to seduce him. To keep her happy, George began to steal his master's money, and when his misdeeds were about to be discovered, he murdered his own uncle and stole his gold. After the evil deed was done Milwood cast him aside, but when he was arrested he confessed, revealing her part in his downfall, and they were both executed. The moral of the story is spelled out in the third verse:

> Take heed of harlots then,
> And their enticing trains;
> For by their means I have been brought,
> To hang alive in chains,

And the last verse:

> Lo! here's the end of youth,
> That after harlots haunt;
> Who, in the spoils of other men,
> About the streets do flaunt.

Lillo's play introduces extra characters, most notably a second apprentice, George's best friend, named Trueman, and the merchant's daughter Maria, who is everything that Milwood is not, and is secretly in love with George.

A tradition developed for the play to be performed during the Christmas and Easter holidays, as a none-too-subtle moral lesson for apprentices. It is in exactly this way that Charles Dickens introduces 'the affecting tragedy of George Barnwell' into his *Great Expectations* (1860–61). In that novel, Pip is at a loose end in the High Street, on his rare half-holiday, when Mr Wopsle buttonholes him and insists that he come and listen to the story being read aloud:

What stung me, was the identification of the whole affair with my unoffend-ing self. When Barnwell began to go wrong, I declare I felt positively apologetic ... Even after I was happily hanged and Wopsle had closed the book, Pumblechook was staring at me, and shaking his head, and saying: 'Take warning, boy, take warning!' as if it were a well-known fact that I contemplated murdering a near relation.

Many writers believed the ballad was based on a true story, but could never find any evidence to support their theory. A highly unconvincing pamphlet, *Memoirs of George Barnwell*, written by 'a Descendant of the Barnwell Family', was published in 1817. But ordinary people were convinced that the story must be true, and the real-life place-names in the ballad and the play went a long way to provide the necessary evidence for this belief. The basic scene is simply set in 'London', but the uncle was said to live in Ludlow (Shropshire), and the house where he was said to have lived, and the wood in which the murder was said to have taken place, were noted local landmarks. According to Lillo, however, the uncle lived in Camberwell, and again the house could be identified, as, for example, in Volume 6 of Edward Walford and Walter Thornbury's *Old and New London* (1878):

> Camberwell Grove is said to be the spot on which George Barnwell
> murdered his uncle . . . Fountain Cottage – which was till recently
> commemorated by Fountain Terrace, a name which the Metropolitan Board
> of Works have thought fit to abolish – was fixed upon as the residence of
> the unfortunate uncle.

An interesting detail from the ballad is that Sarah Milwood lived in SHOREDITCH (p. 298), famed for its women of easy character.

CAMBERWELL NEW ROAD, CAMBERWELL

Edward Lovett was one of the few folklorists of his generation who took an interest in the people of urban areas, at a time when folklore was generally considered to be a purely rural phenomenon. He was not an academic, so his booklets were written in a racy conversational style, as in the following piece from *Magic in Modern London* (1925), which is set in

Camberwell. It is a shame that the tape recorder had not been invented in his day:

> One day down at Camberwell, during the [First World] War, I saw in the window of a small furniture shop a tray of those little wool figures – called Golliwogs. I went in and asked the chap in charge what they were for. He replied that he was selling them as war mascots, 'to oblige a lady', but that he himself didn't believe in anything of the sort, adding, 'What will be will be.' In the Press of the previous day was a report of a lecture of mine on London superstitions in which I related how a horseshoe covered with red fabric was sometimes hung over the head of a bed to prevent the sleeper from having nightmare. I asked the old gentleman if he had seen this, and he said he had. So I said: 'Did you ever see such nonsense?' 'That isn't nonsense,' said he, 'I do that myself.' I said that might be so, but I didn't suppose that any one else in that neighbourhood did such silly things. His reply was that practically all his friends did the same thing, and that it was regarded as the best cure for nightmare in the world.

CHARLTON PARK

One of the most infamous events in the Victorian Londoner's calendar was Charlton Horn Fair, which lasted for three days, from St Luke's Day (18 October). The parish church dates from 1250 and is dedicated to St Luke, which explains the fair's timing. The festivities were formerly held on the green opposite the church, facing Charlton House, until they were moved to a field at the other end of village when the rowdiness became offensive. There is no doubt that the Horn Fair was very old, but no founding charter has been identified, although a three-day fair, at the feast of Trinity, was granted to the Prior of Bermondsey by Henry III in 1268.

Many fairs had bad reputations in Victorian times, but Charlton had one of the worst. Daniel Defoe was just one of many who disliked it, as he made clear in *A Tour Through the Whole Island of Great Britain* (1724–6):

> Charlton, a village famous, or rather infamous, for the yearly collected rabble of mad-people at Horn Fair; the rudeness of which I cannot but think, is such as ought to be suppress'd, and indeed in a civiliz'd, well-govern'd

nation, it may well be said to be unsufferable. The mob indeed at that time take all kinds of liberties, and the women are especially impudent for that day; as if it was a day that justified the giving themselves up to all manner of indecency and immodesty, without any reproach, or without suffering the censure which such behaviour would deserve at another time.

The feature that gave the fair its name, and unique character, was the wearing of horns. Hordes of visitors wore or carried horns, of every description, the motif appeared everywhere around the fair, and even the gingerbread men had little horns on their heads. It is difficult to convey to modern readers how potent the horn motif was in the popular culture of the seventeenth to nineteenth centuries. The root of the humour lies in the saying that a cuckolded man (i.e. a man whose wife has been unfaithful to him) has been made to 'wear the horns'. Horns, therefore, had a ribald sexual connotation that was thought immensely funny. Given this background, it is no surprise that a suitably ribald legend grew up to explain the origin of the fair:

King John, being wearied with hunting on Shooter's Hill and Blackheath, entered the house of a miller at Charlton, to repose himself. He found no one at home but the mistress, who was young and beautiful, and being himself a strapping fellow, handsome withal, and with a glossing tongue, he, in a very short time – or as we would say in the present day, in no time – made an impression upon her too susceptible heart. He had just ventured to give the first kiss upon her lips when the miller opportunely came home and caught them. Being a violent man, and feeling himself wounded in the sorest part, he drew his dagger, and rushing at the king, swore he would kill them both. [The king hastily revealed his identity.] The miller, putting up his weapon, begged that at least he would make him some amends for the wrong he had done him. The king consented, upon condition also that he would forgive his wife, and bestowed upon him all the land visible from Charlton to that bend in the river beyond Rotherhithe where the pair of horns are now (1840) fixed upon the pole. He also gave him, as lord of the manor, the privilege of an annual fair on the 18th of October, the day when this occurrence took place. His envious compeers, unwilling that the fame of this event should die, gave the awkward name of Cuckold's Point to the river boundary of his property, and called the fair 'Horn Fair' it has borne ever since.

Revellers at the notoriously raucous Charlton Horn Fair all wore horns – a potent symbol of adultery. The lower panel depicts a 'Skimmity Riding' or 'rough music' (see p. 358).

This is how the story is described in Edward Walford and Walter Thornbury's *Old and New London* (1897), quite clearly an *ex post facto* concoction to explain the ribaldry and the horns, and it is also likely to be a bowdlerised version, suitable for publication. One can imagine that for the hordes of fair-goers who had such fun with the dressing-up and the cuckoldry theme, the 'kissing' in the story would be understood as a euphemism for something far more serious.

Based on this story, a tradition developed that the fair should be opened by a grand procession, headed by a man carrying a pair of horns on a pole, and people dressed up as the miller, his wife, and the king. Cross-dressing (men as women and vice versa) was another regular feature of the fair, as indicated in the autobiography of William Fuller, the government double-agent and confidence-trickster, in *The Whole Life of William Fuller* (1703):

I remember being there upon Horn-Fair day, I was dressed in my landlady's best gown and other women's attire, and to Horn Fair we went, and as we were coming back by water, all the clothes were spoilt by dirty water etc. that was flung on us in an inundation, for which I was obliged to present her with two guineas to make atonement for the damages sustained.

The most likely explanation for the horn motif is naturally more prosaic than the story. The local church is dedicated to St Luke, and the fair was held on that saint's day. The traditional symbol for the saint, appearing in most paintings of him, is an ox with horns, and it is likely that in earlier times the fair was opened by a procession, from the church to the fairground, headed by someone carrying the saint's symbol on a pole. If this is correct, it is also likely that the horns would have been displayed while the fair was open, to indicate that the fair was officially in operation, as was the case at numerous other fairs with official symbols.

Given its raucous nature, it as no surprise that Charlton Horn Fair was one of the first to be suppressed under the Fairs Act of 1871, which was deliberately designed to make it easier to abolish annual gatherings that the authorities considered undesirable.

Croom's Hill, Greenwich

Croom's Hill was the setting for a point-of-death apparition story published by ghost writer F. G. Lee in his influential 1885 book *Glimpses in the Twilight*. Tom Potter, a restless young man, was a problem to his widowed mother and their friends, but finally ended up going to sea. He parted from his mother at the Hammonds' house, where she was working at the time, and while he was away on a trip to the West Indies, she married again and became Mrs Cooper. One night in September 1866, a newly employed housemaid (who therefore knew nothing of the name Potter) was on duty when the doorbell rang. Mary the housemaid answered it, and Mrs Hammond could hear something of the conversation from her room. She was surprised to hear the voice of Tom, and called out:

'Mary, who was that at the door?' The servant replied, 'Oh, ma'am, it was a little sailor boy; he wanted his mother. I told him I knew nothing of his mother, and sent him about his business.' Mrs Hammond, whose anxiety was aroused, asked the servant what the boy was like. 'Well, ma'am, he was a good-looking boy in sailor's clothes, and his feet were naked. I should knows him again anywhere. He looked very pale and in great distress; and when I told him his mother wasn't here, he put his hand to his forehead, and said, 'Oh dear, what shall I do?'

Mary was taken to see Tom's old schoolmaster and shown some photographs of boys from a few years before. Without hesitation, she picked out Tom Potter's picture. A month later they received news that Tom had died in Jamaica, calling for his mother, two days before being seen at the Hammonds' door.

CULLING ROAD, BERMONDSEY: F. A. ALBIN & SONS

The well-known funeral director Barry Albin Dyer, from Bermondsey, devoted a chapter to superstitions in his fourth book, *Bury My Heart in Bermondsey* (2004), and included many other examples in his other books. The majority are relatively well known from elsewhere, although as is to be expected in his line of work, he had gathered a higher proportion of beliefs concerned with death and funerals than one would find in other collections.

Barry's list includes widely known generally unlucky actions such as placing new shoes on the table, opening an umbrella indoors, putting red and white flowers together, and dreaming of a birth (which signifies a coming death, and vice versa). Specific death omens include: a mirror falling off the wall and breaking; a broken clock suddenly chiming; a bird (especially a robin), white moth, or butterfly entering the house; thirteen people sitting down at a table; and the idea that if three people are photographed together, the one in the middle will be the first to die. Two of the superstitions he recorded are unusual, perhaps even unique: if one drops an umbrella on the floor, that there will be a murder in the house; and if the left eye twitches there will be a death in the family.

Others are concerned with what must happen after a death, including advice to stop the clock, open all the windows, undo all the locks, place a lighted candle in the window, and cover all mirrors while the body is in the house – otherwise the person who next sees their reflection will be the next to die. Everyone should touch the dead body to prevent having nightmares about them, and if the dead person's eyes are left open it is sure they will be looking for the next person to go with them.

All of these have been recorded many times before across the country, although it is surprising to find so many still in circulation in the late twentieth century.

Another group of superstitions are concerned with the funeral itself: if petals fall from the back of a hearse when it is leaving the cemetery another funeral will be quick to follow; it is unlucky to count the cars at a funeral; a funeral on a Friday heralds another death in the family in the year; and one must avoid travelling through a tunnel to the funeral, so as not to take anyone underground before their time.

Finally, two beliefs involve one of the most basic principles of superstition, that nature itself is intimately connected with human affairs: thunder following a funeral means that a dead person has certainly reached the gates of heaven; and if the deceased has lived a good life, flowers will grow on the grave, but only weeds if not.

GREENWICH

Greenwich Fair was one of those fairs that had no founding charter or other legal standing but had simply grown of their own accord. Working-class Londoners – especially servant girls and apprentices–had been flocking to Greenwich for many years, and by the second half of the eighteenth century a full-blown pleasure fair had developed, twice a year, at Easter and Whitsun, which drew huge crowds and enjoyed a national reputation. All the major fairground people attended, and the place heaved with rides, play booths, menageries, dancing booths and shows of all descriptions, gingerbread sellers, fortune-tellers, Aunt Sallies, and other smaller fry. Many of the popular writers and artists of the day described the scene, often with amused affection, such as Charles Dickens, in his *Sketches by Boz* (1836):

> In earlier days, we were a constant frequenter of Greenwich Fair. We have proceeded to, and returned from it, in almost every description of vehicle. We cannot conscientiously deny the charge of having once made the

Play booths and menageries were popular attractions at Greenwich Fair. The crowds of people drawn by these attractions were liable to turn rowdy, and, as was the fate of so many London fairs, it was eventually closed down.

passage in a spring-van, accompanied by thirteen gentlemen, fourteen ladies, an unlimited number of children, and a barrel of beer; and we have a vague recollection of having, in later days, found ourselves the eighth outside, on top of a hackney-coach, at something past four o'clock in the morning, with a rather confused idea of our own name, or place of residence.

For many years the fair received a generally good press. *The Times* (13 April 1814) praised it for its 'order, regularity and good conduct'. But there were some who saw it in a very different light, for example dramatist J. R. Planché, who recorded his visit to the fair in 1820 in his *Recollections*:

On each side of the road, four or five deep, a line of human beings extended as far as the eye could reach; men and women, boys and girls, the majority of the adults of both sexes in every possible stage of intoxication, yelling, screaming, dancing, fighting, playing every conceivable antic, and making every inconceivable noise.

By the mid nineteenth century the fair had lost most of its supporters, and, lacking any legal basis, it was easy to suppress in 1856, with the satirical magazine *Punch* having the last word:

Obituary: Died, on Easter Monday, that terrible old nuisance, Greenwich Fair; not a bit lamented by anyone who knew it, pickpockets and gents alone perhaps excepted. The deceased had been for many years in a bad way, and at the last had sunk to so low a state that it was evident that its existence must be put a stop to.

GROVE PARK: ALLOTMENTS

Between 1973 and 1974 an unusual bout of poltergeist activity reportedly took place in the sheds of the men who ran the Grove Park allotments. The disturbances were fully investigated by members of the Society for Psychical Research, who claimed that they witnessed some of the strange events, and the case was written up in Betty Puttick's *Supernatural England* (2002). As usual, much of the poltergeist's activity consisted of throwing things about, but this time they were not only small portable things such as cups and saucers, but heavy bags of fertiliser, and the level of violence seems to have been greater than usual. In addition, numerous items went missing or turned up in impossible places. The activities finally petered out, but as poltergeists are usually blamed on hysterical females, and none was involved here, the case goes unexplained.

See also BEVERSTONE ROAD, THORNTON HEATH, p. 365; BRIMSDOWN, ENFIELD, p. 196; CHELSEA, p. 138; PLAISTOW, p. 293; REVERDY ROAD, BERMONDSEY: NOS 56 AND 58, p. 342; STOCKWELL, p. 414; SUTTON LANE, CHISWICK: SUTTON COURT-HOUSE, p. 173.

HIGH STREET, LEWISHAM

One of the regular sights on a May Day in London was the Jack-in-the-Green: a man inside a wooden frame about eight feet tall, entirely covered with greenery, ribbons, and other decorations. He was accompanied by a musician and various characters who danced and collected money. The Jack first appeared in the late eighteenth century, and was originally part of the milkmaids' and chimney sweeps' annual celebrations, but later took on a life of his own and appeared as the central character in a May Day street performance that lasted in some areas until the time of the First World War.

Lewisham was only one of the many areas with a local Jack-in-the-Green troupe, but, by chance, this one is better documented than most as it was described and photographed a number of times between 1890 and 1903. We therefore know much more than usual about the accompanying characters, as, for example in the careful description made by Leland Duncan and published in A. R. Wright and R. E. Lones's *British Calendar Customs* (Vol. II, 1938):

> May day, 1894, at Lewisham. In the High Street, at the inn near St Mary's church, we saw a Jack with a Queen of the May, two maidens-proper, one man dressed as a woman, and a man with a piano-organ. The organ was playing a quick tune and the Queen and the maidens danced round the Jack with a kind of 'barn-dance' step, the Jack turning the other way. The man-woman sometimes danced with the maidens, turned wheels, and collected pence. The Jack was a bottle-shaped case covered with ivy leaves and surmounted by a crown of paper roses. The Queen wore a light blue dress and had a crown similar to the Jack's. The senior maiden wore a red skirt and a black body; the junior wore a white dress; each wore a wreath of roses. The man-woman wore a holland dress, and over it a short sleeveless jacket; his face was blackened, and he had a Zulu hat trimmed with red, the brim being turned up. The man-proper [apparently the one with the piano-organ] wore dark grey gaiters (long ones) a dark suit with ribbons on it, and a grey night-cap, with red, blue and green ribbons; his face was blued all over.

See also MAY DAY IN LONDON, p. 318.

Kent Street, Southwark

A localised version of the widespread notion that living animals can exist inside people's bodies was printed on a broadside in London in 1664 (reprinted in the *Euing Collection of English Broadside Ballads* (1971)).

A WARNING for all such as Desire to Sleep upon the Grass
By the Example of Mary Dudson maid-servant to Mr Phillips a gardener, dwelling in Kent Street, in the borough of Southwark: Being a most strange, but true relation how she was found in a dead-sleep in the garden, that no ordinary noise could awake her. As also how an adder entered into her body, the manner of her long sickness, with a brief discovery of the case at length by her strange and most miraculous vomiting up of about fourteen young adders, and one old adder, on August 14, 1664, about fourteen inches in length, the maid is yet living. The like to this hath not been known in this age.

See also KENTISH TOWN, p. 335; NEW MALDEN, p. 404; SILVERTOWN, p. 300; VERE STREET, p. 119.

Ladywell

There were several medicinal wells in what is now the borough of Lewisham. Indeed, in the middle of the seventeenth century the area was briefly inundated with Londoners visiting the famous waters, which were found where Sydenham Wells Park now stands. But the most obvious modern trace of the local healing waters is represented by the place-name Ladywell. Robert Cope's *Legendary Lore of the Holy Wells of England* (1893) records a legend about the discovery of the medicinal qualities of the well:

The manner in which the virtues of the water were discovered is curious. A poor woman afflicted with a loathsome disease, whose case had been given up as hopeless by the doctors, was advised to try the water, not because of any known virtues therein, but because her habitation was near by the springs. She used the water outwardly and internally with such good effect, that, although her distemper had assumed serious and malignant symptoms, she

In the early seventeenth century, a parishioner at West Wickham's St John the Baptist church left 20 shillings a year to ensure that an annual sermon was preached giving thanks for deliverance from the Gunpowder Plot. The tradition continued until the late 1970s.

found herself quickly restored by its daily use. From this circumstance the spot acquired some popularity and patronage.

The tradition developed that the waters should be given free , 'as God hath freely bestowed His favours upon the water', and an attempt to enclose the well and charge for its use was, reputedly:

... frustrated by the Divine hand in a striking manner. The water lost its virtue, taste, its odour, and effects, proving that in behalf of the Poor (incapacitated to right themselves) God sometimes immediately steps in for their assistance.

Some local historians thought that the name of the well was a later addition, and therefore could not be the reason for the name of the area. But the Bridge House Estate Map of 1592, which can be seen in Lewisham Local History Library, clearly shows the 'Lady Well', close to the parish church, which is dedicated to St Mary the Virgin. When the area developed in the late eighteenth century, it naturally took the name of its most prominent feature.

LAYHAMS ROAD, WEST WICKHAM: ST JOHN THE BAPTIST CHURCH

A special prayer to give thanks for deliverance from the Gunpowder Plot was composed and it was included in the Book of Common Prayer, to be used in the annual celebrations decreed for 5 November, so ensuring that every parish adhered to the rule of official remembrance. A number of individuals also felt sufficiently strongly on the subject to give money (often in their wills) to endow a sermon to be preached each year on the day. Sir Samuel Lennard, who lived at Wickham Court, was one of these, and when he died in 1618 he left twenty shillings per annum to the minister to preach 'in memory of the Gunpowder Plot', and he also ensured a congregation by leaving a shilling apiece to forty poor people who turned up to listen. The official prayer was removed from the prayer book in 1859, but the sermon was still being preached at St John the Baptist, West Wickham, in the late 1970s.

See also GUY FAWKES NIGHT, p. 338.

MAIDENSTONE HILL: THE BLACKHEATH CAVERNS

The Blackheath Caverns are three large chambers that have been cut into the chalk about sixty feet below the surface, with an entrance around Maidenstone Hill and Point Hill. They were almost certainly created for extracting chalk, but their original date is not known. They were rediscovered by accident by a builder in 1780, and became a popular drinking place until public criticism prompted their closure, and the entrance was sealed. They were opened up again during the Second World War to see if they could be used as air raid shelters, but they were not deemed suitable and were sealed up again in 1946.

As with all caves and tunnels, a variety of stories have gathered around the caverns. While they were used as a drinking club, they gained the name Jack Cade's Cave. Cade was the leader of the Kentish rebellion in 1450, and subsequent writers have taken the name as proof that the caves existed in his time, or before. The following appeared in *The Mirror of Literature* magazine (1829), and is typical of the flights of fancy that caves bring on:

> Cave at Blackheath: Allow me to hand to you an account of a very curious cavern at Blackheath, fortuitously discovered in the year 1780 . . . It is situated on the hill (on the left-hand side from London), and is a very spacious vaulted cavern, hewn through a solid chalk-tone rock, one hundred feet below the surface. The Saxons, on their entrance into Kent, upwards of 1300 years ago, excavated several of these retreats . . . After these times, history informs us the caves were frequently resorted to, and occupied by the disloyal and unprincipled rebels, headed by Jack Cade, in the reign of

Guy Fawkes Night

An engraving by George Cruikshank (1792–1878) depicting the parading of a Guy – one of the most popular Guy Fawkes' Night traditions in the nineteenth-century. Shown here carried on poles, as though on a sedan chair, Guys were paraded through London by adults and children alike.

For centuries, Guy Fawkes Night was one of the most popular times of public celebration in the year, but it has lost ground in recent years, and Hallowe'en has largely taken its place as the main autumn festival for children. Bonfires, bells, effigies and fireworks have always been characteristic of the night, but different aspects have been prominent at different times. In the nineteenth century, for example, one of the strongest traditions in urban areas was the parading of a guy – a stuffed effigy usually seated on a chair on a cart, or carried on poles like a sedan chair. In some cases the guy was made and carried by children, and this was gradually transformed into the static 'penny for the guy' custom that was so characteristic of twentieth-century Bonfire Nights. But adults also paraded guys, and they often made a spectacle of the affair, with people dressed as clowns, men dressed as women, and musicians and drummers, in attendance. A description of such events appeared in *The Times* on 4 November 1802 in a report of a court case:

> The great annoyance occasioned to the public by a set of idle fellows, going about previous to and on the 5th of November, with some horrid figure dressed up as Guy Faux, and which assembling a mob, is the cause of many depredations and disorders; has very properly determined the Magistrates to punish all such offenders in future. Yesterday therefore, five men and a boy were apprehended in St Martin's Street, with a cart, in which was a figure as the effigy of Guy Faux, and one of the party as a priest, habited in a white smock frock and large wig, and the boy riding on horseback as the Sheriff conducting the offender to the place of execution. They were immediately brought before Mr Graham, at Bow Street, and it being proved upon oath, that the prisoners were seen begging and

receiving money, they were all, except the boy, committed to prison as idle or disorderly persons.

This writer's tone does not imply familiarity with the custom, which perhaps can be taken as an indication that it was new, or at least not common at the time, but by mid-century this kind of performance was widespread in London and other big towns. Two more court cases, from November 1868, involve characters dressed as clowns, and illustrate how the custom must have looked at that time. In the first, a 32-year-old labourer dressed as a clown entered a tobacconist's shop in Bethnal Green and began capering and somersaulting. An alleged accomplice then dashed in and grabbed a bundle of cigars and ran out. The tobacconist claimed that the clown deliberately got in his way when he tried to give chase. In the second case, reported in *The Times* on 7 November 1868, William Ball of Bethnal Green was accused by Joseph Burton, a chemist in Cambridge Heath Road, Hackney, of conspiring to steal his watch:

> On Thursday night [Burton] was standing at his door looking at an effigy of Guy Fawkes which was being carried past, accompanied by a large crowd, when the prisoner, who was one of the attendant clowns, thrust a white hat in front of him and said, 'Please to remember the 5th of November.' A boy came up and stood near him, and a minute afterwards he missed from his pocket a gold watch.

Despite the problems detailed in these accounts, these examples are relatively tame compared to what happened in many places later in the evening, when the 'bonfire boys' took over the neighbourhood, made fires in the streets, set off fireworks indiscriminately, rolled blazing tar barrels, and engaged in petty vandalism, which was little short of mob rule. These antics led to the forcible suppression of mass Guy Fawkes celebrations in many places in the second half of the nineteenth century, and ushered in the era of more controlled private back-garden celebrations and the safely organised public displays of the twentieth century.

See also CHALK FARM ROAD, CAMDEN, p. 202; CHURCH ROAD, BATTERSEA, p. 368; HAMPSTEAD HEATH, p. 218; HARROW SCHOOL: GROUNDS, p. 150; HIGH STREET, PLAISTOW, p. 293; LAYHAMS ROAD, WEST WICKHAM, p. 336.

Henry VI, about AD 1400, who infested Blackheath and its neighbourhood, since then by several banditti, called Levellers, in the rebellious times of Oliver Cromwell, The cave consists of three rooms, which are dry, and illuminated; in one of which, at the end of the principle entrance, is a well of soft, pure and clear water, which, according to the opinion of several eminent men, is seldom to be met with.

Modern websites take the fancy further and claim, among other things, that the chambers were created in prehistoric times by worshippers of the 'Horned God', and that the caves themselves were hewn 'by tools made of antlers'. The Horned God is very popular on the Internet.

MONTAGUE CLOSE: SOUTHWARK CATHEDRAL

Southwark Cathedral occupies a site that has been devoted to religious purposes for over 1,000 years. Its full name is the Cathedral and Collegiate Church of St Saviour and St Mary Overie. The latter part of the name simply means St Mary 'over the river', but a fine legend has been constructed to explain it more fully. It concerns the 'rich ferryman of Southwark' and his daughter Mary.

Before any bridge had been built over the Thames there was only a ferry, to which various boats belonged, to transport passengers between Southwark and Churchyard Alley. The boats provided the main link between London and south-eastern counties, so the traffic was extremely heavy. John Overs held the franchise from the City of London to run the ferry, and over the years his wealth grew steadily until he became a very rich man. Although of humble beginnings himself, he could have lived as well as the highest alderman, had he so wished, but John Overs was a classic miser. Nevertheless, this ferryman had a beautiful daughter, Mary, who he brought up to be something of a lady, though he would not allow suitors to come anywhere near her. One young gallant, however, whose name has not been preserved, did manage to see Mary in secret, and win her heart, while her father was out ferrying.

Completely unaware of his daughter's clandestine trysts, Overs the ferryman hatched a plan to save some money. He calculated that he could save a day's food bill if he played dead, because his staff and servants would have to undergo at least one day's fast while mourning for him. So, with Mary's reluctant agreement, he lay down in his coffin and his death was announced, unaware of the unfortunate chain of events he was unleashing. For a start, his staff did not act according to plan by going into immediate mourning. Instead, they promptly broke open his larder and wine cellar and started to celebrate. Lying in state in his open coffin, the 'dead man' stood this as long as he could, but eventually sat bolt upright and started to climb out, hampered somewhat by his shroud. Startled into action, the nearest apprentice grabbed a broken oar, whacked him on the head, and 'struck out his brains'. The apprentice later claimed that he thought he was defending the company against the Devil, and was acquitted, but Overs was found to have been 'accessory and cause of his own death', which was tantamount to saying he had committed suicide.

This being the case, Mary found that the only way to get him buried in consecrated ground was to bribe the friars of Bermondsey Abbey, while their abbot was away. But on his return, he noticed the new-made grave, discovered the deceit, and had poor John Overs' body exhumed. The Abbot tied John's body to the back of an ass, which he turned out into the street, leaving it to God to decide where his final resting place would be. Perhaps divinely inspired, the ass wandered off to the local place of execution, and shook the body off its back at the very foot of the gibbet, which is where the ferryman was ignominiously laid to rest.

The problems over her father's burial were not the only ones faced by poor Mary at this time. Her young gallant suitor was down in the country when he heard of the ferryman's unexpected death, and set out immediately to be at the young heiress's side in her time of need. Galloping to her aid, his horse stumbled, and the young man broke his neck on the highway. Ever-faithful Mary would take no other suitor, and decided to retire into a cloister. Amongst other good deeds, she used her money to build and endow the church of St Mary Overy, and the priests there later built London Bridge.

W. Taylor's *Annals of St Mary Overy* (1833) includes an engraving of an effigy of a skeletal figure, partly wrapped in a cloak, which was said to be a memorial to the ferryman. Unfortunately, there is no evidence to support this supposition.

The full story was published in chapbook form in 1637, and again in 1744 as *The True History of the Life and Sudden Death of Old John Overs, the Rich Ferryman of Southwark*. These build on earlier versions, such as the one in John Stow's 1598 *Survey of London*, which simply state that when the ferryman and his wife died they left their riches to their daughter Mary, who then founded the church.

OLD KENT ROAD

Building grottoes in the late summer was an extremely widespread children's custom in the London area, and a note in the journal *Folk-Lore* (1905) details a relatively early example from the Old Kent Road:

> Some fifty years ago [i.e. about 1855] my landlady, then a child in the (at that time) well-to-do suburb of the Old Kent Road, used herself to make these grottoes, using for the purpose oyster-shells, which were procured from a fishmonger and most carefully cleaned, and greeting the passers-by with the following jingle:
>
> > Please do remember the grotto:
> > It's only once a year.
> > Father's gone to sea;
> > Mother's gone to fetch him back,
> > So please remember me.

Grotto-building lasted in many areas well into the middle of the twentieth century.

See also GROTTOES AND SPRING GARDENS, p. 402.

REVERDY ROAD, BERMONDSEY: NOS 56 AND 58

One of the regular tricks that poltergeists play is throwing things, and occasionally there is one who does nothing but, as was reported in *The Times* on 27 April 1872:

> Psychic Force: A correspondent of the *Pall Mall Gazette*, who says he was an eye-witness, vouches for the following story: From 4 o'clock on Thursday afternoon until half-past 11 on Thursday night the houses 56 and 58 Reverdy Road, Bermondsey, were assailed with stones and other missiles

coming from an unseen quarter. Two children were injured, every window was broken, and several articles of furniture were destroyed. Although there was a strong body of policemen scattered in the neighbourhood, they could not trace the direction whence the stones were thrown.

See also BEVERSTONE ROAD, THORNTON HEATH, p. 365; BRIMSDOWN, ENFIELD, p. 196; CHELSEA, p. 138; GROVE PARK: ALLOTMENTS, p. 333; PLAISTOW, p. 293; STOCKWELL, p. 414; SUTTON LANE, CHISWICK: SUTTON COURT-HOUSE, p. 173.

ST MARGARET'S HILL, SOUTHWARK

A fair was granted here by charter of Henry VI in 1444 (confirmed by Edward IV in 1462), but although on the southern side of the river, Southwark was so important to London that it fell under the City's jurisdiction, and the rights were therefore given to the Corporation of London. The original grant was for three days, 7–9 September, and it was generally called Lady Fair because 8 September is the Nativity of 'Our Lady', the Virgin Mary; however, it was sometimes also referred to as 'St Margaret's Fair' from its position on St Margaret's Hill. The fair was opened each year by the Lord Mayor and sheriffs, who would ride across the bridge in great state.

In its heyday, Southwark Fair was second only in importance to St Bartholomew's, which was held in late August. It was thus highly convenient for show-people to move straight from one to the other, and, both fairs were well known for their play booths, which offered a wide range of dramatic performances. These were not simply rag-tag offerings by poor show-folk, they were presentations of many of the latest plays, involving leading actors of the day. The fair was also famous for its singing and dancing, tumbling, and animal performances. Seventeenth-century diarist John Evelyn wrote the following about it:

13 September 1660
I saw in Southwark, at St Margaret's fair, monkeys and apes dance, and do other feats of activity, on the high rope; they were gallantly clad *à la mode*, went upright, saluted the company bowing and pulling off their hats, they saluted one another with as good a grace, as if instructed by a dancing-master;

Animal performances such as this bear and monkey show were popular attractions at Southwark Fair. The diarist John Evelyn recorded visiting the fair in 1660 and seeing 'monkeys and apes dance, and do other feats of activity, on the high rope'.

they turned heels over head with a basket having eggs in it, without breaking any; also, with lighted candles in their hands, and on their heads, without extinguishing them, and with vessels of water without spilling a drop. I also saw an Italian wench dance, and perform all the tricks on the high rope, to admiration; all the court went to see her. Likewise here was a man who took up a piece of iron cannon of about 400 lb weight with the hair of his head only.

And when Samuel Pepys visited the fair, it was Jacob Hall who was thrilling the crowds:

21 September 1668
I turned back and to Southwark Fair, very dirty, and there saw the puppet-show of Whittington, which was pretty to see; and how that idle thing doth work upon people that see it, and even myself too. And then to Jacob Hall's dancing on the rope, where I saw such action as I never saw before, and mightily worth seeing.

It is also worth noting that Pepys took the precaution of leaving his money and valuables with his waterman at the Bear inn, in case his pockets were 'cut' at the fair. Many other eighteenth-century writers mention the fair, and it was immortalised in Hogarth's famous 1733 painting.

Like all the London fairs, Southwark eventually outstayed its welcome, as large gatherings of people grew to be regarded as a public nuisance. It was proscribed by order of London's Court of Common Council in 1762, and when some showmen tried to erect their booths in September 1763, they were forcibly prevented by the local authorities.

See also CLOTH FAIR, SMITHFIELD: HAND AND SHEARS PUB, p. 13.

SHOOTER'S HILL

Blackheath can point to several houses and places that are said to be haunted. Indeed, Shooter's Hill seems to have had a reputation second to none, not only for ghosts, but for all manner of unsavoury happenings, which was not helped by the occasional bodies of executed criminals on the gibbets. Samuel Pepys wrote the following after a journey from Dartford to London:

> *11 April 1661*
> Mrs Annie and I rode under the man that hangs from Shooter's Hill, and a filthy sight it was to see how his flesh is shrunk on his bones . . .

And according to Charles Dickens, in his *Tale of Two Cities* (1859), even at the end of the eighteenth century the area was still the occasional haunt of gentlemen of the road.

After the days of the highwayman, Shooter's Hill and the adjoining locality became the scene of many a grim and mysterious tragedy, some real and some supernatural. One in particular, recorded by Elliott O'Donnell in his *Ghosts of London* (1932), was marked by the phantom of a woman in a white dress, gliding about the ground, and known locally as the White Lady. He claimed to have spoken to several locals in the late 1890s who remembered hearing tales of this ghost in previous years, including one Mr Johnson who reported what his father had told him as a child. Mr Johnson's father was returning home to Lewisham one evening, at a time when Shooter's Hill was still a very lonely and deserted locality after dusk, when:

> . . . he heard a cry, expressive of such awful terror and despair that he at once came to a halt. While he stood listening, it was repeated, and it seemed

to come from a spot close at hand. He called out, but there was no reply, only a death-like silence. Then, after an interval of a minute or so, the cry was repeated, and a woman, in a white dress, rose from the ground, some little way ahead of him. The moonlight being, so it seemed, focussed on her, he as able to see her very distinctly, and thinking she was ill and wanted assistance, he ran towards her. To his intense surprise, however, when he was within a few yards of her, she vanished.

Mr Johnson continued on his way, but a few moments later the blood-curdling cry rang out again. He ran the rest of the way home.

O'Donnell also records that the skeleton of a young woman was unearthed near Shooter's Hill in 1844. She had died of a terrible blow to the back of her head, relatively recently, as the corpse still bore quantities of 'beautifully-braided golden hair'. He states that the ghost stories were in circulation before this discovery was made, and implies therefore that the find validated the report of the haunting.

The chronology in such cases is crucial, but we are not given the evidence on which to decide the matter, and it is much more likely that the stories only circulated after the skeleton was found.-

One of O'Donnell's favourite notions was that certain places are imbued with an influence or power that compels certain people to commit violent crimes, and he uses the Shooter's Hill area as evidence to support this theory. In addition to the unidentified skeleton, there were two other murder cases in Victorian times in the neighbourhood. In April 1871, a servant girl named Jane Maria Clousen was bludgeoned to death with a hammer in Kidbrooke Lane, and there were widespread rumours of her ghosts being seen in the vicinity. And in August 1898, a widow named Mrs Tylor was likewise murdered in Kidbrooke Park Road.

SOUTHWARK

Rough music was a custom whereby members of a community signalled their dislike of the domestic activities of other members by parades and raucous noise. Many of the semi-ritual features of rough-music incidents could be brought to bear in other contexts, and were clearly deeply embedded in working-class consciousness in London. The following piece, recorded in the *Annual Register* for 1770, concerns workers in the hat-dyeing industry in Southwark, and is a good example of such action in a trade dispute:

> [They] took one of their brother journeymen into custody, whom they charged with working over hours without any more pay, and for taking under price. They obliged him to mount an ass, and ride through all the parts of the Borough where hatters were employed ... a label was carried on a pole before him, denoting his offence; and a number of boys attended with shovels, playing the rough music; at all shops they came to in their way of business, they obliged the men to strike, in order to have their wages raised.

See also ALBERT ROAD, ADDISCOMBE, p. 358.

WALWORTH ROAD: CUMING MUSEUM

The Cuming Museum, housed in the Old Walworth Town Hall at 151 Walworth Road, was opened in 1906, and was based on an eclectic collection bequeathed to the borough by Henry Syer Cuming. But for the folklorist, it is their collection of objects connected with superstition and belief, amassed by Edward Lovett, which is of major interest.

Lovett (1852–1933) was born in Islington, and moved to Croydon with his parents sometime in the 1860s. He set up home for himself in Outram Road, Addiscombe, about 1882, where he stayed until he moved to Caterham in 1922. He spent his working life as a bank clerk, rising to the position of chief cashier at the Bank of Scotland, in London, by the time of his retirement in 1912.

But in his spare time he roamed the streets, docks, and markets of London, collecting information and obtaining objects that illustrated the beliefs and superstitions of the ordinary people. He collected hundreds of items and pieces of folklore, mostly from small shopkeepers, market-stall holders, sailors, itinerants, servants, strangers on the train, and so on. He made a particularly important collection of dolls – including many home-made examples from the poorest of families – and he was also passionately interested in mascots and amulets, which make up the bulk of his surviving collections. His writings show clearly that the carrying of mascots was

The Flooding of the River Thames

A stereotypical representation of a soothsayer. In the early sixteenth century, fortune-tellers and astrologers agreed that the Thames would flood the city, and many families decided to flee London in an attempt to avoid the catastrophe. Perhaps unsurprisingly, the prophecy turned out to be false.

London has never had any shortage of soothsayers, fortune-tellers, prophets, and astrologers ready and willing to predict dire events and catastrophes about to befall us, but the sixteenth and seventeenth centuries seem to have been particularly credulous times. Perhaps it is simply that developments in printing allowed prophets to spread their ideas more widely, and to leave a paper trail for us to follow centuries later.

Particular times of stress, such as the Civil War, the Great Plague, and the Great Fire, were well-known catalysts for such apocalyptic prophecies, but an earlier example, discussed by the arch-sceptic Charles Mackay in his excellent *Extraordinary Popular Delusions* (1841), seems to show that no external impetus is needed:

A still more singular instance of the faith in predictions occurred in London in the year 1524. The city swarmed at that time with fortune-tellers and astrologers, who were consulted daily by people of every class in society on the streets of futurity. As early as the month of June 1523, several of them concurred that, on the 1st day of February 1524, the waters of the Thames would swell to such a height as to overflow the whole city of London, and wash away ten thousand houses. The prophecy met with implicit belief. It was reiterated with the utmost confidence month after month, until so much alarm was excited that many families packed up their goods, and removed into Kent and Essex. As the time drew nigh, the number of these emigrants increased. In January, droves of workmen might be seen, followed by their wives and children, trudging on foot to the villages within fifteen or twenty miles, to await the catastrophe. People of a higher class were also to be seen in wagons and other vehicles bound on a similar errand. By the middle of January, at least twenty thousand persons had quitted the doomed city, leaving nothing but the bare walls of their home to be swept away by the impending floods. Many of the richer sort took up their abode on the heights of Highgate, Hampstead, and Blackheath; and some erected tents as far away as Waltham Abbey on the north, and Croydon on the south of the Thames. Bolton, the prior of St Bartholomew's, was so alarmed that he erected, at a very great expense, a sort of fortress at Harrow-on-the-Hill which he stocked with provisions for two months. On the 24th of January, a week before the awful day which was to see the destruction of London, he removed thither, with the brethren and officers of the priory and all his household. A number of boats were conveyed in wagons to his fortress, furnished abundantly with expert rowers, in case the flood, reaching so high as Harrow, should force them to go farther for a resting place. Many wealthy citizens prayed to share his retreat; but the prior, with a prudent forethought, admitted only his personal friends, and those who brought stores of eatables for the blockade.

Come the day, of course, the Thames refused to co-operate:

The tide ebbed at its usual hour, flowed to its usual height, and then ebbed again, just as if twenty astrologers had not pledged their words to the contrary. Blank were their faces as evening approached, and as black grew the faces of the citizens to think that they had made such fools of themselves ... On the morrow, it was seriously discussed whether it would not be advisable to duck the false prophets in the river. Luckily for them, they thought of an expedient which allayed the popular fury. They asserted that, by an error (a very slight one), of a little figure, they had fixed the date of this awful inundation a whole century too early. The stars were right after all, and they, erring mortals, were wrong. The present generation of cockneys was safe, and London would be washed away not in 1524, but in 1624. At this announcement, Bolton the priest dismantled his fortress, and the weary emigrants came back.

Where were the astrologers and prophets in 1953, when the Thames really did flood? They could have saved over 300 lives.

particularly widespread during the First World War, and he cites a bewildering range of items that were used in this way, including lucky cards, coins, dominoes, golliwogs, and assorted figurines.

It appears that the selection of a particular item as a mascot was mostly a matter of personal choice, but some patterns do emerge. There seems to have been a preference for things found by chance, or given 'for luck' by a loved one, and many were unusual or even defective everyday items such as a bent coin, a stone with a hole in it, or a left-handed whelk. A personal story told to Lovett by a nurse in 1918 illustrates something of the arbitrary nature of the subject:

> Her father with two of her friends were called up together. The night before they left home they met at her father's house, and the four sat down to a game of whist. When they had finished the last game, the nurse gathered up the cards, tearing the last card on the table into four pieces 'for luck', a piece each. The youngest man contemptuously threw his piece into the fire, saying that he did not believe in such rubbish. Some time later the three men went to France. In the first action they were in the man who had acted in the way described was taken prisoner by the enemy, but the other two came through in safety.

Lovett's anecdotes clearly show that other superstitions were also rife during the war, such as the following, which involves a child's caul. An extremely widespread belief, dating back at least 500 years in Britain, was that a child born with a caul (a section of the amniotic membrane over its face) would always be very lucky, and, in particular, would never drown. An extension of this idea was that anyone who simply possessed one of these cauls would be safe from drowning, and before the war Lovett had bought a couple of examples at shops near the London docks for eighteen pence each. But on the appearance of the German submarine menace, he found they were selling for £2 each (a 26-fold increase).

Lovett's collection also includes numerous items carried to ward off ailments such as rheumatism and cramp, and to help children cut their teeth, and also information on love philtres used by girls to encourage wooers, and on many more aspects of working-class London life, such as the tattooing of their boyfriends' names on girls' arms.

Lovett gave numerous lectures, and contributed occasional articles to newspapers and journals, but he never wrote up his experiences in full. His most substantial publication was *Magic in Modern London*, printed by the

Croydon Advertiser Office in 1925, but even this was only a hundred pages long, and is purely anecdotal.

His great strength was as an indefatigable gatherer, and the fact that he was a maverick in the relatively genteel world of folklore research adds to his interest for and value to subsequent generations. He was a fieldworker rather than an armchair scholar; he collected in London, when most folklorists were concerned with rural traditions; he collected objects rather than just verbal traditions; and he was concerned with the present-day as well as the past. But it is perhaps fortunate that he did not publish all his thoughts on the matter, as his lecture notes and articles demonstrate that he was not a deep thinker and had a highly simplistic notion of evidence, being prone to jump to conclusions on flimsy connections. Perhaps he was being wise, therefore, rather than just folksy, when he wrote in the introduction to *Magic in Modern London*:

> Although many of my records are quite remarkable and most suggestive,
> especially when one thinks of the people from whom they were gathered,
> it may be thought that I have a theory to account for the contents of this
> little book which covers so many years of personal enquiry! I not only have
> no theory, but as regards my personal opinion as to the reason why these
> remarkable beliefs in magic still exist in modern London, I simply say 'I
> don't know!'

Objects collected by Lovett can also be found in the Horniman Museum in Forest Hill, the Science Museum, the Imperial War Museum, the Museum of Childhood in Edinburgh, the Pitt Rivers Museum in Oxford, and the National Museum of Wales in Cardiff.

WOOLWICH

An item that appeared in *The Times* on 28 June 1844 reveals one of several related procedures believed infallible in locating the body of a drowned person:

> On Tuesday a fisherman residing in Woolwich named Michael Sullivan had
> been drinking rather freely during the morning, and contrary to the
> dissuasive arguments of his friends, proceeded in his boat to the middle of

the river to catch whitebait, and while engaged in hauling in his net was observed by several persons on shore to overbalance himself and fall into the river. Drags were immediately procured, and every attempt made to recover his body without success. Some of his friends insisted upon trying the following singular plan to discover the body, but without the anticipated result: A bundle of straw was taken to the middle of the river on a boat, and on arriving as near as possible at the spot where he fell overboard, the straw was set on fire while floating on the surface of the water, and allowed to be carried onwards by the tide, then running down, the parties in the boat expressing a firm belief that the fire would go out and the smoke cease to be evolved over the place where the body had settled in the river. The experiment failed entirely, as after considerable labour in dragging the river for some distance round the place where the straw ceased to burn and to smoke, the parties gave up further trial as hopeless, and the body has not yet been found.

This idea of floating burning straw was reported in other parts during the nineteenth century, but an older method, noted in 1581, was to float a piece of bread, loaded with quicksilver, which it was similarly thought would settle above the body. A related method was to fire a gun across the river, or to bang a drum loudly on a boat, and this was thought to bring the body to the surface.

WOOLWICH DOCKYARD

Until the early twentieth century many people took their trade affiliations very seriously, and the traditional year was enlivened by various processions, feasts, and other annual gatherings. This was particularly the case in areas where a local industry, such as ship-building, brought together a large number of similarly employed men. A letter published in William Hone's *Every-Day Book* (1825) describes in detail the activities of the blacksmiths' apprentices at Woolwich, every 24 November, which was the eve of the feast of St Clement, claimed by seafarers, foundry-workers, and blacksmiths as their patron saint.

One of the senior apprentices was chosen to serve as 'old Clem' and dressed up in a greatcoat, an oakum wig, and a mask with a long white

The sheer number of shipbuilders working in Woolwich Dockyard gave rise to many colourful traditions. On the feast of their patron saint St Clement, blacksmiths' apprentices took part in a lively parade in which one of their number dressed up as the character of 'old Clem'.

beard. He was seated in a large wooden chair, under a wooden crown and anchor, and flanked by four scenes, representing the blacksmiths' arms, anchor smiths at work, Britannia with her anchor, and Mount Etna. Before him stood a wooden anvil, and in his hands were a pair of tongs and a wooden hammer. A mate, also masked, attended him with a wooden sledgehammer, and they were surrounded by a number of other attendants, some of whom carried torches, banners, flags, battle-axes, tomahawks, and other accoutrements of war. Clem's chair was mounted on the shoulders of six men, and he was carried in procession, with drum and fife, around the town, stopping at nearly every public house, of which there were many. At each stop, set speeches were made, and money collected from onlookers:

> Gentlemen all, attention give,
> And wish St Clem long, long to live.

OLD CLEM: I am the real; St Clement, the first founder of brass, iron, and steel, from the ore. I have been to Mount Etna, where the god Vulcan first built his forge, and forged the armour and thunderbolts for the god Jupiter. I have been through the deserts of Arabia; through Asia, Africa and America; through the city of Pongrove; through the town of Tipmingo; and all the northern parts of Scotland. I arrived in London on the twenty-third of November, and came down to his majesty's dockyard, at Woolwich, to see how all the gentleman Vulcans came on there. I found them all hard at work, and wish to leave them well on the twenty-fourth.

THE MATE: Come all you Vulcans stout and strong,
Unto St Clem we do belong.
I know this house is well prepared
With plenty of money and good strong beer,
And we must drink before we part,
All for to cheer each merry heart.
Come all you Vulcans strong and stout,
Unto St Clem I pray turn out;
For now St Clem's going round the town,
His coach and six goes merrily round. Huzza, -a, -a.

After having gone round the town and collected a pretty decent sum from all and sundry, they retired to a public house, for a celebratory dinner.

SOUTH-WEST LONDON

The London Boroughs of Croydon, Lambeth, Merton,
Richmond upon Thames, Sutton, Wandsworth
and the Royal Borough of Kingston upon Thames

ACKERMAN ROAD, BRIXTON

As reported in Richard Davis's *I've Seen a Ghost! True Stories from Show Business* (1979), actor and comedian Roy Hudd tells of the only 'supernatural' experience he has ever had. Over and over, since childhood, he had dreamed the same dream, in which he would be standing outside a particular house, with steps and stone pillars. He would go up to the front door and enter, and then walk through the rooms, and sometimes the cellar. Nothing bad or scary would happen, but it was always the same house.

Years later, Roy and his wife were invited to visit two actor friends who had just moved into a flat in Ackerman Road, Brixton. As they drew up outside, Roy instantly recognised the house of his dreams, and to everyone's amazement could describe the rooms before entering them. They decided that the only possible explanation was that a previous occupant – Dan Leno, the well-known music-hall artist in Victorian times – had somehow impinged himself on Roy's consciousness. Roy was prompted to made a particular study of Leno and his career, which he later turned into a television programme.

An 1896 cartoon of Dan Leno (1860–1904), a well-known Victorian music-hall artist who once lived in a house in Ackerman Road, Brixton. Years after Leno's death, actor and comedian Roy Hudd (b. 1936) had a recurring dream about the house, prompting the suspicion that there was some strange and unexplained link between the two performers.

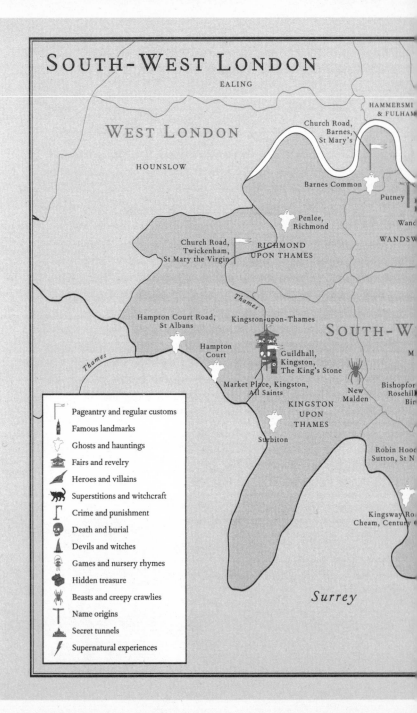

SOUTH-WEST LONDON

EALING

WEST LONDON

HOUNSLOW

HAMMERSMI
& FULHAM

Church Road,
Barnes,
St Mary's

Barnes Common

Putney

Penlee,
Richmond

Wand

Church Road,
Twickenham,
St Mary the Virgin

RICHMOND
UPON THAMES

WANDSW

Thames

Hampton Court Road,
St Albans

Kingston-upon-Thames

SOUTH-W

Hampton
Court

Guildhall,
Kingston,
The King's Stone

M

Thames

Market Place, Kingston,
All Saints

New
Malden

Bishopfor
Rosehil
Bir

KINGSTON
UPON
THAMES

Surbiton

Robin Hood
Sutton, St N

Kingsway Ro
Cheam, Century

Surrey

Pageantry and regular customs

Famous landmarks

Ghosts and hauntings

Fairs and revelry

Heroes and villains

Superstitions and witchcraft

Crime and punishment

Death and burial

Devils and witches

Games and nursery rhymes

Hidden treasure

Beasts and creepy crawlies

Name origins

Secret tunnels

Supernatural experiences

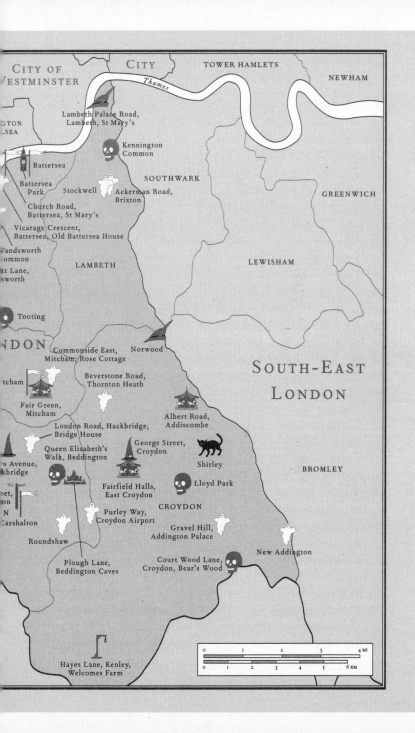

CITY OF WESTMINSTER

CITY

TOWER HAMLETS

NEWHAM

Thames

Lambeth Palace Road, Lambeth, St Mary's

Kennington Common

SOUTHWARK

GREENWICH

Battersea

Battersea Park

Stockwell

Ackerman Road, Brixton

Church Road, Battersea, St Mary's

Vicarage Crescent, Battersea, Old Battersea House

Wandsworth Common

LAMBETH

LEWISHAM

Lane, sworth

Tooting

NDON

Commonside East, Mitcham, Rose Cottage

Norwood

SOUTH-EAST LONDON

Beverstone Road, Thornton Heath

tcham

Fair Green, Mitcham

Albert Road, Addiscombe

London Road, Hackbridge, Bridge House

Queen Elizabeth's Walk, Beddington

George Street, Croydon

Shirley

BROMLEY

s Avenue, kbridge

Fairfield Halls, East Croydon

Lloyd Park

et, on

N

Carshalton

Purley Way, Croydon Airport

CROYDON

Roundshaw

Gravel Hill, Addington Palace

New Addington

Plough Lane, Beddington Caves

Court Wood Lane, Croydon, Bear's Wood

Hayes Lane, Kenley, Welcomes Farm

0   1   2   3   4 MI

0   1   2   3   4   5   6 KM

ALBERT ROAD, ADDISCOMBE

Rough music is the term given to a phenomenon that was widespread from the sixteenth century, not only in this country but also in Western Europe, where it was called the *charivari* in France and the *scampanate* in Italy. In essence, it describes the rough and mocking behaviour indulged in by people who wanted to express disapproval of individuals in their community. In Britain, the type of social 'misdemeanour' that most attracted the attention of the rough-musickers was almost always domestic, and usually concerned with people who had stepped outside the accepted parameters of sexual morality. These included widows or widowers marrying too soon after the death of their spouse, major disparities in age or class between bride and groom, blatant adultery, wife-beating, and, very commonly, shrewish wives who henpecked their husbands. Nevertheless, in some cases there is a hint of other underlying motives, such as the desire to stoke a dispute over money and property, or just plain vindictiveness and bullying. Because the custom was both festive and punitive, it was great fun to take part in, and while apologists will claim it was a legitimate and democratic method of social comment and community control, it is clear that the practice included all the usual faults and potential dangers of mob rule and vigilantism.

The exact form varied from place to place and as occasion demanded, and went by various names – *riding the stang*, *lew-belling*, the *stag hunt*, *ran-tanning*, *skimmington* or *skimmity riding*, or simply *a riding* – and there were many set pieces and recurrent features. Indeed, the participants often believed that the law could not touch them as long as they observed certain parts of the ritual, such as parading for three successive nights only, and they carefully avoided naming names in their accusatory declaration. In most recorded examples, the police appear to have taken no action to stop the proceedings.

The procedure usually took place after dark, and included a procession followed by a demonstration outside the house of the victim. The 'music' was rough indeed, being a cacophonous din, provided by the crashing of pots and pans, dustbin lids, hammers on shovels, stones rattled in tins, and so on, accompanied by thundering drums, screeching horns, and always raucous shouting and screaming.

A key feature was the parading of effigies, dressed to resemble the intended victims, which were usually burnt, shot to pieces, or otherwise mistreated as a climax to the event. In some cases, a human was used in the

Hogarth's famous print of 1726, *Hudibras Encounters the Skimmington*, illustrates the custom of 'rough music', whereby people took to the streets to mock those who had won their disapproval. The tradition persisted well into the nineteenth century, a particularly well-documented incident occurring in Albert Road, Croydon, in 1870.

parade instead of an effigy, and in earlier reports there seems to have been an unwritten rule that in the case of domestic strife the nearest neighbour should play the part of the offender. Nevertheless, if the protesters could get hold of the miscreants, it was they who were paraded and very roughly handled, although rarely, as far as we know, actually killed. An extremely common element was the placing of the human victim or effigy sitting backwards on horse or donkey, which was regarded as shameful and inherently very funny. Another recurrent feature was the carrying of a shirt or petticoat on a pole, like a banner, as illustrated in Hogarth's famous print *Hudibras Encounters the Skimmington* (1726), and a pair of horns, indicating cuckoldry and sexual inadequacy, was also often prominently displayed.

Rough music is frequently regarded as a predominately rural custom, but a number of cases have been reported from London over the years, including some of the earliest known examples. The merchant-tailor Henry Machyn, for example, recorded the following in his diary in 1562/3:

> The 22nd day of February, was Shrove Monday, at Charing Cross there was a man carried of four men, and before him a bagpipe playing, a shawm and a drum playing, and 20 links burning about him, because his next neighbour's wife did beat her husband; therefore it is ordered that his next neighbour shall ride about the place.

John Stow recorded a similar incident in his *Survey of London* (1598), in which a draper in the parish of St Michael, Cornhill, caught the local priest paying attentions to his wife. Samuel Pepys mentioned a 'riding' in Greenwich on 10 June 1667 for 'the constable of the town, whose wife beat him', and a French visitor to London, Henri Misson de Valbourg, described the following in an account of his travels published in 1698:

> I have sometimes met in the streets of London a woman carrying a figure of straw representing a man, crown'd with very ample horns, preceded by a drum, and follow'd by a mob, making a most grating noise with tongs, grid-irons, frying pans, and saucepans; and I ask'd what was the meaning of all this; they told me, that a woman had given her husband a sound beating, for accusing her of making a cuckold, and that upon such occasions some kind neighbour of the poor innocent injur'd creature generally perform'd this ceremony.

The various forms of rough music and allied customs of social protest and control were clearly widespread over several centuries, but we rarely have much more information than is given in these tantalisingly brief reports. Occasionally, however, an incident is described in more detail, as in the following case brought before the magistrates in Croydon, and reported in the *Croydon Chronicle* on 2 July 1870 and the *Croydon Advertiser* on 9 July 1870.

Georgiana Rutland, a live-in housekeeper to Mr Brockway, a shoe-maker, was accusing a local builder, Joel Cox, of being the ringleader in a fracas that had taken place outside their house in Albert Road, Addiscombe. On a previous night, a crowd had gathered and a male effigy had been burned, and on this night a female figure, which had been got up to resemble Mrs Rutland, was treated in the same way. Mrs Rutland described what had happened:

> On Monday night, the 27th June, there was a congregation of roughs in front of my governor's house, and at half-past ten an effigy was brought; I suppose it represented me. (Laughter.) The mob brought it to the front of the house, and illuminated it. (Renewed laughter.) A procession had been formed, headed by the defendant, Joel Cox, who was encouraging the roughs to go up and open my door. They commenced throwing glass bottles, stones and bricks at the door and windows.

Mrs Rutland sent Brockway and her son out the back way to fetch the police.

Meanwhile the stones came pouring into the house and one of them struck my dear little child, whilst I was sitting crouched behind the door. The roughs, under Joel Cox's instructions, tried to break open the door and drag us out. I heard Cox say distinctly, 'Go ahead, my boys; drag them out and kill them all.'

In the ensuing cross-examination of Mrs Rutland and other witnesses, nobody denied that the gathering of between 100 and 200 'roughs' and the stoning of the house and burning of the effigies had taken place, but it was disputed that Cox was the ringleader, and he was acquitted. However, the astonishing thing is the whole affair seems to have been taken as a joke by the defendant's counsel and many others in the court. They made great play of the fact that Brockway had escaped out the back, and had been told by Mrs Rutland not to attend the court hearing. It was also stated that Brockway had a wife elsewhere in Croydon, and it was implied that he and his 'housekeeper' were living as man and wife. Mrs Young, who lived opposite to Brockway, commented: 'I was rather amused at seeing the effigy burned.' The newspaper reports certainly give no hint of sympathy for a woman and child being threatened and assaulted in such a distressing manner.

Eleven years later, both newspapers carried a short report of another incident, only a few hundred yards away from Albert Road. According to the *Croydon Advertiser* on 1 October 1881:

A thrice married man has been getting it warm in the Leslie Park Road, where he lives. It is said that he has married his third wife six weeks after the death of the second, and his neighbours and friends have thought fit to demonstrate their approval of this proceeding in a very marked manner. They have smashed his windows, discharged fireworks outside his house, treated him and his bride to rough music, and indulged in various other manifestations of ill-feeling.

The *Chronicle* points out that the man was aged forty, and his wife was a young barmaid. Police were called to disperse the crowd, but no arrests were made.

See also SOUTHWARK, p. 346 *and illustration on* p. 328.

BARNES COMMON

According to Elliott O'Donnell in his *Ghosts of London* (1932), Barnes Common enjoyed something of a reputation for hauntings in the later nineteenth century, and it is interesting to note the way he skilfully links a number of stories into one effective narrative. He starts with the generalised statement:

> It was said that people crossing the Common at night saw black-robed women, suddenly and inexplicably, appear, and, just as suddenly and inexplicably, disappear.

He then throws in a factual event – the finding of parts of the body of a murder victim, Mrs Thomas, in 1879 – followed by some vague sightings of the ghost of a woman dressed as a nun whose face lacked eyes and eyesockets. Next comes a more concrete sighting, by a youth who stated that, while passing the cemetery gates:

> . . . he suddenly saw a woman who, from her dress, appeared to be a nun, gliding along, in a curious zig-zag fashion, on the opposite side of the road. There was something so eerie and unnatural about her that he took to his heels and ran.

And, finally, the same young man relates a well-rounded and detailed story concerning an occurrence at the home of Mr and Mrs West, and the latter's sister, Miss Dester. One evening, when Mr West was in poor health, Miss Dester went to the front door before retiring for the night:

> To her astonishment, standing in front of her, at the foot of the steps leading out of the garden, was a woman, dressed, to some extent at least, as a nun. She had her arms folded across her breast, and was staring hard at Miss Dester.

Corroborating details follow: a servant maid also saw the figure and was very frightened (maids in ghost stories always are); and – an example of probably the commonest detail in modern ghost legends – the family dog, which usually barked vigorously at strangers, cravenly hid behind Miss Dester and managed nothing more than a growl. Miss Dester slammed the door, and went to bed.

Next morning, Mrs West told Mr Dester that her husband had had a very bad night, and was particularly agitated by the strange woman, dressed as a nun, 'who never took her eyes off him'. The poor man died later the same day.

O'Donnell does not explain why the first manifestations of the nun had no eyes, while the later ones clearly did.

BATTERSEA

Battersea is one of the many places across London in which children had a custom of making grottoes around late July or early August. Local resident Ted Pepper gave this account of grotto-making in March 2008:

> I remember that this practice was well established in Battersea in the 1930s. It would appear that by word of mouth the grotto day was established and then the process started. Firstly the grotto was outlined by an initial border usually of pebbles or ideally sea shells. This could be square or oblong, but I favoured a semi-circle against a convenient wall. Then the enclosure was filled virtually by anything, small china ornaments, discarded paste jewellery, coloured marbles, etc. The size varied according to the contents displayed. It was left to the ingenuity of the builder with regard to the display. Some were haphazard in appearance, others presented in elaborate patterns. Perhaps at this point it should be established that this ritual was not a celebratory exercise, but had a mercenary objective. Sitting by one's creation, a passer-by would be greeted with the mantra, 'Please remember the grotta.' Substituting a glottal stop for the double t in 'grotto' will give some idea of the local dialect.

This was clearly the type of 'flat' grotto reported from MITCHAM (p. 399). *See also* GROTTOES AND SPRING GARDENS, p. 402.

BATTERSEA PARK

Battersea Park, one of the riverside jewels of South London, has a murky past. It was previously called Battersea Fields, and for a while in the nineteenth century, according to local historian Ernest Hammond in *Bygone Battersea* (1897):

. . . possessed a notoriety which has left its stigma on Battersea even to the present time, though half-a-century has elapsed since this scene of lawless disorder was converted into a beautiful park.

Most writers agreed with him. The area had always been problematic, as it was low-lying, marshy, and prone to flooding when the tides overflowed the river bank. Some of it was farmed, but it was a dreary, desolate place, about 300 acres in extent, that had acquired a reputation for being a quiet spot ideal for duelling. On one famous occasion in 1829, the Duke of Wellington, then Prime Minister, and the Marquis of Winchelsea faced each other with pistols, but the former fired wide, and the latter up in the air, and then apologised.

But the place went from bad to worse, and by the 1830s was notorious for disreputable behaviour, attracting 'riff-raff' from all over London. Ernest Hammond writes:

> Prize-fighting, gambling, immorality, and disorders of the vilest kinds, rendered the place positively disgraceful, while the weekly fair, held on Sunday, was an institution around which concentrated every evil under the sun. As many as 15,000 people have been landed at the pier at Battersea on these occasions, while the influx from the roads would bring the numbers up to 40,000 or 50,000 people.

The Red House inn was at the centre of all this activity and, of course, did extremely well out of it. In addition to food and drink, it specialised in bird-shooting, and had an enclosed four-acre ground, where live pigeons were

supplied at five shillings per dozen, starlings at four shillings, and sparrows at two shillings. This 'sport' drew people of all classes, including the nobility and gentry, and added to Battersea's raffish reputation.

The local vicar led a concerted effort to reclaim the area for respectable residents, having the brilliant idea of turning it into a royal park. An Act of Parliament to this end was passed in 1846, and work commenced on clearing and

Battersea Fields, a large marshy area where Battersea Park now stands, was a popular location for duels.

improving the site. A million cubic yards of soil, which had been excavated in the creation of the London docks, was spread across the land to raise its level significantly, the Red House was closed in 1852, and Queen Victoria formally opened Battersea Park in 1858.

See also ROYAL PARKS, p. 90.

BEVERSTONE ROAD, THORNTON HEATH

In February 1938, the Croydon suburb of Thornton Heath hit the headlines when major poltergeist activity was reported at a house in Beverstone Road. This occurrence came hot on the heels of another well-publicised 'poltergeist infestation' at Bethnal Green, which of course may not be entirely coincidental. Both events were thoroughly investigated by Dr Nandor Fodor (1895–1964), a Hungarian lawyer, who at the time was living in England and was employed as Director of Research with the International Institute for Psychical Research. Fodor's report on the Thornton Heath affair was suppressed by the Institute, but was finally published in book form, twenty years later, as *On the Trail of the Poltergeist*.

The Thornton Heath poltergeist suddenly struck an apparently ordinary household of husband and wife, their 21-year-old son, and a lodger. The usual activity took place around the house – crockery smashing, wardrobes falling, eggs flying, things disappearing and reappearing elsewhere, and so on. For a short time, the house was infested with journalists and psychic investigators, and it became clear that the occult activity, if such it was, centred on the wife, who Fodor called Mrs Forbes. Fodor naturally took a great interest in Mrs Forbes, and arranged for her to visit his laboratory in London on several occasions, where all sorts of strange things continued to happen. In particular, small items that Mrs Forbes had left at home kept appearing in the studio – a phenomenon that psychics call *apports*. These are shy little devils. They only appear when no one is looking, usually behind the investigators' backs, and they particularly like to materialise when some other activity is occurring, in order to distract attention. Other small items that Mrs Forbes had handled in shops also miraculously appeared in the car on the way home, and so on.

Despite catching Mrs Forbes in the act of throwing these apports in the studio, and knowing full well that she had secreted small items about her body with the clear intention of defrauding the investigating team, the good doctor was still apparently convinced that some of the occurrences in the house were genuine, and came up with the idea that they were not caused by an external 'spirit' but were the result of forces channelled through the mind of a person suffering from such a deep and powerful neurosis that she was either attracting or causing these phenomena herself. Basing his ideas on amateur Freudian psychiatry, he automatically assumed that the root of the problem must be sexual, and if Fodor's account of her earlier life is to be trusted, Mrs Forbes certainly supplied enough evidence of previous sexual trauma. She also reported lots of weird vivid dreams, which were perfect grist for Fodor's Freudian mill.

The brilliant core of this theory is that even if a poltergeist 'victim' such as Mrs Forbes is shown to be a fraud, it can be argued that something else is acting through her, or that she is not acting under her own volition, or simply that the human mind has great powers as yet unexplained by science. Such ideas now form part of the standard repertoire of ways to explain supposed poltergeist phenomena, but at the time they rocked the small world of spiritualist and psychic belief to its very foundations, and cost Dr Fodor his job with the Institute. A bitter war ensued, with blast and counter-blast in the specialist press and claim and counter-claim in the libel court. Dr Fodor went to America and became a leading light in the psychic world. It is not known what happened to the poltergeist.

See also BRIMSDOWN, ENFIELD, p. 196; CHELSEA, p. 138; GROVE PARK: ALLOTMENTS, p. 333; PLAISTOW, p. 293; REVERDY ROAD, BERMONDSEY: NOS 56 AND 58, p. 342; STOCKWELL, p. 414; SUTTON LANE, CHISWICK: SUTTON COURT-HOUSE, p. 173.

BISHOPFORD ROAD, ROSEHILL: MECCA BINGO HALL

The Gaumont cinema was opened 1937, but was converted to a Top Rank bingo club in 1960, and is now the Mecca Bingo Hall. It is haunted by an active ghost, nicknamed Fred by the staff, who has been causing trouble since at least the early 1970s. Neighbours regularly hear the sound of an organ being played loudly in the middle of the night, despite the fact that the organ was removed from the building years ago, while some have reported seeing 'a man in grey'. Other reported happenings have mostly been the standard pub-haunting fare of beer taps being mysteriously turned on and glasses falling off the shelves.

Explanations of Fred's unrest include various unverified claims that people have died in the building – a builder working on its construction, a nightwatchman, another builder working on the conversion, and a boiler-man who fell down a flight of steps – and the predictable notion that the cinema was built on a plague pit. But a visiting clairvoyant claimed to see a man dressed as a cavalier, which is much more jolly.

CARSHALTON

Like many other places in London, Carshalton had its grotto-builders, and they were remembered in the *Wallington & Carshalton Times* on 16 April 1981:

> In the 1940s, 'grotters' were a not uncommon sight on Carshalton pavements during the summer. These mysterious little mounds of earth, shells, leaves, flower petals, bits of chalk and stones were guarded jealously by their young architects, and passers-by were greeted with the plaintive cry of 'Penny for the grotter'. We didn't know why we made them. Like tin can Tommy, tops, dabs, knock down Ginger, lengthy skipping sagas and other street activities which all had their seasons, their origins were unknown to us. We just played them because all the other kids did.

See also GROTTOES AND SPRING GARDENS, p. 402.

CHURCH ROAD, BARNES: ST MARY'S CHURCH

Bequests inaugurating regular doles of food to the poor are common across the country, but occasionally an added detail makes the charity a little more interesting than the run-of-the-mill case. The testator might incorporate a play on his or her own name, as in the Barnes Rose Tree Charity. Local resident Edward Rose's will, dated 18 December 1652, left land to be used to finance a distribution of bread to the poor every Good Friday, but also bequeathed five pounds 'for making a frame or partition of wood in the churchyard, where he had appointed his burying place, and ordered three rose trees or more to be set or planted about the place where he should be so interred'.

CHURCH ROAD, BATTERSEA: ST MARY'S CHURCH

One of the regular customs of parish life before the mid nineteenth century was the ceremony of BEATING THE BOUNDS (p. 370). The Battersea churchwardens' accounts include many references to the custom, as shown in the extracts reprinted in John Taylor's history of the parish, *Our Lady of Battersey* (1925), covering the period from 1600 to 1830. They show expenditure on bread, cheese and drink, dinners, wands (for thrashing the boundary marks), points for the boys (decorated laces as mementoes, sometimes referred to as 'ribbons'), and in special years 'for gunpowder and fireing ye guns'. Taylor adds a footnote: 'The writer remembers the beating of Battersea bounds c. 1884, when wands were carried in accordance with ancient custom, and the parish boundaries duly impressed on the bodies of the boys who took part in the ceremony.'

Oddly enough, Penge, which is now part of Bromley borough, was for centuries a detached part of Battersea parish, given to them in the year 957. The importance of the custom of beating the bounds is shown by the fact that Battersea parish officials did not forget to journey there to carry out the perambulation. Thus there are entries such as the one in 1661: 'Spent for a dynner for the parish agoeing the bownds of the parish at Penge £3 8s.'

The churchwardens' accounts also reveal details of other customs and observances that have now passed into history. The parish bell-ringers, for example, were paid extra money for ringing on certain occasions such as the King's birthday, coronations, 'when the Queen was delivered', and the day of Elizabeth I's accession, which was a major celebration with Protestant overtones:

> *1600* Laid out the 17th of November for four ringers. Spent more the same day for bread and drink and candles for the Ringers 4d

Elizabeth's day was soon to be eclipsed by 5 November, which remained one of the most popular 'ringing nights' in many parishes right into the twentieth century:

> *1633* To the ringers upon Gunpowder Treason 2s
> *1650* Gunpowder Plot – to Ringers 2s 6d

Another interesting entry appears under 1675: 'Gave Elizabeth Bannestar, for carrying the child to be touched by the King 2s.' This is a

The Battersea churchwardens' accounts include numerous references to the tradition of 'beating the bounds'. Once a widespread custom, it involved walking around the borders of a parish, using long wands to thrash out the boundary marks.

reference to the disease scrofula, which was popularly known as *the King's Evil* because it was believed that it could be cured by the touch of the ruling sovereign. Accredited sufferers could be sent by parish officers to see the King, and in cases of need, the parish would also pay expenses, which presumably explains the two shillings paid to Elizabeth on this occasion.

See also GUY FAWKES NIGHT, p. 338.

CHURCH ROAD, TWICKENHAM: ST MARY THE VIRGIN CHURCH

There was previously a widespread custom in local churches for good neighbourhood and brotherly love to be symbolised at Easter by a meal in the church, or the dividing of cakes or bread among the parishioners. In Twickenham parish church, this took the form of dividing two large cakes among the young people on Easter Sunday. But the custom ran into trouble

Beating the Bounds

The 'beating of the bounds' ceremony took place at several London churches as well as the Tower of London, shown here in a photograph from 1905. This annual custom, in which long wands were used to beat the boundary markers, took place in order to pass the knowledge of the parish boundaries on to younger generations.

Beating the bounds, an annual religious custom that was later secularised, used to take place in every parish in the country at Rogation-tide, which was the Monday, Tuesday, and Wednesday immediately before Ascension Day, the fortieth day after Easter Sunday.

Rogation derives from the Latin *rogare*, 'to ask', and during the three-day festival parishioners, led by their clergy, would process around the parish, blessing the fields and holding services to ask God for his continued protection and beneficence. The procession included religious regalia such as large crosses, banners, and effigies of saints, and was a popular and colourful early summer event, which involved the whole community. The festival originated in Gaul in response to a specific run of disasters, but religious leaders quickly recognised its community value and it soon became an annual event, introduced into Britain in the eighth century.

The Reformation changed the custom radically, but did not destroy it. The carrying of crosses and saints was too closely identified with the Roman Catholic faith, but the processions themselves were rebranded as secular occasions and made to serve the purposes of parish administration, which was taking on an ever-expanding range of roles. The focus of the procession shifted to walking round the boundaries of the parish both to check that there had been no encroachments or illegal building, and to make sure that everyone knew the extent of the parish in detail. The local clergy still took part, of course, and they usually held a short service, or led a hymn, at certain strategic landmarks, which were often named Vicar's Oak, Gospel Oak, or something similar.

In the days before accurate maps, it was essential that the knowledge of boundaries was passed on to younger generations, and an important function of the process was to teach them to local boys. A number of peculiar customs grew up around this. The participants often carried flexible wands, and when they reached a particular boundary marker they would literally beat it with their sticks. In many cases, boys were whipped with the wands at each stone, or 'bumped' on them, or even held upside down. Sometimes they were encouraged to run on ahead to find the next marker and the first one there was rewarded. It was also thought important, even perhaps legally binding, that the whole of the boundary be followed, at least by a representative. Boys were therefore useful to scale walls, crawl through hedges, wade through ponds – wherever the official boundary took them.

At certain points refreshments were given, and there was often a dinner provided for the great and the good in the evening. But parishes vary considerably in shape and size, and in some of the larger ones it took two or three days to get all the way round. As the custom lost its importance, it became common to beat the bounds only every now and then, and in most places it died out completely during the nineteenth century. It is often revived, however, to celebrate an anniversary or other special occasion in the parish, and is still thought of as a useful way of engendering community knowledge.

See also CHURCH ROAD, BATTERSEA: ST MARY'S, p. 368; SYDNEY STREET, CHELSEA: ST LUKE'S CHURCH, p. 174; TOWER OF LONDON: BOUNDARIES, p. 54.

when the Puritans came to power in the Interregnum. They regarded it as a popish relic and so Parliament decreed that the custom of sharing food be transmuted into a distribution of bread to the poor, and this was carried out by throwing it to them, as at SUSSEX GARDENS: ST JAMES'S CHURCH (p. 116).

See also CLEMENT'S LANE: ST CLEMENT EASTCHEAP, p. 12.

COMMONSIDE EAST, MITCHAM: ROSE COTTAGE

Rose Cottage in Mitcham has several ghost traditions, which James Clark tries to piece together in his *Strange Mitcham* (2002) booklet, but they remain a somewhat disparate bunch of stories. The building dates from the late eighteenth century and has gone through various stages of remodelling over the years. Ghostly happenings were first reported in the 1920s, with the figure of a stately middle-aged lady (nicknamed Lady Jane by the residents) seen walking from room to room, apparently doing no harm to anyone. Her costume is variously described as being from 60 years ago, or 600 years ago, which is clear evidence of (mis)copying from one source to another. Later reports, however, describe more of a poltergeist than a ghost, with things crashing to the ground, others disappearing, doors refusing to open, and so on. There are also rumours of a murder in the house, and a connection with another killing at Southend in 1894, by someone who was renting a room in the cottage.

COURT WOOD LANE, CROYDON: BEAR'S WOOD

Harry Hill, a resident of New Addington housing estate, was featured in the *Croydon Advertiser* on 3 January 1986 relating a ghost story from when he was a boy scout (sometime around 1950). It concerns a character called Digger Harry, and Bear's Wood, off Court Wood Lane. Digger and his wife lived for many years in a lonely cottage in the wood. But when his wife died, he became paranoid about being separated from her if she were taken away to a cemetery, so he buried her in the woods, and told no one. Suspicions were eventually raised, and Harry was arrested for murder, but he still refused to say what had happened to his wife. Because of his extreme age, he was released some months later, but unfortunately he had by then forgotten where his wife's body was buried, and he died soon afterwards. Quite naturally, his ghost still walks the wood, shovel on shoulder, endlessly searching for his wife. Mr Hill commented that the first sighting of the ghost was in 1932, and it has been reported regularly ever since.

CULVERS AVENUE, HACKBRIDGE

A pair of very strange occurrences at Mullard's radio factory at Culvers Avenue, which operated from 1927 to 1993, gave the area a short-lived reputation for the supernatural. A piece in the parish magazine of All Saints church in April 1977, repeated in the local press, explained that in 1937 one of the radio sets being packaged up for shipping suddenly burst into flames before the very eyes of an astonished workman, even though it was not plugged in.

As he and his companion stood by, fanning the remaining smoke away with their hands, they heard a hideous cackle. Turning towards the laughter, they saw what looked like a decrepit old gypsy woman, clawing the air and grinning toothlessly. Then, before either of them could move, the old woman, like the smoke, disappeared.

A few days later a similar thing happened, but this time they saw the same hideous creature tied to a tree, still cackling defiantly, surrounded by burning

It was once believed that Mullard's radio factory in Culvers Avenue was haunted by the apparation of a witch who had been burned on that very spot 300 years earlier. In fact, as this eighteenth-century chapbook shows, the traditional punishment for witches was hanging, not burning.

faggots. The story they were told to explain these apparitions was that 300 years earlier, an old woman called Mother Chisley had been burnt as a witch on the very spot, because her prophecies were too close to the mark.

Quite apart from the cartoon-character description of the witch, more likely to provoke laughter than belief, the credibility of the explanation is undermined by the fact that, despite popular misconceptions, the punishment for witchcraft in England was hanging, not burning.

FAIR GREEN, MITCHAM

The two biggest fairs for the South Londoner in the nineteenth century were at Croydon and at Mitcham, but while the former was suppressed in 1868, the latter has managed to survive several attempts to get rid of it, and is still a popular feature of the local scene. It is held for three days, 12–14 August, and has always been sited on or close to what is still called the Fair Green – first on Upper Green, then on Three Kings Piece, and now on Mitcham Common.

It is said that Elizabeth I granted it a charter because she was so pleased with the festivities when she visited the town. She did, in fact, visit the area five times between 1591 and 1598, but no charter, or mention of one, has ever been found. In fact, the earliest reference to a fair in Mitcham that anyone has been able to find dates only to 1732, when Christopher Halstead, a fiddler, happened to die there. Nevertheless, the fair now has a perfectly legitimate customary status, and apart from an interruption during the Second World War, and for a short period when the showmen were in dispute with the council, it has a documented history of at least 275 years.

Before the nineteenth century, a fair was a major event in the local calendar, not least because many special regulations concerning local trade and even legal proceedings came into force for its duration. It was therefore essential that it was clear to all parties when the fair was in operation and when not. Most fairs were opened and closed with the reading of a proclamation by the fair's owner, or the local mayor, and in many places a large symbol was carried around the fairground on a pole at the opening, and then kept on display to show that the fair was in operation. At Mitcham, as also at neighbouring Croydon, the symbol of the fair was a large wooden key, about four foot long, and painted gold. It is often thought to have been an ancient fixture, but no documentary evidence for its use can be found before about 1911, and it may have been a late addition.

Another interesting feature at Mitcham Fair was the popularity of oysters – primarily because of the coincidence of its date with the opening of the oyster season. This goes some way to explain why the custom of grotto-making at MITCHAM (p. 399) survived to an unusually late date.

FAIRFIELD HALLS, EAST CROYDON

Croydon had three ancient fairs, granted by charters in 1276, 1314, and 1343. One was held in the first week in July, and was nicknamed the Cherry Fair. It lingered on till 1852, but for most of its time was overshadowed by the autumn fair, which lasted the longest and was widely known as *the* Croydon Fair. Originally chartered for three days around St Matthew's Day (21 September), after the change of the calendar in 1752 it began on 2 October, and was held on the ground near East Croydon called the Fair Field, now occupied by Fairfield Halls.

Most of the old fairs had gimmicks or idiosyncrasies that made them famous, and Croydon's October fair was generally known as the *Walnut fair*, as so many nuts were consumed there. It was also, however, a good time of year for roast meat, as remembered by local resident Thomas Frost, who knew the fair well in the 1830s, in his *The Old Showmen* (1881):

> All the inhabitants of the town prepared for visitors, for everyone who had a relative or acquaintance in Croydon was sure to make the fair an occasion for a visit. Two time-honoured customs were connected with the October fair, everybody commencing fires in their sitting rooms on the first day of the fair, and dining on roast pork or goose. The latter custom was observed even by those who, having no friends to visit, dined in a booth; and the number of geese and legs of pork to be seen roasting before glowing charcoal fires in grates of immense width, to the rear of the booths, was one of the sights of the fair.

The local pubs also did a roaring trade. The Greyhound Inn alone cooked a hundred geese each day of the fair. Thomas Frost also recalled the opening ceremonies:

The October fair at Croydon was opened as soon as midnight had sounded by the town clock, or, in earlier times, by that of the parish church; the ceremony consisting in the carrying of a key, called 'the key of the fair', through its principal avenues. The booth-keepers were then at liberty to serve refreshments to such customers as might present themselves, generally the idlers who followed the bearer of the key; and long before daylight the field resounded with the bleating of sheep, the lowing of cattle, the barking of dogs, and the shouting of shepherds and drovers.

Thomas Frost mentions 'the lowing of the cattle' because Croydon Fair was a major cattle and horse market, as well as a pleasure fair. All the major metropolitan circuses, menageries, and shows put in an appearance, and there were the usual roundabouts, dancing booths, gingerbread sellers, toy stalls, boxing booths, card-sharpers, pickpockets, fat women, living skeletons, giants, and dwarves. The presence of wild animals in the town always caused a stir, and Thomas Frost recounts a particularly memorable experience that took place early on morning in 1842:

> One of Wombwell's elephants escaped from confinement, and at the early hour of three in the morning was seen, to the amazement and alarm of old Winter, the watchman, walking in a leisurely manner down High Street. He was in the habit of being taken every morning by his keeper to bathe in Scarbrook pond . . . and on such occasions he was regaled with a bun at a confectioner's shop . . . near the Green Dragon . . . The elephant reached the confectioner's shop, and, finding it closed, butted the shutters with his enormous head, and, amidst a crash of wood and glass, proceeded to help himself to the delicacies inside.

But it was not only elephants who caused problems at the fair. Until 1861, Addiscombe Military College, which trained officers for the East India Company's private army, stood a mile or so from central Croydon. The cadets, always a lively presence in the town, sometimes got out of hand, as described by Colonel Vibart, the author of the standard history on the subject, *Addiscombe: Its Heroes and Men of Note* (1894), who had himself been a cadet in his youth:

> It was usual to give leave to the cadets to go to the fair; fifty on each day, out of uniform, so as to avoid mischief, if possible. It goes, however, without saying that mischief was found. One amusement of the cadets was to hire all the donkeys they could, and make a charge of cavalry among the stalls to their own great satisfaction, but to the dismay of the stall-keepers.

In around 1844 the cadets got even more out of hand, and there was a major fracas between them and the fair-people, resulting in their being banned from the fair from then on.

In retrospect, the 1840s could be seen as the last decade that the fair enjoyed general support in the town. The first indication that things were changing was when it became clear that the livestock and pleasure aspects of the fair were heading in different directions, so they were separated, and held in different locations on different dates, and this made it easier for critics to move for the suppression of the 'undesirable' pleasure fair. In common with many other outer London fairs, the death knell started to sound when the railway came to town. In Croydon, it took over twenty years, but the forces of opposition gained in strength in direct proportion to the crowds swelling the town, as reported in the *Croydon Chronicle* on 6 October 1866:

> The annual pleasure and pastimes of the people were held in Mr West's field, and attracted an immense concourse of persons, chiefly from London and suburbs, the inhabitants of Croydon being conspicuous by their absence. If possible, the caterers for public amusement were inferior to past years, while the element of ruffianism showed an unmistakable increase. Gambling, although 'strictly prohibited' was carried on, we might say, at almost every step; and what with the stink, the noise, the oaths, the drunkenness and fighting, there was no lack of 'enjoyment' for those whose tastes were easily supplied.

The period also saw a major change in the way popular entertainments were seen by those in authority, and their friends on the local newspapers, such as the *Croydon Chronicle*, which reported on 6 October 1855:

> Croydon fair, as regards the pleasure portion, will soon disappear, as the people have now new habits, new feelings, and are becoming gradually better educated, they will not require the noisy unprofitable mirth which they derive from visiting a fair, but will seek for pleasure in the Crystal Palace, and such other buildings as will afford them rational delight, and bear the next morning's reflection.

Under the provisions of the Metropolitan Fairs Act, the Croydon Bench of Magistrates prohibited the fair in October 1868. There was some rioting in protest, but Croydon's last fair eventually succumbed and is now no more.

GARRATT LANE, WANDSWORTH

Garratt Lane commemorates the small hamlet of Garratt, which used to lie halfway between Wandsworth and Tooting. For the second half of the eighteenth and into the early nineteenth century, it was nationally famous for its annual mock-mayor ceremony.

Mock mayors and MPs were once quite common across England. At a time when the franchise was restricted to the upper echelons of society, and real elections were occasions of great pomp and circumstance, it is not particularly surprising that the more humble among England's inhabitants would enjoy parodying the events. Their taste for the burlesque was encouraged by the publicans, who would do a roaring trade during the festivities.

The pattern was similar everywhere, and every part of a real election and inauguration was a potential target. The candidates often had silly names, such as Squire Blow-Me-Down, Sir Buggy Bates, or Lord Twankum; they made speeches that promised preposterous things, for example no work and free beer; they took fanciful oaths of allegiance; and they handed out mock punishments. They were usually paraded around the community on chairs, amid much cheering and drinking, and they often wore deliberately shabby clothes and carried burlesque regalia, such as a cabbage stalk for a mace.

It is not clear when the mock elections in Garratt started, but the earliest on record took place in 1747 on Garratt Green, near the Leather Bottle. It was said locally that the mock elections began when the people of the village who had formed a society to oppose the enclosure of local common land celebrated their success by continuing to elect officers, but this is unlikely to be true.

The Garratt elections were given a huge publicity boost with the staging of Samuel Foote's popular play *The Mayor of Garratt* (1763), and thousands of onlookers began descending on the hamlet in subsequent years.

Two of the Garratt mayors became widely known characters in their own right in the 1780s and 1790s. Sir Jeffrey Dunstan, a second-hand wig-dealer, and Sir Harry Dimsdale, a muffin-seller, achieved some celebrity and were invited to gatherings and parties in London, where they made speeches and were plied with drink. The humour of the day was certainly robust and by modern standards crude. But even though the real mayors

Sir Harry Dimsdale, a muffin-seller, and Sir Jeffrey Dunstan, a second-hand wig-dealer, were the most famous Mayors of Garratt. There used to be an annual event in the small hamlet, now commemorated by South London's Garratt Lane, in which local people were elected in a mock-mayor ceremony that parodied the pomp of official mayoral elections.

and members of Parliament probably deserved the ribbing they received, a large element of cruelty was involved in choosing those who stood as mock mayor. They were often selected because they had some kind of disability or were 'feeble-minded', which was regarded as intrinsically funny at the time. John Thomas Smith gives a flavour of the proceedings in his *Book for a Rainy Day* (1861), under the heading of 1787:

> Sir Harry Dimsdale, a short feeble little man, was brought in to St Anne's watch-house, charged by two colossal guardians of the night with conduct most unruly. 'What have you, Sir Harry, to say to all this?' asked the Dogberry of St Anne. The knight, who had been roughly handled, commenced like a true orator, in a low tone of voice, 'May it please ye, my magistrate, I am not drunk; it is *langour*. A parcel of the bloods of the Garden have treated me cruelly, because I would not treat them. This day, sir, I was sent for by Mr Sheridan to make my speech upon the table at the Shakespeare Tavern in Common Garden; he wrote the speech for me, and always gives me half a guinea, when he sends for me to the tavern. You see

I didn't go in my Royal robes; I only put 'um on when I stand to be member'
... Sir Harry was advised to go home, which, however, he swore he would
not do at midnight without an escort. 'Do you know,' said he, 'there's parcel
of raps now on the outside waiting for me.' The constable of the night gave
orders for him to be protected to the public house opposite the west end of
St Giles's church, where he then lodged. Sir Harry hearing a noise in the
street, muttered, 'I shall catch it; I know I shall.' 'See the conquering hero
comes' (*cries without*). 'Ay, they always use that tune when I gain my
election at Garratt.'

Sadly, Dimsdale died in the workhouse in 1810, aged fifty-four.

Many mock-mayor celebrations across the country were forcibly
suppressed by the local authorities in the first half of the nineteenth
century, as much because they were drunken riots as because they pierced
the civic pride of the real officials. But others simply faded away as the
jokes wore thin and they lost local support. The Garratt mock-mayor
ceremony seems to have been one of the latter, as it faded out in the late
1790s, and an attempted revival in 1826 did not succeed.

GEORGE STREET, CROYDON

In his *Reminiscences of a Country Journalist* (1886), local-born Thomas Frost
remembered Croydon when it was a bustling market town around 1820,
and recorded some of the traditions then current in George Street. A house
in the street, which had formerly been the George Inn, was reputed to be
haunted:

A century or more ago, several travellers and pedlars were known to
have been entertained in the house, and were never seen afterwards.
They were supposed to have been murdered by the people of the inn,
which was thereupon believed to be haunted by their troubled spirits . . .
[there was also] a closet in the house, the door of which had been nailed
up by some former tenant, perhaps a century before, and had never been
opened since.

Many strange stories were told about another resident, a singular old
woman called Mother Hotwater:

It was while staying with some friends at Addington Palace that Henry James was told a gruesome story about some dead servants and some children that inspired his *The Turn of the Screw*.

One of these was that she had a closet into which she placed the household gear whenever it needed cleaning; and on opening the door on the following morning found the work done. Some domestic sprite, akin to the brownies of Scotland, cleaned the knives, and performed any similar office that the old woman required of it. Among the needlewomen and domestic servants of the town it used, years ago, to be a common saying when they were busy, 'I wish we had Mother Hotwater's closet' . . . Another tradition attributed to the old witch a prophecy that, when she had been dead a hundred years she would rise from her grave. It is said that the time when this prediction should have been fulfilled is past, but the year of the dame's decease is unknown.

GRAVEL HILL: ADDINGTON PALACE

Addington can claim a little piece of one of the most famous of Henry James's stories, *The Turn of the Screw*, first published in 1898. The author got the idea for the plot, in a which a lonely governess becomes convinced that the house she is working in is haunted, and the children she is caring for are possessed, while staying with his friends, the Benson family at Addington Palace. In a letter, James writes:

> On one of those two memorable – never to be obliterated – winter nights that I spent at the sweet Addington, your father, in the drawing-room by the fire, where we were talking a little, in the spirit of recreation, of such things, repeated to me the few meagre elements of a small and gruesome story that had been told him years before and that he could only give the dimmest account of – partly because he had forgotten details and partly – much more – because there had been no details and no coherency in the tale as he received it, from a person who also but half knew it. The vaguest essence only was there – some dead servants and some children. This essence struck me and I made note of it . . .

The 'father' in this letter was Edward White Benson, Archbishop of Canterbury from 1882 to 1896, who enjoyed Addington Palace as one of the country residences belonging to his office.

GUILDHALL, KINGSTON: THE KING'S STONE

Kingston is very proud of its title as the Royal Borough of Kingston, a title given because in Saxon times, for nearly a hundred years, it was the place where coronations took place. Seven kings were crowned there: Edward the Elder (899); Athelstan (924); Edmund (941); Edred (946); Edwy (955); Edward the Martyr (975); and Ethelred (978).

The King's Stone, said to be the stone on which the Saxon kings were crowned, has moved around in its time. It was previously in the Saxon chapel of St Mary, and was later sited in the marketplace and used as a mounting block. It was rescued from this indignity in 1850, and finally came to its present position of honour when the new Guildhall was built in 1935. It is of hard sandstone, and is now mounted on a heptagonal plinth protected by suitably Saxon-like iron railings. The names of the kings are inscribed around the plinth, along with a coin of each reign, presented by the British Museum.

It would be neat if we could say that the name of the town derives from the King's Stone, as has often been assumed, but it does not. In fact Cyningestun was already in use long before the first known coronation, and means a royal estate or palace.

In all, seven Anglo-Saxon kings were crowned at Kingston. This engraving shows the King's Stone as it was sited in the nineteenth century.

HAMPTON COURT

Hampton Court Palace was commissioned by Cardinal Wolsey in 1515, who was forced to give it to Henry VIII in 1525. Henry VIII and his wives appear in folklore traditions all over the country, so it is unsurprising that two of the dead wives are said to haunt the palace. Jane Seymour – Henry's third wife, who died following childbirth, having given the King his long-awaited son – is said to have been seen walking calmly downstairs from the Queen's apartments dressed in white and carrying a candle. Katharine Howard – the fifth wife, who was beheaded – has provided a more lively spectacle as her ghost apparently re-enacts the scene when she escaped from the guards who had come to arrest her, and ran to the chapel in which Henry was saying Mass. Her screams and frantic footsteps to the chapel door have reportedly been heard.

These tales of celebrity royal ghosts have the taint of tourist-lore about them, and were probably invented quite recently. In an unusually rational chapter of his 1907 book *Haunted Houses*, Charles Harper discussed the

Derby Day

Gustave Doré's (1832–83) illustration brilliantly captures the division between upper-class people going to the races and the rabble who lined the streets to watch them go past. It was traditional for wealthy race-goers to throw coins to the working-class children.

Horse-racing has been taking place on Epsom Downs since at least 1661, but the Derby Stakes, named after Edward Smith-Stanley, 12th Earl of Derby, was first run in 1779. It soon became one of the most prestigious flat races in the world, and Derby Day in the nineteenth century was one of the great days out for Londoners of all classes. As Blanchard Jerrold wrote, rather breathlessly, in *London: A Pilgrimage* (1872), in his collaboration with the artist Gustave Doré:

> On Derby morning, all London wakes at cock-crow. The first flicker of light breaks upon thousands of busy men in misty stables; breaks upon a vast encampments of the Romans [Gypsies] and other less reputable wandering tribes on the Downs; breaks upon lines of loaded pedestrians footing it from London, to turn a penny on the great event. Horsey folk issue from every beer-shop and inn on the road. The beggars are in mighty force; the tattered children take up their stations. Who wants to see samples of all degrees of Cockneys, has his golden opportunity today …
>
> On the Downs London is in the highest spirits, and all classes are intermingled for a few hours on the happiest terms. Strolling amid the booths and tents we find elbowing each other, bantering, playing, drinking, eating and smoking; shoals

of shop-boys and clerks, tradesmen in attire, mechanics in holiday dress, wondering foreigners, gaudy ladies, generally of loud voice and unabashed manner.

In areas such as Croydon and Sutton, the tattered children's station was beside the road through which the vehicles bound for Epsom had to pass. They lined the streets to watch the posh people go by in their fancy carriages, and to catch the coins traditionally thrown to them by the passing toffs. When the meeting was on a weekday annoyed schoolteachers recorded low attendance:

Princess Road School, Croydon, head-teacher's log-book
Week ending 1 June 1872
The attendance has considerably improved, and would have more so had not many of the boys stopped away on Wednesday to see the people go to and return from the Derby.

Well into the twentieth century working-class Londoners would make a day of it on the Downs. In her memoirs *Please to Remember* (1982), Ellen Morris recalled the scene on the Isle of Dogs in about 1920:

It was from the Manchester Arms that parties used to go off to the Derby. There were usually three or four horse-drawn brakes full of merry people sitting round the sides of the flat, open vans. It was some sort of tradition that they wore funny hats. I remember my father borrowing a straw bonnet from one of my dolls, decorating it with a large feather, and looping the elastic round his nose.
. . . A crowd gathered to watch the fun as, with some heaving and pushing, larger ladies were hoisted aboard. As each brake departed with a crack of the whip and a chorus of 'gee up', the crowd cheered and the horses set a smart pace up Manchester Road as if glad to be going to Epsom Downs. Children did not go to the Derby. I spent the day with my friend in the pub. We watched from an upstairs window waving to those below. Her parents gave us a handful of pennies and as each party pulled away we flung the coins out into the street. Scrambling and pushing the children would pick the pennies up, there always seemed enough for all. But by the time the last brake left some of them grew cunning and held out caps and skirts to catch the falling money, looking up and laughing. Derby Day was always a favourite.

Hampton Court ghosts with Mr Ernest Law, a resident of thirty-five years' standing. Mr Law dismissed the supposed sounds of Katharine Howard as the wailing of cats, and made the point that there had been a marked upsurge in celebrity ghost stories in his time, prompted by sensationalist press coverage. He also, however, told a much more down-to-earth story that he had heard in his time at the palace.

> Late in the 1860s, a lady who occupied apartments in the Palace . . . assured her friends that she was frequently troubled by the rappings made by two invisible beings, who in this way exercised upon the panelling of her rooms. She complained to the Lord Chamberlain, and the Lord Chamberlain passed on the complaint to the Office of Works, with the result that in due course, after the matter had circulated through the requisite number of departments, she was informed that the jurisdiction of the First Commissioner did not extend into the spirit world. The sequel is singular. In 1871 when workmen were excavating in the cloister or covered way of Fountain Court, nearly opposite the entrance to this lady's rooms two human skeletons were uncovered, at a depth of about two feet below the pavement. It was supposed that they were the remains of two soldiers of the time of William III, but it does not appear what was the evidence that led to this supposition.

Other Hampton Court stories that do not feature Henry's wives include the tales of the ghost of Mrs Sibell Penn, and the experiences of PC 265T in February 1907. Mrs Penn was reputedly the devoted nurse to the future Edward VI, and a trusted servant to the royal family, until her death from smallpox in 1562. She was buried in the old church at Hampton, but when that building was demolished in 1821 and replaced, her tomb was moved to the porch of the new building. It is this removal which the ghost-believers have identified as the reason for her reappearance.

Residents of one of the grace-and-favour apartments began to be disturbed by a strange whirring sound, and the muffled voice of what sounded like a grumpy old woman. In true narrative fashion, it was finally discovered that close to their flat was a secret room, bricked up and unused for centuries, in which was found an old-fashioned spinning wheel, and the wooden floor under the treadle was worn away with constant use. Other sightings have also been identified as Mrs Penn. An excellent example is reported by J. A. Brooks in his *Ghosts of London* (1991), which concerns the Revd J. G. M. Scott's redoubtable great-aunt Edith, ninety years old and living at Hampton Court:

Commissioned by Cardinal Wolsey in 1515, Hampton Court Palace was taken over by Henry VIII when the cardinal fell from favour. Two of the king's wives – Jane Seymour and Katherine Howard – are said to haunt the palace.

I was woken up in the night by someone bending over my bed and looking into my face. 'What do you want?' I said, 'You must go away. What do you mean by coming into my bedroom?', and she said, 'I want a home, I want a home.' So I said, 'Well I'm sorry, you can't have one here; this is my bedroom and you must go away.' And she did, but when I thought about it in the morning I really felt quite ashamed of myself, because we had a spare room upstairs, and she could have had that.

The story of PC 265T is another from Charles Harper's book. One night in 1907, the policeman was on his usual duty at the east front of the palace, standing close to the main gates, when he saw a group of figures approaching along Ditton Walk. There were two gentlemen in evening dress and seven or nine ladies, which he thought might be late-night revellers returning home, but as they got closer he noticed that they made no sound except 'what resembled the rustling of dresses'. The constable prepared to open the gates for the party, but they changed direction and headed for another set of gates, and as they did so they re-formed into processional mode, two by two, with the men at the front. Then, as the PC watched, they melted into thin air.

One last tale, printed in the magazine *All the Year Round* on 22 June 1867, is a nice example of a point-of-death wraith story. An English woman who was living in Germany with her daughter Maud fell ill and, fearing the worst, entreated Maud to write to her old friend Mrs B, to ask her to come to Germany to say goodbye and to take care of the girl. Mrs B received the letter, but put off setting out for Germany, partly because her husband was away, and partly because she did not believe her friend to be in real danger. The story continues:

> Mrs B resided at Hampton Court, and here it was that, on the night of the 9th of November, a curious incident occurred. Retiring to her room between eleven and twelve, she rang for her maid, and the latter not appearing as promptly as usual, went to her still open door to listen if she were coming. Opposite to her was a wide staircase, and up this came noiselessly, a figure which the lamp held by Mrs B showed to be that of a lady dressed in black, with white gloves. A singular tremor seized her. She could neither stir nor speak. Slowly the figure approached her, reached the landing, made a step forward, and seemed to cast itself on her neck; but no sensation accompanied the movement! The light fell from her hand; she uttered a shriek that alarmed the house, and fell senseless to the floor . . .
>
> In a few days . . . came a letter from little Maud announcing that her mother was no more; that her latest thoughts were directed to Mrs B, and her sole regret was the not being permitted to embrace her before her spirit passed away. She had died a little before midnight on the *ninth of November*.
>
> Mrs B hastened to Germany to claim her orphan charge, and then was added a noteworthy confirmation of the vision. Little Maud, in one of their conversations, observed, 'Mamma had a curious fancy. On the night she died, she made the baron [her husband] promise that she should be buried in her black satin dress – *with white kid gloves*.' The request had been complied with.

Not only is this tale well told (as is to be expected in a journal edited by Charles Dickens) but it has an understated tone, which adds much to its veracity. Setting the story in two different countries accentuates the impossibility of naturalistic explanation, the coincidence of the time of death and the wraith's appearance is found out later, for dramatic effect, and the neat corroborating detail of the white gloves clinches it, and we simply must believe.

HAMPTON COURT ROAD: ST ALBANS

Prolific novelist Winifred Graham lived at St Albans, a large riverside house on Hampton Court Road, in the first half of the twentieth century. She believed in all things spiritual, and her house seems to have had more than its fair share of supernatural happenings, which she described in her 1947 autobiography *Observations*. One was experienced by her mother, who was herself reputed to be 'very psychic', as befitted a seventh child of a seventh child. The mother's room had two large windows, overlooking the roof of a veranda. One morning, at daybreak:

> ... she woke with a start to see three people, standing as she believed on the roof of the veranda, gazing in at her window. They made an astonishing group. One was a woman looking simply terrible, with her head hanging down and her clothes and hair dripping wet. Two men were supporting her, also apparently in great distress. Mother had no time to think how they could have got there, but sprang from her bed and rushed to the window, calling out: 'What is it? What is the matter?'

But the figures vanished as she approached. The explanation soon arrived. They heard of an accident that had happened in the night, just down the river at the Karsino ferry. A car carrying two men and a woman had somehow ended up in the river instead of on the ferry. Despite frantic attempts to get her out, the woman had died. One of the passengers was Tommy Hamm, a well-known racing driver at Brooklands, and when his photo appeared in the newspaper, Winifred's mother recognised it as one of the men at her window.

On the first night that Winifred's mother and father spent in the house, they took a stroll along the river, in the bright moonlight.

> When returning to the lawn my father suddenly said: 'Do you see anything peculiar in that magnolia tree?' 'Why yes,' she replied, 'a man is hanging there!' Hurriedly they rushed towards the tree, seeing the hanging figure all the time quite distinctly. Then as they reached the bough it disappeared.

A week later they were invited to a ball at a neighbour's house. During the evening, they fell into conversation with another local resident:

Are you the Mr Graham who has bought St Albans, that lovely old house where the man hanged himself on the magnolia tree? . . . I don't really know much about it, except that I heard it was a footman who got into trouble over money and people say his ghost haunts the garden.

The next ghost was seen by a maid, who excitedly reported that she had met 'a most beautiful lady in a low necked dress' on the stairs. She was 'surrounded by a bright light which showed up her jewels and sweet expression in her eyes'. Winifred's mother thought the description sounded like Nell Gwynne, who had apparently built the original house for her son. She fetched out a photograph of an old portrait, and sure enough the maid recognised her beautiful lady. The family always hoped that Nell would appear again, but she never did.

The last story concerns a young curate from Hampton parish church, who was a regular visitor at St Albans. One day he arrived in an excited and breathless state, after cutting through the churchyard as usual.

As I was strolling along thinking of nothing in particular, I suddenly heard the strangest noises like a multitude of voices calling to me from the graves – as if they were asking me to come to them. I was so petrified with fear I took to my heels and ran as fast as I could, while the ghostly voices called after me, until I was out of earshot.

Even as he told the story he said he could still hear the voices ringing in his head. He was young, strong and healthy, so nothing more was said, but within a few months he was dead.

See also THE STRAND: NORFOLK STREET, p. 113.

Hayes Lane, Kenley: Welcomes Farm

For a short time in 1921 and 1922, Welcomes Farm in Kenley was put in the spotlight as the site of a mysterious murder that included the supernatural element of a prophetic dream, a motif also found in other cases, such as the famous murder of Maria Marten in the Red Barn, Suffolk, in 1827.

Petty crooks and confidence tricksters Bill Dyer and Eric Gordon-Tombe bought the place, ostensibly to run it as a stud farm but actually to burn it down for the insurance money. When their plans went wrong the two men disappeared. Dyer was discovered in Yorkshire by local police who were investigating a different fraud, and he was killed by his own gun while struggling with them to avoid arrest. Meanwhile, Gordon-Tombe's parents had become convinced that his disappearance was not voluntary, and his mother reported a recurrent dream that her son was trapped underground and calling for help. The police were persuaded to search the farm more thoroughly, looking in particular for wells and other underground areas, and Eric's body was eventually found jammed into a disused cesspit. He had been shot in the back of the head, presumably by Dyer. The story has the added frisson that the famous occult writer Dennis Wheatley was a close friend of the two men and may, or may not, have been involved in some of their schemes.

HIGH STREET, CARSHALTON

A spring situated on the corner of the High Street and Church Hill, now dry and filled in, but encircled with railings and graced with a stone marker, has for some years been known as Anne Boleyn's Well, and a legend tells why. George Brightling's *History and Antiquities of Carshalton* (1872) relates the usual version of the story:

> One day, the King [Henry VIII], with his wife (Anne Boleyn) were about paying a visit to Sir Nicolas Carew, at Beddington Park. Proceeding from Nonsuch Palace on horseback, and reaching as far as Carshalton Church, the Queen's horse began prancing about, and struck its hoof into the ground, causing a spring to burst forth. The inhabitants, to commemorate the event, erected a stone dome over it, and named it Anne Boleyn's Well, which remains to this day. A bowl is attached by a chain to the neat iron railings which surround it, so that thirsty travellers can at all times drink to the memory of Anne Boleyn.

This story breaks down on the simple fact that Anne Boleyn was executed in 1536, before Nonsuch Palace was built, and the legend does not seem to be particularly old. As so often happens in such cases, it appears that the story was created in relatively modern times, to explain an existing name which had lost its meaning.

The well is shown, but not named, on the Arundel map of Carshalton, drawn about 1610–20, but in 1693 the local parish register recorded the death of a two-year-old boy, 'dround in bullin well'. It has been suggested that the name *bullen* is derived from *de Boulogne*, a family of landowners who lived in the area in the twelfth century, but there is no solid evidence to back up this derivation. Sutton council website points out that *bullient* in the seventeenth century meant boiling or bubbling, so it could simply have been a 'bubbling spring'.

It is also not quite clear when Anne Boleyn's name was first applied to the well. It was certainly being used in the early 1830s, but in the same period the well was referred to in the local vestry minutes as 'Anna Bullen's Well' or 'Bullen Well'. Some modern well researchers have assumed, apparently without evidence, that the well was a holy one, previously dedicated to St Anne, but this theory seems to have its basis in modern legend.

KENNINGTON COMMON

An example of the *dead man's hand*, which it was widely believed would cure tumours on the face or neck, occurs in the *Annual Register* on 19 April 1748:

> James White, aged 23, and Walter White, his brother, aged 21, were executed at Kennington Common for breaking open and robbing the dwelling house of farmer Vincent of Crawley . . . While the unhappy wretches were hanging, a child about nine months old was put into the hands of the executioner who nine times, with one of the hands of each of the dead bodies, stroked the child over the face. It seems that the child had a wen [swelling or tumour] on one of its cheeks, and that superstitious notion which has long prevailed of being touched is looked on as a cure.

The cure worked best if the dead hand was taken from someone who had been executed or committed suicide.

A nineteenth-century engraving of the Shrove Tuesday football match at Kingston-upon-Thames. There were virtually no rules, anyone could join in, and by 1840 it was being described as 'prejudicial to the morality of the Town'.

KINGSTON-UPON-THAMES

Regular Shrove Tuesday football games used to be a common all across the country, but most had died out by the nineteenth century. The last surviving game in Greater London was the one that was held in Kingston-upon-Thames. *Football* in this context is not the controlled rule-bound sport of modern times, but was an extremely rough-and-ready event, which took over the streets of the town for a whole day. Anyone could join in, and the sides were often chosen according to territory – the upper town versus the lower, for example. 'Goals' were usually landmarks a mile or more apart. The ball could be kicked, carried, or thrown, and physical contact was commonplace.

The earliest reference we have to any ball game is in William Fitz Stephen's *Description of London* (*c*.1180):

> Each year upon the day called Carnival – to begin with the sports of boys (for we were all boys once) . . . After dinner all the youth of the City goes

out into the fields to a much-frequented game of ball. The scholars of each school have their own ball, and almost all the workers of each trade have theirs also in their hands. Elder men and fathers and rich citizens come on horse-back to watch the contests of their juniors, and after their fashion are young again with the young; and it seems that the motion of their natural heat is kindled by the contemplation of such violent motion and by their partaking in the joys of untrammelled youth.

By 'Carnival' he means Shrove Tuesday. The poet and playwright John Gay records going for a walk in Covent Garden in his *Trivia: or the Art of Walking the Streets of London* (1716), and spotting the same degree of fervour with which the game was played:

> Here oft my course I bend, when lo from far
> I spy the furies of the foot-ball war
> The 'prentice quits his shop to join the crew
> Encreasing crowds the flying game pursue.

As with many people who meet a football crowd, his first thought was 'Whither shall I run?'

The early history of the game at Kingston is not documented, but it was already well established by 1797, at which point it was firmly believed locally that the game had been played for a thousand years, and that the players had an inalienable right to continue the custom, by an ancient charter. They also had an origin legend, as recorded in the *Illustrated London News* on 28 February 1846:

Kingston was one of the strongholds of the Anglo-Saxons; and tradition relates that the Danes, in a predatory excursion, were stopped here by the firm stand made against them by the townspeople, until assistance arrived from London, when the enemy was defeated; and the Danish general being slain, his head was cut off, and kicked about the place in triumph. This happened on a Shrove Tuesday; whence the origin of the custom; the football being regarded as the symbol of victory.

This explanation is given for games all over the country, so is likely to be apocryphal. The teams here were organised by two 'clubs' – Thames Street and Townsend – and, as elsewhere, the play was rough:

When the ball is driven into the river, the sport is 'fast and furious'; the antagonists dash into the stream, and wade about in the struggle. A few years since, when the Shrove tide was so high as to be above the arch of the bridge, one of the players leaped after the ball from the parapet into the river, and was carried by the force of the stream through the arch, but was providentially rescued on his appearance on the opposite side.

Some of the leading members of the community tried to suppress the custom throughout the early nineteenth century, and in 1840 it was dubbed an 'obstruction to the passengers, a great annoyance to the peaceable inhabitants, subversive of good order, and prejudicial to the morality of the Town'. But the game still enjoyed the support of many local dignitaries, who took their stand by equating 'old English customs' with English freedoms and resisting the abolitionists and reformers. By the 1860s, however, the game had lost these influential supporters, partly because it was attracting too many people from outside and was increasingly out of control, but also because of a rising tide of mid-Victorian civic pride.

The police moved in on Shrove Tuesday in 1867, and although they met with resistance, the game was soon suppressed. A brief attempt to continue it in local fields was not successful.

Other places in south-west London known to have had street football games include Barnes, Cheam, Mortlake, and Richmond, and it survived at Dorking in Surrey until the late 1890s.

See also RUISLIP, p. 172.

KINGSWAY ROAD, CHEAM: CENTURY CINEMA

The best-known ghost story from Cheam concerns the Century Cinema, which was built in 1937 but has now been demolished. Various incidents of supernatural phenomena have been recorded, usually focusing on strange sounds, particularly footsteps, which were often described as 'shuffling'. One manager arranged for a group of local reporters to spend the night there, and although they saw nothing, they heard plenty of unexplained and scary noises. But the most detailed account appeared in the *Sutton Guardian* on 29 August 1991. It was based on the memories of Joyce Gibbs, who used to work at the Century in the late 1940s and early 1950s, and who was convinced that the building was haunted:

After dark the cinema took on a disturbing life of its own and everyone would dread night duty. You had that feeling, it was a horrible feeling, cold, as if you were being followed . . . Usherettes particularly disliked climbing the stairs which led to the circle and the staff room. Once she and a fellow usherette heard footsteps behind them. They looked around but no one was there.

The basic story of the cinema ghost is repeated in many standard collections of English ghost stories, and in every case the explanation given concerns an incident that occurred while the cinema was being constructed. A workman engaged in the building simply disappeared from the job one day, leaving behind his jacket, his lunch, and, most tellingly, his unopened wage packet. Nobody ever found out what happened to him, and so theories of foul play, or at least a fatal accident, have arisen. Mrs Gibbs thought that he must have been murdered and bricked up in a wall. Yet the story is even more unconvincing than most origin-tales, with a palpable 'generic' feel about it, and it is not clear who first connected the hauntings and the disappearing workman story. The fact that no one ever quotes his name, or gives a verifiable reference, strongly suggests that it in itself is simply an *ex post facto* invention, constructed to explain the reported ghostly happenings.

LAMBETH PALACE ROAD, LAMBETH: ST MARY'S CHURCH

In Lambeth's parish church of St Mary a painted window depicts a man with a pack on his back and a dog at his feet. This man is usually referred to as the Lambeth Pedlar. This is probably the third version of the window, and it has been moved from its original position in the church. The previous one, installed in 1703, along with nearly all the other glass in the church, was unfortunately destroyed by enemy action during the Second World War, but copies appear in various publications, such as Thomas Allen's *History and Antiquities of the Parish of Lambeth* (1826). It is not known when the original was painted, but it was certainly in place by 1608, as the churchwardens' account for that year includes an entry for 'two shillings paid to the glazier for a panel of glass for the window where the picture of the pedlar stands'.

It has long been said that the picture was erected to commemorate a sixteenth-century pedlar who left money and land to the parish, provided that his dog could be buried in the churchyard, or, as another version has it, be commemorated in the church. According to this story, the land was thereafter called the Pedlar's Acre. No trace of such a benefactor can be found, but there certainly was a piece of land called Pedlar's Acre from at least 1690 onwards, situated on the south bank of the Thames, where County Hall now stands.

Some writers, however, have suggested a different lineage, in which the picture of the Lambeth Pedlar has become curiously tangled with the story of Henry Smith, London alderman and major benefactor to Surrey and other places, who died in 1627. Smith was a wealthy man, and when he died he left numerous legacies, including money for the poor in every parish in Surrey, but for some unknown reason a tradition grew up after his death that he had spent some time travelling around the county as a beggar. He was always accompanied by his dog, and so was therefore generally known as Dog Smith. The story tells that he always begged a bone for his dog, as well as food for himself, but that in one particular place he was whipped out of the parish, and so this particular parish alone was omitted from his benefactions. In some versions of the story the whipping occurred in several parishes. The earliest known version is in John Evelyn's additions to Bishop Gibson's new edition of Camden's *Britannia*, published in 1695. There is, however, no real foundation to the story, although it is repeated in a number of otherwise respectable histories of Surrey. Nor is there anything to connect him to the picture in Lambeth, although as one of the recipient parishes his name would have been familiar there.

Other writers, however, connect the story of the Lambeth Pedlar with the more famous one of the Swaffham Pedlar, or Tinker (*see* LONDON BRIDGE, p. 36), but the only similarity here is that both seem to have been invented simply to explain an illustration of a pedlar and his dog, which were probably originally erected, in this prosaic world, as a rebus to commemorate a person or family named Chapman, an old word meaning 'pedlar'.

LLOYD PARK

As mentioned elsewhere in this book, every open space is reputed to be a plague pit these days, and poor old Lloyd Park is one of them. But there is worse news for unsuspecting park visitors. According to local resident Phil Conway, whose story was reported in the *Croydon Advertiser* on 8 August 2003, people have described feeling an overwhelming terror there:

One person claimed that while he and a friend were in the park together they both began to feel as though some unseen menace was lurking nearby. The feeling grew until they were unable to speak, and both bolted to the park's exit. Experts in paranormal research have attributed these experiences to a ghoul, an entity which is reported to feast on dead flesh.

There is no other information about this ghoul, or which particular 'experts' identified it.

LONDON ROAD, HACKBRIDGE: BRIDGE HOUSE

According to a report in the *Sutton Herald* on 28 October 1993, some young people who were squatting in Bridge House, a listed building on London Road, Hackbridge, got more than they bargained for:

They said they had heard the sound of tapping and footsteps coming down the stairs. They went into the hall and saw this woman in black Victorian dress with a veil and a walking stick. The young girl with them fainted; the boys picked her up and ran for it.

At least this shows the spirit of chivalry is not totally dead, and perhaps owners of other buildings with unwelcome tenants might learn a trick or two here.

MARKET PLACE, KINGSTON: ALL SAINTS' CHURCH

Barbara and Tracy Russell included the following unusual ghost story in their booklet on local folklore, *Mysterious Kingston* (1996). An old couple were keen that they should be buried side by side. The husband died first, in 1860, and was duly buried in All Saints' churchyard, but by the time his wife died a few years later, a new cemetery, now known as the Memorial Gardens, had been brought into use, and she was laid to rest there. It is said that every year, just before Christmas, the husband's ghost can be seen walking across to his wife's grave, and returning a few days later.

A most singular custom also used to take place at All Saints', each year at Michaelmas (29 September), until the early nineteenth century. According to Edward Wedlake Brayley's *Topographical History of Surrey* (1850), members of the congregation on that day brought nuts into church, and spent the whole service cracking and eating them:

> The custom was not restrained to the junior branches of the congregation, but was practised alike by young and old; and the cracking noise was often so powerful, that the minister was obliged to suspend his reading, or discourse, until greater quietness was obtained.

The day was thus called locally Crack Nut Sunday. No real explanation for this behaviour has ever been put forward, although Brayley offers the opinion in a footnote that it had something to do with the election of the bailiffs. It is certainly the case that in many other communities the day of the election of the new mayor or other local officers was marked with some strange behaviour (often called a Lawless Hour), but this may simply be coincidence. Michaelmas was a popular date for civic terms of office to start, and it is also seen traditionally as the beginning of the nutting season. The only other evidence we can bring forward is a passage in Oliver Goldsmith's immensely popular *Vicar of Wakefield* (1766) in which the narrator lists the things done at certain seasons (for example eating pancakes at Shrove), and says, 'they religiously cracked nuts on Michaelmas Eve.'

MITCHAM

The children's custom of grotto-building was found all over the Greater London area, but Mitcham has the distinct honour of being the last known place where the practice was carried out each year. In a letter printed in *The Times* on 26 November 1957, a correspondent claimed that 'Grotter Day' was still very much alive and well:

> In the streets surrounding a large factory at Mitcham, Surrey, home-going workers are besieged once a year in July with requests to 'Please remember the Grotter', and find themselves picking their way carefully over structures of stones, shells and flowers. I have often asked the children concerned the 'why and wherefore' of the grotto, but they have no explanation.

Grottoes, such as the one on the left of this picture, were formerly built by children all over London. They were usually made of shells and stones, and passers-by were encouraged to give money to 'remember the grotto'. The last recorded grottoes were erected in Mitcham in the 1950s.

Grottoes were usually beehived-shaped constructions, about two feet high or more, made of shells, stones, and clinker, decorated with flowers, and built on the street so that passers-by could be asked to give money to 'remember the grotto'. The shells point to one theory why Mitcham children kept the tradition going. Mitcham Fair, held in the second week in August, was well timed to catch the beginning of the oyster season, and large quantities of this delicacy were eaten there. Children therefore had ready access to the shells from which to make their grottoes.

But this theory begins to break down when considering the evidence that the children made their grottoes *before* the fair. It appears that children made them in order to get money to spend there. Indeed, a survey of current Mitcham residents who remember making grottoes in the 1950s hardly mentions shells at all. Their grottoes were quite different:

> My brother and I used to make an anchor made of earth and pinch the flowers out of the gardens to decorate it. We used to stand at the top of

Mount Road in the late 40s and the 50s; the money we made we spent at the fair.

We used to get earth and soak it in water to make mud, and then stick flower heads into the mud. They actually looked quite pretty. When people used to come along the children used to say 'penny for the grotto' . . . Any money given was put away to use at Mitcham Fair . . . This was in the 50s.

We would have a baking tray of our mum's, cover it with earth, and then find small flower heads to cover all the earth, and try to get some twigs with leaves on them to make a little wood in one corner. A little to one side of the centre we used to put a jam jar lid filled with water and pushed it into the earth so that it would not come out. When we had finished we went to the top of Quicks Road where it meets Merton Road and put it on the pavement for anyone to see.

I used to make a grotto every year, along with the other kids around there. We used to do this to collect money for the old Mitcham Fair. You had to get a good pitch, though. I did mine either outside the Star pub, the old Bath Tavern, or just on the corner of the street outside of Charlie Brook's shop, which is where the fish shop is now. Every year I got a good whacking, though, as I used to take my dad's best roses . . . You had to have good soil too, no stones or lumps in it. My poor dad's garden did go through it.

This is something of a mystery, as photographs from Mitcham from around the same time clearly show hive-shaped grottoes made of stones or shells, but these flat earth grottoes are more similar to the 'spring gardens' found elsewhere in London.

See also FAIR GREEN, MITCHAM, p. 374; GROTTOES AND SPRING GARDENS, p. 402.

NEW ADDINGTON

New Addington, an estate on the Kent side of Croydon, was planned as a 'garden village' in the 1930s, but was developed in the post-war period as a huge overspill council estate. In January 1986, Harry Hill, a resident of the estate, told the *Croydon Advertiser* a story that is quite different from the usual local ghost story. It concerns a man walking home from work at a

Grottoes and Spring Gardens

Children often used oyster-shells – in plentiful supply during August and September's oyster season – to build 'grottoes' by the side of the road. A lit candle would have been placed in the opening at the front.

With the exception of asking for a 'penny for the guy' in November, the most widespread custom in the London child's year was formerly the building of a 'grotto'. Sometime in late July or August the children of the poorer districts of London would decide that it was Grotto Day, and would busy themselves constructing a grotto on the pavement, by which they hoped to solicit coins from passers-by. There are reports from much further afield (as far away as Norfolk and Swansea), but the vast majority of examples come from Greater London.

The grotto was of conical shape, somewhat like an old-fashioned bee-hive, and anything from two to four feet in height. The basic building material for a grotto, at least in the nineteenth century, was oyster shells. Oysters at that time were a poor man's food, sold and eaten by the million in London streets, so their shells were in plentiful supply when the season started in late August or early September. But in later years other materials are mentioned, including other shells, clinker, and stones, and, in addition to flowers and grass, various other items were used for decoration, such as glass, beads, ribbons, and even pictures. An almost invariable feature was an opening at the front in which a lit candle was placed, and children took the provision of the candle very seriously. A number of informants recorded that if no candle could be got beforehand, the first money collected was always spent on providing illumination.

The children greeted any passer-by with a request to 'Remember the grotto!', and they had a rhyme, which they chanted or sang:

Please remember the grotto
Only once a year
Father's gone to sea

Mother's gone to bring him back
So please remember me
A penny won't hurt you
A ha'penny won't break you
A farthing won't put you in the work'us

The earliest known reference to the grotto custom is in 1823, but it would be no surprise if its origin was found to be in the eighteenth century. Certainly, by 1833 it must have been already widespread, as it was mentioned twice in the august pages of *The Times* in terms implying general familiarity.

As with other children's street customs, there were many adults who disapproved of grottoing and who wished to see it abolished, mainly because it was regarded as begging. But the custom lasted well into the twentieth century, and grottoes were still a regular feature in many areas until the 1930s. By the post-war period, however, they were a rarity, and probably the last place to see regular grotto-making was MITCHAM, in the 1960s (*see* p. 399).

Nearly all the writers who have commented on the custom have assumed that it is a relic of the veneration of St James, and by repetition this explanation has gradually gained the status of received wisdom. St James's Day is 25 July (Old Style 5 August), and his accepted symbol is the scallop shell. But St James's popularity peaked many centuries before the first mention of grottoes, and the coincidence of shell motif and time of year has apparently led to a false connection being made. There is no reason to believe that Grotto Day is anything more than a custom to celebrate the start of the oyster season.

Some of the descriptions of grottoes from the late nineteenth century onwards, however, reveal a very different style of construction, which is similar to a less well-known but similar street custom that took place in the spring. At this time, some children made 'gardens' of flowers, grass, stones, and other decorations on the pavement, and their distinguishing feature, apart from the time of year, was that they were flat, rather than three-dimensional affairs. Some children called this custom 'Tommy on the Tub's Grave', a name that has never been explained.

See BATTERSEA, p. 363; CARSHALTON, p. 367; HORNSEY, p. 231; LEYTONSTONE, p. 286; OLD KENT ROAD, p. 342.

local factory who found that he had lost his wallet and wages, so he retraced his steps. As he neared the valley land in Queen Elizabeth's Drive:

> . . . a young fair man wearing a leather flying jacket, approached him. Speaking with a foreign accent but in good English, the young man asked if the man had lost a wallet which he had found. The man took the wallet, thanked the youth and returned towards home again. But just as he was going he looked over his shoulder and was surprised to see that the youth had simply disappeared – especially strange as they were on open land.

When he got home and told his wife about this strange encounter, she remembered the story of the Second World War German pilot who had baled out of his blazing plane, and landed, badly injured, on that very spot. Apparently, some locals had wanted to 'finish him off', but others had protected him until the authorities arrived. The young airman died in hospital. Not only this, but she managed to find an old photograph of the German airman, and her husband immediately recognised him as his wallet-finding friend.

NEW MALDEN

A story submitted to the journal *Folk-Lore* in April 1926 describes an interesting variation on the horrific idea that animals can live inside humans:

> A trained nurse (a working-class girl) living at New Malden, told me this story as current among the school children near her home. A young girl ate frog-spawn while on a visit to the sea-side, and an octopus has grown inside her. Its 'fangs' (tentacles) have spread into every part of her body, and one is wrapped round her heart: if it gives a pull 'her heart will come away'. The nurse's mother, taking the story quite seriously, assented: 'I should suppose it would.' They have taken the girl to Kingston Infirmary, but they can't do anything for her; and now they're just waiting for the King's consent to smother her. Nurse took credit to herself for being too sensible to believe the story.

See also KENT ST, SOUTHWARK, p. 346; KENTISH TOWN, p. 233 SILVERTOWN, p. 404; VERE STREET, p. 119.

NORWOOD

The formerly wild and desolate area of Norwood, named after the extensive North Wood that once covered the area, is where two counties, Surrey and Kent, and five modern London boroughs, meet – Croydon, Bromley, Lambeth, Lewisham, and Southwark. Until the mid nineteenth century, when rapid development transformed the area, it contained not only extensive woods but also acres of open wasteland, and had a reputation of danger and mystery. For centuries it was famous for the Gypsies who lived there, and gave rise to numerous rumours and stories among the settled populations of the surrounding areas.

Travellers all over the country were often feared and despised, harried by the authorities and moved on by farmers – except when they were needed as migrant labour. At the same time, however, they were seen as romantically wild, and blessed with occult powers – a reputation that they themselves traded on. Many a servant girl, or indeed her mistress, enjoyed the frisson of a visit to a genuine Gypsy fortune-teller, or would have their palm read at the back door for a shilling when no one was looking.

Samuel Pepys's wife, Elizabeth went to see the Norwood Gypsies on 11 August 1668:

> This afternoon, my wife and Mercer and Deb went with Pelling to see the gipsies at Lambeth and have their fortunes told, but what they did, I did not enquire.

The Norwood Gypsies were particularly famous in the seventeenth and eighteenth centuries. Painters, poets and musicians spread their fame far and wide, pantomimes portrayed them, and in the nineteenth century a number of cheap fortune-telling chapbooks were published with titles such as *The Original Norwood Gipsy* or *The Circle of Fate, or the New Norwood Gipsy*. Engravings of a character named Margaret Finch appeared, and she was usually referred to as 'The Queen of the Norwood Gypsies'. Margaret died in 1740, reputedly at the age of 108. Another artistic stereotype can be found in the romantic engravings of 'The Gypsy Encampment' at Norwood, which illustrate visiting women having their fortunes told. A nice little detail in some of these pictures is the young woman's suitor, who, having escorted her to the camp, hides behind a tree listening to the Gypsy's patter. It is clear that he has bribed the fortune-teller to say favourable things about him.

Famed for over 200 years, the Norwood Gypsies were believed to have knowledge of the occult and were frequently consulted by those seeking to have their fortunes told. Here, a young woman consults a gypsy while her suitor hides behind a tree – it was not uncommon for young men to bribe the fortune-tellers to say something favourable about them.

By the nineteenth century, Gypsy women were not above being treated as a tourist attraction at places of entertainment such as Beulah Spa, as indicated by Thomas Frost's *Reminiscences of a Country Journalist* (1886):

> An old woman, the mother, I believe, of Gipsy Cooper, of pugilistic renown, was for many years allowed to pretend to reveal the fortune of all inquirers who crossed her palm with a piece of silver at the Beulah Spa Gardens, a once famous summer resort which has long ceased to exist.

See also ANERLEY WOOD, p. 309; EPPING FOREST, p. 268.

PENLEE, RICHMOND

The following ghost story appeared in the *Surrey Magazine* (1899/1900), quoting 'A lady novelist, writing in the winter of 1880':

> I was living at Penlee, Richmond, Surrey. I went up into the night nurseries one evening, according to my custom, before sitting down to dinner, and had a chat with my little boy, between four and five years of age. I found

him sitting up in bed nibbling a biscuit. Suddenly he fixed his eyes on the door, which I had left ajar, and then, slowly turning his head several times, seemed to watch the movements of someone from the door into and around the room. I saw no one. 'Is that Uncle George?' he asked presently, and then added a moment later, 'Oh, he has gone now.' I may add that I did not let this circumstance be mentioned in the house for fear of alarming the servants or children; but a short time afterwards the cook came to me and told me that twice 'that gentleman in the red silk dressing-gown had come into her room at night, and that he strongly reminded her of the General' (the gentleman who was the Uncle George spoken of by my little boy). A few years after leaving this house I went there once on a visit to it, in the summer of 1880, and slept in the room adjoining the one in which my boy had had his ghostly experience. I awoke one night without apparent cause, and, raising myself on my elbow, saw, seated at the foot of the bed, a woman in a neat servant's dress, with a cap (an old black one like that of a housekeeper) lying beside her. She turned her face towards me so that I had a clear view of her features. Then she disappeared, and I realised the fact that she was no member of the household but a supernatural character.

PLOUGH LANE: BEDDINGTON CAVES

'Shudderus', the anonymous author of 'Haunted!', an article published in the *Croydon Review and Timetable* in January 1880, details what must be the longest secret tunnel in the country:

Close to the spot, at the commencement of the road to Bandon-Hill, is a cave, which is said, and with some show of reason, to have been a robbers' cave. Having inspected the cave, I can vouch that there is nothing very remarkable about it. Rumour goes so far as to say that the cave originally extended right away to Brighton, and that by its means smuggled goods were introduced to Surrey and thence to London. The cave was discovered, I was told, by some person who was ploughing above it, and who suddenly found himself in the robbers' den. In confirmation of this assertion my informant pointed to the figure of a man and a plough on the sign-board at host Watkinson's hostelry as being a picture of the identical man and of the plough he was directing at the time.

The Plough Inn marks the spot where the Beddington caves begin.
These caves are rumoured to run all the way down to Brighton and are
alleged to have been used by all sorts of people – from smugglers to Sir
Walter Raleigh.

The Beddington Caves are in fact well known, with an entrance near
the Plough Inn on Plough Lane, and have excited many a wild theory as
to their extent, origin, and use. Even if they do not run all the way to
Brighton, they are usually confidently said to be at least two miles in
length, and, apart from providing a helpful route for smugglers, they have
been claimed as an emergency escape tunnel for Romans living at the
nearby villa; and as a secret access for Catholic priests after the
Reformation, extending to Nonsuch Park or Archbishop Whitgift's palace
in Croydon. It is said that the ghost of Sir Walter Raleigh still walks them.
The cold water of science ruins most of these theories, as the local geology
makes it impossible for the tunnels to run for two miles without cutting
through solid chalk, diving under the River Wandle, negotiating other
waterlogged gravels, at a very steep gradient, and so on. In fact, they
probably run only a hundred yards or so, and were almost certainly made
to extract sand, which was sold for domestic scouring purposes. It is
interesting to note that no reliable documentary evidence for the tunnels'
existence can be found before the 1860s.

PURLEY WAY: CROYDON AIRPORT

For years after its closure in 1959, the terminal building of the old Croydon Airport was neglected and half-empty. Fortunately, there is now a thriving visitors' centre and museum, run by the Croydon Airport Society. In May 1970, however, the caretaker told an *Evening Standard* reporter that he had heard voices coming from the empty conference room:

> I have been here at eleven at night and I swear I have heard people talking in our conference room. Matter of fact, I couldn't get my dog to come up the stairs, and she'd come up them other times of day. I could hear these two men talking, mumbling all the time. I thought the first time I heard it that I must be dreaming so I opened the door and went in, but I couldn't hear this murmuring when I was in there. And when I came out it was there again. I'm not the only person that's heard this, others have, and they always say there's two people involved.

See also ROUNDSHAW, p. 413.

PUTNEY

Folklore stories about how particular places got their names are extremely common, and most are relatively uninspiring or based on false etymologies. But a cute little story about how Putney and Fulham got their names is included in Francis Grose's *Provincial Glossary* (1787):

> According to vulgar tradition, the churches of Putney and Fulham were built by two sisters, who had but one hammer between them, which they interchanged by throwing it across the river, on a word agreed between them; those on the Surrey side made use of the word 'put it nigh!'; those on the opposite shore, 'heave it full home'; whence the churches, and from them the villages, were called Putnigh and Fullhome, since corrupted to Putney and Fulham.

A Victorian engraving of the annual Oxford and Cambridge Boat Race, between Putney Bridge and Mortlake, which first took place in 1829.

PUTNEY BRIDGE

The Oxford and Cambridge Boat Race, which takes place each year in March or April, was the idea of two friends, one from each university, in 1829. Every year, over a quarter of a million people line the banks of the Thames to watch, and the live television coverage reaches millions of others in their homes. The course starts at the University Stone beneath Putney Bridge, and finishes at Mortlake, just before Chiswick Bridge.

Almost from the start, the race attracted good crowds. Gustave Doré and Douglas Jerrold's *London: A Pilgrimage* (1872), for example, contains two chapters on the race, and several evocative engravings entitled 'All London at a Boat Race', detailing the huge numbers of people gathered for the day. But the real mystery about the boat race was how such an event caught the imagination of ordinary Londoners who had no chance of going to a university, or even knew where Oxford and Cambridge were. Children especially took vociferous sides in a contest that had apparently no connection with their lives at all. An anonymous contributor to *Middlesex Within Living Memory* (1996) remembered:

> Each year in the 1930s there was great excitement and rivalry as the day approached of the Oxford and Cambridge University Boat Race. We each

had to support either Oxford or Cambridge and wear a favour to declare our allegiance. These favours were usually made of dark blue or light blue celluloid in the form of a rosette and we purchased them at the local sweetshop. Children who had a lot of pocket money often wore a little celluloid doll dressed in the colour of their 'side' and with a big furry hat on its head. Even to this day I am still 'Cambridge', mainly because my brothers were 'Oxford'.

And Ellen Morris writes of her childhood on the Isle of Dogs about 1920 in *Please to Remember* (1982):

> The Oxford and Cambridge boat race saw a division of the sexes. It was amazing how passionate we could get over something we were not able to see. Blue was the colour of the day, lengths of ribbon pinned to shoulders or hats. Girls always supported Cambridge with ribbons of light blue. The boys were for Oxford and dark blue was their colour.
>
> > Cambridge the winner, Oxford the sinner
> > Put it in a matchbox, and throw it in the river,
>
> or vice versa for boys. The battle raged until the result was known, then the chants would turn to taunts. Boat Race Day divided families throughout England, the poor who would never go to university, cheering for the sons of the rich who raced rowboats along the Thames.

QUEEN ELIZABETH'S WALK, BEDDINGTON

An article entitled 'Haunted!', written by 'Shudderus' and published in the *Croydon Review and Timetable* in January 1880, appears to have been written by someone who knew Beddington well, although he inexplicably calls it Carshalton:

> Queen Elizabeth's Walk, and the sand pits at Carshalton are said to be haunted, and the story goes that some spirit whose body has been cruelly murdered at this spot, haunts the place of his doom. The locality favours a supposition that it was a place where dark deeds were possible years ago. Another story attaches to this place. At the top of the sand pit may be seen a figure carved upon the trunk of a tree. This, probably the work of some

idle villager or lounging excursionist, is said to be the handiwork of a person as a preliminary to suicide. The branch of the tree used to be pointed out on which the personage hung himself.

ROBIN HOOD LANE, SUTTON: ST NICHOLAS'S CHURCH

In the south-west corner of the churchyard of St Nicholas is a large square mausoleum, known as the Gibson tomb. It was erected in 1777 by sisters Elizabeth and Mary Gibson to house the remains of their family, most notably their parents, who had both died in 1776. Their father, James, is somewhat of a mystery, although his story is presumably one of rags-to-riches, as he was variously described as a sailor, a distiller, a wine merchant, a miller, and eventually Master of the Worshipful Company of Ironmongers. Nor is it known why Sutton was chosen for the family's memorial, as they seem to have come from Walthamstow, and Mary and Elizabeth lived in Hampstead.

Elizabeth died in 1787, and Mary in 1793, and they both left money for charitable purposes, including the purchase of shoes and stockings for the poor of the parish. Mary also left instructions in her will for the family tomb to be inspected by the rector of St Nicholas's once every year on 12 August, and any necessary cleaning and repairs carried out. He was also required to deliver a memorial sermon. The shoes and stockings stopped being distributed years ago, and the sermon is no longer given, but the inspection is still carried out each year, and the tomb is kept in good condition. The tomb is, in fact, older than the church, as the original St Nicholas's was demolished in the 1850s to make way for the current building.

Various legends about the tomb have circulated at times, including the idea that the sisters were concerned about grave-robbers, and that the key to the tomb was to be taken by ship and thrown into the River Jordan. This is a regular motif in legends, when something needs to be irretrievably lost, although it is more usually the Red Sea. Within living memory, local children believed that if you walk seven times round the tomb, a ghost will appear from the urn on the roof. This also is a localised version of an extremely common children's legend, told of graveyards up and down the country, which nearly always involves walking round a particular tomb a certain number of times, to make some creature appear.

ROUNDSHAW

Following the closure of Croydon Airport in 1959, the 1,800-house Roundshaw Estate was built on the site, and it is perhaps inevitable that several ghost stories told of the area are all linked to the airport. Workmen sleeping on the unfinished site reported being woken by the sound of community singing, and various suggestions have been made as to whether this was an echo of the airmen relaxing, or people sitting out an air raid in the shelter there. It has even been suggested that they are the voices of those killed in the main raid on the airfield in 1940, but it is not clear why air-raid victims would be singing.

Another workman had a supernatural experience nearby, according to a report in the *Croydon Advertiser* on 31 August 1979:

> Early one morning in late 1971, a council workman was shifting rubbish on Roundshaw, when he saw a motor cyclist tearing round the boiler house and then shoot past him at full speed. An odd event at the best of times. But this rider had no face. Local legend has it that the phantom rider was a Battle of Britain airman who was killed when his plane crashed at the end of the runway.

Francis Stewart's *Around Haunted Croydon* (1989) claims that this motor-cyclist has been seen by other residents.

Another well-known story linked to the airport is the repeated sightings of spectral nuns around the estate, dating from the mid 1970s onwards. These nuns are often mentioned in ghost articles in the local press, but are treated most fully in Andrew Green's *Phantom Ladies* (1977). He claims that three nuns were aboard a Spencer Airways Dakota bound for Rhodesia in January 1947 which crashed into another plane before take-off, and all on board were killed. Sightings are often of the trio, but single nuns have also been reported.

See also PURLEY WAY: CROYDON AIRPORT, p. 409.

SHIRLEY

On 6 March 1998, the *Croydon Advertiser* reported that a pensioner from Shirley had called the Meteorological Office in Bracknell, Berkshire, in a state of distress after seeing her garden and street covered in dead frogs. She apparently had assumed that it had been raining frogs in the night as there was no pond near her. This anonymous Shirley resident would probably not have been so distressed if she had known that showers of frogs, fish, snails, and other small creatures have been reported from all over Britain, and elsewhere in the world, for hundreds of years. Indeed, writing in the *Guardian* on 12 May 1998, a representative of the Tornado and Storm Research Organisation (TORRO) claimed to have over one hundred examples from the UK alone, and John Michell and Robert Rickard comment in their *Phenomena: A Book of Wonders* (1977) that they have enough material on frog and fish falls to 'fill up a fat book'. The only unusual detail in the Shirley case is that the frogs were dead – they are normally described as surprisingly lively after their supposed ordeal.

This phenomenon has never been satisfactorily explained. Some have argued that the frogs are not usually observed in the act of falling, and are therefore not transported by the shower itself but brought out into the open by the rain. However, this does not explain the fish that have been found miles from the sea or any substantial lake. The most popular explanation is that mini-tornadoes or highly localised whirlwinds whisk these small animals into the sky and carry them for miles. But if this were the case, we would presumably expect to find showers of other light, perhaps inanimate, things much more commonly. Showers of wheat have been reported, but in the vast majority of cases it is small living creatures that appear, as if the tornado somehow knows what to pick up and what to leave behind.

STOCKWELL

A house in the small village of Stockwell achieved some notoriety in 1772 as the scene of an impressive supernatural occurrence, called at the time 'the Stockwell Ghost'– although we would now refer to it as a *poltergeist*, a German word meaning 'noisy ghost' that was first used in English in the

1840s. On the morning of Twelfth Day (6 January), at the home of Mrs Golding, an elderly lady living with her servant Anne Robinson, all the cups, saucers, and plates in the kitchen suddenly started falling to the ground, eggs flew across the room, water boiled in a pail, and even the furniture moved and trembled. Severely frightened by these occurrences, Mrs Golding first invited friends to stay, and later took refuge in a neighbour's house, but the disturbances followed her there and her host packed her off home again. After two days of this uproar, it finally dawned on Mrs Golding and her friends that not only did the disturbances always take place when servant Anne was present, but that she herself was the only one not frightened by the whole affair. She was dismissed, and the disturbances immediately ceased. The affair was written up in a pamphlet: *An authentic, candid, and circumstantial Narrative of the Astonishing Transactions at Stockwell in the County of Surrey, on Monday and Tuesday, the 6th and 7th days of January 1772.*

So the story would have rested, as another unexplained poltergeist phenomenon, if William Hone had not provided an explanation in his *Every-Day Book*. Hone reported a conversation he had had with the Revd Brayfield, of Camberwell, in 1817, who had known Anne Robinson in later life. She had readily admitted to him that she had faked the whole affair – placing items precariously, and using horse hairs and wires to move things about, and in some cases simply throwing or pushing things herself. Her work was clearly made easier by the gullibility of those around her, and the fact that they were so frightened that they would not look directly at objects, in case they moved. Hone's account also includes the telling phrase, 'subsequent conversations magnified many of the circumstances beyond the facts'.

See also BEVERSTONE ROAD, THORNTON HEATH, p. 365; BRIMSDOWN, ENFIELD, p. 196; CHELSEA, p. 138; GROVE PARK: ALLOTMENTS, p. 333; PLAISTOW, p. 293; REVERDY ROAD, BERMONDSEY: NOS 56 AND 58, p. 415; SUTTON LANE, CHISWICK: SUTTON COURT-HOUSE, p. 173.

Surbiton

An unusual kind of ghost story is set in a suburban train travelling from Hampton Court to Waterloo. It was contributed by the novelist Mrs Winifred Graham to Townshend and Ffoulkes's *True Ghost Stories* (1936):

> I was lucky enough to find an empty carriage at Hampton Court. At Thames Ditton, the next stop, quite an ordinary-looking man got into the carriage and sat down at the far end from me. We took no notice of each other, and in the usual course of events I should have continued reading my paper without giving him a thought. But I suddenly had the most dreadful feeling about him. In fact it was so strong that I could hardly support his presence, and something seemed to say: 'Take in every detail of that man's appearance, because you may have to identify him again.'

Mrs Graham was so unnerved by this feeling that she decided to get out at the next station, but as the train drew in, and before she had made any move, the man calmly gathered up his things and left the train. Greatly relieved, she settled back and closed her eyes for a while. She opened them again as the train pulled into Vauxhall:

> ... when to my unutterable horror, I saw the very same man seated in front of me ... he sat very still, gazing quite calmly and normally at me ... I got out and ran the whole length of the train, desirous of nothing except to put distance between us. Then I jumped, panting, into a compartment, terrified lest I should meet him again at Waterloo.

Tooting

A footnote in W. E. Morden's *History of Tooting-Graveney* (1897) refers to a piece of land called 'Shoulder of Mutton Field' in Tooting on which neighbouring Mitcham parish collected rates. The local explanation was that a dead body was discovered in the field, which Tooting residents refused to bury. Mitcham, however, buried the body, and subsequently took the rates from the field. Exactly the same notion is found in many other places, to explain a detached piece of land located in another parish, and is akin to a deeply held, but spurious belief that a right of way is automatically created over any land across which a dead body is carried.

See also WHIPPS CROSS ROAD, WALTHAMSTOW, p. 305.

VICARAGE CRESCENT, BATTERSEA: OLD BATTERSEA HOUSE

The writer A. W. M. Stirling (1865–1965) lived at Old Battersea House, built in 1699 and one of the finest buildings in the area. She published many anecdotes about the history of the house in her *Merry Wives of Battersea* (1956), including one concerning 'the late Lady C.', who was apparently somewhat psychically gifted. Lady C. came to tea one Sunday, and when they met again a few days later referred to that occasion and asked if Mrs Stirling had had a guest who was going to a fancy dress ball. She continued:

'I was waiting for you alone in the hall, when I glanced up and saw a man looking over the banisters on the upper landing. To my surprise he was wearing a plumed hat, a gay coat, with, what particularly struck me, some remarkable odd-shaped diamond buttons, and jack-boots which I could see through the balustrades of the landing.'

As she gazed at the figure, it slowly descended the stairs:

'I distinctly heard his sword strike against the oak stairs with every step he trod, but when he reached me he took no notice of my presence. He brushed rudely against me as he passed, and, without apology, walked on through the swing doors opposite and disappeared.'

The figure reminded Lady C. of the great Duke of Marlborough, who was a distant relation, and Mrs Stirling then confirmed that the Duke had been a regular visitor to the house when it was owned by his friend, Lord Bolinbrooke. Lady C. informed Mrs Stirling of ghosts in her house on several occasions, at one time warning her not to sit on an old fifteenth-century Italian armchair because it was already occupied by a man in Elizabethan garb, holding a rapier.

WANDSWORTH

An article on strange experiences, which includes a story about out-of-body apparitions in Wandsworth, was published in the *Surrey Magazine* (1900). A young lady wrote to a gentleman friend as follows:

Has anything happened to you? Please let me know at once, for I have been so frightened. Last Tuesday evening I was sitting in the dining room when I happened to look up and I could have declared that I saw you standing at the door looking at me. I put my handkerchief to my eyes and when I looked you were gone, and thought it must be only my fancy; but last night (Monday) while I was at supper, I saw you again just as before, and was so frightened I nearly fainted. Luckily only my brother was there or it would have attracted attention. Now, do write at once and tell me how you are. I really cannot write more now.

These strange apparitions were said to have occurred because the young man who had appeared to the lady, with his friend, had been experimenting with 'mesmerism' (what we would now call 'hypnotism'). He had appeared before her while in a trance but was fully aware of what was going on, and on waking he described the scene each time, and the lady's reactions. He agreed to give up the experiments because the lady found them so frightening – a particular shame because if he had perfected the technique and given classes to others, the skill would be a useful one.

WANDSWORTH COMMON

Another story that appeared in the *Surrey Magazine* (1900) related to poltergeist-type activity at a house near Wandsworth Common, which was being used, in May 1887, as livery stables:

The late occupants of it, a man, his wife and a child, had to leave it because they could get no rest at night owing to the fearful noises which went on incessantly. The sister-in-law of these people told Mrs H. S. Ireland that one night whilst she was in the house, she was taken by the shoulders and roughly shaken from side to side. Her husband stretched out his hand to take hold of her, but he felt, right up his arm to his shoulder, a shock, as it were, of electricity, which made him cry out. Nothing was seen. In the same room the clothes would be pulled off the bed at night on to the floor, and then would rear up again on to the bed. Since these people left it is said that no less than five families have respectively occupied the house as tenants, but they, one and all, left it as soon as possible. It is now to be permanently untenanted.

The motif of a house lying empty because of supernatural occurrences is extremely common.

See also BERKELEY SQUARE: NO. 50, p. 70; BRIMSDOWN, ENFIELD, p. 196.

BIBLIOGRAPHY

Abbott, G., *Ghosts of the Tower of London* (London: Heinemann, 1980).

Addison, William, *English Spas* (London: Batsford, 1951).

——, *English Fairs and Markets* (London: Batsford, 1953).

Alexander, Matthew, 'Shrove Tuesday Football in Surrey', *Surrey Archaeological Collections* 77 (1986) 197–205.

Andrews, William, *Bygone Middlesex* (London: William Andrews, 1899).

Ashton, John, *Chapbooks of the Eighteenth Century* (London: Chatto & Windus, 1882).

Attwood, John, *Dick Whittington: Fact and Fable* (London: Regency Press, 1988).

Aubrey, John, *Remaines of Gentilisme and Judaisme* (1686–7) and *Miscellanies* (1696), in John Buchanan-Brown (ed.), *John Aubrey: Three Prose Works* (Carbondale: Southern Illinois University Press, 1972).

Ayto, John, *The Oxford Dictionary of Rhyming Slang* (Oxford: Oxford University Press, 2002).

Baker, Alan, *Ghosts and Spirits* (New York: TV Books, 1998).

Baker, Roy (ed.), *Strange Stories from the Tower of London* (Harrisburg, PA: Historical Times, 1983).

Barber, Richard, *Living Legends* (London: BBC, 1980).

Barlow, Derek, *Dick Turpin and the Gregory Gang* (London: Phillimore, 1973).

Barron, Caroline M., 'Richard Whittington: the Man Behind the Myth', in A. E. J. Hollander and William Kellaway, *Studies in London History* (London: Hodder & Stoughton, 1969).

Bate, G. E., *And So Make a City Here: The Story of a Lost Heathland* (Hounslow: Thomasons, 1948).

Beer, R., and Pickard, C. A., *Eighty Years on Bow Common* (Booklet, no publisher, no date).

Bell, Walter George, *The Great Fire of London* (London: Bodley Head, 1923).

Bennett, Gillian, *Traditions of Belief: Women, Folklore and the Supernatural Today* (London: Penguin, 1987).

——, *Bodies: Sex, Violence, Disease and Death in Contemporary Legend* (Jackson: University Press of Mississippi, 2005).

Binder, Pearl, *The Pearlies: A Social Record* (London: Jupiter, 1975).

Bondeson, Jan, *The London Monster: A Sanguinary Tale* (New York: Da Capo, 2002).

Boulton, William B., *The Amusements of Old London* (London: John Nimmo, 1901).

Brand, John, *Observations on Popular Antiquities* (London: Bohn, 1849).

Brandon, David, *Stand and Deliver! A History of Highway Robbery* (Stroud: Sutton, 2003).

Brooke, Alan, and Brandon, David, *Tyburn: London's Fatal Tree* (Stroud: Sutton, 2004).

Brooks, J. A., *Ghosts of London*, 2nd edn (Norwich: Jarrold, 1991).

Browne, Edgar, *Phiz and Dickens* (London: James Nisbet, 1913).

Burford, Jo, and Wotton, Joy, *Private Vices – Public Virtues: Bawdry in London from Elizabethan Times to the Regency* (London: Hale, 1995).

Burns, William E., *An Age of Wonders: Prodigies, Politics and Providence in England 1657–1727* (Manchester: Manchester University Press, 2002).

Bushell, Peter, *London's Secret History* (London: Constable, 1983).

Cameron, David Kerr, *The English Fair* (Stroud: Sutton, 1998).

Celoria, F., 'Folklore Collected around 1860–1893 in London and Middlesex by John Philipps Emslie', *London Studies* 1 (1974) 38–86.

Chambers, Paul, *The Cock Lane Ghost: Murder, Sex and Haunting in Dr Johnson's England* (Stroud: Sutton, 2006).

Chambers, Robert, *The Book of Days* (London: Chambers, 1864).

Clark, James, *Strange Mitcham* (Mitcham: Shadowtime, 2002).

Cope, Robert Charles, *The Legendary Lore of the Holy Wells of England* (London: Elliot Stock, 1893).

Coxe, Antony D. Hippisley, *Haunted Britain* (London: Hutchinson, 1973).

Crystal, David, *The Stories of English* (London: Allen Lane, 2004).

Currie, Ian, *Frosts, Freezes and Fairs* (Coulsdon: Frosted Earth, 1998).

Daniel, George, *Merrie England in the Olden Time* (London: Richard Bentley, 1842).

Dash, Mike, 'Spring-Heeled Jack: To Victorian Bugaboo from Suburban Ghost', *Fortean Studies* 3 (1996) 7–125.

Davis, Richard, *I've Seen a Ghost! True Stories from Show Business* (London: Hutchinson, 1979).

Day, Sidney, *London Born* (London: Harper Perennial, 2006).

Ditchfield, P. H., *Old English Customs Extant at the Present Time* (London: George Redway, 1896).

Doré, Gustave, and Jerrold, Douglas, *London: A Pilgrimage* (London: Grant, 1872).

Druett, Walter W., *Harrow Through the Ages*, 3rd edn (Uxbridge: King & Hutchings, 1956).

Dyer, Barry Albin, *Bury My Heart in Bermondsey: Memoir of a Funeral Director* (London: Hodder & Stoughton, 2004).

Dyer, T. F. Thiselton, *British Popular Customs* (London: George Bell, 1876).

Edwards, H., *A Collection of Old English Customs and Curious Bequests and Charities* (London: John Bowyer Nichols, 1842).

Ellis, Bill, 'The Highgate Cemetery Vampire Hunt: The Anglo-American Connection in Satanic Cult Lore', *Folklore* 104 (1993) 13–39.

——, *Raising the Devil: Satanism, New Religions and the Media* (Lexington: University Press of Kentucky, 2000).

Emslie, John Philipps, *see* Celoria, F.

Errand, Jeremy, *Secret Passages and Hiding Places* (Newton Abbott: David & Charles, 1974).

Finny, W. E. St Lawrence, 'Medieval Games and Gaderyngs at Kingston-Upon-Thames, *Surrey Archaeological Collections* 44 (1936) 102–36.

Fitz Stephen, William, *Description of the City of London* (*c.*1183; published as *Norman London*, New York: Italica, 1990).

Fodor, Nandor, *On the Trail of the Poltergeist* (New York: Citadel Press, 1958).

——, *The Haunted Mind: A Psychoanalyst Looks at the Supernatural* (New York: Garrett, 1959).

——, *Between Two Worlds* (New York: Parker, 1964).

Frost, Thomas, *The Old Showmen and the Old London Fairs*, new edn (London: Chatto & Windus, 1881).

——, *Reminiscences of a Country Journalist* (London: Ward & Downey, 1886).

Gamble, Rose, *Chelsea Child* (London: BBC, 1979).

Gartenberg, Patricia, 'An Elizabethan Wonder Woman: The Life and Fortunes of Long Meg of Westminster', *Journal of Popular Culture* 17:3 (1983) 49–58.

Gattrell, V. A. C., *The Hanging Tree: Execution and the English People 1770–1868* (Oxford: Oxford University Press, 1994).

Golland, Jim, *Fair Enough? Pinner Fair: The Last 200 Years* (Harrow: Herga Press, 1993).

Gover, J. E. B., et al., *The Place-Names of Middlesex* (Cambridge: English Place-Name Society, 1942).

Graham Winifred, *Observations, Casual and Intimate* (London: Skeffington, 1947).

Grant, James, *Sketches in London*, 2nd edn (London: Thomas Tegg, 1840).

Granville, Wilfred, *A Dictionary of Theatrical Terms* (London: André Deutsch, 1952).

Green, Andrew, *Phantom Ladies* (Folkestone: Bailey Bros. & Swinfen, 1977).

Greenwood, James, *Low Life Deeps* (London: Chatto & Windus, 1876).

Hahn, Daniel, *The Tower Menagerie* (London: Simon & Schuster, 2003).

Haining, Peter, *Sweeney Todd: The True Story of the Demon Barber of Fleet Street*, updated edn (London: Robson, 2007).

Hall, Mike, *Tales of Old Middlesex* (Newbury: Countryside Books, 2001).

——, *Haunted Places of Middlesex* (Newbury: Countryside Books, 2004).

——, *Middlesex Tales of Mystery and Murder* (Newbury: Countryside Books, 2005).

Hallam, Jack, *Ghosts of London* (London: Wolfe, 1975).

Hammond, Ernest, *Bygone Battersea* (London: Dyer, 1897).

Hare, Augustus, *The Story of My Life* (London: George Allen, 1896–1900).

Harper, Charles G., *Haunted Houses: Tales of the Supernatural* (London: Chapman & Hall, 1907; 2nd edn, London: Cecil Palmer, 1924; 3rd ed., London: Cecil Palmer, 1927).

Hole, Christina, *Haunted England* (London: Batsford, 1940).

——, *English Custom and Usage* (London: Batsford, 1944).

——, *English Folk-Heroes* (London: Batsford, 1948).

Hone, William, *The Every-Day Book* (London: The Author, 1825).

——, *The Table Book* (London: Thomas Tegg, 1827).

——, *The Year Book* (London: Thomas Tegg, 1832).

Hopkins, R. Thurston, *Life and Death at the Old Bailey* (London: Herbert Jenkins, 1935).

——, *Ghosts Over England* (London: Meridian, 1953).

——, *Banker Tells All* (London: Frederick Muller, 1956).

Howard, Margaret M., 'Dried Cats', *Man* (November 1951) 149–51.

Hutton, Ronald, *The Rise and Fall of Merry England: the Ritual Year 1400–1700* (Oxford: Oxford University Press, 1994).

——, *The Stations of the Sun: A History of the Ritual Year in Britain* (Oxford: Oxford University Press, 1996).

Ingram, John, *The Haunted Homes and Family Traditions of Great Britain* (London: Reeves & Turner, 1912).

Ingram, Martin, 'Ridings, Rough Music and the Reform of Popular Culture in Early Modern England', *Past and Present* 105 (1984) 79–113.

——, 'Ridings, Rough Music and Mocking Rhymes in Early Modern England', in Barry Reay, *Popular Culture in Seventeenth-Century England* (London: Croom Helm, 1985) 166–197.

Jarvis, T. M., *Accredited Ghost Stories* (London: J. Andrews, 1823).

Judge, Roy, *The Jack-in-the-Green*, 2nd edn (London: Folklore Society, 2000).

Kent, William, *London Worthies* (London: Heath Cranton, 1939).

——, *London Mystery and Mythology* (London: Staples Press, 1952).

——, *London in the News Through the Centuries* (London: Staples Press, 1954).

Kightly, Charles, *Folk Heroes of Britain* (London: Thames & Hudson, 1982).

Kimberley, Ken, *Oi Jimmy Knacker* (Kettering: Silver Link, 1998).

Larwood, Jacob, *The Story of the London Parks* (London: Chatto & Windus [1881?]).

Lee, Frederick George, *Glimpses in the Twilight* (London: William Blackwood, 1885).

Liechtenstein, Princess Marie, *Holland House* (London: Macmillan, 1874).

Linebaugh, Peter, *The London Hanged: Crime and Civil Society in the Eighteenth Century* (London: Allen Lane, 1991).

Lovett, Edward, *Magic in Modern London* (Croydon: The Advertiser, 1925).

McGrath, Melanie, *Silvertown: An East End Family Memoir* (London: Fourth Estate, 2002).

Machyn, Henry, *The Diary of Henry Machyn*, ed. John Gough Nichols (London: Camden Society, 1847).

Mack, Robert L., *The Wonderful and Surprising History of Sweeney Todd: The Life and Times of an Urban Legend* (London: Continuum, 2007).

Mackay, Charles, *Extraordinary Popular Delusions and the Madness of Crowds* (London: Richard Bentley, 1841).

McMains, H. F., *The Death of Oliver Cromwell* (Lexington: University Press of Kentucky, 2000).

Madders, Jane, and Horseman, Grace, *Growing Up in the Twenties* (Bovey Tracy: Cottage Publishing, 1993).

Man, Myth and Magic (London: Purnell, 1970–72).

Maple, Eric, *Supernatural England* (London: Robert Hale, 1977).

Mason, Charlotte Craven, *Essex: Its Forest, Folk, and Folklore* (Chelmsford: J. H. Clarke, 1928).

Matthews, William, *Cockney Past and Present: A Short History of the Dialect of London* (London: Routledge, 1938).

Maxwell, Gordon S., *Highwayman's Heath: The Story in Fact and Fiction of Hounslow Heath in Middlesex*, 2nd edn (Hounslow: Thomasons, 1949).

Mayhew, Henry, *London Labour and the London Poor* (London: Griffin, Bohn, 1861).

——, *The Morning Chronicle Survey of Labour and the Poor* (Horsham: Caliban, 1982).

Menefee, Samuel Pyeatt, *Wives for Sale* (Oxford: Blackwell, 1981).

Merrifield, Ralph, *The Archaeology of Ritual and Magic* (London: Batsford, 1987).

Michell, John, and Rickard, Robert J. M., *Phenomena: A Book of Wonders* (London: Thames & Hudson, 1977).

——, *Living Wonders* (London: Thames & Hudson, 1982).

Middleton, Jessie Adelaide, *The White Ghost Book* (London: Cassell, 1916).

Misson, Henri, *Misson's Memoirs and Observations in his Travels over England*, trans. Mr Ozell (London: D. Browne, 1719).

Morris, Ellen, *Please to Remember* (unpublished typescript in Tower Hamlets Local Studies Library, 1982).

Murphy, Ruth, and Wichelow, Clive, *Mysterious Wimbledon* (London: Enigma, 1994).

——, *More Mysterious Wimbledon* (London: Enigma, 1995).

O'Donnell, Elliott, *Haunted Places in England* (London: Sands, 1919).

——, *Ghosts of London* (Philip Allan, 1932).

——, *Haunted Britain* (London: Rider, 1948).

——, *Haunted People* (London: Rider, 1950).

——, *Phantoms of the Night* (London: Rider, 1956).

——, *Haunted Waters* (London: Rider, 1957).

Opie, Iona, and Opie, Peter, *The Singing Game* (Oxford: Oxford University Press, 1985).

Parker, Penny, *Merton in Pictures Book 3: Mitcham Fair* (Merton: Merton Library Service, 1991).

Payne, Jessie, *A Ghost-Hunter's Guide to Essex* (Romford: Ian Henry, 1980).

Perfect, Charles, *Ye Olde Village of Hornchurch* (Colchester: Benham, 1917).

Phillips, George L., 'Mrs. Montagu and the Climbing-Boys', *Review of English Studies* 25 (1949) 237–44.

Playfair, Guy Lyon, *This House Is Haunted: An Investigation of the Enfield Poltergeist* (London: Souvenir, 1980).

Pringle, Patrick, *Stand and Deliver* (New York: Dorset Press, 1991).

Pusey, Richard, *Essex Rich and Strange* (London: Robert Hale, 1987).

Puttick, Betty, *Supernatural England* (Newbury: Countryside Books, 2002).

Richardson, Ruth, *Death, Dissection and the Destitute* (London: Routledge & Kegan Paul, 1987).

Richardson, Ruth, and Hurwitz, Brian, 'Jeremy Bentham's Self-Image: An Exemplary Bequest for Dissection', *British Medical Journal* 295 (1987) 195–8.

Roberts, Chris, *Cross River Traffic: A History of London's Bridges* (London: Granta, 2005).

Rolph, C. H., *London Particulars* (Oxford: Oxford University Press, 1982).

Roud, Steve, *The Penguin Guide to the Superstitions of Britain and Ireland* (London: Penguin, 2003).

——, *The English Year* (London: Penguin, 2006).

Rumbelow, Donald, *The Triple Tree: Newgate, Tyburn and Old Bailey* (London: Harrap, 1982).

Russell, Barbara, and Russell, Tracy, *Mysterious Kingston* (Wimbledon: Twilight Books, 1996).

Sharpe, James, *Dick Turpin: The Myth of the English Highwayman* (London: Profile, 2004).

Shepard, E. H., *Drawn from Memory* (London: Methuen, 1957).

Shoemaker, Robert, *The London Mob: Violence and Disorder in Eighteenth-Century England* (London: Hambledon, 2004).

Smith, A. W., 'An Introduction to East London Folklore', *East London Papers* 2 (1959) 63–78.

Smith, Alan, 'Notes on the Folk-Life of the East London Child', *Folklore* 69 (1958) 39–42.

Spargo, John Webster, *Juridical Folklore in England, Illustrated by the Cucking-Stool* (Durham, NC: Duke University Press, 1944).

Spence, Lewis, *Legendary London* (London: Robert Hale, 1937).

Spraggs, Gillian, *Outlaws and Highwaymen: The Cult of the Robber in England from the Middle Ages to the Nineteenth Century* (London: Pimlico, 2001).

Squiers, Granville, *Secret Hiding-Places* (London: Stanley Paul, 1933).

Stewart, Frances D., *Around Haunted Croydon* (Croydon: AMCD, 1989).

——, *Surrey Ghosts Old and New* (Croydon: AMCD, 1990).

Stirling, A. W. M., *The Merry Wives of Battersea and Gossip of Three Centuries* (London: Hale, 1956).

——, *Ghosts Vivisected* (London: Hale, 1957).

Stow, John, *A Survey of London* (1598, revised 1603; London: Routledge, 1912).

Strange, K. H., *The Climbing Boys: a Study of Sweeps' Apprentices 1773–1875* (London: Allison & Busby, 1982).

Strutt, Joseph, *The Sports and Pastimes of the People of England*, new edn, edited by William Hone (London: Tegg, 1833).

Thompson, E. P., *Customs in Common* (London: Merlin, 1991).

Thorne, James, *Handbook to the Environs of London* (2 vols., London: J. Murray, 1986; reprinted in 1 vol., London: Godfrey Cave, 1983).

Timbs, John, *Walks and Talks About London* (London: Lockwood, 1865).

Told, Silas, *An Account of the Life and Dealings of God with Silas Told* (London: Gilbert & Plummer, 1786; 2nd edn, entitled *The Life of Mr Silas Told, Written by Himself* . . . 1790).

Torre, Henry John, *Recollections of School Days at Harrow* (Manchester: Charles Simms, 1890).

Townshend, Marchioness, and Ffoulkes, Maude, *True Ghost Stories* (London: Hutchinson, 1936).

Trow, M. J., *Boudicca: The Warrior Queen* (Stroud: Sutton, 2003).

Turner, E. S., *Boys Will Be Boys* (London: Michael Joseph, 1948).

Underwood, Peter, *Gazetteer of British Ghosts* (London: Souvenir, 1971).

Varley, Frederick John, *Oliver Cromwell's Latter End* (London: Chapman & Hall, 1939).

Walford, Edward, *Greater London* (London: Cassell, 1883–4).

Walford, Edward, and Thornbury, Walter, *Old and New London* (London: Cassell, 1872–8).

Weinreb, Ben, and Hibbert, Christopher, *The London Encyclopaedia* (London: Macmillan, 1983).

Westwood, Jennifer, *Albion: A Guide to Legendary Britain* (London: Grafton, 1985).

Westwood, Jennifer, and Simpson, Jacqueline, *The Lore of the Land: A Guide to England's Legends, from Spring-Heeled Jack to the Witches of Warboys* (London: Penguin, 2005).

Wheatley, Henry B., *London Past and Present*, 3 vols. (London: Murray, 1891).

Wiles, David, *The Early Plays of Robin Hood* (Woodbridge: Brewer, 1981).

Wolveridge, Jim, *Ain't it Grand (or This is Stepney)* (Stepney: Stepney Books, 1976).

Wright, A. R., and Lones, T. E., *British Calendar Customs: England*, 3 vols. (London: William Glaisher, 1936–40).

INDEX